JAPAN'S FOREIGN POLICY, 1945-2003

JAPAN'S FOREIGN POLICY, 1945-2003

1945-2003

The Quest for a Proactive Policy

BY

KAZUHIKO TOGO

SECOND EDITION

BRILL

LEIDEN · BOSTON

2005

 This book was published with financial support from the International Institute for Asian Studies (IIAS), Leiden, the Netherlands.

This book is printed on acid-free paper.

Library of Congress Cataloging-in-Publication Data

A C.I.P. record for this book is available from the Library of Congress.

ISBN 90 04 14796 9

PRINTED IN THE NETHERLANDS

CONTENTS

GLOSSARY

ABM	Anti-Ballistic Missile
ADB	Asian Development Bank
AECF	Asia-Europe Cooperation Framework
AMF	Asian Monetary Fund
APEC	Asia-Pacific Economic Cooperation
ARF	ASEAN Regional Forum
ASEAN	Association of Southeast Asian Nations
ASEAN-PMC	ASEAN Post-Ministerial Conference
ASEM	Asia-Europe Meeting
B/D	Barrels per Day
BHN	Basic Human Needs
CDF	Comprehensive Development Framework
CEP	Comprehensive Economic Partnership
CIS	Community of Independent States
COP	Conference of Parties to the United Nations Framework Convention on Climate Change
CSCA	Conference on Security and Cooperation in Asia
CSCE	Conference on Security and Cooperation in Europe
CTBT	Comprehensive Test Ban Treaty
DAC	Development Assistance Committee
DPRK	Democratic People's Republic of Korea
EASR	East Asian Strategic Report
EC	European Community
ECAFE	Economic Commission for Asia and the Far East
ECSC	European Coal and Steel Community
EEC	European Economic Community
EROA	Economic Rehabilitation in Occupied Areas
EU	European Union
EURATOM	European Atomic Community
EVSL	Early Voluntary Sectoral Liberalization
FDI	Foreign Direct Investment
FSX	Fighter-Support Experimental
FTA	Free Trade Agreements
GARIOA	Government and Relief in Occupied Areas
GATT	General Agreement on Tariffs and Trade

GDP	Gross Domestic Product
GHQ	General Headquarters
GNP	Gross National Product
GSP	Generalized System of Preferences
HIPC	Heavily Indebted Poor Countries
IAEA	International Atomic Energy Agency
ICRC	International Committee of the Red Cross
IDA	International Development Association
IEA	International Energy Agency
IMF	International Monetary Fund
IMTFE	International Military Tribunal for the Far East
INF	Intermediate-Range Nuclear Forces
INTERFET	UN Sanctioned International Force in East Timor
IT	Information Technology
ITO	International Trade Organization
JBIC	Japan Bank of International Cooperation
IBRD	International Bank of Reconstruction and Development
JDA	Japan Defence Agency
JETRO	Japan External Trade Organization
JICA	Japan International Cooperation Agency
JSDF	Japan Self-Defence Forces
JSP	Japan Socialist Party
KEDO	Korean Peninsula Energy Development Organization
KWP	Korean Workers Party
LDC	Least Developed Countries
LDP	Liberal Democratic Party
LLDC	Least among Less-Developed Countries
MAFF	Ministry of Agriculture, Forestry and Fisheries
MAPA	Manila Action Plan for APEC
METI	Ministry of Economy, Trade and Industry
MFN	Most-Favoured-Nation
MITI	Ministry of International Trade and Industry
MOFA	Ministry of Foreign Affairs
MOSS	Market-Oriented, Sector-Selective
MTCR	Missile Technology Control Regime
NAFTA	North American Free Trade Agreement
NATO	North Atlantic Treaty Organization
NCND	No Confirmation No Denial
NDPO	National Defence Program Outline
NEACD	Northeast Asia Cooperation Dialogue

NGO	Non Governmental Organizations
NIEs	Newly Industrialized Economies
NPCSD	North Pacific Cooperative Security Dialogue
NPT	Non Proliferation Treaty
OAPEC	Organization of Arab Petroleum Exporting Countries
ODA	Official Development Assistance
OECD	Organization for Economic Cooperation and Development
OEEC	Organization for European Economic Cooperation
OMA	Orderly Market Agreement
OPEC	Organization of Petroleum Exporting Countries
OPTAD	Organization for Pacific Trade, Aid and Development
OSCE	Organization for Security and Cooperation in Europe
PAFTAD	Pacific Trade and Development Conference
PBEC	Pacific Basin Economic Conference
PECC	Pacific Economic Cooperation Conference
PKO	Peacekeeping Operations
PoW	Prisoners of War
PPP	Purchasing Power Parity
PRC	People's Republic of China
RC	Republic of China
SACO	Special Action Committee on Facilities and Areas in Okinawa
SALT	Strategic Arms Limitation Talks
SDF	Self-Defence Forces
SDI	Strategic Defence Initiatives
SII	Structural Impediment Initiatives
TAC	Treaty of Amity and Cooperation
TICAD	Tokyo International Conference on African Development
UAE	United Arab Emirates
UN	United Nations
UNCTAD	United Nations Conference on Trade and Development
UNDHA	United Nations Department of Humanitarian Affairs
UNDOF	United Nations Disengagement Observer Force
UNDP	United Nations Development Program
UNGOMAP	UN Good Offices Mission in Afghanistan and Pakistan
UNIIMOG	UN Iran-Iraq Military Observer Group

UNTAC	UN Transitional Authority in Cambodia
UNAMET	UN Assistance Mission in East Timor
UNTAET	UN Transitional Administration in East Timor
UNMISET	UN Mission of Support in East Timor
USTR	United States Trade Representative
VERs	Voluntary Export Restraints
WMD	Weapons of Mass Destruction
WTO	World Trade Organization
WW I	World War I
WW II	World War II

ACKNOWLEDGEMENTS

I would like to express my sincere gratitude to all who have encouraged and helped me in writing this book. It was only thanks to the good will of so many people that I was able to write this book as one of my first projects after my retirement from the Ministry of Foreign Affairs in the spring of 2002.

My particular thanks go to the University of Leiden, which became the founding father of this project. Prof. Dr. W.R. van Gulik helped enormously by settling me with this project at Leiden University. Dr. L.E.H. Vredevoogd, and his successor Mr. A.W. Kist, Presidents of the University of Leiden, as well as Prof. Dr. Douwe D. Breimer, Rector Magnificus of the University, all kindly encouraged me to pursue this endeavour.

I owe a deep debt of gratitude to Prof. Dr. Rikki Kersten of the Centre for Japanese and Korean Studies of the University of Leiden, who gave me the opportunity to teach a class at the University, using the draft text of this book as reference material. Professor Kersten continued to be of invaluable assistance, and her comments on both the content and the language were vital in bringing this work to publication. Without her determination and support this book would not have been published.

The students of Leiden University who attended my class 'Japan and the World' in the spring term of 2003 have made no small contribution to the improvement of the contents of this book through their active classroom participation.

My particular thanks go also to the International Institute for Asian Studies (IIAS) which supported the publication of this book. Prof. W.A.L. Stokhof, Director of IIAS, Mr. Wouter Feldberg and Ms. Josine Stremmelaar, staff members of IIAS, have constantly encouraged me to bring this project to its completion.

There are many individuals to whom I owe special thanks as well. Mrs. Elizabeth van der Wind-Hamill helped me enormously in improving the English. Mrs. Muriel Hussin gave me many valuable comments and advice on the text itself. I am also grateful to Ambassador Takeshi Kagami for his extremely insightful comments. I also owe many thanks to Prof. Dr. Arthur Stockwin of the University of Oxford and Prof. Dr. Peter Pantzer of the University of Bonn who have continuously encouraged me to publish this book.

My friends in the Ministry of Foreign Affairs in Tokyo helped me in gathering information which brought further accuracy to this book, including statistical data, the latest unpublished materials and old speeches.

Mr. Albert Hoffstädt of Brill Netherlands and Mr. Patrick H. Alexander of Brill USA took the vital decision to publish this book by Brill Academic Publishers. Without them, this book would have never taken its current shape, and I am immensely grateful for their decision. Ms. Tanja Cowall did most of the detailed work related to the publication. Dr. Koen Donker van Heel contributed immensely in copy editing. Mrs. Tamaki Yoshida, a student at the Leiden University, helped me a lot in bringing the index into shape. Thank you very much.

And last but not least, mention has to be made to the Ailion Foundation and the Canon Foundation. Both have contributed generously and unselfishly, enabling me to write this book. Mrs. Corrie Siahaya-van Nierop of the Canon Foundation followed this project with great interest.

All in all, I thank all my friends and members of my family who continuously encouraged, helped and supported the writing of this book. Without their support this book might never have been published.

INTRODUCTION

In the spring of 1995 I was serving as Deputy Chief of Mission at the Japanese Embassy in Moscow. President Yeltsin was in power, implementing his reform policy and preparing for the election in the following year. The political situation was very tense. It was interesting and stimulating for a diplomat to serve in this historic period of transition in Russia.

One day, I was conversing with my long-time friend in the Russian Foreign Ministry, the then Deputy Minister in charge of Asia and the Pacific region, Alexander Panov. I began outlining a vague idea I had, to give lectures at one of the leading universities or institutions in Moscow on Japan or Japanese foreign policy.

"Is it not useful to give some deeper knowledge on Japan or Japanese foreign policy to a younger generation in Russia?" I asked Deputy Minister Panov.

"Do you think that a diplomat like me could make a significant contribution?"

Deputy Minister Panov not only supported this idea, but also showed a great interest in implementing it. Almost instantaneously he suggested that I should focus on MGIMO, the Moscow State Institute of International Relations. MGIMO was a university established during the Soviet regime primarily for those 'elite students', who were considering a career in the Foreign Service. After the demise of the Soviet Union, the majority of Russian diplomats are still MGIMO graduates.

Things proceeded smoothly and in the autumn of 1995 I was given a rare opportunity to give a one-term lecture to MGIMO undergraduate students on 'Japanese Foreign Policy 1945–1995'. I spent a fair amount of time during that summer preparing for the lecture both in contents and language. Colleagues and friends were helpful in gathering material and I devoted all my private Russian language lessons to studying technical and specialized terms. As a member of the Japanese Foreign Service, I had specialized in the Russian language since joining the service in 1968 and had already served twice at the Embassy in Moscow, in the early seventies and the mid-eighties. But to cover over a dozen different themes on

Japanese foreign policy 1945–1995 in Russian required thorough preparation.

Despite my initial anxieties, the lectures proceeded very smoothly. In the oral examination, or *zachet* in Russian, all 23 students passed.

Particularly for a diplomat of my generation, whose memory of the Soviet Union was one where freedom of speech was totally suppressed, my experience at MGIMO was astonishing. At no time throughout the course of the lecture was I approached by anyone from the university or elsewhere. The content of the lectures was left entirely to my own discretion. I felt it a particular honour that such complete trust was shown to a diplomat from Japan, given the prevailing and painful situation regarding the unresolved territorial issue of the 'four islands' located to the northeast of Hokkaido.

When the lectures ended at the end of 1995, there emerged an idea from the university whether the major content of my talks could not be outlined in a form of a book or a reader for other students, who had not followed the course. It was another honour for me that such a proposal was offered and I naturally accepted it. For half a year I struggled with my notes and the recorded minutes of my lectures, assisted by an Embassy staff member and native speaker. In July 1996, I managed to produce, virtually on the eve of my departure to Tokyo to assume a new post in the Foreign Ministry, a book in Russian, entitled '50 Years of Japanese Foreign Policy (1945–1995)'.

During the latter part of the 1990's, the book has played a discrete role, so I hope, in enhancing deeper understanding in Russia and among Russian speaking neighbouring countries, of the development of Japanese foreign policy after World War II. On a personal note, I had several surprising encounters when unexpected visitors to Japan from Central Asia or the Russian Far East, not to mention Moscow, told me that they had read my book and referred to particular passages that had caught their attention.

My teaching experience in Moscow and the publication of '50 Years of Japanese Foreign Policy (1945–1995)' made me realize that the combination of teaching and daily work at the Foreign Ministry is very helpful in clearing one's mind and expanding the scope of one's thinking. After my return to Tokyo in 1996, I continued lecturing, this time at Japanese universities. I gave courses at the Sofia University Undergraduate School 1996–98 and Keio University Graduate School 1999–2000. In essence my lectures remained the same. However, this time I added a substantial section regarding

Japanese foreign policy from the Meiji Restoration to World War II.

When I retired from the Foreign Ministry in the spring of 2002, after serving for a short while as ambassador of Japan in the Netherlands, I entered a new phase in my life and thought it to be a worthwhile task to put down in writing a synthesis of Japanese foreign policy in the era I had lived through. What I wrote seven years ago in Russian in Moscow served as a good starting point for this task.

Thus, from the autumn of 2002 onwards I began to write, this time in English, primarily for a European and American audience, a reader about the foreign policy of Japan from 1945 to 2003.

While I was in the process of writing my first draft, I was given an opportunity to combine my writing with teaching. Professor Rikki Kersten of the Leiden University Centre of Japanese and Korean Studies suggested that I teach a class at Leiden University in the spring term of 2003 and use my manuscript in my teaching. This was an exciting offer!

Some twenty students attended my class 'Japan and the World'. Each week they received a draft text of the chapter to be discussed the following week. The teaching process naturally gave me further opportunity to clarify and deepen the contents of my writing. Some of the comments given by the students have contributed substantially to the formulation of this book.

It was against this brief background that my book was written.

Much like the one which I wrote seven years ago, this book was written based primarily on the assumption that the readers did not have prior knowledge of Japanese foreign policy. Students who are studying Japan as well as those who have a general interest in the subject matter are welcome to read this book.

The author naturally is flattered if experts on the subject are able to derive any meaningful impression from the contents of this book.

With these points in mind, my three objectives while writing this book were:

First, I wanted to introduce the basic facts, which constituted the major framework of postwar Japanese foreign policy. I tried to be careful in selecting the most important facts that a reader is advised to know if he or she is interested in the development of Japanese foreign policy after World War II.

Second, the intention of the author was to describe not only the facts, but also to give an analysis of the reason and logic through which Japanese foreign policy has developed. In other words, knowing 'what happened' is essential, but knowing 'why it happened' is what shapes the depth and meaning of history.

Since the author had been in the Japanese Foreign Service until quite recently, it is most purposeful to present, as far as possible, the 'inside views' of the Ministry of Foreign Affairs and the government of Japan. Naturally all 'inside views' presented here are written 'as I saw them' and the government of Japan bears no responsibility for their content. But probably the more I could tell my own views, the more insights readers could have about the inner perspectives of the formulation of Japanese foreign policy. I particularly tried to show the interrelationships between the external events which shaped foreign policy and the internal factors which in many cases conditioned foreign policy.

Third, through my experience in teaching at Leiden University, I felt that one of the liveliest discussions in class developed around my personal experiences, which I explained candidly. Why not include some of these experiences in this book? Naturally, there are so many colleagues of mine who could tell so many inspiring personal stories, but since I happen to write this book, why not tell 'my experiences'? At the suggestion of the students, these episodes are highlighted in a box form in the text. I hope that they will help make the conduct of Japanese foreign policy a little friendlier to those newcomers.

In this context, I also did not hesitate to give some accounts on my grandfather Shigenori Togo, twice Foreign Minister of Japan at the beginning and the end of the Pacific War, and my father Fumihiko Togo, who held a key position in the Foreign Ministry at the time of the revision of the Security Treaty with America and the reversion of Okinawa. I hope that these family experiences may also help in giving a little more animation to the subject in this book.

After the Prologue, which covers the period from the Meiji Restoration to World War II, this book consists of 12 Chapters. Other than Chapter 1, which describes the postwar situation until the conclusion of the San Francisco Peace Treaty, each of the 11 Chapters is dedicated to individual issues, which constitute major spheres in postwar Japanese foreign policy.

Given the limited size and the introductory nature of the book I had to omit some important aspects, such as Japan's policy toward South America and science and technology in general. More words could also have been spent on Africa and on cultural relations. I apologize to the reader for these omissions and those fellow countrymen who have been working in these areas.

I also apologize for some inevitable complexity which emerged, because of the vertical structure of this book. The reader must refer back eleven times through the course of historical development to obtain a full view of the major events which have taken place over a period of half a century. So as to cope with these structural difficulties, I endeavoured to give cross references on major intersecting points and introduce a summary of horizontal analysis in the Conclusion.

In closing, let me add that the major portion of this book is dedicated to the historical analysis of postwar Japanese foreign policy. But writing the history led me to identify seven agendas for future Japanese foreign policy at the threshold of the 21st century. In addition, as the book shows, the success and failure, the dynamism and limitations of postwar foreign policy in Japan have been strongly conditioned by the way Japan dealt with the past. Five limitations emerged from the past while writing this book.

These seven future perspectives and five past limitations are summarized in the concluding chapter.

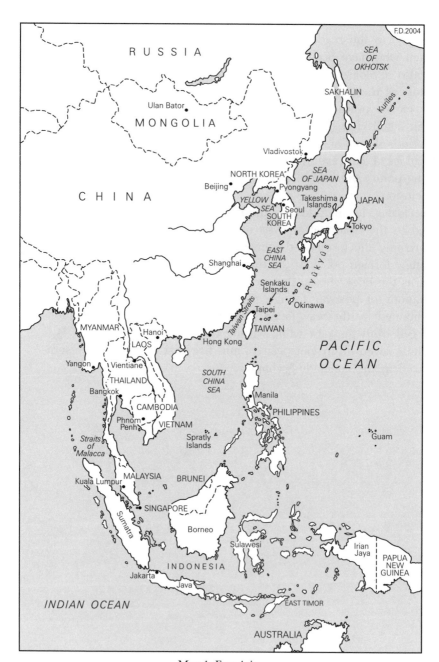

Map 1. East Asia

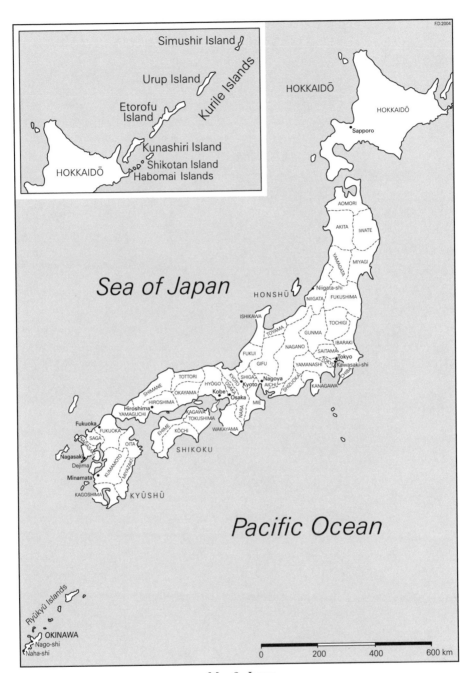

F.D.2004

Simushir Island

Urup Island

Kurile Islands

Etorofu
Island

Kunashiri Island

Shikotan Island

Habomai Islands

HOKKAIDŌ

HOKKAIDŌ

HOKKAIDŌ

Sapporo

Sea of Japan

AOMORI

AKITA

IWATE

YAMAGATA

MIYAGI

HONSHŪ

Niigata-shi

NIIGATA

FUKUSHIMA

ISHIKAWA

TOCHIGI

TOYAMA

GUNMA

IBARAKI

NAGANO

SAITAMA

FUKUI

GIFU

YAMANASHI

TOKYO

Tokyo

Kawasaki-shi

CHIBA

TOTTORI

SHIGA

Nagoya

SHIZUOKA

KYOTO

AICHI

KANAGAWA

SHIMANE

HYŌGO

OSAKA

Kyoto

OKAYAMA

Kobe

Osaka

MIE

HIROSHIMA

NARA

Hiroshima

YAMAGUCHI

KAGAWA

WAKAYAMA

Fukuoka

TOKUSHIMA

FUKUOKA

EHIME

KŌCHI

SAGA

SHIKOKU

Nagasaki

OITA

Dejima

KUMAMOTO

Minamata

MIYAZAKI

KAGOSHIMA

KYŪSHŪ

Pacific Ocean

Ryūkyū Islands

OKINAWA

Nago-shi

Naha-shi

0   200   400   600 km

Map 2. Japan

PROLOGUE: FROM THE MEIJI RESTORATION TO THE PACIFIC WAR

1. *From the Meiji Restoration to the Japan-Russia War*

The Meiji Restoration

In 1868, what is called the 'Meiji Restoration' took place in Japan. There are no other events as important and crucial in the history of modern Japan than those which took place in this Restoration. So much so, that any reader who is interested in Japan must grasp their essence.

Before the Restoration Japan was a feudal society, orderly, stable, rich and in its own way with a highly civilized culture. It was governed by a class of warriors (*samurai*), which effectively controlled the class of farmers, producers and merchants. The country was divided and governed by warlords (*daimyos*) and above the daimyos stood the Shogun, the ruling warlord of the Tokugawa dynasty who resided in *Edo* (present-day Tokyo).

In the early 17th century, the Tokugawa Shogun introduced a tight regime of control over political and economic contacts with the outside world. This policy later became known as the policy of *Sakoku*, or period of isolation. The country had been cut off notably from the Western world for two and a half centuries. The only exception was the relationship with The Netherlands, whose representatives were allowed to stay on a fan-shaped artificial island constructed within Nagasaki Bay in Southern Japan.[1] The Netherlands were a natural choice for the Tokugawa Shogun to preserve diplomatic relations with, because the 17th century was the 'Golden Age' for the Netherlands. Dutch ships took the lead on the seven seas and merchant and other activities expanded.

---

[1] It has long been perceived both in Japan and among Western researchers on Japanese history that, except for the Netherlands, Japan was completely cut off from the outside world during the *Sakoku* period. But recent scholarly works indicate that this isolation primarily applied to the West and that Japan had maintained its contacts with China and Korea (Leitch, Kato, Weinstein, *Japan's Role in the Post-Cold War World*, Greenwood, 1995, p. 10).

In 1853 the peace and tranquillity of feudal Japan were shattered by the sudden arrival of American gun boats, led by Commodore Matthew C. Perry, at a bay not far from *Edo*. It is not easy for contemporary Japanese to truly appreciate the extent of the shock to the psychology of the Japanese people, but for the Japanese of one and a half centuries ago, the black, iron-covered, steam engine driven gun boats were surely as shocking as gleaming spaceships from outer space would be for us today.

At any rate, by the middle of the 19th century the Tokugawa and other feudal leaders came to understand the hard reality that Great Britain, France, Russia, the Netherlands, Germany, and the United States were each trying to expand their sphere of influence by reaching out to Asia, particularly to China, so close to Japan. It was a painful process, entailing a lot of confusion and some bloodshed, but it was implemented amazingly fast, and in 1868, the Tokugawa Shogun relinquished power to a new government, which was shaped by a group of influential 'reformist' warlords, united under the authority of the Emperor Meiji.

The Imperial tradition that originated in Japan from the beginning of Japanese history,[2] played an important role during her formative years and then through the feudal years. During the Tokugawa Shogunate the Imperial House was carefully preserved as a centre of spiritual and cultural value in Kyoto, the ancient capital of Japan. It then played a critical role in the unification of the country during these difficult years of Japan's modern history.

It is now of paramount importance to understand how the Meiji government leaders saw the world and what conclusions were derived from their vision. The Meiji government leaders were aware that Japan was surrounded by incomparably strong imperialist powers. For Japan, to survive and remain as an independent nation, there was an absolute necessity to understand exactly where she stood and what she should do, so as not to be engulfed by these imperialist powers. Thus from 1871 to 1872 for nearly a full two years, the newly established government sent an extraordinary mission to America and major European countries, headed by five top leaders

---

[2] One of the oldest narrative histories, the *Nihonshoki*, says that the first Emperor assumed the throne in 660 BC. Historians maintain that it was around the 7th century that the Imperial system came into existence.

of the new government under the leadership of Tomomi Iwakura and accompanied by more than 40 of the 'best and brightest' of the new Meiji government. Their eagerness to learn, their humbleness and courage in facing the unknown, their intelligence to absorb things fundamentally new, while displaying a natural pride in the culture and history from which they originated, all left a strong impression in the countries they visited.[3]

The delegation came back to Japan with a shared understanding that, for Japan to coexist with the countries they had visited, Japan should become strong. The ultimate criterion of strength was military power, but that strength could be developed only if it was based on a strong and stable political structure and a powerful, prosperous economy. *Fukoku-Kyohei*, which meant 'rich country and strong military' became the motto of the time. Japan therefore focussed its energy primarily on the internal development of politics, industry, trade, society, education, and the military. Realism became the key approach of the Meiji government, to ensure the survival of the country.

Foreign policy agenda: revision of unequal treaties and border demarcation

At a time when the Meiji government's efforts were directed primarily towards the creation of a strong government based on a strong economy, two major issues weighed heavily in the area of foreign policy. These two issues were essential if Japan was to secure equal footing with the Euro-American powers of the international community. Both issues commanded the general support of the Japanese people.

The first issue was the revision of the 'unequal treaties', which the Tokugawa Shogunate was forced to conclude during the 1850's with the United States, the Netherlands, Russia, Great Britain, France, Portugal and Prussia (Germany). These treaties included special clauses to grant consular jurisdiction to foreigners. They were allowed to

---

[3] The Iwakura Mission travelled altogether for 632 days, visiting the following 12 Euro-American countries and other Southeast Asian countries as well: USA, UK, France, Belgium, the Netherlands, Germany, Russia, Denmark, Sweden, Italy, Austria, and Switzerland (S. Izumi, *Dodotaru Nihonjin (The Dignified Japanese)*, Shodensha, 1997, p. 91).

live inside the foreign residential area, where they were subjected to consular jurisdiction and exempted from Japanese jurisdiction. Other clauses in these treaties deprived Japan of the right to determine its own customs duties. Both clauses gave one-sided privileges and benefits to the other contracting party. The revision of these clauses became an essential task for successive foreign ministers and as a result of their strenuous efforts the consular jurisdiction clauses were abrogated by 1899, but customs duties clauses were only revised by 1911. Indeed, it took 40 years for Japan to overcome this issue, which symbolized the burden under which the Meiji government had started its governance.

The second agenda was that of border demarcation with the neighbouring countries.

With Russia, with which Japan had to demarcate the northern border, the Tokugawa Shogunate had already concluded the Treaty of Commerce and Friendship in 1855, which defined the southern limit of the Russian border from the Kurile Islands down to the island of Urrupu and the northern border of Japan up to the island of Etorofu. Whereas the sovereignty of Sakhalin was left undefined in this treaty, a new Treaty of Exchanges concerning Sakhalin and the Kurile Islands was concluded in 1875, stipulating that Sakhalin belonged to Russia and the Kurile Islands to Japan.

In terms of the southern border, Japan and China went through complicated negotiations over the islands of Okinawa. Japanese control over the islands was considerably strengthened by the beginning of the 1880's, but the final settlement had to wait until the Japan-China War in 1895.

In the 19th century the islands of Ogasawara, located to the south of Honshu, the main island of Japan, had been visited by several British and American vessels, and at the same time immigrants arrived from Japan. Japan's announcement to exercise sovereignty in 1875 was met with basic understanding by other interested parties, such as the US, the UK and Germany.

The Korean peninsula and the Japan-China War

Thus over the 1880's Japan's internal political, economic and military strength gradually began to accumulate. Some of the border issues were being resolved. The Meiji Constitution was enacted in 1889. Against the background of these developments Japan began to conceptualize more acutely her position in Far Eastern Asia and the world.

The overall consensus of the government and intellectuals of Meiji, based on their realism, was probably that the Euro-American nations' power was simply overwhelming in contrast to that of the Far Eastern Asian nations, including Japan.

The only credible way for Japan to overcome that situation was to continue to become stronger, even at the expense of becoming different from the surrounding Asian nations. In 1885 such a view was crystallized in the formula presented by a leading intellectual of the era, Yukichi Fukuzawa, in his well-known paraphrase *Datsu-A-Nyu-Ou*, which meant 'Getting out (=*Datsu*) from Asia (=*A*) and entering into (=*Nyu*) Europe (=*Ou*)'. In another words, 'catching up with the West' became a real motto of the time.

Admittedly, in the debates among intellectuals and philosophers there were some views that Japan should become united with other Asian countries such as China or Korea, against the oppression of Western imperialism, but those views were not shared by the majority and were in general kept outside the scope of governmental policy-making.[4]

By the 1890's these internal, external and conceptual developments led Japan to a search for a stronger basis to implement a policy of 'catching up with the West'. The key question which emerged was the notion that Japan needed to secure the surrounding areas to ensure her own security and development. A statement made in 1890 by Aritomo Yamagata, one of the prominent leaders of the Restoration, outlined the necessity for Japan to protect 'the cordon of sovereignty', which meant the area under Japanese sovereignty within the demarcated border, and 'the cordon of influence', which meant those adjacent areas, where Japan's own security was also affected.

In actual terms, for the leadership of the Meiji government, the area within 'the cordon of influence' primarily meant the Korean peninsula. The Korean peninsula in fact stretched from the continent

---

[4] In 1885 a minority opposition party leader, Tokichi Tarui, published his theses calling for a unification of Japan and Korea and its alliance with China to counter a Russian threat. His view did not command much support (M. Ikei, *Nihongaikoushi Gaisetsu (Overview of the Japanese Foreign Policy) 3rd Edition*, Keio University, 1997, pp. 63–64).

to the Japanese islands like a 'dagger' and it could be so perceived that the geopolitical conditions of the peninsula made it a conduit for threats from the continent to Japan. In 1872, just after the return of the Iwakura Mission from its trip abroad, it already became a serious political issue whether Japan should not take more effective measures to keep the peninsula outside the sphere of influence of other powers, such as China or Russia. That approach was then rejected as being too hasty and premature, but from then on, these underlying motives did not disappear.

The first real contention over the Korean peninsula developed with China in the middle of the 1890's.

In the spring of 1894, an agrarian-religious revolutionary movement called the *Ton-Haku* rebellion began in Korea. The Korean government, faced with the danger of a revolutionary movement, decided to invite Chinese military forces into their country in an effort to suppress that movement. The Japanese government saw further danger for an expanded role by China in the peninsula and decided to send its own army to counter the Chinese move. After the suppression of the *Ton-Haku* rebellion Japan successfully pressured the Korean government to break off its special relationship with China. China could not accept that situation and war broke out between Japan and China in July. In the course of half a year, to the surprise of everyone including Japan, a swift victory over China both on land and at sea was attained and in April 1895 the two countries agreed on a peace treaty. The major achievements for Japan were the independence of Korea, the annexation of Taiwan (Formosa) and the Pen Fu islands (Pescadores) as well as the Liaotung peninsula, and a sizable reparation payment of 300 million yen.

The unexpected victory brought great relief, rejoicing and a sense of achievement for the Japanese people. Six days after the signature of the peace treaty, however, Russia, Germany and France made a common demarche against Japan to renounce the rights of annexation of the Liaotung peninsula. Russia took the lead in this Triple Intervention. Though stunned by this totally unexpected demarche, the government had carefully discussed the three options it could take: to reject it, to convene a multilateral conference or to accept it. Japan had no further military capability to risk a war against the three intervening countries. Foreign Minister Munemitsu Mutsu maintained strongly that a multilateral conference carried the risk of unleashing other issues. There was no other option than to accept the intervention. The news of the return of the Liaotung peninsula permeated the country like a high voltage electric shock from government leaders to the 'man in the street'. Soho Tokutomi, a well-known intellectual at the time, wrote: "I may say that the return of the Liaotung peninsula has practically determined the fate of the rest of my life. After I heard the news, I virtually became a different person. All my reflection and consideration boils down to the question of a lack of power. If you do not have power, then any justice or action is not as valuable as a half penny."[5] That became the mood of the country and the whole nation recharged its energy to work, work and work to make Japan a strong country, politically, economically and militarily.

Another serious realization, which occurred in the foreign policy arena, was that in facing the three countries intervention, Japan did not have any ally to support the Japanese cause. The danger of isolation in the conduct of foreign policy was the single greatest lesson the Meiji leadership had had to learn. Thus there emerged strong support to seek an alliance with a major power in world politics. Japan's search for an ally met with a positive reaction on the part of Great Britain, which increasingly shared an acute common concern over the expansionist tendency of Russia in the southern and eastern part of the Eurasian continent. The first Anglo-Japanese alliance was concluded in 1902.

The Russo-Japanese War

After the Triple Intervention, it was the relationship with Russia that became the most sensitive for Japan. Russia not only took the lead in the intervention, but also acquired the Liaotung peninsula under lease. Faced with mounting pressure from this gigantic neighbour from the north, the most delicate area for Japan was once again the Korean peninsula. Some influential Japanese[6] argued that a reasonable balance was to let Korea stay under the Japanese 'sphere of influence' and let Manchuria, which was between Korea and Russia, remain under the Russian 'sphere of influence'. This concept was

---

[5] Ikei, *op. cit.*, p. 76.
[6] Top Meiji leaders like H. Ito, K. Inoue and others shared this view (Ikei, *op. cit.*, p. 83).

then called 'the concept of exchange between Korea and Manchuria'. When Russia concluded an agreement with China in 1902 on Russia's withdrawal from Manchuria, the situation seemed to have improved substantially. The repeated failure of Russia to withdraw its troops within the prescribed deadline of the agreement, but moreover, some signs that Russia was taking concrete steps to establish a military presence in Korea, ignited a deep anxiety among the Japanese leadership. Thus the tension between Japan and Russia mounted.

The war broke out in February 1904, and again, the Japanese military gained a fast and unexpected victory. On land, the army secured the Liaotung peninsula and in March 1905 gained a major victory at Shenyang. The navy secured an unprecedented victory— which would long be remembered in the history of naval battles— at the Tsushima Straits against the Baltic Fleet in May 1905.

The Meiji government, with its acute sense of realism, grasped every opportunity to conclude the war. It was fully aware that the supply of materials, weaponry, logistics and finance simply did not allow the continuation of warfare for long. Under President Theodore Roosevelt's mediation, the peace treaty negotiations took place in August 1905 at Portsmouth on the east coast of the United States. The treaty was signed in September 1905: in addition to the recognition of Japanese supremacy in Korea, both Russia and Japan agreed on the withdrawal of their troops from Manchuria; Japan gained the right to lease the Liaotung peninsula and the right to control the southern Manchurian railroad between Changchun and Ryuushun; Japan also annexed the southern half of Sakhalin Island.

The people of Japan believed that the content of the 1905 Peace Treaty was miserably poor in contrast to the dramatic victory achieved on the battlefield. No reparations and the land they acquired was just the southern half of Sakhalin! They took it as an outrageous betrayal of the country. Demonstrations reached a dangerous level when a delegation headed by Foreign Minister Jyutaro Komura came back from Portsmouth and a curfew had to be introduced to protect the delegates on their journey home.

There was a serious dilemma for the government in its relations with the people through the media. The leadership was well aware of the weakness of the position of its own country. However, it was essential for the government not to let this recognition of its own weakness be made known to Russia. This knowledge could have weakened the Japanese position both on the battlefield and at the negotiating table. Information therefore simply could not be disclosed to the public. The Japanese people only had access to successive news reports on the outstanding victory on the battlefields and therefore developed an illusionary vision of the strength of the country as well as a false expectation of the anticipated gains from the 1905 Peace Treaty.

Despite all these difficulties and complications Japan won the war and with this unexpected and unprecedented victory the first phase of the post-Meiji Restoration ended. Japan's victory was generally welcomed by the Asian countries, albeit that the complications related to the outcome of the peace treaty made Japan feel that 40 years of united efforts to 'catch up with the West' or *Datsu-A-Nyu-Ou* allowed her to climb the ladder very quickly. To the surprise of the Japanese themselves more than anyone else, Japan had finally achieved her goal of being equal with other major players of the international community.

2. WW I and the Washington Conference

The psychological impact of the Russo-Japanese War

The second phase of the post-Meiji Restoration started with a very different psychological set-up. The objective of 'climbing the ladder' had been fulfilled and Japan saw herself at the top of a plateau, where it had more freedom for choices and options. But that freedom was combined with a dilemma and a contradiction which made the Japanese implementation of foreign policy a more complex and intricate exercise. Six points are worth mentioning regarding the psychological make-up of the Japanese during this period:

(1) First, an inevitable inclination to the notion of 'the Gospel of Power' cannot be negated. Japan itself now became a much bigger country comprising Korea, which it annexed in 1910, the southern half of Sakhalin, Taiwan and the Pescadores. The primary area of its 'sphere of influence' now moved into the southern part of Manchuria.

(2) Second, an acute sense of realism stayed active among some of the government leadership and intellectuals and they knew well that victory came not only through military power, but also by a careful coordination of external relations to avoid isolation and to

create allies. For them, it was essential to ensure a good understanding among the major Euro-American powers on the conduct
of Japanese policy in the East-Asian continent. In many instances,
they were aware of the danger of a growing perception of 'the yel-
low peril' theory, and therefore in some instances even carefully dis-
tanced Japan from identifying itself with Asiatic values.

(3) Third, in the private sector, on the contrary, those views identifying Japan's future with Asia and Asiatic values gained further
momentum against the background of the Japanese victory over
Russia. A well-known statement by Tenshin Okakura, a philosopher
and artist that "Asia is a single unity" was pronounced in 1902.
There emerged harsh criticism from private sector intellectuals that
government policy seeking understanding among Western nations
was too compromising and void of ideals. It is also interesting to
note that among those private sector views in support of Japan's
positioning in Asia, the voices emphasizing Japan's specific and leading role became more prominent than those who stressed the necessity of equal partnership with Asian countries.

(4) Fourth, in the new era of complexity, among the optimists
there emerged a new concept that given the unique achievement
Japan had made over the last 40 years, she might have a specific
mission to fulfil to the betterment of the world, namely to act as a
catalyst for the harmonization of Western and Eastern values. That
concept was labelled as *To-Zai-Yuuwa*. *To* meant east, *Zai* meant west,
and *Yuuwa* meant harmony or fusion: 'Harmony of East and West'.
As romantic and idealistic as it may sound in retrospect, this notion
grasped the hearts of many intellectuals in the period after the Russo-
Japanese War.

(5) Fifth, among the pessimists, however, the post Russo-Japanese
War situation created a call for a new identity. Japan, which tried
to catch up with the West, was still very different from the real
West. She was obviously different and wanted to be different from
the rest of Asia. What is Japan and who are the Japanese? What
specific values can Japan introduce as a lone, new-born country from
the Far East? Pessimists could not find an answer to this question.

(6) Last, in the area of domestic policy, it should be noted that
the decades which followed the Russo-Japanese War until the
Manchurian Incident were generally recognized as a lively period,
in which various democratic movements gained strength. Within the
rights and obligations of the Meiji Constitution, the first prime min-

ister from political parties was selected in 1918 and in 1925 a universal manhood suffrage law was enacted.[7]

The foreign policy agenda after the Russo-Japanese War

The victory over Russia fundamentally changed Japan's relationships with the major powers surrounding her in the Asia-Pacific region.

First and foremost, the United States, which acted as a mediator in concluding the Portsmouth Peace Treaty, began to harbour serious concerns on the nature of Japan's rapidly growing power.

In Eastern Asia the United States was concerned that the way Japan was expanding its influence to Manchuria and possibly China would go directly against American interests, embodied in the 'Open Door Policy' expressed by Secretary of State John M. Hay in 1899. In 1905, at the time the peace treaty was negotiated in Portsmouth, a leading railroad owner Edward H. Harriman visited Japan and made an agreement on the joint management of the southern Manchurian railroad, which Japan was going to gain from Russia. This agreement was later revoked upon the return of Foreign Minister Jyutaro Komura from his peace treaty negotiations at Portsmouth. Komura was convinced that the railroad, which was going to become the key element for the governance of southern Manchuria, had to be owned by Japan. In 1909 Secretary of State Philander C. Knox put forth a proposal to place all Manchurian railroads under international control, but the proposal could not be accepted by Japan, which already saw Manchuria as a vital area under its sphere of influence.

In the Pacific it was the growing strength of the Japanese navy that troubled America. Admiral Heihachiro Togo, who commanded the historic victory at the Tsushima Straits over Russia, became more a symbol of a threat than of glory. America began serious efforts to expand and strengthen her own naval power. In 1907, the first American plan, called 'the Orange Plan' was drafted, the purpose of which was to counter a possible war against Japan in Pacific. In this newly emerging and tense situation, Japan also saw it as necessary to create an even stronger navy. It became the objective for

---

[7] This period is also known as the 'Taisho democracy', after Emperor Taisho, who reigned from 1912 to 1926, between Emperor Meiji and Emperor Showa.

the Japanese admiralty to create fleets of 8 battleships and 8 cruisers.

To make the situation worse, discrimination against Japanese emigrants, who established themselves primarily on the west coast of the American continent after the Meiji Restoration, erupted. In 1906 the city of San Francisco gave an order to segregate Japanese students from studying with other 'white children'. In 1913 a law was enacted in California to exclude the first generation of Japanese emigrants from land ownership. These developments confused and irritated the Japanese leadership and fuelled anger and strong emotion among the public.

Notwithstanding those emerging difficulties, the leadership of the two countries displayed a sense of realism that it was not in the interest of either country to go on a collision course. The 1905 Katsura-Taft Memorandum, which recognized Korea and the Philippines as within each country's respective sphere of influence, was one example. The 1908 Takahara-Root Agreement, in which both countries agreed to preserve the status quo in the Pacific region and to observe in China the independence, territorial integrity and the principle of equal opportunity for third powers, was another example.

In contrast to the emerging tension with the United States, the relationship with Russia, with which Japan had fought a desperate war, improved phenomenally. The first accord was concluded in 1907, primarily based on the necessity for both sides to ensure post-war stability and the preservation of a balance of power in south and north Manchuria. That first accord developed into the second accord in 1910. It became clear that both countries shared a common concern *vis-à-vis* the United States for their expanded economic activities in Manchuria. The third accord was concluded in 1912, and finally the fourth one in 1916. The fourth accord was even looked upon as an alliance between Russia and Japan.

The nature of the Japanese-British alliance also changed. From the European point of view, Germany rather than Russia emerged as a major threat to the status quo. From that point of view Britain had no objection to the enhanced relationship between Japan and Russia as outlined above, as well as the strengthening of the Japanese-French relationship, which came to be realized by the Japan-France Accord of 1907. Thus the alliance relationships of Britain, France and Russia, each supported by Japan, a newly emerging power in the Far East, took shape. These complex multilateral relationships, rather than a narrowly defined bilateral relationship with Japan, came to be preferred by Great Britain. That arrangement also suited Japan well.

At the same time, Great Britain had another serious reason to distance itself somewhat from Japan. The growing tension between Japan and the United States increasingly put Britain in an awkward position. In the event that a crisis should occur between Japan and the United States, Britain did not want to put itself in a position to have to fight against the United States. Thus the third Anglo-Japanese alliance in 1911 excluded America from the objective of the agreement.

World War I and the Paris Peace Conference

In August 1914 World War I broke out in Europe. There Japan saw a great opportunity to show her new role in global politics and to expand and strengthen her position, particularly in Eastern Asia. It cannot be denied that the notion of a 'Gospel of Power' gained further momentum.

When asked by Great Britain to join the war on 7 August, Japan sent an ultimatum to Germany on 15 August and declared war on 23 August. Given the alliance relationships with the British, French and the Russians, that was a natural choice.

The area where Japanese activities were expected to be performed was not in Europe but in the Far East. The first Japanese objective was to take over German interests in the region. Japan immediately attacked and occupied Chintao, a major German basis in the region located on the Shandong peninsula. The Japanese navy occupied some of the South Pacific islands which had been under German control as well.

The second, and probably a more important objective for Japan, was to establish her sphere of influence firmly inside China, where political turmoil had been mounting for years. In October 1911 a revolutionary movement exploded there, which led to the establishment of the Nanjing Provisional Government headed by Sun Yat-sen in January 1912. In Beijing, after reigning for 300 years, the Qing Dynasty resigned and in February 1912 a new republic led by Yuan Shi-kai, the leader of the northern warlords, was created.

The country was politically far from being united, but a strong feeling of nationalism united the people. The notion of the 'sphere of influence' on the part of outside powers was losing its traditional ground. But, in a situation where world power attention was directed primarily to Europe, Japan saw a unique opportunity to enlarge her traditionally accepted 'sphere of influence'. In January 1915, Japan presented its 21 Clauses to the newly formed Chinese government. They included such clauses as Japan's right to inherit German privileges over the Shandong peninsula, to extend her special privileges in Manchuria and Mongolia, and to dispatch her counsellors in financial or military administration to the Chinese government. The Chinese were violently opposed to the Japanese requests, particularly the last part, where Japan requested her right to intrude on internal matters in China. After five months of bitter and thorny negotiations an agreement was reached on the basis of 14 clauses, excluding all parts related to Japanese intrusion to internal matters. Japan achieved certain policy objectives, but severe psychological damage was done to the Chinese government and people.

In 1918 the war was terminated and the Peace Conference was convened in Paris in January 1919. Japan was invited there as one of the five principal victor countries together with Great Britain, France, Italy and the United States. It was the first occasion, where Japan was included in such a multilateral forum as one of the leading countries of the world. It was an honourable occasion and the delegates to the conference went there with a strong sense of pride.

However, as it turned out, the conference offered many opportunities for Japan to think seriously about the future of her foreign policy. How to ensure Japan's right over the Shandong peninsula and the South Pacific islands, which she inherited from Germany, was, in a practical sense, the only area for Japan to speak out upon and defend her interests. After prolonged and bitter debates, particularly with the Chinese delegation, Japan achieved her objective to secure her rights on the Shandong peninsula. But this in turn invited an outburst of anti Japanese feeling in China, as a result of which the peninsula was given back to China only three years later. Thus the 1919 Peace Conference resulted in enhanced anti-Japanese emotions in China, further complicating difficulties for future Japanese policy there.

On all other issues related to the question of global peace, security and justice which were of major importance for many delegations, such as the question of the establishment of the League of Nations, the Japanese delegation remained virtually mute and was even labelled as 'the silent delegation'. From the point of view of substance, the foreign policy thinking of the delegation was ill-equipped to follow major issues of future decades. The only exception, where Japan made a conspicuous proposal in relation to global issues, was the proposal to include a clause into the League of Nations Charter on racial equality, which was not adopted but is still remembered as a farsighted step towards the future.

There was also a huge vacuum of professional experience to participate in multilateral foreign policy. Thus the conference was instrumental in assisting Japan to comprehend her fundamental weakness.

The Russian Revolution and Allied intervention

Another important world event occurred during World War I, namely, the Russian Revolution. Great Britain and France, in particular, became much concerned with the fate of this neighbouring country and decided to go ahead with intervention. The United States was more cautious in her approach but they decided to go ahead in July 1918, when they heard news that Czechoslovakian troops were caught by a Bolshevik surge in the central part of Siberia. Japan waited cautiously until the US decision was taken, but once the decision was taken, following the US, her activities became more conspicuous than others. In August 1918 Japan dispatched troops to Siberia. By autumn their numbers totalled 73,000, eight times more than agreed upon with the United States, occupying a tangible part of Siberia and Northern Sakhalin. The army stayed in Siberia until 1922, as the last troops to have occupied Soviet territory.

It took another three years, until 1925, before Japan and the newly born Soviet Union fully normalized their relationship based on the Convention of Basic Principles. Japan withdrew from Northern Sakhalin in the same year but acquired the rights for oil excavation in the northern part of Sakhalin.

The intervention left a deep scar in the mind of the Soviets about Japan's actions in their homeland. Japanese casualties numbered 3,500 plus huge expenditure and brought relatively small benefits. It became a bitter lesson and a clear warning for Japan in relying too much on the 'Gospel of Power'.

The Washington Conference and foreign policy under the Washingtonian order

Now that the two major events of the 1910's, World War I and the Russian Revolution were over, the major countries of the world gathered in Washington from November 1921 until February 1922 to discuss acute outstanding issues pertaining to the peace and security of the world. As the situation in Europe was basically resolved by the Paris Peace Conference, the outstanding crucial issues which remained were primarily those related to the Asia-Pacific region.

To this day opinions vary in Japan on the evaluation of this conference. Some maintain that it was a process of unwilling Japanese subordination to American pressure, which dominated the arena. Others argue that it represented serious efforts on the part of Japan to associate with and contribute to the emerging new values in international relations. There are also views, that whether it was a willing or unwilling process, Japan managed to preserve her sphere of influence over Manchuria and keep her power base as she then intended. Whichever the evaluation, Japan took an important decision to adhere to the conclusion of the 1919 Peace Conference, which set the basic tone of international relations during the 1920's.

The first agreement made was on naval arms reduction. The key issue was the ratio to be applied to battleships between the United States, Great Britain and Japan. Japan's basic position was to achieve a ratio of 10:10:7, but it finally agreed to the proposal made by America, that of 10:10:6. There remained within the Japanese navy differing views on the adequacy of this agreement, but the majority in Japan accepted it as an unavoidable compromise. As a footnote, this agreement was supplemented later in 1930 at the London Naval Conference on cruisers and other auxiliary ships with a ratio of 10:10:6.97.

The second agreement was on China. A treaty was signed by all nine participants of the conference: the USA, Great Britain, France, Italy, Japan, Belgium, the Netherlands, Portugal and China. It was an incarnation of the traditional open door policy maintained by America. Those fundamental clauses such as respect for the sovereignty, independence and territorial integrity of China, as well as the right to equal opportunities in trade and commercial activities for foreign countries, were included. The fact that the treaty did not derogate the existing rights of foreign governments over China nor include any clause on measures to be taken against a violation of the treaty, allowed Japan to maintain her sphere of influence in Manchuria and elsewhere. The treaty embodied, however, new principles of international relations which went beyond the traditional thinking of imperialism and the notion of respective spheres of influence. It was not without importance to note that Japan abided with those newly emerging principles.

The third agreement was on the Asia-Pacific region in general. By that time, the Anglo-Japanese alliance had significantly lost its *raison-d'être*, because both Russia and Germany, which could have become their common threat, were fundamentally weakened. American uneasiness concerning the alliance had to be taken into account as well. Thus an idea emerged to restructure the alliance so as to include America. France was invited as a fourth partner with a view to soften an inflated impression of American participation. Thus a quadrilateral treaty, comprising America, Britain, Japan and France, was signed to replace the Anglo-Japanese alliance.

The talks within and at the fringe of the conference became instrumental as well for Japan in engendering two decisions mentioned above, the return of the Shandong peninsula and the withdrawal from Northern Sakhalin.

In 1924 Kijuuro Shidehara became Foreign Minister for a period of three years. After an interval of two years, he was re-appointed in 1929 for two-and-a-half more years. As one of the plenipotentiaries of Japan to the Washington Conference, Shidehara's political thinking was deeply rooted in the spirit which governed the conference.

First, he maintained strongly that Japan should follow the major trend of international relations. From that perspective he emphasized the importance of a new foreign policy aiming at justice, peace and the role of the League of Nations, but in reality it was a reflection of the importance he attached to Japan's relations with America and Great Britain.

Second, a strong emphasis on economic rather than military policy was sought. One of his reasons to further the relationship with the United States was based on a sober recognition, that about one third of Japanese trade was shared with the United States. On the continent, such measures as the 21 Clauses' demand against China, or the Siberian intervention against the Soviet Union were counterproductive, just fuelling nationalism against Japan and inviting suspicion by surrounding countries. A more peaceful approach to expand economic interests was preferred.

Third, his approach was characteristic for non-intervention in the internal affairs of China. It conformed well to the two principles mentioned above, but at the same time, it was based on a certain realism related to the internal situation in China. China was in turmoil. The new government in Beijing, established in February 1912 under the leadership of Yuan Shi-kai, could not reconcile its rivalry *vis-à-vis* the revolutionary government in Nanjing led by Sun Yat-sen. In 1921 Sun Yat-sen created a new Nationalist Party Government in Kwantong. In the same year the communist party was formed. In 1924 the Nationalist Government and the communist party went into the first round of coalition. In 1926 the Nationalist Government under the leadership of Chiang Kai-shek began the gigantic Northern Expedition and established a new government in Nanjing in 1927. To take sides in any of these movements seemed to be difficult and risky. The wisest policy was to stay away from internal turmoil.

Shidehara' s approach created a fresh image, a new approach to foreign policy, which combined external, economic and military elements within a unified structure. Unfortunately, his position gradually met with severe opposition, particularly from nationalistic forces inside the country.

The first attack was on his China policy. For many, his approach seemed to be too weak, conciliatory and lacking creative ideas for the preservation and consolidation of Japan's interests in China. It became the primary reason for his resignation in 1927.

During his second tenure of office from 1929 criticism of his economic policy mounted again. The worldwide recession, which exploded during the same year, made Shidehara's position not very convincing in the eyes of many Japanese. Shidehara was, on the one hand, a strong advocate for the protection of Japanese economic rights and privileges, but his fundamental thinking to rely on the principle of open trade with China sounded less convincing under the extreme recessionary international economic situation, for those who maintained the necessity of preserving the traditional sphere of influence for Japan's economic interests.

On his approach towards the harmonization of foreign policy with Anglo-American forces, towards the end of the 1920's, emphasizing Asiatic values and the necessity for Japan to adhere to its destiny within the surrounding countries under her sphere of influence became more vocal in many echelons of society. They maintained that Japan needed to expand her influence to areas which ensured a self-sufficient basis for economic development, that not only Manchuria and outer Mongolia but China in its entirety had to be viewed from that perspective, and that the American approach shown at the naval disarmament talks, emigration issues, or the creation of the Washingtonian order was not conducive to the national interest of Japan.

Foreign policy orientation to emphasize Asia and Japan's role in Asia, thus far a minority view and held primarily by the limited private sector to seek an expanded sphere of influence, thereafter became more vocal. In various echelons of society the Japanese military forces, primarily the army, became the chief advocate of this view.

Between 1927 and 1929, Giichi Tanaka became the Prime Minister, concurrently serving as Foreign Minister. He took a more active, interventionist and sometimes militaristic policy towards China, while emphasizing the necessity of preserving an economic approach and paying due attention to the understanding of the major surrounding countries such as the United States or Great Britain.[8]

At any rate, we have reached the end of the second phase of prewar history. It was a period when Japanese foreign policy was seriously searching to find a way to ensure its national interest. The 'Gospel of Power' directly inherited from the victory of the Russo-Japanese War was clearly there. However, that was not the only theme. A sense of realism, idealism, new directions for economic and pacifist tendencies, all of these directions were there.

As we now enter the third stage, from the Manchurian Incident to the War in the Pacific, we see that these various trends gradually converged in a single direction towards Pearl Harbour in December 1941. But that conversion was not a predetermined direction devoid of hesitation, confusion, and efforts to choose the future course of the nation from several alternatives, which then still seemed to exist.

---

[8] Giichi Tanaka, a former army general, has often been portrayed as representing military views during his tenure as Prime Minister. But Akira Iriye maintains that, although Tanaka did not have the non-interventionist and economy-oriented approach characteristic in Shidehara, Tanaka's position reflected the traditional imperialist type of balance of power approach under the Meiji government. Tanaka did not share the militaristic approach of securing Japan's primary interest by physical power and, if necessary, intrigues, characteristic in the Kwantung army. He therefore stood somewhere in between Shidehara and the military (A. Iriye, *Nihonno Gaikou (Japanese Foreign Policy)*, Cuukou Shinsho, 1995, p. 101).

3. *From the Manchurian Incident to the War in the Pacific*

The Manchurian Incident

When the world plunged into the global recession in 1929, Japan was not spared. All aspects of life on the Japanese mainland, in the annexed territories, and in those areas under her sphere of influence, suffered. Notably, a sense of crisis emerged in Manchuria, particularly among the leading officers stationed there, called the Kwantung army. They were convinced that the national interest of Japan could only be secured through the establishment of a self-sufficient area for its economic development and that it was absolutely essential to keep Manchuria firmly under the Japanese sphere of influence. They became worried about the way the Manchurian economy was hit by the world recession, such as the decline in the soybean market. They were also fundamentally troubled by the behaviour of the local Manchurian leader Zhang Xue-liang. His father was assassinated by the Kwantung army in 1928, and Zhang Xue-liang assumed an overt policy of support of the Nationalist Government.

In September 1931 the Kwantung army blew up a railroad near Shenyang. Based on the pretext that it was instigated by Chinese rebels, the Kwantung army moved fast to occupy a vast area of Southern as well as Northern Manchuria. The government in Tokyo repeatedly tried to stop their escalation, but in vain. Public opinion, partly frustrated by the economic and political difficulties at home, ardently welcomed this development of securing and consolidating an area under a Japanese sphere of influence.

The incident rapidly developed from a military to a political one. In March 1932 a new independent Manchurian State was established under the heir of the former Qing dynasty and Japan recognized it as an independent state in September. The reality, however, was that not only the diplomatic and military policies of the country but also internal matters fell under Japanese governance in many instances. A 'puppet state', as we now call it, was created.

China strongly objected to the Japanese moves and immediately took the case to the League of Nations, where heated debates began. In January 1932 the Secretary of State of the United States, Henry L. Stimson made the American position clear, namely that it did not approve of the Japanese action. Though there was an absence of any concrete sanctions or measures to curb the Japanese moves, on a moral basis, the US clearly sided with the Chinese position. Meanwhile, a mission from the League of Nations headed by Sir Victor A.G.B. Lytton was sent to the Far East and a report was formulated in October 1932. The report advised that Manchuria be kept under the Chinese sovereignty with extensive rights for self-determination and that an agreement should be reached between Japan and China on the nature of this status. The special status of Manchuria in relation to Japan, as it was recognized by the League of Nations, was not enough for Japan, which insisted that the newly born 'puppet state' should be recognized by the international community. A vote on the report took place on 24 February 1933, with 44 votes for the report, one against (from Japan), and one abstention, which was Thailand. The Japanese delegation ceremonially left the room and one month later Japan formally withdrew from the League of Nations. The realistic avoidance of isolation learned in the aftermath of the Japan-China War in 1895 thus met with severe defeat.

For Japan the independence of Manchuria became essential to secure this area under its own sphere of influence and to ensure the development of a self-sufficient economy, particularly in terms of natural resources. After the Manchurian Incident Japanese external policy began to bear a strong notion of 'national interest' and 'national defence', which was primarily aimed toward establishing a self-supporting sphere of influence, based, above all, on military power. Various policy options and ideas as they had appeared after the victory of the Russo-Japanese War and developed through the 1910's and 1920's, were gradually replaced by this single direction. The notion that Japan was the leading power to represent a new Asia became strong in supporting this direction.

The military took the lead in this direction, and the government in general supported it. On the domestic front, the Taisho Democracy was gradually replaced by rigid control, restricting freedom of thought and expression.[9] Though society was filled with tension, the majority of the Japanese people, either with ardent enthusiasm supported it, or, with tacit approval, acknowledged it.

---

[9] The Peace Preservation Law which had already been enacted in 1925 became the basis of control.

Undeclared War with China

After Manchuria came under Japanese control in the form of the 'puppet state', the primary attention of the army and some of the Tokyo-based leaders shifted to the situation in China. China was still in turmoil. The nationalist government finally unified the country in December 1928, but the leadership struggle between the nationalists and the communists was far from over. It developed into an open fight between the two political forces, but strong Chinese indignation against Japan's oppressive moves was the underlying reason the nation united.

Admittedly there was serious concern in Japan that a deeper involvement in China would not ensure a stable sphere of interest. But Japan actually chose a path toward deeper involvement.

In July 1937 a minor clash between Japanese and Chinese troops near Beijing took place, which became the beginning of the 'Undeclared War with China'. In September 1937 the second round of coalition between the nationalists and the communists took shape. Faced with stern opposition from the nationalist government now united with the communist forces, the Japanese military actions spread to the south, and in December 1937 they attacked Nanjing, where later it became known that the worst atrocities during the war with China were committed by the Japanese army.

In the latter part of 1937 some efforts to seek an armistice with China had been conducted, but by early 1938 no agreement had been reached. Although further efforts to reach a ceasefire were not terminated, the emphasis now shifted to the establishment of a regime that would be friendly to Japan. After series of endeavours, consultations and manipulations, a 'puppet government' headed by Wang Ching-wei was established in March 1940. From the point of view of seeking accord with the real fighting power, namely the nationalist-communist government, this step was nothing but another step towards further complications.

Relations with global powers in Europe

From the time of the withdrawal from the League of Nations, while engaging itself in the exercise of strengthening her sphere of influence in Manchuria and China, Japan also tried to re-establish a viable policy of alliances with the major powers of the world, in continuation with her policy of realism to avoid isolation and seek understanding of Japan's policy objectives. At the aftermath of the Manchurian incident, there were at least three options open to Japan in this regard.

The first approach was to regain the confidence of Great Britain and America. Some maintained that it might be possible to resort to the Anglo-Japanese alliance. Others tried to exert influence to improve relations with the United States. An attempt was made by Japan to conclude agreements such as the Takahara-Root Agreement of 1908, but all these efforts did not bear fruit.

The second approach was to seek harmony with Russia, possibly in the form of a nonaggression treaty. It did not prove to be successful either.

Thus the third approach began to acquire a higher priority. That approach was to enter into a new alliance with Germany and possibly with Italy. At a time when Japan was expanding her activities around the Chinese continent, in Europe Adolf Hitler's Germany was rapidly gaining power. Increasingly, military officers, politicians and foreign ministry officials emerged, who sympathized with and admired the German success in dismantling the existing status quo.

In 1936 the Anti-Comintern Pact was concluded between Japan and Germany. This step led to serious deliberation in 1938 and 1939, whether or not to conclude an alliance between Japan, Germany and Italy. Hitler's invasion of Poland in September 1939 heightened the debates between those who supported Germany and those who thought that further action to narrow the proximity with Germany might fatally alienate America. The final decision regarding the conclusion of the treaty was taken by Yosuke Matsuoka, a retired Foreign Ministry official who became the Foreign Minister in July 1940. His strategy was that stronger ties with Germany and Italy would consolidate Japan's position and allow her to enter into a reasonable agreement with America. Thus in September 1940 the so-called Triple Alliance was concluded.

Although the idea of concluding a nonaggression agreement with Russia failed, the necessity to ensure a more secure relationship with this country, which undoubtedly was gaining strength under her new leader Iosif V. Stalin, came to be shared by many government leaders and diplomats. Particularly the two border incidents which took place in 1938 at Lake Khasan (Zhangufeng) outside the northern Korean border in the Soviet Union and in 1939 at Nomonhan

(Khalkhin Gol) near the Outer Mongolian border in northern Manchuria, where Japan was overwhelmingly defeated, created a serious
concern among the army about the possibility of a direct clash with
the Soviet Union. On Stalin's side, he also found reasons to enter
into accord with Japan with a view to prepare for a possible clash
with Hitler. Foreign Minister Matsuoka seized this opportunity and
in April 1941 a neutrality pact was signed between Japan and the
Soviet Union.

Relations with America until the Pacific War

Whether it was so intended or whether it was a result of several
chains of events which led to an unavoidable consequence, towards
the end of the 1930's tension between Japan and the United States
rose to a dangerous level.

For America, Japan's rigorous way of expanding her sphere of
influence from Manchuria into mainland China simply could not be
overlooked.

In July 1939 America decided to abrogate the Treaty of Commerce
and Navigation with Japan as a first step to introduce sanctions
against Japan. After the expiration of the treaty in January 1940,
America introduced an approval system for the export of gasoline
and scrap iron. It caused economic damage to Japan, but contrary
to US expectations, rather than adopting a more conciliatory policy
with regard to America, Japan developed an acute fear of a possible shortage of basic industrial and strategic resources such as oil or
steel, and decided to further expand her sphere of influence to ensure
those resources, this time in September 1940 to the northern part
of Indochina, where there had emerged a power vacuum because
of France's defeat in Europe.

To make the situation worse, Hitler's decision to attack Stalin in
June 1941 and the initial amazing victories over the Soviet army
invigorated the Japanese army, and in July 1941 it entered the southern part of Indochina. The United States almost immediately reacted
to this and froze Japanese assets in America and in August declared
an overall embargo on oil to Japan. At that point the imminent danger of war should have been felt by everyone.

Last minute efforts, however, to avoid the war continued. Already
in April of that year a 'draft Understanding' was proposed by the
American side, based on some agreements which had been negoti-

ated among private individuals of the two countries, concerned about the state of affairs. The key issues were the Triple Alliance and China. On the alliance between Japan, Germany and Italy, Japan underlined its defensive character and the US stated her intention not to take active part in the war in Europe. On China, America agreed to recommend to the Chinese government a settlement with Japan, with such conditions as ensuring China's independence, the Japanese army's withdrawal, recognition of Manchuria, and an open door principle. Yosuke Matsuoka, however, upon his return from Moscow after signing the Neutrality Pact, refused to accept this 'draft Understanding' as a basis for negotiations and came up with a totally new and rigorous proposal, which naturally disappointed the Americans and was rejected by them. Thus the first opportunity, if any, of a final stage agreement was gone.

In July Prime Minister Fumimaro Konoe, having realized that Foreign Minister Matsuoka's approach to the US was not conducive to bring about peace with America, reshuffled his cabinet and selected a new Foreign Minister. In August, after the turmoil from Japan's move to southern Indochina and the sharp American reaction against it, Konoe still fervently hoped that a summit meeting with President Franklin D. Roosevelt might rescue the two countries from disaster. For two months that wish had been on the table, but no zeal was expressed by the Americans and in September it was virtually rejected in a reply that substantive rapprochement between the two sides on major issues should come first.

Thus in Tokyo on 6 September Prime Minister Konoe agreed to adopt a basic plan to allow a decision in October to wage war with America, should any effort for peace not be successful. Nevertheless he made one last endeavour to present Japanese views on the major issues, to which the Americans reacted just politely. Konoe resigned from the post of Prime Minister on 16 October. Thus the second opportunity for peace under Konoe was gone.

General Hideki Tojo replaced Konoe on 18 October as Prime Minister. The new cabinet abrogated the September decision on taking the decision to enter the war in the Pacific, and under the strict guidance of the new Foreign Minister Shigenori Togo, prepared two proposals to avoid war with the United States.

Plan A was to resolve major issues with mid to long-term perspectives. On trade it accepted in general, the principle of non-discrimination in all Pacific regions including China. On the Triple

Alliance it specified that Japan had no intention to arbitrarily modify the interpretation of self-defence. On China, Togo made an enormous effort to propose a time frame for the withdrawal of the Japanese army from China. An immediate withdrawal of troops from Indochina was also proposed, once peace was established in the Far East or in China.

Plan B was to propose short term quick solutions in the event that no agreement was reached on the basis of Plan A. It basically proposed to bring the situation back to the way it had been in early July, namely, that the US would suspend its oil embargo against Japan and that Japan would withdraw from the southern part of Indochina.

Negotiations took place in Washington in November on the basis of these two plans, but on 26 November the Secretary of State Cordell Hull handed over an American counter proposal, now known as 'the Hull Note', which was taken by the Japanese side as an American ultimatum. Disregarding all the preceding points of negotiations, America asked Japan to virtually nullify the Triple Alliance, to implement a complete withdrawal of the Japanese troops from China and Indochina, and to withdraw its support of the Wang Ching-wei government. The disappointment of Togo and all those who had worked for the success of the negotiations was beyond words. Thus the third and the last opportunity to save the situation was gone.

The Pacific War

On 1 December the Japanese government formally took the decision to go to war with the United States on 8 December. The Japanese Navy attacked Pearl Harbour on that day and the Japanese memorandum declaring war, which was due to have arrived half an hour before the attack began, reached Cordell Hull fifty minutes after the attack had begun. The delay was due to clerical reasons, namely the preparation of the statement at the Japanese Embassy in Washington. Though the delay was not intentional it was nonetheless inexcusable, and caused great damage to Japan by creating the infamous image of a sneak attack in the minds of Americans and people all over the world.

The initial stage of the war proceeded with a complete Japanese victory. Until the middle of 1942, Japan occupied most of Southeast

Asia. During those initial months of Japan's victory its moves were welcomed by some local leaders and people. However, the conduct of some members of the Japanese army increasingly raised indignation. In particular, the Japanese occupation left a severe scar in the hearts and minds of the British, Dutch and Australian people.

In Japan the population rejoiced at the victory. Foreign Minister Togo made a powerful speech in his New Year address of 1942 to members of the Foreign Ministry to urge them to concentrate their efforts for an early closure of the war, but unlike the situation at the time of the Russo-Japanese War in 1904, diplomatic efforts to terminate the war did not succeed.

The military situation meanwhile began to deteriorate as early as the middle of 1942. In June Japan lost a historic naval battle at Midway; in February 1943 it had to abandon an important strategic island in the Pacific Ocean, Guadalcanal. In the course of 1944 US troops successively occupied South Pacific islands such as Palau and Saipan.

Inside the country in September 1942 Togo resigned from the post of Foreign Minister in protest against the establishment of a new ministry governing the occupied area. General Tojo tried to consolidate his leadership, but major setbacks on the military front became clearly recognizable and he had to resign in July 1944. The task of the Kuniaki Koiso cabinet, which succeeded the Tojo cabinet, was to bring the war to an end at an appropriate moment in time. The new cabinet hoped for such an occasion immediately after another conspicuous victory was made on the battlefield.

Such an occasion did not occur and in April 1945 Koiso resigned and Kantaro Suzuki formed the cabinet. For the second time Shigenori Togo assumed the position of Foreign Minister. In accepting this post he insisted on the assurance from the Prime Minister that the Prime Minister's objective was to end the war as soon as possible.

One of the most important mechanisms Togo created was an entirely informal, confidential, off the record meeting, constituted by 6 top leaders of the conduct of the policy of war. They consisted of the Prime Minister, Foreign Minister, Minister of War, Minister of Admiralty, the Chief of Staff of the Army, and the Chief of Staff of the Navy. The main subject debated at this 'Top 6 Meeting' was the question of mediation through the Soviet Union. The Soviet Union was the only global power with which Japan was not at war. The military had therefore some interest in confirming its neutrality and if possible letting it play a friendly role towards Japan. Japan did not know that in February at Yalta, Stalin agreed with Roosevelt and Churchill that the Soviet Union would enter the war with Japan three months after the German capitulation. Thus, diplomatically Japan's quest for mediation did not bear any fruit. But the long process of candid discussions strictly restricted in the 'Top 6 Meeting', at a time when an open discussion on the termination of war could easily become a target for assassination, later became the psychological basis of bringing the war to an end.

On 26 July the Allied Powers, the United States, Great Britain and China issued the so-called Potsdam Declaration prescribing the conditions to end the war: 1) The Japanese territory would be confined to the four main islands and other smaller islands to be determined by the Allies; 2) Armed forces and all military power which led the war would be dissolved and eliminated; and 3) Japan would become a democratic and peaceful country with the possibility to regain its economic strength and eventually participate in world trade relations.

Togo and others took the declaration as a serious proposal to bring the war to an end, but extremely unfortunate and inadequate media reporting created the impression that Japan 'ignored' the proposal.

On 6 August the atomic bomb was dropped on Hiroshima, which literally annihilated the city.

On 8 August the Soviet Union declared war against Japan and on the following day marched through Manchuria to the south.

On 9 August another atomic bomb was dropped, this time on Nagasaki.

On 10 August top leaders of the government gathered in front of the Emperor to decide on Japan's response to the Potsdam Declaration. In the minds of all those present, there was one issue which the Potsdam Declaration did not touch upon. That was the question of 'Japanese statehood (*kokutai*)', which in fact meant the question of the Emperor or the Imperial system in Japan. There was no doubt in the minds of everyone present that after the capitulation the Imperial system had to be preserved. Thus Foreign Minister Togo maintained that Japan should accept it with only one condition, i.e. that the statehood of Japan would be preserved. General Korechika Anami, the Minister of War, explained the military position, namely that three more conditions in relation to occupation, disarmament, and war criminals should be requested. The Prime Minister asked for an Imperial decision and the Emperor decided to adopt the Foreign Minister's view.

On 12 August the Allies reply to the Japanese response was announced: the fate of Japan's statehood was left to the free will of the Japanese people.

On 14 August a full fledged cabinet meeting was held to decide on the Allies reaction. Togo's view was that the response from the Allies was sufficient to allow the acceptance of the Potsdam Declaration and bring the war to an end. General Anami and a few others maintained their objection and doubts. The Prime Minister asked for a second Imperial decision. The Emperor decided with clear and compelling reasons that the Potsdam Declaration must be accepted. The Emperor's decision was accepted unanimously.

On 15 August Japan formally capitulated.[10]

---

[10] General Anami committed *seppuku* (*Hara-kiri*, disembowelment, a ritual way of committing suicide by the *Samurai*) on that day. Being the Minister of War, General Anami had messages he' had to deliver, but he played an invaluable role to curb the emotion of the soldiers and bring about an orderly capitulation. His death is remembered as an act of honour.

CHAPTER ONE

AFTER THE WAR:
NEW VALUES AND THE PEACE TREATY

1. *The defeat and new values*

In August 1945—for the first time in its history—Japan was defeated by outside forces. It was not only defeated, but the country was reduced to the size it was before the Meiji Restoration; most of the larger cities were in complete ruin as a result of American bombardments; and American forces were about to occupy the country.

> I was born in January 1945 and was a baby of eight months when the war ended so I have hardly any recollection of the immediate postwar period. Nevertheless, I still have flash-back type memories in which I see a large field very near to my house surrounded by the ruins of bombed-out buildings, clumps of grass and wild flowers growing here and there. The vast sky of Tokyo, with an amazingly beautiful sunset in brilliant red and gold, served as a colourful backdrop to these ruins, grass and flowers. It is a strange and hollow memory, mixed with a sense of tranquillity.

Symbolically enough, what that small boy felt in an empty field in Tokyo might very well have been an accurate reflection of what the Japanese people felt at the aftermath of the war.

The end of the war meant the end of certain values which led to the war. It should therefore be said that it was this complete destruction and loss of values that governed the actions and spirit, of at least those of the preceding decade, and perhaps even many years leading up to this period. But the majority of the Japanese people did not, or rather could not analyse and reflect upon the values and significance of the events which led to the war. The shocks were so great and struck the very heart and soul of the majority of the people. Such was the void which engulfed Japan for a while after 15 August 1945.

It is certainly true that for the majority of the people who fought in the war, there was a purpose in fighting. They thought that they were sacrificing their lives for the good of the country, for the good of those who were dear to them, for the good of the community in the Asia-Pacific region. However, the war was lost. Were the values for which they had fought lost? Were the causes for which they had fought valid? If not, what was wrong and who was responsible? The majority of the people of Japan could not, or did not, answer these questions. Rather than entering into serious reflection of the past or grieving for the end of an era, they were engulfed in this void from which they gradually re-emerged, filled with certain intuitive feelings from which new values gradually emerged.

Right or wrong, this was the reality with which Japan entered the postwar period. There were of course minorities. There were those, like generals and soldiers from the many battlefields, who, knowing that the era that had cherished their values was about to close and knowing that they would not be able to find a new set of values to replace the old ones, chose to end their lives.

There were those who already knew, or at least who thought that they knew what Japan had done wrong before and during the war. Some were political prisoners, who were released from prison after the war.

There were those who tried to separate objectively right from wrong in the actions of prewar Japan and explain or defend them as intelligently as possible. Some realists in the emerging new Japanese government and defendants at the International Military Tribunal for the Far East (IMTFE) were amongst them.

Over the past half century Japan has travelled a painful path in search of the answer, as a consensus to society, to be shared by all foreign countries with which Japan fought the war, to these questions which remained unanswered in the void which enveloped postwar Japan. Some answers have been found, but not all of them. The uncertainty which a great many Japanese were left with after the past war eventually became one of the underlying reasons why the issues related to the past became such complicated issues in the postwar relationships with some of Japan's major partners such as China, as we will see in Chapter 4, or Korea, as we will see in Chapter 5.

But let us first examine the individual values on which postwar Japan began to build itself. These values were peace, democracy and imperial tradition, which were gradually blended with the values of economic reconstruction.

Pacifism

The first feeling that emerged among the Japanese people in the postwar period was probably one of profound relief, mixed with a sense of happiness that the war was over. "The war is over, peace has come, we need not die, we do not want to die, and we do not want it to happen again." Pacifism as described and as defined above became an underlying feeling amongst the Japanese people. There was no doubt that the Japanese people truly appreciated the value of peace and that they did not want to let another war happen in or around Japan. A revival of militarism was remote in the mind-set of the outstanding majority of the Japanese people.

At the same time, it was a pacifism that was very passive in nature. It was a pacifism to say: "Leave us alone on war related issues." "We are not going to disturb you, but please do not disturb us." Several political situations eventually further nurtured this passive approach to pacifism, as we are going to see in relation to the Peace Treaty below, to Japan-US political relations in Chapter 1, and to Japan's involvement in UN peacekeeping operations in Chapter 12.

In the conduct of postwar foreign policy, however, there was realism and awareness that peace could not be achieved without endeavours and sacrifices, and in order for Japan to come back as a full-fledged partner in the international community, Japan had to share a greater responsibility for the maintenance and creation of peace and security. But that realism had to go through a long process of internal debates and political persuasion, before Japan could fulfil a more responsible role.

Democracy

The second feeling that emerged was probably another feeling of relief, but this time from the oppressive elements of society. A great majority of the Japanese people was happy that they were not constantly pressured by the weight of the controlling organs of society, such as the military or the police or others. People must have felt that excessive control of society and excessive leadership by the military affecting their daily life had become too much of a burden.

It must be noted, however, that it was wrong to observe that Japanese people were just simple victims of an oppressive totalitarian and military regime. On the contrary, the majority of the Japanese people supported the strengthening of the Japanese 'sphere of influence' through the Asian continent and wholeheartedly welcomed victory on the battlefields during the initial months after the beginning of the Pacific War.

Thus the postwar Japanese democracy began with some fundamental complexities, if not contradictions. Firstly, 'democracy', 'human rights' or 'people's sovereignty',—whatever they meant—were well suited to the people's inner inclination that they were happy to have been relieved of the heavy burden of control by society. But secondly, for the majority of the Japanese people, these democratic values were very much an object for learning and were placed at the centre of the society for absorption from the occupying forces. They were not values created or voluntarily sought, but rather given from outside for inner consumption. Thirdly, the majority of the Japanese accepted these values without going through a serious process of digesting them, in contrast to the values which they themselves had upheld before the war, drawing the clear conclusion as to what was right and what was wrong, what was inevitable and what were those mistakes which could have been avoided.

Lastly, for those intellectuals and social activists whose spirits were associated with the Taisho democracy, the new era of democracy was what they had already been longing for for many decades. They saw continuity, rather than rupture, in the postwar Japanese democracy. They became a basis for developing democracy in Japan. Many of them naturally became strong critics of Japanese paths from the Manchurian Incident to August 1945. Thus in the areas of foreign and security policy, an important part of postwar Japanese intellectuals became more supportive of the passive pacifism of the public opinion than the realism developed by the government.

The Emperor and the Imperial system

The third feeling, which was still preserved in the psychological hollow of the Japanese people, despite the rupture from the past, was the feeling toward the Emperor or to the Imperial tradition. I explained in some detail the importance which the notion of 'statehood (*kokutai*)' had, when the Potsdam Declaration was debated in the summer of 1945. The unanimous approach taken by the government leadership then was a reflection of the feeling shared by the Japanese people. This issue became a crucial issue during the first year of the occupation and the enactment of the constitution, as we are going to see in Section 3 below.

In comparison to the issue of peace and democracy the issue of the Imperial tradition had not appeared on the surface of everyday life for the majority of the Japanese people. But in a quiet manner the Imperial tradition had been kept as an underlying spiritual and cultural value, ensuring tradition and continuity, as a symbol and discrete unifier of the country. Even in external relations, the Imperial tradition had made substantial contributions toward the betterment of Japan's relations with foreign countries, as will be described in brief in Chapter 8 on Japanese-European relations.

Economic reconstruction and development

These three issues, namely peace, democracy and the Imperial system became fundamental points, which the postwar Japanese government in turn had to resolve during the initial postwar years.

The basic direction of these three major political agendas was established in the new constitution adopted in November 1946, as we will see in Section 3 below. The fourth element in considering postwar Japanese development, namely Japan's concentration on economic recovery and economic development, started to take shape thereafter.

That was the last element, but probably the most powerful and important element, which occupied the minds of by far the largest majority of the Japanese people. Material welfare, more than any of the three preceding abstract values, filled effectively the psychological hollow of the Japanese people after the end of the Pacific War.

We are going to look at these issues either in relation to Chapter 3 on Japan-US economic relations, or in Chapter 11 on Japanese multilateral economic diplomacy.

2. *The American occupation*

In addition to these essential aspects of the material and psychological situation of the Japanese people after the war, it is essential to

understand the nature of the American occupation so as to grasp
the reality of the postwar situation and its recovery in Japan. An
important part of the overall success of the postwar Japanese recovery is due to the successful policy of the American occupation. Several
reasons for this achievement can be given:

First, the content of the policy objectives of the occupation must
be pointed out. The key policy objectives with which General Douglas
MacArthur, the Supreme Commander of the Allied Powers, arrived
in Japan were 'democratization' and 'demilitarization'. They were
clearly stated in President Harry S. Truman's policy statement of 6
September 1945 entitled 'Early US policy toward Japan after its
capitulation'.[1] The two objectives corresponded well with the basic
psychology of the Japanese people as described above and this fortunate matching of basic policy orientation became the basis of the
successful occupation.

Second, the wisdom of 'indirect governance' has to be mentioned.

As early as August 1942, Japanese experts at the State Department
began their work to consider the modality of the postwar Japanese
occupation.

Up until 1944 however, America was envisaging a policy similar
to what was applied to Germany after its capitulation, namely a joint
occupation of Allied Powers and an introduction of direct military
control to implement US policy objectives in a straightforward manner.

After President Roosevelt passed away in April 1945 and some
tension arose in US relations with the Soviet Union, President Truman
adopted a more flexible approach based on advice given by Japanese
experts of the State Department, that "Japan should be democratized but the punishment and demolition of their moderate political
forces should be kept to a minimum and Japan should be restored
as a friendly nation to the United States."[2] The Potsdam Declaration,
which acknowledged the role of the Japanese government in the
postwar period, was already a reflection of that flexible policy approach.
Thus the Japanese government itself could and did play an important role in furthering democratization and demilitarization effectively
and smoothly during those critical years of American occupation.

---

[1] Ikei, *op. cit.*, p. 232. The title of this policy statement was translated from
Japanese by the author.
[2] Ibid.

Third, it was noteworthy that the occupation was implemented primarily by the Americans, different from Germany and different from Korea. Japan did capitulate early enough to give sufficient authority to President Truman to implement an American occupation and not a joint occupation by the Allied multilateral forces. Stalin proposed Soviet occupation of the northern part of Hokkaido and there were other plans such as a quadrilateral occupation of Japan by America, Britain, China and the Soviet Union. But the emergence of Cold War tension and the difficulty already experienced in the German quadrilateral occupation were enough reasons for President Truman to reject all these plans, and with a symbolic involvement of Commonwealth forces, the occupation was primarily implemented by the American forces. Thus, effective and smooth governance through the coordinated and unified policy implementation of the American command was ensured throughout the country.

Fourthly, there was the humanitarian and reconstruction aid America provided from the beginning of the occupation up to the conclusion of the Peace Treaty in 1951, which we are going to see in a little more in detail in Chapter 10. During the days immediately following the end of the war, the American help became the key element for Japanese survival. In general it was highly appreciated by the people.

It is sometimes asked why Japan as a whole became so pro-American after the war. As we are going to see in Chapter 2 and 12, there was certainly strong vocal public opinion which criticized American 'imperialism' and 'expansionism'. But in general, for a country with which it had fought war for four years with all these civilian casualties, the Japanese people became extremely friendly towards America. The convergence of values, successful policy guidance and American assistance could be included as reasons for this.

There are increasing voices lately in Japan that resent the Japanese behaviour in the postwar period, which 'blindly' followed American directions, accepting as an inevitability the atomic bombing of Hiroshima and Nagasaki;[3] the carpet-bombing of major cities which caused so many civilian casualties;[4] the results of the trial in the

---

[3] The death toll of Hiroshima was 201,990 and Nagasaki 93,967 (H. Takeuchi, *Ano sensouha ittai nandeattaka (What was that War?)*, Harashobou, 1997, pp. 207–208).
[4] The death toll of Tokyo was 97,031 and of 63 other cities 86,336 (Peter Duus, *Modern Japan*, Houghton Mifflin, 1998, p. 249).

IMTFE and Article 9 of the Constitution enacted by General MacArthur. It is only hoped that these views will bring a fair and objective view of the history, and not an emotional explosion of ultra-nationalism.

3. *The new constitution*

Probably the most important decision taken in the course of the first year by the Japanese government under occupation was the adoption of the new constitution.

General MacArthur's headquarters, which was then called the GHQ, were of the view that the Meiji Constitution did not fulfil the requirements of the new policy objectives and either a new constitution had to be adopted or it had to be fundamentally amended.

From October 1945, Kijyuuro Shidehara, a former Minister for Foreign Affairs during the 1920's, whose approach was based on internationalism, economic values and respect for Chinese internal matters, and was well remembered in the United States, became Prime Minister at the age of 73. Shidehara was profoundly enthusiastic in introducing reforms towards demilitarization and democratization, but when it came to constitutional reform his approach was lukewarm. A special committee was nonetheless established under Cabinet Minister Joji Matsumoto in October 1945. Matsumoto made a policy statement for the revision of the Meiji Constitution in December 1945, the gist of which were the following: to increase the power of the parliament, to make cabinet ministers responsible to the parliament, to ensure fundamental rights for each individual, but to leave intact the Imperial Powers of Governance. An unofficial summary of his draft was presented to GHQ on 1 February 1946. The GHQ considered this version totally unacceptable and on 13 February produced their own version and handed it over to the Japanese government with a strong request that it should be fully taken into account in their deliberations. The Japanese government accepted it and on 6 March produced 'a summary of a draft revision of the constitution', in which all the major clauses of the current constitution were already included.[5]

---

[5] I. Sato, *Nihonkokukenpo Gaisetsu (The Constitution of Japan)*, Gakuyou Shobou, 1993, pp. 47–50.

What actually happened in the intricate discussions between GHQ and the Japanese government and in particular between General MacArthur and Prime Minister Shidehara from January to March 1946 has since been a mystery. Researchers, scholars and politicians have tried to find out the truth. Particularly in the context of the debates which are conducted today in Japan on the revision of the constitution, it became very important to know to what extent Japan's own thinking was reflected in the 6 March draft constitution.

Recent research indicates that an important meeting took place between Shidehara and General MacArthur on 24 January 1946, and that in that meeting Shidehara expressed his earnest wish for the preservation of the Imperial system and a fundamentally pacifist direction. General MacArthur was deeply moved by his plea, and thus Shidehara's plea became the source of inspiration for the general to come up with the GHQ version in mid-February.[6]

As interesting as it might be to know what happened in that crucial three-month period, I must now move on to the analysis of the basic content of the constitution as it was promulgated on 3 November 1946.

Sovereign right of the people

The first notion expressed was the notion of 'people's sovereignty'. It was a direct and fundamental realization of the first US policy objective of democratization. The preamble states that "The Japanese people do proclaim that sovereign power resides with the people."[7] Article 11 ensures that "The people shall not be prevented from enjoying any of the fundamental human rights. These fundamental human rights guaranteed to the people by this Constitution shall be conferred upon the people of this and future generations as eternal and inviolate rights." Article 41 reads that "The Diet shall be the highest organ of state power, and shall be the sole law-making organ of the State." In short, all articles, which are familiar in all modern democratic constitutions, are stipulated with clarity.

---

[6] M. Iokibe, *Sengo Nihongaikoushi (Postwar Japanese Foreign Policy)*, Yuuhikaku, 2001, pp. 45–50.

[7] www.okakogi.go.jp/People/miwa/document/law/ConstitutionOfJapan.html 2003-11-06. All other quotations from the constitution are from this website.

Article 9 and the renunciation of war

The second notion expressed was the notion of pacifism, which is clearly in line with the second US policy objective of demilitariza-tion, but expressed in rather dramatic language.

First there is a sentence in the Preamble: "The Japanese people have determined to preserve our security and existence, trusting in the justice and faith of the peace-loving peoples of the world."

And then Article 9 reads as follows:

> Aspiring sincerely to an international peace based on justice and order, the Japanese people forever renounce war as a sovereign right of the nation and the threat or use of force as means of settling international disputes.
>
> In order to accomplish the aim of the preceding paragraph, land, sea and air forces, as well as other war potential, will never be main-tained. The right of belligerency of the state shall not be recognized.

The three steps in the mounting logic of Article 9 are very power-ful. Japan would renounce the use of force as a means of resolving disputes, therefore Japan would not possess armed forces, and thus the right of belligerency would not be recognized. As we will see below, exactly what the constitution prohibited under Article 9 was not entirely clear, but whatever the scope for interpretation, there was no doubt that a strong message, to keep Japan from militarism and military activities, was forcefully prescribed.

That basic message of pacifism suited well the feelings of the Japanese people in the psychological hollow I have described above; they wished to be left in their own world, with peace and without war. That message could have been a reflection of genuine idealism for the creation of a peaceful world expressed by Kijyuuro Shidehara. That message certainly met the objective of demilitarization by the occupying forces under General MacArthur. The need to adhere to that message was strongly backed up by those who feared a possi-ble revival of Japanese militarism both inside and outside the country.

The strong inclination towards pacifism, however, became a seri-ous stumbling block for those who considered that, regardless of the subjective wishes of the Japanese people wanting to avoid war, objec-tive conditions in the world and around Japan necessitated an ade-quate allocation of power. And if Japan wanted to become a member of the international community bearing her responsibility for the maintenance and creation of peace, she had to take measures and act. Some of the interpretations deriving from Article 9 seemed to go directly against this thinking. Thus right from the beginning when Article 9 was born, it was destined to become a battlefield of serious contention over Japanese peace and security policy.

Let me restrict myself to two issues which directly emerged from the interpretation of Article 9.

(1) The first issue was the question of the right of self-defence and the role of the Self-Defence Forces (SDF).

The interpretation of the 'realists' was the following: Yes, Japan renounced war, but only as a means of resolving international disputes. Japan did not renounce war when it came to self-defence. Therefore Japan was allowed to maintain armed forces for self-defence purposes. The right of belligerency was not recognized but this provision did not exclude the right to self-defence.

The interpretation of the 'idealists' was completely the opposite: Yes, Japan renounced war, and this meant that she renounced all kinds of war, both as a means to resolve international conflicts and in self-defence. Japan possesses an abstract right to self-defence, without resorting to the use of armed forces. Naturally any possession of armed forces is unconstitutional. The negation of the right of belligerency was an overall conclusion of all previous points.

We will see in section 6 the outcome of this constitutional debate in the process of the conclusion of the Peace Treaty.

(2) The second issue was the question of the right of collective self-defence. As is prescribed in the United Nations Charter in Article 51: "Nothing in the present Charter shall impair the inherent right of individual or collective self-defence." Japan, from the point of view of international law, clearly enjoys the right of not only individual but also collective self-defence. Since the enactment of the constitution, however, not only among the pacifists but among the realists, it has been generally interpreted that Article 9 allows only the exertion of minimal forces for self-defence and therefore prohibits the exertion of collective self-defence. The consequence of that interpretation was that any action which could be interpreted as going beyond the minimal right of individual self-defence in the arena of collective self-defence would be 'unconstitutional'.

Japanese security policy has been seriously affected by this interpretation, as we are going to see in Section 5 (Peace Treaty), Chapter 2 (the Japan-US Security Treaty), and in Chapter 12 (International Peace Cooperation Law) and plants significant seeds of contention.

Article 1 and the role of the Emperor

The third notion expressed in the constitution was related to the Imperial tradition. Article 1 of the Constitution states that:

> The Emperor shall be the symbol of the State and of the unity of the people, deriving his position from the will of the people with whom resides sovereign power.

As I have already explained, for the leadership of the Japanese government under occupation it was essential for the Imperial system to continue. Prime Minister K. Shidehara was said to have made an earnest plea for the preservation of an honourable role for the Emperor at his crucial meeting with General MacArthur on 24 January.

For General MacArthur it was clear that the Imperial Powers of Governance as prescribed in the Meiji Constitution were unacceptable. The Imperial system had to be democratized. At the same time, the general must have been aware of the importance that Japan attached to the notion of Japanese 'statehood (*kokutai*)' at the time of the acceptance of the Potsdam Declaration. From the point of view of the Japanese government all responsibility for the events which took place from the 1931 Manchurian Incident up to August 1945 lay in the hands of the government, with the sole exception of the decision to capitulate. General MacArthur himself was said to have been genuinely impressed by Emperor Hirohito's candour, courage and determination to devote himself to the good of the people. At the same time, among the other Allied Powers there were views that the Emperor's personal and administrative responsibility for conducting the Pacific War should be pursued. In order to preserve the Imperial system in Japan General MacArthur had to move fast and convince other political forces which favoured pursuing the Emperor's responsibility.

Thus the carefully worded role of the Emperor as 'the symbol of the State' struck the right balance with the definition of 'people's sovereignty' and a powerful and unfaltering inclination towards 'pacifism'. This seems to be the conclusion drawn from January to March 1946, during the most severe winter Japan had ever experienced.

Article 1 of the Constitution was born under such circumstances. In my view an interesting question remains unanswered: how does the present-day status of the Emperor as the 'symbol of the State' compare with the maintenance of Japanese 'statehood (*kokutai*)' as it was envisaged in August 1945? For those who accepted the Potsdam Declaration with the sole condition of the maintenance of Japanese 'statehood', to what extent are they satisfied with Article 1 of the Constitution? What would they say about the way the Japanese Imperial system has been maintained and developed since the enactment of the constitution?

4. Political reforms and economic recovery

The major objectives of GHQ and the Japanese government in the initial years of the occupation were the political reforms, parallel to their efforts to create a new Constitution. As early as October 1945, General MacArthur had outlined five items, where urgent reforms were required: the liberation of women, the liberalization of education, the democratization of the economy, the organization of labour unions, and the abolition of laws and regulations which oppressed freedom. Under the Shidehara cabinet and several cabinets which succeeded it, postwar political reforms rapidly took shape until approximately the end of 1947.

Just to outline some major reforms: the dissolution of the Zaibatsu (gigantic enterprises with their affiliated companies constituting one capital network, which were viewed as the basis of arms production) in November 1945; new election laws, which included women's right to vote and a new law on trade unions in December 1945; agricultural reform in October 1946; an anti-monopoly law and a local self-government law in April 1947; a new law governing police activities and the abolition of the Ministry of the Interior in December 1947.

From the beginning of 1948, when these postwar political reforms had more or less taken shape, the attention of GHQ as well as of the government were directed to the question of economic recovery. The economy had not yet been able to rid itself of the turmoil of the postwar situation. By 1948 Japan's industrial production had not reached half of the pre war production of the mid-1930's. Several missions arrived from the United States to inspect the state of the economic recovery, and the major impression they gathered was that there was an urgent need to introduce a sound macroeconomic policy to curb inflation, to balance the budget and encourage industrial production based on the rules of the market economy.

The dissolution of the Zaibatsu started a slow-down and excessive strikes by the newly born trade unions came under stronger control. The Nine Principles for Economic Stabilization issued by GHQ in March 1948 embodied this policy towards the industrial recovery. An American economist, Joseph Dodge, visited Japan from February to March 1949 and announced a new policy direction, named the 'Dodge Line', aiming at further decentralization, a stronger anti-inflationary policy, and the unification of the exchange rate to 1\$=360yen. A new budget trying to balance tax and expenditure was immediately adopted, and admittedly with pain and social tension, a new policy for economic stabilization began to take shape.

At a time when public attention was primarily directed towards political reforms and postwar economic recovery, the last vestige of the war had to be executed as was mentioned in the Potsdam Declaration: "Stern justice shall be meted out to all war criminals."

The International Military Tribunal for the Far East (IMTFE) was held from May 1946 till November 1948. The prosecution waged two major offences: joint conspiracy to execute aggression after the Manchurian Incident and the execution of, or the failure to, prevent atrocities. Among the 25 leaders who were sentenced as class A war criminals, 7 of them, who were found guilty of either or both of these crimes, were sentenced to death. The majority of the accused, 16 of them, received a life sentence.[8] Shigenori Togo, in a determined defence, argued that he had done everything to prevent the war against the United States from happening, but that there remained no choice but to go to war after the Hull Note.[9] All his endeavour

---

[8] In addition to the IMTFE, seven Allies convened tribunals on war crimes inside and outside Japan: Australia, China, France, the Netherlands, the Philippines, UK, and USA. Out of the 5,700 indicted, 984 were sentenced to death (Records of Debates at the House of Councillors, 1991-11-01 Addendum).

[9] During the trial Shigenori Togo left many notes which represented his views regarding the war, such as the following:

"Such a major event as a war cannot be initiated by one or two persons. In the case of the Pacific War, it reached a situation where "no-one could stop the flow of history". That was a very different situation from the situation under an absolute dictatorship or under Hitler.

The war between Japan and America was a war to regulate conflicts of interests between Japan and the Allies. It was not waged as a war of aggression. If one intends to examine Japan's responsibility for having conducted a war of aggression, then it is they who have created or enhanced the following directions who must be held responsible:

1) The capitalistic and nationalist direction to make Japan strong;

to let Japan capitulate on 15 August 1945 was outside the scope of prosecutors' interest. He was sentenced to 20 years in prison. Mamoru Shigemitsu, who succeeded Togo as Foreign Minister during the war, was sentenced to 7 years.

My grandmother, Edi Togo, Shigenori's wife of German origin, and my mother, Ise Togo, the only daughter of Shigenori and Edi, were always present at the tribunal. Many years later, when I began to understand a little about the history, my mother once told me:

"I can never forget the day when the sentence was pronounced. As usual, I was with your grandmother at the court. When the sentencing began, there was utter silence in the court room. But each time the death sentence was pronounced, all who were in the court room breathed in so deeply that those sounds are still vivid in my ears.

But you know, Kazu, when the verdict was pronounced for your grandfather, 20 years of imprisonment, deep in my heart, I told to myself: "We won!" Yes, 20 years seems to be a harsh sentence now, particularly for someone who did everything to prevent the war from happening and who contributed so much to ending the war, but he was the Foreign Minister at the time of Pearl Harbour. His situation was very precarious. Every one of us was fighting. Yes, 20 years—that was a victory for us."

Togo died in prison in 1950, one month after finishing his memoirs, later translated into English as The Cause of Japan.

Togo left the following passage in his memoirs regarding the last conference in the Imperial presence on 14 August 1945:

---

2) The imperialist direction to strengthen military power, considering that it was impossible to make Japan strong while it walked at a tortoise-pace; and

3) The militaristic direction to oppose outside pressure, which endeavoured to prevent these developments (on occasion through the use of military force)." (Shigehiko Togo, *Sofu Togo Shigenorino Shougai (Life of my grandfather Shigenori Togo)*, Bungeishunjyu, 1993, p. 414).

"The Tokyo Tribunal could bring about justice based on crimes against peace and humanity. After WWI, it was so desired but not implemented. Even if there . had been arbitrary judgment by the victor, the world is making gradual progress and mankind has now reached the stage where it is capable of implementing such justice. One has to acknowledge that there has been a significant improvement." (Ibid., p. 457).

The Emperor then spoke:

'It was not lightly, but upon mature consideration of conditions in and outside the country, and especially of the direction the war has taken, that I previously determined to accept the Potsdam Declaration. My determination is unaltered. I have heard the dispute over the recent reply given by the Allied Powers, but I consider that in general they have confirmed our understanding. As to paragraph 5 of the Declaration, I agree with the Foreign Minister that it is not intended to subvert the statehood of Japan; but, unless the war is brought to an end at this moment, I fear that the statehood will be destroyed, and the nation annihilated. It is therefore my wish that we bear the unbearable and accept the Allied reply, thus preserve the State as a State and spare my subjects further suffering. I wish you all to act with that intention. The War and Navy Ministers have told me that there is opposition within the Army and the Navy; I desire that the Services also be made to comprehend my wishes.'

All attendants wept at these well-reasoned and gracious words, and at perceiving the Emperor's emotions. It was an inexpressibly solemn and moving scene; as we retired down the long corridor, while returning in our cars, and at the reconvened Cabinet meeting, in our thoughts, each of us wept again.

In remembering these moments today, the scenery clearly re-appears in my sight, and my eyes are blurred with tears. The future of Japan is infinite, but having led the war to its end, having alleviated the suffering of our people, and having spared the lives of several millions of people, I am now sublimely happy and feel that my work is over and what will now become of my life is no longer of importance.[10]

5. *The 1951 San Francisco Peace Treaty*

Preparatory stage to the Peace Treaty

The shift of American policy from a rigorous implementation of political reforms to economic reconstruction was also closely related to the changes which occurred in the international situation surrounding America and Japan, namely the beginning of the Cold War.

The Cold War began in Europe. In March 1946 Winston Churchill had already made his well-known speech on the Iron Curtain, with

---

[10] Shigenori Togo, *Jidaino Ichimen (The Cause of Japan)*, Chuukoubunko, 1989, p. 530, translated by the author, based on the English translation by Ben Bruce Blakney and Fumihiko Togo, Simon and Schuster, 1956, p. 334. The last quoted paragraph is not included in the aforementioned English translation.

which the Soviet Union surrounded its satellite countries. In March 1947 President Truman expressed his determination to assist Turkey and Greece, which faced the Iron Curtain, and in June made a call for an overall reconstruction plan of a free Europe, called the Marshall Plan. In June 1948 the closure of Berlin began and in April 1949 the North Atlantic Treaty Organization (NATO) was created. Tension mounted rapidly.

In Asia tension grew, but in the initial years, in a more restrained manner. Korea, a former Japanese territory, was occupied by the Soviet troops in the north and by the US troops in the south at the 38th parallel. In China a civil war erupted between the nationalists and the communists after the Japanese capitulation. The outcome of this rivalry became clear in October 1949 when the People's Republic of China was established on the Chinese continent under the communists, and the nationalists fled to Taiwan in December and established the Republic of China there.

Against this background of emerging tension of Cold War, particularly in Europe, and the steady progress of Japanese political reforms, General MacArthur touched upon the question of a possible conclusion of the Peace Treaty in March 1947. As early as the autumn 1945 the Japanese Ministry of Foreign Affairs, at the advice of top political leaders, had began their study of a possible peace accord with the Allied countries. Serious study was conducted particularly around the issue of the future of Japan's security, the role of the United Nations and a possible arrangement with the United States to entrust Japan's security. Preliminary contacts between America and Japan began in the latter part of 1947 but this early endeavour proved not to have produced any result.[11]

In the course of 1948 the US government had kept a cautious approach to a 'premature peace' with Japan. Rather than contemplating the political task of re-establishing Japan as a member of the international community, they considered it more important to ensure a rapid economic recovery so that Japan would gain a stable economic basis, particularly against the background of mounting Cold War tension. Thus, a new Japanese policy was formulated in October 1948 in an US government document NCS13–2, and as we saw in the preceding section, the Nine Principles for Economic Stabilization

---

[11] Iokibe, *op. cit.*, pp. 56–63.

in December 1948 and the 'Dodge Line' in March 1949 were implemented.

In the autumn of 1949 the overall situation began to change. The Cold War tension in particular had mounted to such a level that an independent democratic Japan became a desired political reality in the Far East. In September a US-British Foreign Ministers meeting took place, in which the important decision was taken that an early conclusion of the Peace Treaty would be sought with Japan. In November, the State Department had already made a public statement that a first draft of the Peace Treaty with Japan was being prepared. With a view to expedite the process for the Peace Treaty, President Truman appointed a special envoy, John F. Dulles, a former republican senator, to handle the Peace Treaty issue with Japan.

Dulles visited Japan in June 1950, during which time an incident of great significance took place, which affected not only the fate of the Japanese Peace Treaty but also the fate of the entire situation in the Far East for many years to come: the Korean War.

The United States immediately reacted and under the flag of the United Nations joined the war. We will see how this operation was carried out under the UN flag in Chapter 12. In October 1950, when the American counterattack went north beyond the dividing line of the 38th parallel, Chinese volunteer troops intervened. This determined the Cold War structure in the Far East, in particular, in the eyes of the American leadership, that Communist China belonged to the socialist expansionist block and Taiwan to the democratic free world. Cold War tension had now peaked in the Far East.

More than any other element, this newly emerging situation around the Korean peninsula made Japan an indispensable member of the democratic camp in the Far East. The Peace Treaty with Japan had to be concluded fast, if necessary among the democratic countries only, and make Japan re-emerge as a partner on an equal footing within the democratic camp.

Internally, however, Japan was split between realism and idealism. Tension in the international situation spilled over in domestic political and social strife.

The government position was firm. It was led by Prime Minister Shigeru Yoshida, who assumed this post for a year from 1946 to 1947, and then for six years from 1948 to 1954. A former diplomat, who belonged to the generation between Shidehara and Togo, he had a clear vision to lead the country based on the good tradition of the prewar realism of Japanese foreign policy. As I understand it, his thoughts may be summarized in the following principles:

(1) In the emerging new situation of the Cold War, it is in Japan's interest to side with the United States. Since Japan's own power is insufficient and is not supposed to be enough to meet security dangers around the country, a security agreement with the United States will become necessary.

(2) Japan's future lies in its power of economic recovery. The abovementioned security environment is most conducive when concentrating on economic development. Given the fundamental character of the Japanese economy, namely that it is a trading power across the oceans, it is all the more important to create a strong tie with the United States.

(3) Japan has created a society more 'Western' than 'Asian' in its pre war development. Despite World War II, there were traditional ties between Japan and the Anglo-American powers. In the postwar policy direction it is a natural course to develop a policy friendly to America and Britain.

Thus for Yoshida the choice of going ahead for a conclusion of a peace treaty with those 'willing countries' led by America to make a 'partial peace' was a natural choice.

Opposition parties led by the socialists, supported by some active vocal public opinion and leading intellectuals of the time, had entirely different views. They were under the strong influence of postwar pacifism, that Japan should renounce the war and that she was going to entrust her security to the good will of the peace loving people of the world. It was unacceptable in concluding the Peace Treaty to leave out some of the major powers with which Japan was at war, such as China or the Soviet Union. A utopian image of socialism permeated their pacifist thinking as well. In December 1949 the Japan Socialist Party adopted a three point resolution of 'comprehensive peace', 'no military bases' and 'neutrality' and called for support from the Japanese people, and in April 1950 all opposition parties except the Communist Party declared a common front in favour of the policy of 'comprehensive peace' and 'permanent neutrality'.

To favour 'partial peace' or 'comprehensive peace', that was the question. Internal debates and tension continued. By the end of 1950, however, governmental leadership under the compelling GHQ guidance spiralled in the direction of 'partial peace'. The first decision on a fundamental choice of Japanese security foreign policy options was made on the path to 'partial peace'.

In November 1950, the United States published Seven Principles to govern the peace treaty negotiations with Japan, which became henceforth the basis for further negotiations. The most important points included; 1) that the Peace Treaty would be concluded between Japan and those countries which were ready, implying that those countries which would object would be left out, 2) that Okinawa would be left under US trusteeship, 3) that the security of Japan would be ensured based on the cooperative responsibility between US forces and Japanese facilities, 4) that the concluding parties waive their claim against Japan, but with exceptions, 5) that Japan would be ensured in principle, a Most-Favoured-Nation treatment until a new agreement to govern economic relations would be concluded with the respective countries.[12]

From the beginning of 1951 concrete negotiations started primarily between the United States and other parties on the terms and conditions of the Peace Treaty.

US special envoy John F. Dulles visited Japan from January to February 1951 and had serious discussions with Prime Minister Yoshida. The two countries reached a basic understanding on the nature and the modality of American forces to be stationed in Japan after the conclusion of the Peace Treaty, as well as the key issue of Japanese rearmament, both issues to be looked at in more detail in the next Section. The status of Okinawa was also discussed and despite a strong Japanese plea to leave Okinawa under Japanese governance, the US position, as outlined in the seven principles above that it should be governed under US trusteeship, remained firm.

The key issue negotiated from April to July between America and Britain was the question of Chinese participation. Great Britain had already officially recognized the People's Republic of China as the sole representative of China in January 1950. The United States continued to recognize the Republic of China (Taiwan) governed by the Nationalist Party as formerly representing China. The original UK proposal to invite the People's Republic of China to the Peace Treaty Conference could not be accepted by the US. After prolonged

---

[12] C. Hosoya, *Sanfuranshisuko kouwaheno michi (Road to the San Francisco Peace)*, Cuuoukouron, 1984, pp. 113–114.

discussions they came to the conclusion that neither the PRC nor the RC should be invited.

Content of the San Francisco Peace Treaty

From 4 to 8 September 1951, the Peace Treaty Conference with Japan was held in San Francisco. 55 countries were invited, but no-one was invited from China or Korea. Among those invited India, Burma and Yugoslavia did not send delegations. The Treaty was signed on 8 September, but dissatisfied with its content, three countries that joined the debate did not sign it: the Soviet Union, Poland and Czechoslovakia.

Let us quickly view the key articles.

Articles 2 and 3 give territorial demarcation.

Japan recognized the independence of Korea. Japan renounced all rights to Formosa (Taiwan) and the Pescadores, and to the Kurile Islands and Southern Sakhalin. Each relevant party to its respective clause was either not present or refrained from signing: Korea, China and the Soviet Union. Thus each article became the beginning of future negotiations between Japan and the respective country for the normalization of their relationship (Article 2).

The Okinawa Islands would be placed under US trusteeship under the auspices of the United Nations, but pending the realization of this scheme the United States was given the right to exercise all administrative rights over the islands (Article 3). Thus, as we are going to see in the next chapter, the question of the reversion of Okinawa would become one of the major issues of Japan's relationship with the United States during the 1960's and the first half the 1970's.

Articles 5 and 6 covered security. The basic principles of the UN Charter, such as to settle disputes by peaceful means and to refrain from the use of force, were reiterated and Japan's right of individual and collective defence was confirmed (Article 5). All occupation forces were to withdraw from Japan, but this did not prevent the stationing of foreign armed forces based on bilateral or multilateral agreements. This bilateral agreement meant the agreement with the United States as we will see below (Article 6).

Article 14 defined the principles governing reparations. While recognizing the basic obligation that reparations should be paid by Japan to the Allied Powers, it also recognized that Japanese resources

were insufficient to meet all requirements if Japan were to maintain
a viable economy. Based on this article Japan strived, particularly
with Asian countries, to agree to a mutually acceptable amount of
reparations.

6. *Japanese security policy and the Japan-US Security Treaty*

When the peace treaty negotiations truly began to take shape from
the latter part of 1950, it became clear in the minds of the United
States and Japan that acceptance of Japan as a member of the international community had to be accompanied with a clear 'security
position' for Japan. Such was the tense Cold War climate, in particular, with the war in Korea raging in full swing. Japan had to
show a clear position on the contribution she was prepared to make
for the peace and stability of the region. That became a prerequi-
site to the Peace Treaty. Thus when US special envoy J.F. Dulles
and Prime Minister Yoshida conducted negotiations from January to
February 1951 on the Peace Treaty, it was more than anything else
the security issues that dominated the negotiations.

The first issue they discussed was the issue of the maintenance of
US forces in Japan after the conclusion of the Peace Treaty. As for
the desirability to keep a substantial number of US forces in Japan
under the then emerging Cold War situation, both sides had no dis-
agreement. Political opposition in Japan, which considered the United
States as dangerous, expansionist and against the cause of peace,
naturally objected, but the basic direction of the path to 'security
ties with the US' was clearly chosen by the Japanese government.
Next on the road to 'partial peace', the second decision on the fundamental choice of Japanese security foreign policy options was clearly
made.

The key issue to negotiate with the Americans was the modality
of US troop stationing. The Japanese wanted to introduce the notion
of collective self-defence under Article 51 of the United Nations
Charter and justify US bases in Japan as an implementation of US
rights and obligations of collective self-defence. The US objected to
this and argued that the US could not exert her right of collective
defence in relation to a country like Japan, which did not even maintain the means of individual self-defence. The US further emphasized
their position by referring to a Senate resolution in 1948 that the

US could conclude a collective security agreement only with those countries, that had power for a "continuous and effective self-help and mutual aid" to the United States (the Vandenberg Resolution). Japan was not eligible for collective self-defence under this resolution. Japan had to accept another formula which would allow a US military presence in Japan.

The next issue discussed substantially was the question of Japanese rearmament. The US side strongly maintained its necessity, however, Prime Minister Yoshida first objected on the ground that there was strong pacifism on the part of the Japanese people and that postwar Japanese efforts should be directed to economic reconstruction. Prime Minister Yoshida expressed nonetheless Japan's readiness to create a *hoan-tai* (Security Force) of 50,000 on land and at sea, to show Japan's alertness to the tense international situation which surrounded her. Article 9 was interpreted in this context, based on a realist's view, and that turned out to be the beginning of the creation of the Self-Defence Forces. The third decision on the fundamental choice of Japanese security foreign policy options was thus taken on the path to the 'minimum forces for self-defence', after the road to 'partial peace' and 'security ties with the US'.

The intention by the Japanese seemed to have met with the basic satisfaction by the US and to have paved the way to the Peace Treaty.

The fundamental structure of postwar Japanese security policy, to hold minimum adequate forces for the purpose of self-defence, and to rely on security relations with the United States to fill in the outstanding gap in facing the reality of the outside world, thus took shape. This security policy of realism was naturally in sharp contrast to, and strongly opposed by, the opposition parties, some vocal public opinion, and those idealist intellectuals, who advanced the 'no armament' and 'neutrality' policy. We need to note that opposition views that the Self-Defence Forces are 'unconstitutional' continued forcefully for another 50 years.

Notwithstanding those differences and the rising tension, the government decision was taken. On 8 September 1951 in San Francisco, on the same day and at the same place as the Peace Treaty was signed, the Security Treaty between Japan and the United States was signed. For the government of Japan, the Security Treaty was an indispensable element of the agreement in San Francisco, comprising another side of the coin of the Peace Treaty.

But the Treaty still reflected the subordinate nature of the relationship between Japan and the United States during the occupation:

On the key issue of collective defence it was agreed that Japan granted the United States the right to deploy their forces in Japan and such forces "may be utilized to contribute to the maintenance of international peace and security in the Far East and to the security of Japan."[13] The gist of the Article was that while Japan was obligated to grant facilities for use by US forces in Japan, the US were not obligated, strictly in the legal sense, to defend Japan;

In addition, the presence of US forces in Japan was determined by administrative agreements between the two governments, but the nature and scope of the US forces sent to Japan were left to a unilateral decision by the United States;

The Treaty was also formulated in such a way that US forces could be expected to intervene in large-scale domestic riots and disturbances in Japan caused by outside powers;

The Treaty did not, however, allow Japan to grant any security related power to any third country without prior consultation with the United States;

Lastly, the Treaty did not have a clear termination clause which, though hypothetically, deprived Japan from her formal right of abrogation.

This subordinate character of the Treaty would become the major agenda of Japan-US relations over the 1950's, as we are going to see in the following Chapter 2.

---

[13] Security Treaty between Japan and the USA, Article I, Ministry of Foreign Affairs (MOFA), *Shuyo Jyouyaku-shuu (Principal Treaties)*, 1991, p. 172.

CHAPTER TWO

THE UNITED STATES:
POLITICAL AND SECURITY RELATIONS

1. *The revision of the Security Treaty*

Post-San Francisco climate

The San Francisco Peace Treaty went into force on 28 April 1952. That was the first major landmark of postwar foreign policy. Japan terminated nearly seven years of occupation and came back to the international community as a full-fledged sovereign power. Notwithstanding the differences regarding what kind of peace Japan should achieve, regaining the status of a sovereign power was a genuine source of relief and satisfaction for most Japanese.

The relationship with the United States entered into a new stage as well. America was no longer the imposing occupying force but became a kind of 'big brother'. In this 'big brother-vs-little brother' relationship, security related issues between the two countries became the primary agenda during the 1950's.

The immediate issue which emerged after San Francisco was the issue of the Japanese rearmament. The 50,000 *hoan-tai* (security forces) committed by Prime Minister Yoshida before the conclusion of the San Francisco Peace Treaty were clearly not sufficient for either side, with the war in Korea continuing amidst the Cold War tension in the Far East. The US maintained in 1952 that land forces of 10 divisions and 300,000 troops should be established. Prime Minister Yoshida agreed to establish a Security Force of 110,000 but no more. In 1953 Japan proposed the establishment of 10 divisions of 180,000 troops comprised of land and other forces. In addition, the Self-Defence Forces were formally established in July 1954.[1] But no clear agreement was reached between the two sides.

---

[1] It is interesting to note that as of March 2002 the Self-Defence Forces currently number 282,795. In addition, there are more than 50,000 in the reserves (http://www.jda.go.jp/j/defense/jda-sdf/kousei/index.html 2003–02–16).

Meanwhile those changes which began from 1953 in external and internal contexts helped to alleviate tension on the rearmament issue between the two governments. On the international side the Korean War ended in July 1953 and another war in Indochina between France and Vietnam also saw an end in July 1954. On the domestic front the Japanese economy faced new difficulties, when the special boom resulting from the Korean War came to an end. The need to direct limited government expenditure to the area most conducive to economic recovery and not to a consolidation of military power had more compelling reasons.

An American nuclear bomb testing at the Bikini Islands in the Pacific, which resulted in a nuclear contamination of a small fishing vessel in March 1954, heightened Japanese anti-nuclear popular feeling as well. This incident triggered the postwar Japanese anti-nuclear movement which already had a strong basis from the Hiroshima and Nagasaki bombs, and clearly raised tension between the two countries. A better management of security relations became an important task for the two governments.

Conclusion of the new Security Treaty

Thus, in the latter part of the 1950's the focal point of political relations between the two countries gradually moved into the area of the revision of the Security Treaty signed in San Francisco in September 1951.

As we saw at the end of the previous Chapter, in many ways the Security Treaty left traces of 'big brother-little brother' relationship.

The first attempt to revise the Security Treaty was in August 1955 by Foreign Minister Mamoru Shigemitsu, who was rehabilitated after the IMTFE and became Foreign Minister in the cabinet led by Ichiro Hatoyama from December 1954 to December 1956. In a personal letter to John F. Dulles, Shigemitsu proposed a mutual defence treaty. The purpose of the revision was to create a new treaty, which eradicated inequality pertaining to the then existing Security Treaty. J.F. Dulles reacted bluntly that Japan neither had the readiness nor the power to conclude a mutual defence treaty. Thus the first attempt did not produce any tangible result.

In November 1955 an important power shift took place on the Japanese internal political scene. The two most influential conservative parties, the Liberal Party, to which Yoshida belonged, and the

Japan Democratic Party, to which Hatoyama and Shigemitsu belonged, merged and created one single conservative party: the Liberal Democratic Party (LDP). Hence began one of the longest periods of one party rule, which came to be called 'the Coalition of Conservatives' or 'the 1955 System'.

Nobusuke Kishi succeeded Hatoyama as the Prime Minister from this newly established Party in February 1957. He appeared to be a powerful Prime Minister, whose internal position was strong, and who was determined to bring Japan back to a respectable position in the international community and, for this purpose, to take concrete action. In May 1957 the first major policy decision on Japanese defence was taken under the 'Basic Policy for National Defence', which stated that:

> The purpose of National Defence is to prevent in advance direct and indirect aggression, to remove it if it takes place, and thus to protect the peace and independence of Japan, which is basing its course on Democracy. In order to achieve this objective (i) the promotion of efforts for peace and establishment of the foundations for national security; and (ii) the development of an efficient defence capability and adherence to the Japan-US Security Agreements are the basic policy.[2]

Kishi was also active in determining a new basis for foreign policy in Asia, which we will see in Chapter 6, but his guiding motive was the creation of a genuinely equal Japan-US relationship. He visited Washington in June and what he had in mind was precisely the revision of the Security Treaty. He proposed that Japan and the United States should enter into a "new era of relationship".

This time the US welcomed Kishi's approach and a basic agreement to prepare a revision of the Security Treaty was achieved between Prime Minister Kishi and President Dwight D. Eisenhower.

Several reasons can be outlined: 1) Japan by then had resumed diplomatic relations with the Soviet Union in 1956 (Chapter 7) and joined the United Nations in the same year. Japan had acquired a more important status among the community of nations and an unequal Security Treaty did not match this picture; 2) Anti-bases movements in Japan, particularly in Okinawa, took serious shape

---

[2] http://www.jda.go.jp/e/pab/wp2002/0201.htm 2002-12-17. The same JDA home page states that "Other Basic Policies for Japan's national defense include an exclusively defence-oriented policy, not becoming a military power, adherence to the three non-nuclear principles and ensuring civilian control of the military."

from 1956 onwards. The death of a Japanese woman in January 1957 at an American base in Sagamihara in the central part of Honshu (Main Island) fuelled anger towards the American military presence. Something had to be done to ease the tension. 3) Kishi showed sufficient sensitivity to the revision of the Security Treaty and knew that proceeding too precipitously was not conducive to a positive outcome.

Both sides took a full year of preparation before entering the negotiation stage. In August 1958 Prime Minister Kishi met with the American Ambassador to Japan, Douglas MacArthur II, a nephew of General Douglas MacArthur, and Kishi declared his determination to conclude a fundamentally new treaty, rather than partially revising the existing one. Foreign Minister Aiichiro Fujiyama visited Washington in September and the negotiations started in October in Tokyo between Foreign Minister Fujiyama and Ambassador MacArthur. 25 official meetings and possibly a greater number of unofficial meetings took place. Fumihiko Togo, who was assigned to the post of the Director of the Security Division of MOFA in April 1957, prepared and interpreted at all of those meetings.[3]

The negotiations proceeded rapidly and by the end of 1958 the basic structure of the agreement had already taken shape. Nevertheless, and primarily because of the need to secure consensus among various domestic political forces on the Japanese side, the actual signing of the agreement took place in Washington on 19 January 1960. The new Treaty of Mutual Cooperation and Security, as it was renamed, revised practically all problems, which had been raised from the Japanese side in relation to the previous Security Treaty of 1951.

On the key issue of the US obligation to defend Japan in case of an armed attack on Japanese territory, the first half of Article V prescribed that:

> Each Party recognizes that an armed attack against either Party in the territories under the administration of Japan would be dangerous to its own peace and safety and declares that it would act to meet the common danger in accordance with its constitutional provisions and processes.[4]

---

[3] Fumihiko Togo, *Nichibeigaiko 30 Nen (Thirty years of Japan-US foreign relations)*, Sekaino Ugokisha, 1982, p. 97.

[4] MOFA, *op. cit.*, p. 135.

The obligation on the part of the United States to defend Japan if attacked lay in the wording "declares that it would act to meet the common danger". This was the first major improvement for Japan over the previous Security Treaty. A careful reader might notice that each side used subtle and effective wording to meet their respective internal requirements. The Japanese side used 'constitutional provisions' referring to Article 9, the interpretation of which does not allow Japan to exercise its right to collective self-defence; the United States side used 'constitutional processes', implying the 1948 Senate resolution, which required "continuous and effective self-help and mutual aid" to allow the United States to engage in a security agreement with a foreign country.

Article VI constitutes another pillar of the Treaty: the first half reads as follows:

> For the purpose of contributing to the security of Japan and the maintenance of international peace and security in the Far East, the United States of America is granted the use by its land, air and naval forces of facilities and areas in Japan.[5]

This basically reflects the rights and obligations in the previous Security Treaty. However, in this connection an important novelty was introduced in the form of an 'Exchange of Notes', signed by Prime Minister Kishi and US Secretary of State Christian A. Herter in relation to Article VI, the essential part being the following:

> Major changes in the deployment into Japan of United States armed forces, major changes in their equipment, and the use of facilities and areas in Japan as bases for military combat operations to be undertaken from Japan other than those conducted under Article V of the said Treaty, shall be the subjects of prior consultation with the Government of Japan.[6]

The Exchange of Notes on prior consultation meant that in the abovementioned changes on 1) deployment of armed forces into Japan, on 2) equipment, and on 3) the use of facilities for combat operations, the US side would make prior consultations with, and obtain approval from, Japan. Japan acquired a legal basis to express its views on the major aspects of US forces activities in Japan. That was unprecedented in security agreements of this kind.

---

[5] Ibid., p. 136.
[6] Ibid., p. 139.

An oral agreement between Foreign Minister Fujiyama and Ambassador MacArthur was further made so as to give a more precise definition of the three points requiring prior consultation and, *inter alia*, the 'major changes in their equipment' was defined as "introduction of nuclear warheads and mid to long-range missiles and the construction of bases thereof".

Clauses on US forces deployment to put down internal riots or restriction to grant security related powers to a third country were eliminated.

An expiry clause was introduced, allowing each party to terminate the treaty with a one year interval after 10 years (Article X).

In addition, the new Treaty incorporated new clauses prescribing basic security principles of the United Nations Charter (Article I), cooperation (Article II), development of capacities to resist armed attack subject to constitutional provisions (Article III), consultation (Article IV), and precedence of UN Charter (Article VII). All these articles can be interpreted as equal footing, and thus, as positive and reasonably useful.

The revision of the Security Treaty created a new structure underlining Japan's new role in the international community.

At the same time the new Security Treaty created an important question of asymmetry. Before the revision, there was an asymmetry in that the US had the right to use the facilities and areas in Japan, but did not have the obligation to defend Japan. After the revision this asymmetry was resolved, because the United States retained the right to use the facilities and areas in Japan while it became obligated to defend Japan when attacked. In addition, Japan was granted the right to prior consultation. But this new equation created a new asymmetry, because while America is obligated to defend Japan when attacked, Japan is not obligated to defend America even if America is attacked. This asymmetry, which is the direct result of Japan's constitutional constraint, remains a fundamental basis of Japan's security relations with America to this day.

Internal debate, tension, riots and parliamentary approval

However, Japanese public opinion led by the opposition parties and under the strong influence of postwar passive pacifism failed to appreciate these achievements and 1960 came to be remembered as one of the most turbulent years of postwar Japanese history.

In January, after the Treaty was signed, it was presented to the parliament for approval and from February to June it was subjected to intensive debate. Meanwhile political opposition inside and outside parliament mounted steadily. Severe riots broke out in the capital. So much so that in June a female university student died in the riot near the Diet buildings and President Eisenhower's visit to Japan was cancelled at the last minute. Although the treaty was ratified on 20 June 1960 and entered into force on 23 June, through the exchange of instruments of ratification, Prime Minister Kishi had to resign and left his post on 19 July.

Why did such mounting protest against the treaty prevail at that time?

We have to go back first to the legacy of pacifism and the call for peace, neutrality, and non-armament. Policy options which arose from the standpoint of 'minimum forces for self-defence' and 'security ties with the US' could not be accepted. The most important argument the political opposition forces created was the theory of 'unwilling involvement': If Japan enters into a new treaty obligation with greater responsibility, there is a higher risk of being unwillingly involved in warfare created by expansionist militaristic America.[7] It is amazing to note how greatly this argument succeeded in provoking public sympathy throughout the country.

Some analysts now contend that the primary reason for the turmoil lay in the internal political situation: people feared Prime Minister Kishi's high-handed approach in dealing with internal politics and in particular the new laws he tried to introduce, such as the law giving more power to police activities. They argued that the fact that the public calmed down so fast after Kishi's resignation was proof that foreign policy issues were not a central part of the confrontation.[8]

---

[7] Just to show some examples of the opposition's logic: "Suppose that Japan is attacked by the use of force under an Article V situation. If the US launched a counterattack before Japan decided to do so, then Japan would run the risk of being unwillingly involved in warfare." (House of Representatives, *Special Security committee Minutes*, 11 March 1960, p. 6/13). "Japan will be unwillingly involved in war because of the prior consultation system. In the current situation Japan has no responsibility. America is acting unilaterally. But once Japan acts after consultation, Japan will be unwillingly involved against our Constitution." (House of Representatives, *Special Security Committee Minutes*, 18 May 1960, p. 36/17–18).

[8] K. Sakamoto, *Sengo Nihon Gaikoushi (Postwar Japanese Foreign Policy)* Chapter 2, M. Iokibe ed., Yuuhikaku, 2001, p. 102.

In the spring of 1960 I was a high school student of 15. I had just passed the public high school entrance exams in central Tokyo. Polemics on the question of the revision of the Security Treaty was a hot issue at school, especially in the 'Social Studies' class. In those days in particular there were many high school teachers strongly inclined towards pacifist views. Kishi's danger had been talked about a little, but it was primarily the security issue that excited us.

The key question was whether Japan would be safer under the new treaty or under the existing old treaty. The majority of views inclined toward the belief that the treaty would bring increased threats and danger for the security of Japan. I remember very well how my father, Fumihiko Togo, became angry when I tried to explain some of the points raised at school and, in turn, how I became isolated at school when I tried to present my own views based on the realism I brought from home.

Whatever the true reasons for the turmoil during the first half of 1960, the fundamental choice the Japanese government made towards the 'security ties with the US' went through a severe test of vigilance, but it survived.

Thence onwards the Japanese people gradually began to live in better harmony with the security relations with the United States, although many contentious issues continued to arise even to this day.

Security debates on the prior consultation system

While we are going to see concrete issues related to the security relations between Japan and America in the following sections and in Chapter 12, I would like to briefly touch upon one issue which is of conceptual and substantial importance, that of prior consultation.

The question of prior consultation was probably one of the most important issues to have been debated so intensively in parliament from the spring of 1960. The focal point was the question of the introduction of nuclear warheads and missiles. The background to this was the two atomic bombs that were dropped on Hiroshima and Nagasaki in August 1945 and the nuclear testing at the Bikini Islands in 1954.

In the course of the debates inside and outside parliament over the years, several interesting issues have emerged for discussion:

(1) Opposition parties, based on the strong anti-nuclear feeling of public opinion in general, pressed the government to commit itself to always say "No" to any prior consultation related to the introduction of nuclear weapons to Japan. As early as the spring of 1960, the government had made a clear "No" statement at the parliamentary debate in relation to a situation where the government might be asked by the Americans to allow the introduction of nuclear weapons to Japan.[9] In January 1968 then Prime Minister Sato stated at parliament the well-known Japanese government policy on 'three non-nuclear principles', namely that it does not possess, produce, nor allow the introduction of nuclear weapons.

The common sense position of the US on the other hand, was to expect at least a careful deliberation on the emerging situation and to expect the possibility of a "Yes" or "No" in such an extraordinary situation.

How could the two countries come to terms, given their contradictory positions?

(2) The long-standing US military position was to never let the position of a nuclear arsenal outside its country become known. That understandable security policy has been defined as the No Confirmation No Denial (NCND) policy. If that was the case, in a situation where the US might wish to introduce nuclear warheads to Japan, would this issue be put forward at the risk of endangering its security and in contradiction to its long term policy of NCND? Would America really ask Japan to allow the introduction of nuclear weapons in a security emergency? In particular, would they ask Japan when it was understood that the answer would be "No"?

(3) Later in the 70's and 80's, a more confusing situation emerged. Several important American officials such as retired Rear Admiral La Rocque and former Ambassador to Japan Edwin O. Reischauer announced in 1974 and 1981, respectively, that a confidential agreement existed in January 1960 that the notion of 'introduction' is separate from the notion of 'transit' and that port visits or the passage of vessels carrying nuclear warheads should be understood as 'transit'

---

[9] Prime Minister Kishi, when asked whether Japan would allow the US to introduce nuclear weapons under the Article V situation if Japan was attacked by outside forces, answered that Japan would not allow such an introduction and that that was the policy of the Kishi government (House of Representatives, *Special Security committee Minutes*, 5 February 1960, p. 26/19).

and not 'introduction', therefore these activities should be outside the scope of prior consultation. Each time such reports appeared in the Japanese or American press, the government of Japan went all the way to deny the existence of such a confidential agreement, but over the years, the idea that some understanding must have existed grew strongly among the public and other interested observers.[10]

The difficulty of giving a clear-cut answer to these questions probably showed the high degree of mutual trust which had developed over the years between the two governments. Both governments probably knew that there were areas where it was not in the interest of the alliance to pursue further and still had no doubt about the credibility of the alliance. We will see how this relation based on mutual trust proved to be of unprecedented value on the occasion of the reversion of Okinawa.

2. *The reversion of Okinawa*

During the first half of the 1960's the relationship between Japan and the United States saw a period of tranquillity, quite amazing compared to the turbulent year of 1960. On television, which was rapidly becoming a symbol of middle class affluence, President John F. Kennedy enjoyed great popularity in Japan, as did Edwin O. Reischauer, the newly appointed American Ambassador to Japan, long-time scholar in the field of Japanese studies and married to a Japanese woman.

In the latter half of the 1960's, however, a new issue moved to the forefront of the relationship. There emerged in Japan a new notion that "Unless Okinawa is returned to her homeland, the post-war period for Japan shall never end".

Okinawa is a group of islands located to the south of Japan. From the beginning of the 17th century the islands were governed by the Kagoshima warlord but were also placed under the governance of the Qing Dynasty of China. Before the Japan-China War in 1894–1895, the Meiji government put Okinawa under its direct control and its victory in the war with China extinguished any objection the latter might have to Japanese governance.

---

[10] Sakamoto, *op. cit.*, p. 103.

In March 1945 the Okinawa islands were severely attacked by the US forces. 550,000 troops, 1400 vessels were concentrated here and after a bloody battle which involved practically all citizens, the islands were occupied in June.[11] 75,000 troops[12] and 150,000 civilians[13] died. Okinawa was virtually the only area where the war was fought inside present-day Japanese territory.

In the San Francisco Peace Treaty the islands were left under US administration. Heavy concentrations of American troops were stationed on the islands and resentment against the US occupation mounted. One of US motivations to revise the Security Treaty in 1960 was to ease the resentment accumulated in Okinawa. The revision of the Security Treaty, however, left another scar on Okinawa. The careful wording of Article V, that America was obliged to react to "an armed attack against Japan in the territories under the administration of Japan" excluded Okinawa from the US obligations. Japanese government might have been unwilling to include Okinawa under the US obligation because of its nuclear arsenal, but from the point of view of the people of Okinawa, that decision represented just another alienation from the mainland.

Eisaku Sato, younger brother to Nobusuke Kishi, took the office of Prime Minister in November 1964 and was determined that his cabinet's priority was to resolve the last vestiges of the Pacific War. In August 1965 Sato was the first postwar Prime Minister to visit Okinawa and declared there that "Unless Okinawa is returned to her homeland, the postwar period for Japan shall never end." In early 1967 Fumihiko Togo became the Director General of the American Bureau in charge of the negotiations for the reversion of the islands.

On the American side the fact that things could not be left as they were gradually came to be understood. Repeated signals from the islands that people there were not content with the US administration alerted Washington. Already in March 1962 President Kennedy announced that "Okinawa is a part of Japan and I hope that the security interests of the free world will enable a complete return of the islands to Japan."[14]

---

[11] Ikei, *op. cit.*, p. 287.
[12] Takeuchi, *op. cit.*, p. 194.
[13] Peter Duus, *op. cit.*, p. 249.
[14] Ikei, *op. cit.*, p. 288.

With this background Sato visited Washington in November 1967 and made his first breakthrough. In a joint communiqué issued by Sato and President Lyndon B. Johnson, Sato expressed his view that a mutually satisfactory timing of the reversion of Okinawa should be agreed "within a few years". The President replied that he fully understood the desire of the Japanese people for the reversion of these islands.

Thus there emerged crucial years in the history of the negotiations on the reversion of Okinawa. On one hand, 'within a few years', indicated that a clear timing of the reversion had yet to be determined. However, on the other hand, so as to achieve this objective, the security status of Okinawa had to be defined, and for that the most difficult issue of nuclear arms had to be resolved.

The international situation surrounding the negotiations created one of the most thrilling conditions for a potential breakthrough. Toward the end of the 1960's, the monopolar position of the United States at the postwar situation underwent a relative decline economically (Chapter 3) and politically. Increasing difficulty because of the Vietnam War (Chapter 6) was one of the reasons for this change. Richard Nixon was elected to the US Presidency in 1969 with a vision and ambition to overcome the new challenge. In July 1969 President Nixon announced the so-called 'Guam Doctrine', which was later named the 'Nixon Doctrine', which stated that America sought a greater role for allied countries in the common efforts to enhance the security of the free world.

The reversion of Okinawa was compatible with his basic philosophy: Okinawa will be returned to Japan as a symbol of a greater and more responsible role to be played by Japan on security matters in the Asia-Pacific region. All the more so, in the immediate strategic situation in and around Vietnam, the role of a stable and reliable Okinawa had to be strongly maintained. The reversion of Okinawa could be accomplished, provided it would not weaken the military function of the islands. But then, what to do about the nuclear arsenal?

However difficult the solution was, towards the latter half of 1969 a general understanding emerged between the two governments. The two sides carefully prepared a joint communiqué to be issued during Sato's visit in November 1969.

On the question of the timing, an agreement was reached to "expedite the consultations with a view to accomplishing the reversion during 1972",[15] that is to say three years starting from the end of 1969.

On the general security status of Okinawa an agreement was also reached that "upon return of the administrative rights, the Treaty of Mutual Cooperation and Security and its related arrangements would apply to Okinawa."[16] 'Related arrangements' implied the prior consultation mechanism.

On concrete issues which could cause threats or tension in the situation in and around the Far East, a clear convergence of views was needed between the two governments so that any possible mobilization of forces from Okinawa would be conducted based on common recognition of the developing situation. Hence the particular importance of the following clauses related to the situation in and around the Far East.

(1) On Korea, "the Prime Minister——stated that the security of the Republic of Korea was essential to Japan's own security."[17] The language is strong and clear and expresses Japan's security concern over the peninsula and since then this part has been called 'the Korean Clause';

(2) On Taiwan, "the Prime Minister said that the maintenance of peace and security in the Taiwan area was also a most important factor for the security of Japan."[18] This came to be known as 'the Taiwan Clause';

(3) On Vietnam, the two leaders "agreed that, should peace in Vietnam not have been realized by the time the reversion of Okinawa is scheduled to take place, the two governments would fully consult with each other in the light of the situation at that time so that the reversion would be accomplished without affecting the United States efforts to assure the South Vietnamese people the opportunity to determine their own political future without outside interference."[19] This was the result of elaborate efforts on the part of the two governments to harmonize the reversion of Okinawa with the precarious situation in Vietnam. It goes without saying that neither of the

---

[15] MOFA, *op. cit., Joint Communiqué between President Richard M. Nixon and Prime Minister Eisaku Sato November 21, 1969*, Para. 6, p. 99.

[16] Ibid., Para. 7, p. 100.

[17] Ibid., Para. 4, p. 97.

[18] Ibid.

[19] Ibid., p. 98.

two governments could imagine then that in 1975, three years after the reversion of Okinawa, South Vietnam would fall and that North Vietnam would re-unite the entire country.

Fair enough, what happened to the 'nuclear' issue? Here we see one of the most thrilling and probably the most successful stories of postwar Japanese foreign policy.

The agreement reached at the communiqué was the inclusion of the following masterpiece of contemporary diplomacy:

> 8. The Prime Minister described in detail the particular sentiment of the Japanese people against nuclear weapons and the policy of the Japanese Government reflecting such sentiment. The President expressed his deep understanding and assured the Prime Minister that, without prejudice to the position of the United States Government with respect to the prior consultation system under the Treaty of Mutual Cooperation and Security, the reversion of Okinawa would be carried out in a manner consistent with the policy of the Japanese Government as described by the Prime Minister.[20]

My interpretation of this paragraph is the following:

(1) 'The particular sentiment of the Japanese people' means the 'three non-nuclear principles' of not possessing, not producing and not introducing nuclear arms.

(2) The fact that the US President 'assured that the reversion will be done in a manner consistent with that sentiment' implies that the US will take away all nuclear warheads and missiles at the time of the reversion. There will be no nuclear arsenal when Okinawa is returned to Japan.

(3) But then what does it mean 'without prejudice to the position of the United States with respect to prior consultation'? I presume, based on common sense, that 'the position' means that if the question is put forward to the Japanese on further introduction of nuclear weapons to Japan through prior consultation, the Japanese answer should be either "Yes" or "No". 'Without prejudice to the position of the US Government' should at least have meant that American expectation should have the right to exist.

(4) There obviously arises a contradiction as I described in the preceding section. Japan maintains the 'three non-nuclear principles' and therefore would not allow an introduction of the nuclear weapons

---

[20] Ibid., Para. 8, pp. 100–101.

even if asked by the American side at a time of emergency. Can we still say that the American expectation is justified?

(5) The key solution to this dilemma was the fact that this question was left unanswered. In other words, the two governments agreed on this text knowing that an unanswered question remains, and yet based on this text the reversion of Okinawa was achieved. What prevailed here was a genuine and high level of confidence between the two governments, which took the form of their trust in 'one mechanism'. The 'prior consultation' mechanism, a mechanism which has never been used in reality to this day, and which, since 1960 became the object of fierce controversy inside Japan, contained the wisdom to overcome a seemingly impossible contradiction between the two sides.

On 21 November 1969 a joint communiqué between Eisaku Sato and Richard M. Nixon was issued in Washington and the most dramatic chapter of the reversion affair was concluded. The Agreement on the reversion of Okinawa was signed on 17 June 1971 and the actual reversion took place, as scheduled, on 15 May 1972. Two months later, having accomplished all of the objectives related to the reversion of Okinawa, Sato retired from the post of Prime Minister.

Fumihiko Togo left in his memoir the following concluding evaluation of the negotiations and the Sato-Nixon meeting in November 1969:

> Recalling the essence of the negotiations, Japan maintained that Okinawa should be returned, so that it would become a normal part Japan. Japan had no intention to jeopardize the security of the Far East after its reversion, but requested that America take certain risks. America took these risks based on their trust of the Japanese Government. That is why the meeting ended with success. What lay behind it was the relative change of position between Japan, with its increasing power, and America, with difficulties in and out of the country.[21]

More than 20 years later, in May 1994, however, an amazing book was published by a Japanese scholar Kei Wakaizumi. The book gave a detailed record of the top secret negotiations which had been conducted between President Nixon and Henry Kissinger on the American side and Prime Minister Sato and his special envoy Wakaizumi himself on the Japanese side, as a result of which highly confidential

---

[21] F. Togo, *op. cit.*, pp. 174–175.

Agreed Minutes were signed between the Prime Minister and the President on 21 November 1969. The gist of these Agreed Minutes was that the Prime Minister declared that if the US government required the re-entry of nuclear weapons and transit rights in Okinawa in time of great emergency the government of Japan would meet these requirements without delay.[22]

Both governments do not confirm the existence of this document.

Fumihiko Togo wrote the following passage in his memoirs published in 1982: "Henry Kissinger's memoirs 'The White House Years' tell that there had been a contact person between Prime Minister Sato and Secretary of State Kissinger. In recalling those days, I do not hold it against the Prime Minister even if it was true. Had he been alive today, I wish I could have told him with a nice smile that he was not terribly kind to us."[23]

Togo passed away in 1985 without having the opportunity to read Kei Wakaizumi's memoirs.

Whatever the true story of the drama of the reversion of Okinawa was, whatever the human efforts displayed therein were, whatever the responsibility each individual was determined to take, Okinawa finally came back under the administration of Japan. It was a clear achievement of postwar Japanese foreign policy. But the Japanese government and the people of Okinawa are continuing to struggle thence onwards to resolve outstanding problems, as we will see below in Section 5.

3. *Host Nations Support and Guidelines for Defence Cooperation of 1978*

All in all, the reversion of Okinawa was a turning point in the relationship between Japan and the United States. Before Okinawa, politico-security issues primarily dominated the relationship. Despite some pleas for an equal partnership, in reality Japan was a junior partner to the United States. After Okinawa a major political issue was overcome in the bilateral relationship and the growing economic power of Japan emerged on the surface, while America's monopolar economic power in the free world was losing its basis.

---

[22] K. Wakaizumi, *Tasakunakarishiwo Shinzentohossu (I wanted to believe that there was no other option)*, Bungeishinjyu, 1995, p. 417.

[23] F. Togo, *op. cit.*, p. 176.

Before Okinawa it was primarily Japan that called for changes in the bilateral political relationship, like the revision of the Security Treaty or the reversion of Okinawa. In that sense the 1950's and 1960's had been proactive and dynamic periods, when Japan tried to rise from the position of little brother to an equal partner. After the reversion of Okinawa it was more the USA that called for changes in the economic bilateral relationship. Japan increasingly stood in a position to meet demands from America. Important changes were occurring in the relative economic balance of power between the two countries.

During those years of trade conflict after the reversion of Okinawa, which lasted at least for a quarter of a century (as we are going to see in Chapter 3), it is important to note that the security relations became, on the whole, an effective bond between the two countries. As in any other areas of foreign policy, this was also the result of strenuous efforts by those who were particularly concerned with the security aspects of the relationship, to make the security ties even sounder and stronger.

Changing circumstances in international relations were not unrelated to Japanese endeavours. The fruits of Detente as we observed in the US-PRC Shanghai Communiqué in February 1972 (Chapter 4), in the SALT I and ABM Treaty in May 1972, and in the Helsinki Final Act in August 1975 (Chapter 8) gradually became replaced by the growing expansionist movement of the Soviet Union. 1975 marked the emergence of socialist regimes in Indochina (Chapter 6) and the expanding influence of the Soviet Union in Africa, for instance in Angola. 1976 came to be called the year of the 'end of Detente'. The cooling off of the bilateral relations between Japan and the Soviet Union (Chapter 7) coincided with this rising East-West tension from the mid-1970's.

So, in 1976 the Japanese government took an important policy decision on defence by adopting the 'National Defence Programme Outline (NDPO)'. It was the second major policy decision on defence after the adoption of the 'Basic Policy for National Defence' in 1957. The newly adopted Outline was based on the 'Concepts of Basic Defence Force'.[24] In accordance with the new Outline "Japan should possess the minimum necessary defence capability for an independent nation so that it would not become a source of instability in

---

[24] http://www.jda.go.jp/e/pab/wp2002/0203.htm 2002–12–17.

the surrounding region by creating a vacuum of power, rather than building a capability directly linked to a military threat to Japan".[25] In the thinking permeating passive pacifists amongst the general public, this was probably an unavoidable approach to seek further understanding and support from the Japanese people for the maintenance of effective Self-Defence Forces.

One week after the NDPO was adopted by the cabinet, however, another cabinet decision was taken to keep the level of defence expenditure in principle below 1% of GNP. That was a decision reflecting the passive pacifists' fear that even such a minimal approach reflected in NDPO might unleash militaristic tendencies in Japan. In reality, the Japanese defence budget steadily increased after the war and with a smooth curve of increase reached 1 trillion yen in 1974. But because the rate of growth of overall GNP had been greater, the defence budget percentage declined from 2% in early 50's to over 1% in early 60's and dropped well below 1% in late 60's. It stayed at that level over the 70's.[26] Thus the introduction of the 1% ceiling did not mean an immediate cut in defence expenditure, but it mitigated the creative aspect of the NDPO and made the tenure of Prime Minister Takeo Miki (December 1974–December 1976), who took the two decisions, remembered more because of passive pacifism.

Under the cabinet of Takeo Fukuda, who took office in December 1976, the year 1978 should be remembered by two important decisions which strengthened the security ties with America.

The first decision was to increase substantially financial support for the expenses incurred in the stationing of American troops in Japan. It was initiated in May by the Minister of State on Self-Defence Shin Kanemaru. It started with the coverage of locally employed Japanese workers and year by year expanded to include the housing expenses of American troops and various auxiliary expenses related to their stationing. It eventually amounted to $3.2 billion in 1990, reached its apex of $6.6 billion in 1996 on dollar basis and since then has been kept at the same level on yen basis, even in the ill-functioning conditions of the Japanese economy.[27] The Host Nation

---

[25] http://www.jda.go.jp/e/pab/kouho/taikou/made_e.htm 2004–07–21.

[26] M.Tadokoro, *Sengo Nihon Gaikoushi (Postwar Japanese Foreign Policy)* Chapter 3, M. Iokibe ed., Yuuhikaku, 2001, p. 121.

[27] The expenditure related to US forces in Japan from 1993 to 2002 are the

Support, as it came to be called, was much appreciated by the Americans and the Japanese host nation support was known to be the most generous one among all US allies.

The second decision was the adoption with the United States of the Guidelines for Defence Cooperation in November. The Guidelines were intended to establish a concrete cooperative scheme under Article V of the Security Treaty with an enlarged and clear role for the Japanese SDF.

Under Prime Minister Masayoshi Ohira, who replaced Fukuda in December 1978, Japan's efforts continued. In his visit to Washington in May 1979 Prime Minister Ohira called America "an ally and irreplaceable friend".[28] Soviet moves then culminated in its invasion of Afghanistan in December 1979. To protest against Soviet action in Afghanistan and to show Japan's solidarity with the West, Japan took a series of measures including the boycotting of the Olympic Games in Moscow in the summer of 1980. Prime Minister Ohira visited Washington again in May 1980 and expressed his commitment to increase the defence budget and assured the US that cooperation under the newly established Guidelines was steadily advancing.

Needless to say, those efforts to further strengthen the security ties were conducted against the opposition of the passive pacifists' anti-American voices. Against that background, the leadership shown by the Fukuda-Ohira line of positive cooperation in the security area was commendable.

However, Prime Minister Ohira died suddenly in June 1980 during a rough election campaign and confusion occurred under his successor Zenko Suzuki, who was a close supporter of Ohira in his faction within the Liberal Democratic Party, but was not necessarily aiming for the seat of Prime Minister. The confusion was heavily conditioned by the passive pacifism which surrounded the suddenly elected and unprepared Prime Minister.

In May 1981 Z. Suzuki visited Washington and had a meeting with newly elected President Ronald Reagan. The communiqué issued after the meeting used the term 'alliance' to describe the Japan-US relationship. Suzuki afterwards maintained that the word 'alliance'

---

following, in 100 million yen: 5612, 5944, 6257, 6389, 6416, 6342, 6619, 6659, 6534, 6392 (Japan Defence Facilities Administration Agency figures).

[28] H. Nakanishi, *Sengo Nihon Gaikoushi (Postwar Japanese Foreign Policy)* Chapter 4, M. Iokibe ed., Yuuhikaku, 2001, p. 181.

had no military connotations and his view was publicly contested by his Foreign Minister Masayoshi Ito and Vice-Minister for Foreign Affairs Masuro Takashima, as a result of which both resigned. Under the general passive pacifist environment the issue of military connotations could have produced such an outcome even as late as 1981.

Meanwhile, at a luncheon meeting at the National Press Club after the presidential meeting, Prime Minister Suzuki referred to Japan's possible role in defending "a few hundred miles around Japan and 1000 nautical miles of sea lanes".[29] The US took his statement as an important commitment to a more responsible role and welcomed it. There was unfortunately no policy decision to that effect and the two administrations had to face difficult months of readjustment due to this emerging discrepancy. In the US Congress calls came for the enhancement of the Japanese defence capability and terminology such as 'defence friction' in addition to 'trade friction' began to appear in the media.[30]

4. The Western Alliance under Nakasone and Reagan

In November 1982 Yasuhiro Nakasone took the seat of Prime Minister and for five years succeeded in consolidating Japan-US relationships in all areas. Together with his counterpart in the United States, President Ronald Reagan, this period was referred to in Japan as the period of 'Nakasone-Reagan' or 'Ron-Yasu'.

It was an interesting matching of policy and personality. President Reagan's view to deal squarely with the Soviet Union echoed precisely Nakasone's strategic thinking, to let Japan play a more responsible role in the conduct of Japan's external policy. On internal economic policy President Reagan's emphasis on small government and on the role of the private sector also coincided with Nakasone's reformist policies, which aimed at restructuring the Japanese economy and society, as we will see in Chapter 3.

---

[29] K. Murata, *Sengo Nihon Gaikoushi (Postwar Japanese Foreign Policy)* Chapter 5, M. Iokibe ed., Yuuhikaku, 2001, p. 193.

[30] After his resignation, Takashima became the Ambassador to the Soviet Union, and I served under him as political counsellor. Occasional accounts of the incidents he encountered as the Vice-Minister reflected his difficulty to defend a realist view inside Japan.

In 1983 the era of Ron-Yasu began. Nakasone visited Washington in January and reconfirmed in a clear manner the once troubled concept of an 'alliance' replete with military connotations between Japan and the United States. He also declared his intention to increase substantially defence expenditure in the national budget and to facilitate the export of arms and arms-related technology from Japan to America.

In May at Williamsburg in America the G7 Summit was held. Nakasone made an impressive debut at this Summit and took the lead in sharing the notion that "The security of our countries is indivisible and must be approached on a global basis",[31] as was included in the Statement at Williamsburg. In concrete terms he made a clear case that the Soviet threat of Intermediate-Range Nuclear Forces (INF) SS20 had to be considered in its entirety. The threat would not disappear until they also withdrew from the Asian part of the Soviet Union, east of the Urals. It was probably the first time in postwar Japanese foreign policy that Japan sent a clear message of her own, regarding an issue of global magnitude in the security area.

In September the Soviet Union shot down a plane belonging to Korean Airlines (KAL-007) off the coast of the Sakhalin islands. Japan and America cooperated closely in bringing this fact to the attention of the outside world and publicly condemned it, including at a session of the United Nations Security Council.

In the early morning of 1 September 1983, I was still in bed in my flat inside the diplomatic quarters in Moscow. I was the political councillor in the Embassy of Japan at the time. A sudden call from Tokyo woke me up. I was told that a Korean Airliner had disappeared under mysterious circumstances off the coast of Sakhalin and that I should immediately contact the Soviet Foreign Ministry to inquire about this case. A written cable had already been sent to the Embassy.

I immediately called the Soviet Foreign Ministry, conveyed my request to the duty-officer, made emergency calls to several colleagues at the Embassy and went to the Embassy. I saw my Soviet counterpart first thing that morning. He was surprised at my early call, clearly did not know anything, promised to inquire and let

---

[31] http://www.mofa.go.jp/policy/economy/summit/2000/past_summit/09/e09_b.html 2003-02-15.

> me know about the results. For the next few days I met him sev-
> eral times and when the undeniable and unbelievable facts grad-
> ually surfaced amidst the rush of media reports, my counterpart's
> reaction became intensely gloomy and subdued.

In November President Reagan visited Japan and made the first
speech by an American President to the Japanese Parliament. It is
said that the speech was so successful that it was interrupted 25
times for applause by the audience. Yasu and Ron highlighted their
personal friendship by spending time together at a winter resort near
Mount Fuji.[32]

Another round of consolidation took place from the latter part of
1986 to the first half of 1987. Just before this period, in July 1986
Nakasone made his third cabinet reshuffle and Tadashi Kuranari, a
relatively unknown politician from the Nakasone faction of the Liberal
Democratic Party, became Foreign Minister. I was appointed as his
private secretary.

The first security issue Japan had to decide then was the Strategic
Defence Initiatives (SDI). The Reagan administration initiated this
grandiose scheme of counterattacking from space, an attack by continental ballistic missiles from the 'Evil Empire' of the Soviet Union.
America had called for Japan's participation in this project. In retrospect the SDI led the Soviet Union to realize that entering into
an arms race with the United States would not pay and could be
harmful to its own economy. It became one of the underlying impe-
tuses for *Perestroika*. For Japan, however, it was a difficult choice from
political, financial, and technological points of view. My minister,
being a man of sincerity, dealt with these security issues extremely
seriously. In particular, in relation to the SDI, he spent many sleep-
less nights studying and studying this complex scheme in search of
an optimum decision for Japan to make. An endless succession of
questions poured onto the desks of my MOFA colleagues in charge
of this issue, from essential to peripheral. Finally he became convinced that joining the research activities would be in Japan's interest. In September 1986 Japan decided to participate in the related
research activities.

The second issue which surfaced was the question of the 'one percent defence budget ceiling', which I already explained in Section 3

---

[32] Murata, *op. cit.*, p. 200.

above. So as to emphasize Japan's readiness to bear greater responsibility for its own defence the Nakasone cabinet decided to remove
this ceiling in January 1987. Foreign Minister Kuranari was in full agreement with this decision, because there was hardly any sound logical
basis to put up this ceiling. President Reagan naturally welcomed it.

The course of history proceeded in its full swing to the end of
the Cold War under Gorbachev's *Perestroika*, leading to the abolition
of the INF in December 1987, and the conclusion of the peace
accord in Afghanistan in April 1988.

Nakasone meanwhile resigned from the post of Prime Minister in
November 1987, to be succeeded by Noboru Takeshita, and President
Reagan was succeeded by President George Bush in January 1989.
Since then, further dramatic changes resulting from Gorbachev's
Perestroika policy occurred in East-West relations: the Soviet withdrawal from Afghanistan in February 1989, the fall of Berlin Wall
in November 1989, the Malta US-Soviet Summit in December 1989,
declaring the end of the Cold War, and the re-unification of Germany
in October 1990.

But the end of the Cold War did not engender a world of peace
and tranquillity. On the contrary, in many areas of the globe old
or suppressed tensions took the shape of concrete clashes involving
bloodshed and unlawfulness.

5. *The end of the Cold War and 'Japan's defeat' in the 1991 Gulf War*

The end of the Cold War brought about profound impact upon
Japan's position in the international community. During the Cold
War, ironically enough, the US-Soviet rivalry gave Japan a mighty
shield, notably in the form of the Japan-US alliance, under which
Japan's security was well protected. But when the Cold War ended
Japan was exposed to new reality and uncertainty which surrounded
the world. Japan was not prepared for that.

The Gulf War of 1990–91 fell upon Japan precisely at this junc-
ture. Japan's lack of preparedness was demonstrated to the extent
that this war is remembered in Japan with bitter national consciousness as 'Japan's defeat in 1991'. The crucial issue of security,
Japan's position in the global community and her relations with the
US were shattered. But the deep sense of crisis, which enveloped
Japan after the 'defeat in the Gulf', in turn, became the basis for
future development. So much intertwined, complex and complicated

and yet very dynamic Japan-US security relations developed over the 1990's to the beginning of the 2000's.

'Japan's defeat' in the 1991 Gulf War and its direct consequences

In August 1990 Saddam Hussein attacked Kuwait and the Gulf War began. Multinational forces waged war against Iraq in January 1991. Japan, however, was unable to react in a timely way with credible financial assistance, and above all, to implement concrete Japanese participation with tangible and visible Japanese personnel. Although Japan contributed a total of $1.4 billion in financial assistance, it received very little appreciation from the international community. Open feelings of disappointment and subdued anger prevailed, particularly in the minds of Americans (Chapter 9). The accumulated passive pacifism starting from the demand for 'comprehensive peace' in 1951, combined with the negation of SDF, the call for the abrogation of the Security Treaty with America, and the call for an emotionally rigid implementation of the three non-nuclear principles, all resulted in a psychological set-up that made even the government unprepared for such an eventuality as the Gulf War. Realists had been worried and thought that something had to be done. Some efforts by Foreign Ministry officials on peace keeping activities had already begun (Chapter 12). But these worries or efforts were far from adequate during the Gulf crisis in 1991.

Japan's 'defeat' in the Gulf War, however, in turn became a serious occasion for Japan to begin its participation in the cause of international peace and security. A sense of crisis, that relying on cheque book diplomacy simply could not be continued, went deep into the hearts and minds of the realists, and the voices of the passive pacifists became considerably subdued.

The government did its best to enact a new International Peace Cooperation Law on Japan's participation in the peacekeeping operations (PKO) under the United Nations in June 1992, and based on this new law Japan made a substantial contribution to the PKO activities, in particular, in Cambodia from September 1992 onwards (Chapter 12).

A sea change in domestic politics

A dramatic change then occurred in Japanese internal politics. From 1992 to summer 1993 several 'reformist' oriented politicians split from the Liberal Democratic Party (LDP) and subsequently created the Japan New Party (led by Morihiro Hosokawa), the *Sakigake* (Harbinger) Party (led by Masayoshi Takemura) and the Japan Renewal Party (led by Tsutomu Hata and Ichiro Ozawa). In August 1993 the LDP lost the election for the first time since the creation of the Coalition of Conservatives in 1955, and a coalition of eight parties headed by Prime Minister Hosokawa was created. In a year's time, that is in June 1994 however, the LDP came back to power in coalition with the long-standing opposition, a minority Japan Socialist Party, under its Prime Minister Tomiichi Murayama.

Murayama, a socialist but now standing on the ruling side, changed the fundamental platform of the Socialist Party, acknowledged the Self-Defence Forces as constitutional, and the Japan-US Security Treaty as admissible. Thus Murayama made one of the most significant contributions to the cause of realism in postwar Japanese foreign policy.

Meanwhile in February 1994 Prime Minister Hosokawa established a group of wise men under the leadership of Yotaro Higuchi, Chairman of Asahi Beer, to recommend Japan's post-Cold War security and defence policy. In August 1994 the Higuchi Commission finalized a report and presented it to Prime Minister Murayama. The report suggested a further consolidated role of SDF in the post-Cold War era. It argued forcefully the importance of the traditional two pillars of security policy: to enhance security relations with the US and to maintain credible defence capabilities. But having taken into account Japan's traumatic experience during the Gulf War and the enactment of the International Peace Cooperation Law, the report also emphasized the role of multilateral cooperation.[33]

Ironically, for the socialists whose power was already considerably weakened at the 1993 election, the 'betrayal of its long standing ideals' became the last blow for its political influence, and after the LDP gained full-fledged power in January 1996, the leading role of the opposition moved to the Democratic Party, newly formed in September 1996. The traditional passive pacifism was no longer the ideology of this newly-born Party. Thus towards the latter part of the 1990's passive pacifism lost its vigour of the 1950's and 1960's.

---

[33] Y. Funabashi, *Doumei Hyoryuu (Alliance Adrift)*, Iwanami, 1997, p. 259.

The Korean crisis and the National Defence Programme Outline

In the background of these internal psychological changes, the emerging post-Cold War tension in the Far East played a substantial role. From 1993 to 1994 there emerged a truly dangerous possibility of North Korea becoming nuclear. America naturally reacted decisively, war could have been close, but finally an understanding emerged between America and North Korea (Chapter 5).

During this crisis defence-related people in the US realized with horror that, should any crisis break out in the Korean peninsula, Japan was not ready to cooperate with US troops because the necessary legal basis was lacking. This realization was shared by their Japanese counterparts and intense coordination began between the two sides.

First, in February 1995, the US Department of Defence published a report called East Asian Strategic Review (EASR), based on the initiative of Joseph S. Nye and Ezra F. Vogel, two Harvard professors, who had joined the Clinton administration. The report stated the US intent to maintain approximately 100,000 troops in Asia.

Second, in November 1995, the Murayama cabinet adopted—as its last contribution to the policy of realism—the third major document of postwar security policy, a new National Defence Programme Outline (NDPO). While preserving the major characteristics of the NDPO of 1976, the new NDPO reconfirmed the importance of Japan-US security relations in the post-Cold War arena and enlarged the activities of the Self-Defence Forces to such areas as participation in international peacekeeping operations or large-scale disaster relief.

Based on these efforts on the two sides, a joint Japan-US joint reaffirmation of their security relations was due to take place at the fringe of the APEC Leaders Meeting in Osaka in November 1995. But because President William J. Clinton was absent from this meeting, the reaffirmation was postponed. While waiting for the next occasion for a summit meeting between the two leaders, two phenomenal crises exploded in and around Japan: Okinawa and Taiwan.[34]

The Japan-US Joint Declaration on Security and the Guidelines for Defence Cooperation

First, in Okinawa: in September 1995 a young Japanese primary school girl was raped by an American soldier. Indignation by the

---

[34] Michael J. Green, 'Defense or Security? The US-Japan defense guidelines and

people of Okinawa flared. After the reversion, Okinawa had remained the key American base in the Far East, and the underlying dissatisfaction and frustration of the people of Okinawa, who felt that they had born far too much of the heavy burden of accepting the American bases, had never been alleviated. By 1994, 40 American bases were concentrated in Okinawa alone, whereas the rest of Japan had only 54 American bases.

Prime Minister Murayama did what he could. The Special Action Committee on Facilities and Areas in Okinawa (SACO) was established under the Security Treaty in November 1995, to find concrete measures to alleviate the burden of Okinawa as much as possible.

Second, around Taiwan: in July and August 1995 the missile crisis over the Taiwan Strait began and it escalated with tense public attention in March 1996. Inevitably tension in the Far Eastern arena rose (Chapter 4).

Thus the primary task for Ryutaro Hashimoto, when he was elected as an LDP prime minister in January 1996, became the restructuring of the unsettled security relations with the United States. Basic direction toward a reaffirmation of the security relationship had already been given by the EASR and the NDPO, but furthermore, the political climate which surrounded the two countries changed substantially from the autumn of 1995 to the spring of 1996.

In April 1996, upon the visit of President Clinton to Japan 'The Japan-US Joint Declaration on Security—Alliance for the 21st Century'[35] was adopted.

The document begins with a philosophical reaffirmation that "the Japan-US security relationship, based on the Treaty of Mutual Cooperation and Security between Japan and the United States of America, remains the cornerstone for achieving common security objectives, and for maintaining a stable and prosperous environment for the Asia-Pacific region as we enter the twenty-first century." It then introduced two key policy agendas "to initiate a review of the 1978 Guidelines for Japan-U.S. Defence Cooperation" and with respect to Okinawa "to carry out steps to consolidate, realign, and reduce U.S. facilities and areas consistent with the objectives of the Treaty of Mutual Cooperation and Security".

China', in: David M. Lampton (ed.) *Major Power Relations in Northeast Asia: Win-Win or Zero-Sum Game*, Tokyo, 2001, pp. 75–79.

[35] http://www.mofa.go.jp/region/n-america/us/security/security.html. All subsequent quotations from this document are quoted from this homepage.

On the latter point an audacious agreement was reached in principle between the two leaders to reallocate the Futenma base, one
of the most important American bases in Okinawa. In December
1996, the final SACO Report confirmed in concrete terms the relo-
cation of the Futenma base.

On the former point, it is important to note that in the minds of
those who were working in the defence-security relationship, the
operational credibility of the defence-security alliance was at stake.
The adoption of new Guidelines a few years after the NDPO, in
line with the precedents in 1976 (the first NDPO) and 1978 (the
first Defence Guidelines) was their primary aim.[36] It took nearly a
year to review the Guidelines and in September 1997 the new
Guidelines for Defence Cooperation were adopted.

Parliamentary debates on the Defence Guidelines

It took nearly another year for Japan to prepare the necessary internal legislation to implement the new Guidelines and after full-scale
parliamentary debates in the spring, in May 1999 a new law named
'The Law Concerning Measures to Ensure Peace and Security of
Japan in Situations in Areas Surrounding Japan' was adopted.

The new law prescribed Japanese Self-Defence Forces logistic support to US forces such as supply, transportation, repair and maintenance, medical services, communications, airport and seaport
operations, and base operations. It also provided for search and rescue activities primarily conducted by the SDF. Vessel inspection
activities were included in the original bill, but omitted during the
parliamentary debate. Use of weapons was allowed to protect the
lives of members of units of the SDF, as well as the lives of those
conducting relevant activities with them, while implementing the
measures mentioned above.

I happened to be in the post of the Director General of the
Treaties Bureau during the period of parliamentary debates over the
new Bill and was fortunate to have participated in its full process.
It was a fascinating occasion to contemplate some of the basic issues
pertaining to Japan's security policy:

---

[36] M.J. Green, *op. cit.*, pp. 80–81.

(1) The most difficult point in defending the new Bill was related to the notion of 'Surrounding Situations (*Shuuhen Jitai*)'. Cooperation by the SDF was envisaged to take place in those "situations in areas surrounding Japan". Those 'Surrounding Situations' were those which "will have an important influence on Japan's peace and security". It was argued that those "situations in areas surrounding Japan" were "not geographical but situational". Opposition parties drew sharp edges into this aspect from several perspectives:

(2) The first concern which had been talked about within the opposition parties and media was that the definition of the 'Surrounding Situations' was so vague that the new Guidelines actually had intended to enlarge the activities of the SDF outside the scope of the Japan-US Security Treaty. The fact that the wording of the 'Surrounding Situations' was first used in the 1995 NDPO, which stretched its reach to the SDF activities based on multilateral international cooperation, might have deepened their concern. Having realized this possible criticism, the government prepared a bill, which clearly prescribed that the activities under the new law were exclusively confined "within the purposes of the Japan-US Security Treaty". Throughout the course of the debate, that government position was well sustained.[37]

(3) But the opposition parties were not satisfied. They argued against the vagueness of the new concept. Even if what was envisaged was restricted within the Japan-US Security Treaty, they requested precise definition regarding the nature of this 'Surrounding Situations'. Toward the end of the debates in late April, the government had to submit a list of exemplary situations which could be considered as 'Surrounding Situations'. But none of the explanations were geographical.

(4) In fact, one of the focal points of the parliamentary debates was to clarify the geographic applicability of the new guidelines to

---

[37] One question still remained: as the 1978 Guidelines were directed at an Article V situation (an armed attack against Japan), the next Guidelines were scheduled to be directed at an Article VI situation (US activities to contribute to the maintenance of international peace and security in the Far East). The notion of the 'Far East' had been extensively discussed during the parliamentary debate in 1960, and a geographical definition was made by the government as "North of the Philippines and Japan and its surrounding areas, including areas under the control of Korea and the Republic of China (Taiwan)". If the purpose of the 1997 Guidelines were exclusively to further cooperation within the Security Treaty, why could it not have referred more straightforwardly to the Article VI situation?

North Korea and Taiwan. That was an impossible task for the government. In reality, the 1993–94 North Korean nuclear crises triggered the endeavours of the two sides to agree to the new Guidelines. The Taiwan crises in 1995–96 heavily affected the political climate when the Joint Security Declaration was adopted. China became particularly sensitive to the fact that the new Guidelines were not directed against it, in particular, in its relations with Taiwan. In such circumstances a statement by the Japanese government indicating any regional connotation could have ignited a huge political emotion on the part of the country concerned. Wisely and bravely, everyone in the defending team stayed away from a 'geographic definition' in relation to any country. Michael J. Green, now working at the White House for the Bush administration made similar remarks about the absolute necessity of keeping silence over this geographic definition, where clarification could only have harmed and undermined regional security.[38]

(5) Notwithstanding the difficulty around the notion of 'Surrounding Situations' and notwithstanding the many heated and emotional debates on traditional or new security agendas, during the five months of parliamentary debates there was not a single occasion where they were interrupted. In the turbulent debates on the new Security Treaty in 1960 or in the heated row in relation to confidential agreements concerning nuclear introduction raised by retired Rear Admiral La Rocque in 1974 or by Professor Reischauer in 1981, so many times the debates were suspended for hours or for days. Yet perhaps in a limited scope, security matters could now be regarded as a matter pertaining to less emotion and more intellectual discourse.

(6) In this context, one of the amazing changes, which I observed in the parliamentary debates, was the question of the interpretation of Article 9 of the Constitution regarding minimal self-defence. For many years after the enactment of the constitution it had almost been a taboo to question the strict interpretation of Article 9, i.e. that Japan was only allowed to exercise minimal forces for individual self-defence. The right of collective self-defence was unconditionally denied by this interpretation. During the parliamentary debates, however, not only those 'rightist' parliamentarians in the Party of Freedom, but also some of the young leading speakers from the Democratic Party, successors to the fallen Socialist Party in oppo-

---

[38] M.J. Green, *op. cit.*, pp. 81–83.

sition, started to argue about the inadequacy of the interpretation of Article 9. The impact of this new attitude of the 'young democrats' is certainly an interesting new phenomenon which is casting influence to current security debates in Japan.

6. *September Eleven and thereafter*

Against this background of a changing political climate, 9/11 in 2001 shook the world. As we are going to see in detail in Chapter 12, Japan's reaction to 9/11 was fundamentally different from that of the Gulf War in 1991. In the context of bilateral alliance the clear and straightforward action taken by Japan really helped in consolidating the relationship.

Japan's support of President George W. Bush in the Iraq War in the spring of 2003 has put security relations between the two countries on an even stronger basis. As I tried to analyse in detail in Chapter 9, there was no better policy option for Japan than ultimately supporting President Bush. At the same time, the way with which President Bush implemented his policy of dismantling Saddam Hussein created an overwhelming impression of US unilateralism, serious transatlantic split, resentment from the Islamic world, many difficult postwar issues in governing Iraq and a new search for a role which the United Nations could play in the coming decades.

Thus important questions remain for the conduct of Japanese foreign policy: how did Japan take into consideration these major issues which were shaking world politics? In addition to the fundamental and ultimate support of President Bush, what policy options and visions has Japan presented to the world and to the United States? Even from the point of view of strengthening the alliance, was it not in the best interest of the two countries that Japan should make an honest and candid exposure of the various policy options open to the US administration?

Whatever the nature and quality of the Japan-US dialogue, Prime Minister Junichiro Koizumi continued to take concrete decisions. The decision in July 2003 to dispatch the SDF to Iraq was another reflection of Japan's eagerness in strengthening the alliance and in contributing to the peace and security of the world. In December 2003 Koizumi actually started sending SDF units to Iraq (Chapter 9).

The three Laws concerning the Response to an Armed Attack adopted in June 2003 to deal with national emergencies is also another development in filling in the long time gap between the reality and passive pacifists led policies.

Meanwhile, the traditional agenda continues. The difficulty of Okinawa remains. A very slow development is emerging in the area of alleviating the burden of the people of Okinawa, e.g. there were 36 American bases in Okinawa in contrast to 52 on the mainland as of 1 January 2003. Since the figure in 1995 was 40 versus 54, the proportionate change was −4 to −2 in 8 years. The two governments need to continue to improve the situation diligently and with care.

7. *The revision of the constitution*

Even with the dramatic changes which have occurred since the 1990's one cannot deny that a vestige of passive pacifism is still there.

But within the existing Article 9 situation, there is much more that Japan could do to become a responsible member of the international community and increase its contribution to and participation in the cause of peace and security in the world: (1) Enactment of outstanding seven laws and parliamentary approval of three treaties in relation to the Laws concerning the Response to an Armed Attack cannot be missed;

(2) Improvement of the 1992 International Peace Cooperation Law should be under consideration (Chapter 12); and

(3) Creation of a permanent legal basis for participation in rear area support to the coalition of forces is also on the agenda (Chapter 12).

After all these prospective changes have taken place, the very question of Article 9 of the Constitution in relation to its extreme minimal interpretation of the right of self-defence may become a viable political agenda.

In January 2000 a Parliamentary Research Commission on the Constitution was established in the House of Representatives for a designated period of five years. On 1 November 2002, the commission published an interim report to show dividing views concerning the revision of Article 9. The question of the revision of the constitution will probably not become a focal point of the political agenda in Japan in the coming 'several years'. But debates around this issue would certainly gain momentum. What is going to happen after the Parliamentary Commission has formulated its views sometime in 2005?

The answer lies in the hands of the people of Japan.

CHAPTER THREE

THE UNITED STATES: ECONOMIC RELATIONS

1. *The situation until the end of the 1960's*

After the war ended in 1945, it became evident that America remained as the single strong economic giant amongst the capitalist countries. Japan and Germany were not only defeated but also completely devastated. Great Britain, France and other major European countries were all severely damaged by the war. It was only on the American mainland that the war had not actually been fought. Thus under the new international economic order based on the Bretton Woods Agreements and GATT (Chapter 11), America became the leader of the free, market-oriented and capitalist world. This uncontested economic power of the United States lasted more or less throughout the 50's and 60's.

Until the end of the 60's, Japan's foreign policy agenda had consisted primarily of such political issues as the Peace Treaty, the Soviet Union, the United Nations, the Security Treaty with America, South Korea, and Okinawa. They were aimed at bringing Japan back as a normal member of the international community and implemented with considerable tension between the realists in the government and the passive pacifists in the opposition. Meanwhile, after the initial postwar turmoil had subsided, people in Japan had turned their attention to, and concentrated their energy on the development of the economy.

Shortly after the 'special boom' related to the Korean War was over, the first economic boom began. It lasted for about two and a half years, from 1954 to 1957. It was called the *Jinmu* boom and was characterized by the investment to increase production capacity of such industries as shipbuilding together with the enhanced consumption of a trio consisting of 'televisions (black and white), refrigerators and washing machines'. It had successfully replaced the postwar trio of 'radios, sewing-machines, and bicycles'. This boom came to a temporary end when the government introduced a tight deflationary financial policy to redress the balance of payment deficit which had resulted from this enhanced consumption.

The second economic boom was the *Iwato* boom which lasted for three and a half years, from 1958 to 1961. The leading industry which enlarged investment capacity was steel. Oil replaced coal as the fuel of industry. Prime Minister Hayato Ikeda, who succeeded Yoshida in 1960, presented an ambitious programme of 'Doubling the national income' in the decade 1961 to 1970 and based on this target, established an annual rise in the GNP of 7.2%.

The Olympic boom from 1962 to 1964 was followed by the *Izanagi* boom[1] of almost five years from 1965 to 1970, probably the most powerful boom to lead of the entire postwar period. The large-scale investment of production capacity in such industries as steel, automotive, petrochemical and others exploded; in the internal consumption a new trilogy of 'three Cs: car, colour television, and cooler (air conditioning)' brightened up the middle-class dream of the Japanese people. Furthermore, the increased internal demand did not create a balance of payments deficit which in turn resulted in a rather substantial trade surplus. The period of 'balance of payments ceiling' was over and the period of 'trade surplus' began. The yearly real GNP growth from 1961 to 1970 averaged 10.9% and the 'Doubling the national income' programme of Prime Minister Ikeda exceeded[2] its initial plan.

That time was called the 'period of high growth'.

The volume of Japan's global trade was $1.8 billion in 1950,[3] $8.5 billion in 1960 and reached $38.2 billion in 1970. America became her No. 1 partner in trade relations, occupying $11.5 billion in total in 1970, constituting more than 30% of its total trade. By that time Japan succeeded in creating a stable basis to engender a global trade surplus, which reached $2.5 billion in 1971.[4]

---

[1] The names of these 3 economic booms, Jinmu, Iwato, and Izanagi are all taken from ancient Japanese mythology, each representing the strength of the nation. It may be a reflection of the psychology and expectation of the people of postwar Japan (A. Suzuta, Konoissatsude *Keizaiga Wakaru (Understanding Economics in One Book)*, Mikasa Shobou, 2000, pp. 166–185).

[2] Tadokoro, *op. cit.*, p. 115.

[3] Glenn D. Hook, Julie Gilson, Christopher W. Hughes, Hugo Dobson, *Japan's International Relations-Politics, Economics and Security*, Routledge, 2001, p. 442.

[4] From JETRO figures (http://www.jetro.go.jp/ec/j/trade/excel/40w02.xls 2003–07–19).

During the 60's trade friction had hardly appeared as a major political issue between Japan and the United States. And yet, already toward the latter part of this decade, the economic development of Europe and Japan had been well underway. Japan's sudden appearance in global trade, in the form of powerful export capabilities, in particular to the United States, became a source of discomfort and irritation on the part of the Americans. It coincided with the changes in the American position in the world. America's relative position declined politically and economically, partly due to her involvement in Vietnam. America could no longer play a monolithic role in the economy of the free world and began to expect other countries, particularly those strong countries like Japan or Germany, to play a more responsible role in running the world economy.

2. Japan-US economic relations in the 1970's

Global economic situation in the 1970's

Richard M. Nixon, who assumed the US presidency in 1969, had to face this changing situation. President Nixon announced a major change in his economic policy in August 1971, consisting of a temporary suspension of the exchange of dollars versus gold, the introduction of a 10% import levy, and a price and wage freeze. In Japan, President Nixon's policy announcement was met with a sense of surprise and next to the first *Nixon-Shokku* (his announcement in July to visit China), it was remembered as the second *Nixon-Shokku*. But Japan had no alternative but to conform to the reality and together with other nations of industrialized countries acknowledged a new exchange rate for Japan of 1$=308yen at the end of 1971 and the introduction of an entirely new international monetary system of a floating exchange rate in 1973 (Chapter 11).

Another incident which shook the foundation of world economy was the so-called Oil Crisis in 1973, which resulted from the war in the Middle East. America assumed strong leadership in enhancing the cooperation of oil consuming countries through the establishment of the International Energy Agency (IEA) in Paris (Chapter 9); macroeconomic policy coordination entered a new stage (Chapter 11). All in all, the advanced market economies, though with pain, had overcome this shock.

In Japan the economy, which enjoyed a 10% economic growth
during the 60's, had continued to develop by 6–8% in the initial
years of the 70's. Prime Minister Kakuei Tanaka, who succeeded
Sato in July 1972, embarked on a new initiative of 'Reconstruction
of the Japanese Archipelago'. In a situation where the private sector production capacity investment could not be kept at the level of
the 'period of high growth', Tanaka wanted to boost the economy
through governmental investments in highways, bullet trains, and
through the activation of Japanese regions which had been relatively
neglected in comparison to the megacities such as Tokyo and Osaka.
But this dynamic spending policy by the government had created
strong inflationary pressure on land and securities. The oil price hike
fell precisely when the Japanese economy was under this inflationary
pressure. Japan suffered, but managed to demonstrate commendable
resilience (Chapter 9).

America also had gradually recovered from the first oil shock and
appeared strong with an unusual global trade surplus in 1975.

Trade conflict 1969–1975

By the time negotiations on the reversion of Okinawa took serious
shape, economic issues already loomed heavily in the background of
Japan-US relations.

The first stage of the conflict had been from 1969 to 1975. President
Nixon had, for most of the time, been on the other side of the
ocean, in the White House, during this period.

Japanese export to the United States had been constantly in surplus during this period, at a level around several billion dollars. This
amount in itself did not seem to have created particular friction
between Japan and the United States.

The element which triggered the first round of the trade conflict
between the two countries was the textile industry. This industry was
one of the leading Japanese industries during the 'period of high
growth' and the American textile producers had become greatly concerned about the mounting Japanese textile exports to the United
States. These textile producers had a powerful basis in the southern
States of the US. President Nixon committed himself during his presidential election campaign of 1968 to restricting Japanese textile
imports, should he be elected.

The Japanese textile industry, based on the principle of free trade, which they thought they had been taught by the Americans, resisted an accommodation with vehemence. Thus the relatively minor issue of a single sector came to bear unusual political importance, and President Nixon brought up this issue with Prime Minister Sato during his talks on the reversion of Okinawa in November 1969. The Prime Minister is said to have committed himself to a 'positive look' on this issue, and in Japan it was even reputed that an 'Okinawa to textile deal' was in the making![5]

At any rate, Prime Minister Sato had an important task to fulfil upon his return to Japan. It took a full two years, until October 1971, before Japan agreed to a Governmental Agreement to a three year voluntary restraint of textile exports to America, and the agreement came at the expense of huge subsidies given to the Japanese textile producers.[6]

Trade conflict 1975–1981

The successful resolution of the textile issue and the respective success of Japan and America in overcoming the oil crisis brought bilateral economic relations to a lull. Fumihiko Togo, who was appointed as Ambassador to America in 1975, wrote that "It was a period, when people said that no wind was blowing between Japan and America".[7]

In the latter half of the 1970's, however, Japan's cyclical development was stronger than that of America. The trade deficit began to grow in America and so did the unemployment rate, together with the closure of some important factories there. In 1978 the American trade deficit *vis-à-vis* Japan had surpassed $10 billion. That figure itself had a gloomy impact on the psychology of the American people.

But just as in the case of textiles, the key factor for trade friction lay not so much in the area of macroeconomy, but in the area of microeconomy in relation to sectoral industry. A new expression

---

[5] *Nawa* in Japanese means 'products made from textile'. There is a play of words here between Oki*nawa* and 'textile'.

[6] C. Hosoya, *Nihongaikouno Kiseki (Traces of Japanese Foreign Policy)*, NHK, 1993, pp. 183–185.

[7] F. Togo, *op. cit.*, p. 233.

called 'torrential rain' appeared in the media, implying that the
vigour of the Japanese export had destroyed or erased industrial
competition in the importing countries. Such low prices in contrast
to the high quality of the Japanese products sold abroad also dis-
seminated the infamous reputation of 'export dumping'.

Three sectors clearly triggered the trade friction: steel, colour televisions and automobiles. It is very important to note that these three
sectors were, in substance and in perception, the most important in
postwar American economic development and affluence. Steel was
the basis for such industries as automobiles, ships, aircraft, and construction, anything the American people found solid and important
in their daily life. Colour television represented technological development, hope for future innovation, and a source of happiness for
the American family life. The automobiles, well, it was the very
symbol of America, of American affluence, and the American way
of life.

These respective industries developed alongside the development
of the American economy itself. Each of them, in its own way, represented America. To feel that each sector might be menaced by
Japanese 'export dumping' and its 'torrential rain' was not acceptable to America.

The American steel industry had already been weakened in its
competitive strength in the international economy *vis-à-vis* Europe
and Japan towards the end of the 60's, when unilateral restrictive
measures to restrain export to America, both by Europe and by
Japan, had calmed the situation. But in 1976, US import of steel
marked a record high of 17.5 million (out of which 7.25 million was
from Japan) tons, followed by the closure in 1977 of a Youngstown
steel factory, a historic symbol of the American steel industry.

Political attention and emotion began to pile up and after tense
negotiations an agreement was reached between Japan and America
in February 1978 to introduce a 'trigger price system', implying the
introduction of minimum price to Japan's export to America. A similar arrangement was made between America and Europe as well.

Faced with a substantial increase in the import of Japanese colour
television sets and the resulting closure of some American companies, the American government held serious negotiations with Japan
and in May 1977 an Orderly Market Agreement (OMA) was concluded. In accordance with this agreement Japan had to voluntarily
restrain its colour television export to under 1.75 million on a yearly

basis for three years. At the same time, having taken into account the aggravating trade relations, major Japanese companies which produced electric appliances began expanding their direct investment in the US market.

Japanese automobile export surpassed the 1 million mark in 1976 and continued to rise. The internal share of Japanese cars on the American market rose from 6.5% in 1973, 9.3% in 1976 to 21.3% in 1980. The American auto industry was not doing well and industry earnings in 1978 turned from positive to negative in 1980.[8] This was partly due to the inability of American car makers to produce energy efficient cars after the oil crisis, but whatever the reasons, strong pressure emerged from the American car industry to "do something" to overcome the situation.

The Carter administration was initially inclined to resolve the issue in line with principles of free trade, i.e. "(1) neither restrict auto imports nor request Japan for Voluntary Export Restraints (VERs); (2) request Japanese automakers to invest in the US; and (3) ask the Japanese government for a further reduction in tariffs and non-tariff barriers on auto and auto parts."[9] But Japanese auto manufacturers were slow in investing in the American markets. Deregulation efforts on the Japanese side did not bring satisfaction in the US.[10] After President Reagan, whose politico-economic thinking was strongly oriented towards free trade, had nevertheless asked Japan to "do something" about this issue, Japan agreed in May 1981 to introduce a voluntary restriction of Japanese car export to America up to the limit of 1.68 million on a yearly basis for three years.[11]

In all the three cases, Japan started the negotiations thinking that they had not done anything wrong, just worked hard, and tried to produce good quality and cheap products to please customers. Nevertheless, each time Japan agreed to take restrictive measures to limit her export to America. The measures were taken in the form of 'voluntary' actions to make them compatible, at least on pro forma

---

[8] M. Satake, 'Trade conflicts between Japan and the United States over Market Access: The Case of Automobiles and Automotive Parts', *Pacific Economic Paper*, no. 310, Australia-Japan Research Centre, Dec. 2000, p. 5.

[9] Ibid., p. 2.

[10] "Honda had already established an assembly plant in Ohio, but Toyota and Nissan, the two major firms, had resisted investing in the United States." (Ibid., p. 3).

[11] Hosoya, *op. cit.*, pp. 187–189.

basis, with the GATT principles of free trade. Thus the US had avoided the form of import restriction. The Japanese decision was, at least partly, based on Japan's improved understanding that there was a need to coexist with other members of the international economic community.

The nature and type of measures taken were the same as the ones taken in relation to textiles mentioned above, i.e. 'Voluntary Export Restraints (VERs)'. The area covered became only larger and more relevant to the fundamental structure of the American economy. Thus, during the 1970's, VERs became the first prescription in the issue of trade friction. At the same time, some efforts had been displayed by both sides to enlarge Japanese direct investment in the US.

Fumihiko Togo wrote in his memoirs the following observation, which is an interesting reflection of the trade friction in the latter part of the 70's in Washington:

> In this period of trade friction, this subject had come up repeatedly in my talks with the leaders in Washington. Senators and Congressmen were particularly keen in taking up this subject. In talking to them, the logic of the Americans had always boiled down to the conclusion that: in terms of logic what the ambassador is explaining sounds very true, but in reality the American economy is sick and it has to be protected against outside torrents until it is cured, and therefore America hopes that Japan will help America so that the present disease can be overcome. If one talks about a torrent from outside countries, so they continued, the most visible example can be none other than Japanese export, or the American deficit with Japan. When the conversation had reached that stage, it became rather difficult to pursue it further, other than telling my interlocutors that the fundamental economic strength of America far exceeded any other country and it was necessary for the Americans to regain confidence in their own economic strength.[12]

To conclude the decade of the 1970's, the Iranian crisis exploded at the beginning of 1979 and the resulting second oil crisis elevated the oil price 2.5 times higher within six months. Japan plunged again into a trade deficit, but kept its growth from falling to minus (Chapter 9). The US economy was severely damaged and went into a cycle of stagflation.

---

[12] F. Togo, *op. cit.*, p. 237. F. Togo left the post of the Ambassador in 1980.

3. *Japan-US economic relations in the 1980's*

Reaganomics and the Plaza Accord

The 1980's are sometimes regarded as the period under President Ronald Reagan, who was President of the United States from 1981 to 1988. In the global economy, the macroeconomic policy which President Reagan had pursued, known as the 'Reaganomics', certainly had a strong impact, including on the arena of Japan-US economic relations.

Before going into the essence of Reaganomics, let me touch upon one equation of international economics that will really help in understanding the problems that arose in the 1980's. This equation is the foundation of macroeconomic analysis that I believe is confirmed in every textbook on macroeconomic theory in every language.[13]

$$Export(EX) - Import(IM) = Saving(S) - Investment(I) + Tax(T) - Gov. \\ Expenditure(G)$$

Just like in every family's bookkeeping, this is an equation which holds true in every bookkeeping system in every country in the world. On a macroeconomic bookkeeping basis, the external transactions are calculated to always match internal transactions. The external transactions are represented by international trade (EX–IM). The internal transactions are calculated as the aggregated amount of private sector activities (S–I) and government activities (T–X). In other words in terms of the activities inside one country, the private sectors invariably engender differences (surplus or deficit) from their savings and investments, and so does the government in relation to its activities in tax and expenditures. The aggregate amount of these differences will always be equal to the differences that emerge from international trade.

With this background knowledge, let us see the Reaganomics and its consequences during the first half of the 80's:[14]

---

[13] M. Fukuoka, *Keizaigaku Nyuumon (Introduction in Economics Third Edition)*, Nihonkeizai Shuppansha, 2000, p. 322.
[14] Murata, *op. cit.*, p. 205.

1) The American economy had suffered a stagflation after the second oil shock of 1979 and President Reagan introduced a substantial tax reduction in order to stimulate the economy. The aim of Reaganomics was that a greater tax cut would increase savings, which would, in turn, stimulate industries' investment and would result in a strengthened supply side of the economy. (In the equation above T<G will be compensated by S>I.)

2) In reality, however, tax reduction only succeeded in boosting consumer spending. It did stimulate the economy, but only through consumption (the American people were inclined towards very little saving) and in the private sector, savings which counted as 9% in early 80's, went down to 3.2% in 1987.[15] This depressed private sector investment to industries. This became part of the background to sector related trade conflicts in the microeconomy. (S>I did not occur.)

3) Notwithstanding the tax cut, substantial government expenditure had continued during the first half of the 1980's, particularly in the military area in the stand against the 'Evil Empire' of the Soviet Union, and a huge budgetary deficit emerged. It marked, on average, over $200 billion from 1983 to 1986.[16] (T<G continued.)

4) The high-level private sector consumption and government expenditure invited a huge trade deficit. It stayed constant at over 100 billion dollars from 1984 through the 80's, peaked in 1987 with $152 billion.[17] (Inevitably, EX<IM enlarged.)

This trade deficit had an enormous impact on Japan-US economic relations. Partly as the result of restrictive measures taken by the Japanese, during the first three years of President Reagan 1981–1983 the trade deficit between Japan and America was stabilized at a level below $20 billion. But the trade deficit began to grow ominously and in 1984 it reached over $30 billion, in 1985 over $40 billion, and in 1986 over $50 billion, and stayed there for three years.[18] For

---

[15] M. Yabunaka, *Taibei Keizaikoushou* (In Search of New Japan-US Economic Relations), Simul Press, 1991, p. 183.

[16] Ibid.

[17] Ibid., p. 13.

[18] Ibid., p. 12. According the US Commerce Department Statistics yearly US trade deficit with Japan from 1981 to 1990 in billion dollars was 15.8, 16.7, 19.3, 33.5, 46.2, 55.0, 56.4, 51.8, 49.1, and 41.1. Figures after 1985 can also be found at the U.S. Census Bureau: http://landview.census.gov/foreign-trade/balance/c5880.html 2003–06–15. Japanese statistics can be found in JETRO figures.

several years thenceforth, the American leadership emphasized on every possible occasion that this imposing figure of '50 billion dollars' was simply unacceptable and concrete measures had to be taken to remedy the situation.

5) On monetary policy, so as to keep the economy from overheating, high interest rates had been maintained. Consequently, investment from abroad drawn by this high interest rate flooded to America, and the dollar became strong. The Japanese yen, which was once valued at 1$=176yen in October 1978, partly as a result of the 'locomotive role' we are going to see in Chapter 11, weakened considerably and reached 1$=278yen by November 1982.[19]

6) This situation meant a sharp increase in foreign credit in America, which suddenly shifted America to the historic position of a debtor nation. American and foreign companies increased their investment in America, and the strong dollar further increased this flow of foreign capital to the American market. American investment abroad declined rapidly in relative terms. ('I' increased without the increase of 'S'. S<I occurred.) The American credit, which counted for $149.5 billion at the end of 1982 diminished to $48.7 billion in September 1984, and by the end of the year 1984 America had become a debtor nation, after a 70 year history as a creditor nation.[20] It went further down to $110.9 billion in debts in 1985 and $663.7 billion in 1989.[21]

Thus Reaganomics resulted, on the one hand, in a stronger growth and subdued inflation in a very short period, but on the other hand, in the famous 'twin budgetary and balance of payments deficits', combined with the historical transformation to make America a debtor nation. That was not what the Reagan administration wanted to happen.

The chief remedy which the US administration proposed was the devaluation of the dollar, to be achieved as the result of a concerted effort by the international financial community. That was a simple, straightforward and powerful measure. In September 1985, the

---

[19] Nakanishi, *op. cit.*, p. 150.

[20] "Amerikano saimu (American Debt)", *Gendaiyougono Kisochishiki (Basic Knowledge of Contemporary Vocabulary) 2002*, Jiyuu Kokuminsha, 2002.

[21] T. Nishino, *Keizaiyougoni Tsuyokunaruhon (Mastering the Language of Economics)*, PHP Bunko, 2000, p. 32.

Ministers of Finance of the leading industrialized nations agreed on a substantial devaluation of the dollar which came to be called the Plaza Accord, followed by the Louvre Accord in February 1987 (Chapter 11). The value of the yen almost doubled in this 2 year period from 1$=240yen to 1$=120yen by the end of 1987.[22]

Did this policy of the sharp devaluation of the dollar and the sharp evaluation of the yen work to reduce Japan's trade surplus *vis-à-vis* America? Well, in principle, it worked. The amount of the US trade deficit *vis-à-vis* Japan declined from its height of $56 billion in 1987 for four years consecutively to $41 billion in 1990.[23] The ratio of the balance of payment surplus to nominal GDP declined from 4.4% in 1986 to 1.3% in 1990.[24]

Naturally, there are many more reasons which caused the sharp decline of Japan's trade surplus *vis-à-vis* America. The impact of the sharp drop in the oil price in the middle of the 1980's is one important element in considering this issue (Chapter 9). All the efforts the two countries made in the arena of market access as we see below are, in addition, indispensable elements. It is also important to note that in Japan in this period of difficulty,[25] companies began to take serious measures for adjustment, for instance to allocate their factories abroad to America, Europe or Eastern Asia. From the era of 'added value trade', whereby Japan imported raw materials and exported added value products, Japan gradually moved into the era of 'globalization' whereby production was based on global scaling. Thus this change in Japan's corporate behaviour toward greater investment abroad is another important element to be taken into account in these efforts toward the reduction of trade surplus. Japan's direct investment to the United States developed notably fast from $1.5 billion in 1980 to $5.4 billion in 1985, and from 1986 recorded a continuous flow of $10 to $30 billion on an annual basis in the latter part of the 1980's.[26]

---

[22] Suzuta, *op. cit.*, p. 197.

[23] US Census Bureau: http://landview.census.gov/foreign-trade/balance/c5880.html 2003-06-15.

[24] Suzuta, *op. cit.*, p. 204.

[25] In Japan the impact of the sharp rise of the yen had been reflected first as a recession for a relatively short period from mid 1985 till the end of 1986. The GDP growth rate of 1986 was 3.1%, which was relatively lower than the preceding and the following years (A. Suzuta, *op. cit.*, p. 196).

[26] The annual figure from 1986 to 1990 was in billion dollars 10.2, 14.7, 21.7, 32.5, 26.1 (Hook, Gilson, Hughes, Dobson, *op. cit.*, p. 450).

Nevertheless, the 'exchange rate adjustment' has proven to be a powerful measure to bring in a new balance within the global economies, and it could certainly be perceived as the second prescription to deal with the trade friction. In contrast to the first prescription, the VERs, this second prescription was certainly macroeconomy oriented.

Enlarging market access

The macroeconomic approach of devaluating the dollar against the yen was one fundamental measure. Protective measures to cope with the 'torrential rain' of Japanese export had already been in place. But these measures were not enough to deal with the trade frictions through the 1980's. The third prescription which the US had advanced was 'market access'. It was by nature microeconomy oriented, but very different from the VERs approach. The primary purpose was to enlarge American export to Japan. From the point of view of the US consumers and the general expansion of global trade, this approach was certainly sounder than the restrictive approach which the first prescription was directed to.

The intensity and variety of sector based negotiations which took place in the second half of the 1980's under President Reagan is overwhelming. We are going to summarize the major negotiations which took place in those Reagan days, but two remarks need to be made beforehand:

First, it is important to note that measures contemplated to enlarge American export varied from challenging Japan's border restriction (such as the negotiations on beef and citrus—(4) below—) to going deep into the structure of Japanese society (such as the negotiations on construction market—(3) below—). The latter perspectives became particularly important, because in discussing these separate sector issues, not only the question of traditional trade disputes of lowering the border barriers such as quotas or tariffs, but also the very structure and texture of Japanese society, which made selling foreign products difficult, had gradually become a focal point.

There emerged views that the tradition, rules and customs in Japan were so different that selling ordinary good quality foreign goods was virtually impossible. This led to sharp criticism against Japan that it was selectively applying these 'inherent Japanese rules' at her convenience for the protection of her internal market, at the expense of foreign products or investments. This made Japan an 'unfair country'. Clyde Prestowitz, a former USTR negotiator to Japan, James Fallows, a former resident journalist in Japan, Karel van Wolferen, a Dutch Journalist residing in Japan, all voiced these views.[27] Some views expressed were indeed correct and stimulating, but whether intentional or not, they raised tensions, and trade negotiations had to be conducted against these tensions.

Second, it is also important to note that the basic approach taken by the Reagan administration was to establish common rules and common approaches to trade and to the trade related structure of the society. It was aimed at harmonizing the principles which governed trade and economic activities, so that the two countries would stand on common ground in competition. For Japan, because some issues touched upon the foundations of Japanese society and some aspects had real political implications, it was often not easy to come to an agreement with the United States. Nevertheless, the outcome of these negotiations show that Japan was in principle forthcoming in its approach in seeking harmonization in the rules and approaches to be taken regarding trade and economic activities. Thus, the third prescription to deal with trade frictions as perceived under the Reagan administration could be defined as the 'market access harmonization' approach.[28]

(1) *Market-Oriented, Sector-Selective (MOSS) talks*
In January 1985 America initiated what came to be called MOSS, Market-Oriented, Sector-Selective talks covering four areas; electronics, wood products, medical equipment and pharmaceuticals, and telecommunications products. It does seem that after careful consideration, the American side chose a 'harmonization approach' and hence the MOSS talks were conducted with reasonable success.[29]

---

[27] Yabunaka, *op. cit.*, p. 23. They came to be known as the 'revisionists' in contrast to the 'chrysanthemums', who emphasized that Japan and the West shared the same fundamental values.

[28] Japan's attitude to this harmonization approach in contrast to 'market access managed' approach is well described in M. Satake's article as quoted above.

[29] "The Commerce Department and the USTR proposed that a certain quantity of imports be set as a target. The other departments insisted on a procedural, issue-by-issue approach under which barriers would be removed in the chosen industry by means of intensive, high-level negotiations. Finally, it was decided that the latter approach would be taken." (M. Satake, *op. cit.*, p. 9.)

(2) *Semi-Conductors*

In June 1985, the American association of semi-conductor producers filed a case against the Japanese semi-conductor producers for 'export dumping' and the closure of their market. Since 1978 America had been marking trade deficits in this area, and Japan's export to America had rapidly been growing from 1979. The semi-conductor, because of its wide usage in so many industries across the board, was considered the key area of industrial competition in the 21st century.[30] The USTR (United States Trade Representative) started an investigation; negotiations were conducted between the two governments; and in July 1986 an agreement was signed between the two sides to expand the US market share in Japan in the following 5 years.

A confidential letter indicated '20%' as the share of foreign origin semi-conductors in the Japanese market in five years time.[31] It is said that the way this '20%' figure had been treated in the subsequent negotiations left a psychological disconnection between some parts of the respective administrations. America took this figure as a Japanese commitment and Japan took this figure as indicative or on a 'best efforts basis'. One may perhaps conclude that this confidential letter is the only exception to the 'market access harmonization' approach during the negotiations under the Reagan administration. We will see some of the consequences it had in the negotiations under President Clinton in section 5 below.

(3) *Construction Market*

From May 1986 to March 1988, the negotiations on American participation in the Japanese construction market were conducted. This was in many ways an unprecedented negotiation: it covered an area related to the transfer of 'services', barely governed by international rules yet; furthermore, it addressed squarely and primarily, internal practices, customs and tradition in Japan. These were areas that were severely criticized by the revisionists. Such words as *Dango*[32] or

---

[30] Ikei, *op. cit.*, p. 329.

[31] Murata, *op. cit.*, p. 203.

[32] *Dango* means a practice in Japanese business. In a competing situation in choosing a constructor for a project, those who have been accepted as inner circle candidates gather and decide, on a consultation basis, who is going to be selected, paying due attention that with time everyone within the inner circle gets his fair

Keiretsu[33] began to appear in the media reports. The negotiations were tough, but they resulted in an opening of the Japanese construction market to foreign companies.[34]

(4) *Beef and Citrus*

From March to June 1988 other important negotiations in relation to the border restrictions on beef and citrus took place, but this time they were traditional in nature. It was the concluding part of ten years of negotiations, as a result of which Japan agreed to move from a quota to a tariff system from 1991 for beef and from 1992 for citrus.[35]

Maekawa Report

In this tense situation, where the trade frictions seemed to be overwhelming, the Japan-US relations, Prime Minister Nakasone took an important initiative. At the end of 1985 a special advisory committee for the Prime Minister was established at his instruction, headed by Haruo Maekawa, a former governor of the Bank of Japan, to consider the nature of the Japanese society and the resulting trade conflicts.

> At the time I happened to be working in the economic affairs department of the Foreign Ministry, and was on temporary assignment in the special task force established in the Ministry to formulate the Foreign Ministry's views to the Maekawa committee. We were excited in producing a new policy, not because we were told to do so by foreign countries but on Japan's own initiatives. We felt that something was wrong in the then existing situation, and were trying to find a new policy to resolve the problem. We

---

share. It becomes very problematic for those who are not in the inner circle, because in many cases entry to inner circles is very difficult.

[33] *Keiretsu* means the relation between the 'parent' company and its 'relatives' companies, in which the latter receive the privileges to enter into a contractual relation with the former. This kind of relationship often originated from geographical, historical and above all personal relationships between the two entities. For those who are inside the *Keiretsu* system it assured a stable business, but for those outside it, it is again problematic, because for outsiders, entry to *Keiretsu* will be very difficult.

[34] Yabunaka, *op. cit.*, pp. 53–69.

[35] Ibid., pp. 81–82.

thought that the new policy should be in line with the 'harmonization' of the Japanese economy with outside economies. We were convinced that the new policy would enhance Japan's national interest in the years ahead. It was truly satisfying for everyone working in that special task force to see traces of our proposal being reflected in the final report as adopted by the Maekawa committee.

Thus, in April 1986 a report was adopted in the name of the chairman of the committee, entitled the 'Maekawa Report'. Five major policy objectives became identified in the report:

1) To make the reduction of Japanese trade surplus a national objective,

2) To increase internal demand so as to expand import,

3) To introduce structural reform to make Japanese industry more oriented to the internal market rather than the external one,

4) To further evaluate the yen,

5) To increase assistance to developing countries, so that the accumulated trade surplus would be of benefit to the world.

Toward the end of the Reagan administration, the declining trade deficit, the successful conclusion of numerous negotiations, as well as the appreciation on the part of the US regarding Japan's efforts e.g. expressed in the Maekawa Report, all these factors created a relaxation in the atmosphere between the two countries. When Secretary Schulz visited Japan in autumn 1988, he made the often repeated statement that "There has never been any period when US-Japan relations were so good."[36]

4. *Trade conflicts from the end of the 1980's to the beginning of the 1990's*

FSX controversy

These were the years under President George Bush.

After the short lull in the autumn of 1988, in 1989 trade figures had already begun to indicate potential trade friction. As I have

---

[36] Ibid., p. 10.

already indicated, the American trade deficit with Japan had been declining steadily from 1988 to 1990. The trade deficit with Europe, however, declined much more sharply than that with Japan: $20.6 billion in 1987, $9.1 billion in 1988, and a surplus figure in 1989! Therefore the comparative weight of the Japanese trade deficit became even heavier than before.[37]

Against this background, the first issue which shook the relationship was the issue of the next generation of fighter planes, called the Fighter-Support Experimental (the FSX). In November 1988 Japan and America agreed that the FSX to be used by the Japanese Self-Defence Forces would be jointly developed with Japanese finance and American technology. After President Bush came to power in January 1989, the US Congress voiced its doubts that the agreement reached would be nothing but an outflow of important American technology, which belonged to the security area. A difficult negotiation took place and an agreement was finally reached in April 1989, which restricted important technology transfer from America to Japan, obligated the Japanese transfer of technology as requested by America, and ensured 40% of the work share on the American side during the actual production. Indignation remained amongst some of the interested Japanese parties, who had originally requested "national development and production".[38] The bilateral relationship was saved by this compromise, but it showed that the traditional hedging from security considerations did not necessarily govern the final conclusion, and that even such an important security matter as the FSX could be subjected to overall trade and political interests.

Super 301 and Structural Impediment Initiatives (SII)

Furthermore in 1988, the United States Congress enacted a new legislation called 'Super 301', which obligated the US government in 1989 and 1990 to investigate countries which had been conducting unfair trade practices against America, to negotiate with these countries which had done so, and to take countermeasures if appropriate remedies were not taken.

---

[37] Ibid., p. 93.
[38] Murata, *op. cit.*, p. 218.

The Japanese government immediately reacted sharply. "The decision taken by the US government is regrettable. Japan will not accept negotiations which presuppose sanctions. Japan, however, is prepared to discuss any matter which the US finds problematic."[39] Japan was alerted with the emergence of US unilateralism in trade. "The core issue was whether America was able to decide unilaterally the trade system of another country is fair or not, and whether it was entitled to take countermeasures unilaterally. Only an overwhelmingly strong country may think that it can take such measures. But how can they be implemented with the presupposition that that country's decision is always right?"[40]

Despite Japan's objection, the newly elected Bush administration in the spring of 1989 selected Japan, Brazil and India as countries that might be conducting unfair trade practices. It was obviously Japan that the Bush administration primarily had in mind. In May 1989 the Bush administration selected three priority sectors in relation to Japan for the Super 301 investigation: super computer, satellite, and timber. In all three areas America sought greater opportunity for American business involvement.

Japan continued to resist, arguing that it could not engage in negotiations which presuppose unilateral introduction of sanctions by America. The American side gradually withdrew from their official statements, referring to the legal basis on which the negotiation was motivated: the Super 301. Negotiations began to proceed in September 1989 as 'normal trade matters'. Though with considerable difficulty, the two sides found mutually satisfactory solutions on all the three sectors by May 1990.[41]

At the same time, in July 1989 President Bush proposed to Prime Minister Sosuke Uno, who had only been at the post for two months from June to August 1989, to initiate the Structural Impediment Initiatives (SII). That was the additional track to address fundamental obstacles within the Japanese market, which made American market penetration difficult.

As we have seen in the analysis of the macroeconomic theory, one of the fundamental reasons for US trade deficit emerges from

[39] Yabunaka, *op. cit.*, p. 102.
[40] Ibid., p. 105.
[41] Ibid., pp. 95–106, 122–143.

the huge budget deficit and high level of consumption. Japan could not accept just being blamed unilaterally about structural problems in Japan without paying attention to these crucial aspects of US economy.

At the same time the Bush administration carefully dissociated the SII from the narrow sphere of the Super 301. It was not in the interest of Japan to entirely reject President Bush's proposal. Japan accepted this proposal on the condition that it would work two ways. US administration agreed to this legitimate Japanese counterproposal.

Thus the SII proceeded with top media attention from September 1989 to June 1990. Under the leadership of Prime Minister Toshiki Kaifu, Uno's successor, the SII became the top priority agenda for Japan. "The Japan-US SII was an historic event equivalent to the revision of the Security Treaty or the reversion of Okinawa. Subjects covered at the talks were wider and deeper than any bilateral talks had ever been. The impact of the talks would have a profound effect on the everyday life of the people in the respective countries."[42] This statement made by Mitoji Yabunaka, a Foreign Ministry director then in charge of the SII, might sound like an exaggeration, but indeed the extent to which each side went into the inner structure of the society was unprecedented.

Both sides went into the fundamentals of their economies in relation to the saving and investment equation, which I touched upon in Section 3 above:

In Japan trade surplus (EX>IM) had to be reduced. Japanese had a long standing practice of high saving (S>I). In order to reduce the trade surplus, a more vigorous investment had to be made. If the private sector equation was difficult to change, then it was particularly the lack of adequate government expenditure (T>G) that should be remedied. Dynamic 'public investment' was therefore expected. Japan finally agreed to introduce a public investment programme of 430 trillion yen (based on an exchange rate of 1\$=100yen, it will be 4.3 trillion dollar) in the next decade.

In America the trade deficit (EX<IM) had to be reduced. The Japanese stressed that weak private sector saving (S<I) and a huge budgetary deficit (T<G) were the causes of the problem. Enhanced private sector saving or restricted government expenditure were

---

[42] Ibid., p. 147.

required. The Americans agreed to the basic objective of reducing the budgetary deficit and even went so far as to signal a tax increase, even against their commitment during the election campaign.

In addition to these fundamentals of each economy, in relation to the Japanese market, the Americans raised such issues as 1) effective land utilization, 2) improvement of the distribution system, including deregulation on large-scale department stores, 3) price mechanism, which inflates internal prices and dumps external prices, 4) antimonopoly law, with a view to strengthening free competition, and 5) the *Keiretsu* as an independent subject.

The Japanese pointed out that 1) America's industry investment was too weak, 2) industry often lacked long-term strategic thinking, 3) government protection of industries in reality weakened their competitive power, 4) too little attention was given to Research and Development, 5) there was not enough governmental endeavour to expand export, and 6) that more attention should be given to education and professional training.

When the final SII report was adopted in June 1990, both sides expressed satisfaction with its result, and combined with the successful conclusion of the three sector negotiations, countermeasures based on Super 301 were withdrawn.[43] SII perhaps represented the height of negotiations in the era of trade conflicts between Japan and the United States. It entered an area of social structure inside each country. It was conducted on a fair and completely reciprocal basis.

It was the threat of US unilateralism which made the climate of the negotiation very tense. But Japan found a way both regarding the Super 301 related negotiations and the SII to overcome US unilateralism. It is also important to note that the basic approach taken by the Bush administration was the 'market access harmonization' approach. It was an approach which Japan found comfortable and was ready to cooperate with in order to find mutually acceptable solutions.

---

[43] Ibid., pp. 147–205.

5. *Japan–US economic relations in the first half of the 1990's*

The nature of trade disputes under President Clinton

The first three years under President William J. Clinton were probably the most difficult years of trade conflicts between Japan and
the United States. In retrospect, however, they were the years when
economic reality increasingly escaped from the necessity of pursuing
such sharp trade disputes. This last phase of trade conflicts in the
20th century therefore leaves an image of striking discrepancy: increasing harsh discourse and decreasing economic imperatives.

Let us first see the economic reality and its perception which led
to these sharp trade disputes.

American trade deficit *vis-à-vis* Japan hit rock bottom in 1990 at
a level of $41 billion and again began to increase yearly to mark a
record high of $65 billion in 1994.[44]

The key issue of the 1992 US Presidential election campaign was
economy. President Bush, despite his overwhelming victory in the
Gulf War in 1991, lost the election in 1992 because of the souring
American economy. The reason for the failure of the American economy was partly cyclical, but there was also a growing frustration
among the American people that a more effective policy had to be
adopted. President Clinton came to power with a message for the
revitalization of the American economy. In this situation the growing trade deficit with Japan was politically unacceptable.

Huge Japanese investment in the United States, at the level of
$10 to $30 billion on a yearly basis in the latter part of the 1980's,
stayed on at the level of $10 to $20 billion in the first half of the
1990's.[45] But it did not mitigate the impression of a Japanese threat.
Japan's investment created an image of buying expensive golf courses
or monumental buildings rather than job creation. The growing
image of a Japanese threat blended with the image of booming
Japanese economy as well. President Clinton's urge to strike a right

---

[44] The yearly US trade deficit with Japan from 1991 to 1994 was, in billion dollars: 43.4, 49.6, 59.4, 65.7 (U.S. Census Bureau: http://landview.census.gov/foreign-
trade/balance/c5880.html, 2003–06–15).

[45] Japan's yearly direct investment from 1991 to 1995 was, in billion dollars:
18.0, 13.8, 14.7, 17.3, and 22.2 (JETRO figures, www.jetro.go.jp/ec/j/trade/ FDI
to, country data 2003–08–04).

score *vis-à-vis* Japan was partly due to this image of a booming Japanese economy at a time when the US economy was in such difficulty.

Indeed, for nearly 5 years, from the end of 1986 to the beginning of 1991, the Japanese economy went through another period of powerful boom with an average growth of over 5%. It was led by soaring land prices and securities. The Tokyo land price jumped 2.7 times for the commercial district and 2.3 times for residential districts from 1986 to 1991. The average Tokyo Stock Exchanges price doubled in two years from 20,000 yen (early 1987) to 38,915 yen (end 1989).[46]

Economists give many reasons for the eruption of the Japanese bubble economy. The first reason can be summarized by saying that Japan had a surplus of money through her trade relations. From 1986 to 1990 Japan had accumulated an yearly average of $70 billion in trade surplus.[47] Some indicate the emergence of the 'oil yen' after the oil price collapse in 1985–1986 as an important element of this trade surplus (Chapter 9). The second reason may be attributed directly to the Plaza Accord and the concerted efforts to strengthen the yen among the leading industrialized nations. There was an expectation that the yen would become further strengthened. To continue investing in dollars could entail further loss due to the continuous devaluation of dollars *vis-à-vis* yen. This 'exchange rate deficiency' invited the further purchase of yen, and the surplus of yen went into land and securities. The third reason, which has been indicated by many, is the extremely low interest rate policy adopted by the Japanese government. The Japanese government pursued the low interest policy, because it was then considered to be the most effective policy to maintain a GDP growth of around 5%. But there was not sufficient demand for enhanced production. Therefore a huge amount of yen searching for profitable objects poured into asset and security markets.[48] Some point out the special impact caused by the low interest rate policy after 'Black Monday' (Chapter 11).

---

[46] Suzuta, *op. cit.*, p. 202.
[47] JETRO figures.
[48] Ibid., p. 203. Nishino, *op. cit.*, p. 351. Murata, *op. cit.*, p. 216.

Rising trade disputes

President Clinton, after his election to the presidency, carefully began to prepare his policy toward Japan. During the initial months of the presidency, President Clinton formulated his Japanese policy, namely that among the three pillars which constituted the relationship—security, international cooperation and economy—the first two were on solid ground, but the last one, the economy, was not in a satisfactory situation.

Thus economic matters became a high priority issue when Prime Minister Kiichi Miyazawa, who replaced Kaifu in November 1991, visited Washington in April 1993. President Clinton emphasized that clear results were needed fast, and that these results had to be measurable. Thus, a 'result oriented, measurable criteria' became the Clintonian approach for the negotiations. This approach had common elements in expanding 'market access' with the third prescription of trade disputes. But instead of its 'harmonization' approach, the Clintonian approach sought measurable results, and therefore gave an impression that trade should be 'managed' to obtain certain objectives. A fourth prescription which could be defined as 'market access managed' was introduced.

Japan was deeply troubled. Prime Minister Miyazawa reacted with clear antipathy towards 'managed trade'. The ill-fated experience of the 20% figure of semi-conductor trade might have loomed behind Prime Minister Miyazawa.

After intense talks in July 1993, at the fringe of the Tokyo Economic Summit, an agreement was reached between the two administrations that 'comprehensive talks' would be initiated to tackle the three most problematic areas: government procurement, insurance, and automobiles. The objective of these negotiations was to give greater business opportunities to American companies in the Japanese market in the respective areas. Japan made it clear that 'managed trade' could not be accepted, but was prepared to discuss issues which the US found problematic.

The two sides made efforts to reach an agreement in February 1994 at the time Prime Minister Morihiro Hosokawa, the newly elected Prime Minister from the non-LDP coalition government as of August 1993, visited Washington, but the two sides could not agree on the implication of 'measurability' and the talks broke down.

In October, however, an agreement was reached on government procurement and Insurance, without introducing, at least from Japanese perspectives, 'measurable criteria'.

On automobiles, serious negotiations had lasted for six months under the American threat of imposing a 100 percent tariff on Japanese luxury cars and the Japanese government's determination to resist it through the WTO's principle of multilateral engagement.[49] An interesting agreement was finally reached in June 1995. In comparison to the first automobile agreement in 1981, there was no restriction on the number of cars to be exported from Japan to the United States. On the American continent, however, the Japanese agreed to increase production and in particular to increase the use of American manufactured auto parts. Concrete numbers were given, but only as unilateral estimates by the Americans. In Japan, an agreement was reached to substantially increase the dealerships which could handle the import of foreign car imports. The numbers given in its context were again, a unilateral estimate by the Americans. Measures to facilitate the obligatory inspection system, which could become an impediment to the smooth expansion of foreign car sales in Japan, were also agreed upon. Thus, at least from Japan's point of view, a commitment to 'measurable criteria' was avoided, and subsequently the threat to unilateral sanction successfully evaded.

It was a period when emotions in the relationship created genuine anxiety.

In America, the notion of 'Japanese unfairness' weighed heavily. In the minds of some Americans the belief was firmly rooted that Japan was different, that it had enjoyed the best of the American values of free trade and an open society, that nevertheless Japan did not open her own society and blocked foreign import and investment, and that Japan was therefore unfair. 'Japan bashing' was the phrase often used to sum up the American attitude.

The end of the Cold War had clear repercussions on this psychological make-up. Now that the major enemy during the Cold War, the Soviet Union, was gone, the only country which was causing real irritation for the Americans was Japan. At a time when America was suffering from an economic downturn, Japan seemed to be the only country that was booming. And yet Japan was not

---

[49] Hook, Gilson, Hughes, Dobson, *op. cit.*, Routledge, 2001, p. 111.

paying enough attention to the difficulties which other countries, including the US, were facing.

In Japan, sentiments not articulately expressed during the Cold War were unleashed. Some Japanese began to express their weariness of American pressure which had lasted for two decades, on the restriction of Japan's export or the opening up of its market, over its border barrier or its internal social structure. Japan's dissociation from the Clintonian measurable and result-oriented approach was serious. Both Prime Minister Miyazawa's visit in April 1993 and Prime Minister Hosokawa's visit in February 1994 created an image of a 'Japan that says No' through the media reports. Public opinion in Japan generally seemed to have welcomed this image. Such media catchwords as 'anti America', 'hate America', 'desert America', or 'despise America' were being reported.[50]

Reconfirmation of everything positive that Japan already shared or could further share with America was sometimes useful in taking the heat off. Within the 'comprehensive talks' which were agreed in July 1993, this positive win-win cooperation was also enlisted. But the win-win cooperation had only limited impact.

I happened to be the Head of Chancery at the Japanese Embassy in Washington for two years in 1992 and 1993, during the last year under President Bush and the first year under President Clinton.

I felt that there was a genuine risk of becoming involved in a vicious circle. Some Americans said with bitterness that "There is no use to speak to the Japanese anymore on essential things in our life. They are so different. Or rather, I do not care whether they are the same or different. I just want results which are useful for America."

Some Japanese responded with the same bitterness that "It is Japan that is pursuing free trade and America that is seeking 'managed trade'. Japan should create an alliance of free traders against America." This statement naturally further alienated the Americans.

It was not easy to overcome this situation.

---

[50] The Japanese catchwords for these 4 expressions were *'HanBei'*, *'KenBei'*, *'KiBei'*, and *'Bubei'*.

Explaining that, in reality, America was considerably richer than Japan did not help much, because Americans were dissatisfied and irritated by the lack of achievement in their own country.

The best I could think of was basically to defend the Maekawa Report, and tell the Americans clearly that "Japan is trying to change our society to make it better attuned to the outside world." To emphasize that it was in Japan's own interest to create a more harmonized society with the outside world was critically important. It brought Japan to a pro-active position. It emphasized commonness in the relationship rather than difference. It brought Japan into an equal footing position with the US. Based on these common grounds, I tried to explain, not apologetically but objectively, that fundamental changes require a certain amount of 'time'.

Examples of success stories of foreign companies, which have sold attractive products, have also helped consolidating my points.

The Americans did not agree, but at least in some cases we succeeded in diverting the heat and alleviating tension.

The collapse of the bubble economy

At a time when the two countries were engaged in one of the most serious trade disputes, important changes took place in the very texture of the Japanese economy: the collapse of the bubble economy.

By the beginning of the 1990's the bubble economy resulted in the price hike of land prices that made it impossible for an ordinary Japanese businessman to buy a house in Tokyo. Faced with strong criticism, the government introduced regulatory measures to restrict the volume of asset trading and a special tax on land to make it costly to own the land, with a view to preventing speculative asset transactions.

This resulted in the so-called 'burst of the bubble' from early 1991. Stock prices peaked at the very end of 1989 and fell into a steep downhill trend to its third value in summer 1992. The land price in major cities dropped in 1994 to 63.2% of the price in 1990.[51] The collapse of land prices in particular, created a huge amount of non-performing loans, because land was, in many cases, used for security in bank lending.

---

[51] Suzuta, *op. cit.*, p. 205.

During the first half of the 1990's, however, the far-reaching impact of the collapse of the bubble economy was not felt by the leadership of either countries. The bubble economy failed but Japan was expected to recover soon. As if to symbolize the confidence of the market to the Japanese economy, the yen reached the highest postwar value of yen 79.75 per dollar in April 1995 (Chapter 11), at a time when the two countries were on a collision course in the automobile trade disputes.[52]

The declining strength of the Japanese economy over the 90's as we perceive it retrospectively, makes one wonder, what it had been that had caused the emotions and antipathy to place the relations in such a dangerous and psychologically vicious circle. One cannot help but think that had anyone known exactly what was behind the decline in the Japanese economy over the first half of the 90's, the trade conflicts between the two countries would have taken a much different shape. In fact, the economic relations between the two countries were taking an entirely different shape after 1995.

6. Japan's economic situation at the turn of the century

After the collapse of the bubble economy in Japan

The impact of the collapse of the bubble economy continued to an extent which no-one had foreseen:

Japanese banks, whose self-owned capital had already been limited, faced the collapse of land prices and quickly tightened their money supply. Because land was used as the major security item for lending, the collapse of prices required them to adopt an extremely cautious approach for further lending. Companies which became unable to procure finance began trimming their facilities and labour forces. Consumers felt anxious about future prospects and put an even greater emphasis on savings.[53] All these factors resulted in a deflationary spiral.

Thus economic growth rate declined and for three years from 1992 registered just below 1%. But successive government measures

---

[52] Nakanishi, op. cit., p. 150.
[53] Statistics Bureau, Ministry of Public Management, Home affairs, Posts and Telecommunications Statistical Handbook of Japan 2001, p. 27.

helped the recovery and the GDP growth recovered to reach 3.0% in 1995 and 4.4% in 1996. A series of measures however, to tackle the accumulated budgetary deficit, caused a fatal deflationary impact and resulted in a growth rate of minus 0.4% in 1997 and minus 2.0% in 1998.[54] In 2002 the economy still found it difficult to enter a sound circle of development.

Unemployment most seriously affected Japan, which once boasted an extremely low unemployment rate, now saw its rapid rise, starting from 2.1% in 1990, 3.2% in 1995, 4.1% in 1998, to a historical high of 5.1% in 2001.

Successive governments have exerted great efforts to tackle the question of non-performing loans. From 1992 up to the middle of 2001, an accumulative amount of non-performing loans which had been fixed reached 74.8 trillion yen, but still 36.8 trillion yen was left unresolved.[55] Prime Minister Junichiro Koizumi made a clear policy declaration in the spring of 2001 that 'the resolution of non-performing loans' is, together with his 'seven points for the structural reform' a major pillar of his economic policy.

Economic relations with America

At a time when Japan was suffering from the non-performing loans and a deflationary economy, America had gone through a powerful period of economic growth. Industrial production, led by a wave of strong information technology, increased private sector investment accompanied by active consumption, and a declining budgetary deficit allowed the American economy to hold a huge trade deficit. In many respects, the Japanese lesson given at SII seemed to have garnered a good response.

Against this background President Clinton departed and George W. Bush became President in 2001. The trade conflicts that had lasted just over half a century, the economic situation that surrounded Japan and the United States, was showing an unexpected change.

Let us look at the trade figures. After the historic high trade deficit of $65 billion in 1994, that figure declined a little for three years, but then began to escalate again in 1998 and from 1999 to 2002

---

[54] Suzuta, *op. cit.*, pp. 207–208.
[55] The figure is from the Financial Agency.

stayed at an amazing level of around $70 billion, including a historically high figure to date of $81 billion in 2000.[56]

The figure is incredible, but what is more surprising is that there was practically no outcry of concern, no voice raised concerning a Japanese economic threat, and even no outcry of criticism of Japanese unfairness. Between the government officials of the two administrations, the question of trade imbalance and the necessity of the further opening of the Japanese market were discussed. But they do not attract the political attention, which once dominated the relationship during a quarter century of trade frictions. The media began to report that instead of 'Japan bashing', the catchword in America's attitude toward Japan is 'Japan passing'.

The change in the psychological atmosphere is clearly due to the changes in the economic situation in the two countries. The basic economic situations in both America and in Japan have changed so much over the 90's, that $83 billion in trade deficits *vis-à-vis* Japan create very little sensation in America.

The environment in Foreign Direct Investment may be helping this psychological set-up somewhat. Japan's yearly investment in the United States basically stayed at the same level of $10 to $20 billion in the latter part of the 1990's. But what was noteworthy was that US investment to Japan which stayed at a level of around $1 to $2 billion from 1986 to 1995 began to grow with some strength, reaching $9 billion in 2000.[57]

Future economic perspectives in Japan

Prime Minister Koizumi conducted a cabinet reshuffle in September 2002 and concurrently appointed Heizo Takenaka, Cabinet Minister for Economic Policy, to the post of Cabinet Minister for Monetary Policy. Takenaka was known to be an advocate of the adoption of fast and rigorous measures to eliminate non-performing loans. Take-

---

[56] The US trade deficits with Japan from 1995 to 2002 in billion dollars are 59.1, 47.5, 56.1, 64.0, 73.3, 81.5, 69.0, 69.9 (US Census Bureau: http://landview.census.gov/foreign-trade/balance/c5880.html, 2003–06–15).

[57] From 1996 to 2001, yearly Japan's investment in the US was, in billion dollars: 22.0, 20.7, 10.3, 22.2, 12.1, 6.3. US investment in Japan during the same period was: 2.1, 1.2, 6.3, 2.2, 9.1, 5.1 (JETRO figures, www.jetro.go.jp/ec/j/trade/FDI to and from, country data 2003–08–04).

naka kept his position at the cabinet reshuffle in September 2003 despite strong criticism from some LDP members, who urged a greater budgetary spending to stimulate the weak and deflationary economy.

As a matter of fact, non-performing loans are statistically slowly diminishing. When and how will they be fundamentally resolved, so that they will not affect the performance of Japanese economy?

By the end of 2003 many analysts state that the economy is at its bottom in 2003 and recovery will take place from 2004. Is deflationary economy really in upturn?

Koizumi is maintaining concrete objectives of structural reform to stimulate social and economic activities: privatization of the post-office and the High-Way Corporation and greater autonomy of local government. How far will it go?

One reason of Japan's economic stagnation is the consumer's sense of uncertainty, in particular, related to pension, medical care and education. What perspectives are there in these areas toward the future?

Japan has to transform itself into a society which is dynamic enough to meet the challenges of the 21st century. The guiding spirit of the Maekawa Report and SII, that Japan needed transformation of its own society for its own interests, is resonant with the current urge for a dynamic reform. 'Competition, flexibility, and creativity' are precisely the elements which Japan needed then and indeed needs now.

The structural reforms to allow foreign competition inside Japan and harmonization of Japanese society with the outside world seem to be precisely the right recipe for the present difficulty.

After all, in the long term, Japan is still an economic giant. After 10 years of economic recession, its GDP is still half of the United States, twice that of Germany, three times larger than France, UK and Italy, and four times larger than China.[58] It has lost a substantial amount of jobs in production and in construction, but managed to create a huge number of new jobs in the service sector. The information technology related industry has taken a leap forward. The private sectors as well as the government are trying to meet the requirements of the environmentally conscious and age conscious

---

[58] MOFA homepage: http//www.mofa.go.jp/mofaj/area/ecodata/gdp.html, 2003–07–05. Recent economic analysis based on Purchasing Power Parity (PPP) does not underpin that comparison. Chinese economy is evaluated by many analysts as being 1.5 times larger than the Japanese.

society. Japanese regions are another source of new demand for the economy. A new aspiration to recreate Japan with a way of life harmonious with its natural beauty and traditional culture are seen, though sporadic, in many corners of society. The real task is to let this aspiration become a powerful socio-economic direction. On the whole the people of Japan are hard working, conscientious, and willing to create new values.

Thus one may assume that the future is not so gloomy, that Japan will overcome today's difficulty, and when it does come back again as a vigorous member of the world economy, even the age of trade conflict might return to the political attention of the international community!

CHAPTER FOUR

CHINA: ECONOMIC DEVELOPMENT AND
WOUNDED FEELINGS

1. *Diplomatic relations with Taiwan and economic relations with mainland China*

Establishment of diplomatic relations with Taiwan

As we have seen in Chapter 1, neither the People's Republic of China (PRC)—that is continental Communist China under Mao Zedong—nor the Republic of China (RC)—that is Taiwan under Chiang Kai-shek—was invited to San Francisco in September 1951 to participate in the Peace Treaty Conference. The fate of the bilateral relationship between Japan and China, whichever China it might be, was left to future negotiations.

After San Francisco, Prime Minister Yoshida took a very cautious approach. In the mid to long-term perspective he foresaw the possibility of a split between communist China and the Soviet Union, and he took ample time before making a decision as to which China to choose and finding a way to develop relations with communist China. One idea openly discussed was to establish a trade representative office in Shanghai.[1] In the emerging Cold War tension in the Far East, this idea did not work. J.F. Dulles, US Secretary of State, made it clear to the Japanese that the only option open for Japan in the Cold War circumstances was to establish diplomatic relations with the Republic of China. On 24 December 1951, Prime Minister Yoshida sent a letter to J.F. Dulles, indicating Japan's intention to establish diplomatic relations with the RC. Japan concluded a separate peace treaty with the RC on 28 April 1952, the day the San Francisco Peace Treaty came into force.

In order to preserve maximum flexibility for future diplomatic options, Japan tried to limit the application of the Peace Treaty with

---

[1] Ikei, *op. cit.*, pp. 246–248. A. Tanaka, *Nichuu Kankei 1945–1990 (Japan-China Relations 1945–1990)*, Tokyo University, 1991, pp. 35–37, 40.

the RC to the territories under its control. The RC's position was that it represented the whole of China. In a complicated structure of the Treaty itself, the Protocol, the Exchange of Notes and the Agreed Minutes, Japan and the RC both achieved their respective objectives by stating that the jurisdiction of the Treaty "shall be applicable to all the territories which are now, or which may here-after be, under the control of"[2] the government of the RC.

The Treaty also included two further important points: that the state of war between Japan and the Republic of China was termi-nated (Article 1) and that the Republic of China waived its right for reparations (Protocol 1 (b)).[3] The fact that Chiang Kai-shek did not demand reparations was viewed as an honourable and generous ges-ture in Japan. As we will see below, both these points had reper-cussions twenty years later, when Japan tried to establish diplomatic relations with mainland China.

Ups and downs in the relationship with mainland China

The People's Republic of China naturally expressed its anger at the conclusion of the Peace Treaty between Japan and Taiwan. After this initial stage of anger, however, Japan and the PRC moved into an interesting two decades of primarily economic relations.

While recognizing the RC as its political partner, the Japanese government did what it could to develop economic relations with mainland China. This policy was called the 'principle to separate political and economic relations' and was supported by the Japanese private sector, which sought to enhance its business interests with mainland China.

One of the main objectives of the communist Chinese government was to gain diplomatic recognition from Japan as the sole repre-sentative of China. Economic relations became an important tool of this political objective. The Chinese policy was called the 'principle of inseparability of political and economic relations'.

---

[2] Exchange of Notes in relation to the Treaty of Peace between Japan and the Republic of China, MOFA, *op. cit.*, p. 125.

[3] Taiwan was entitled to a 'special arrangement' because it formed a part of Japan when the war ended, based on Article 4 (a) of the San Francisco Peace Treaty. Since Japan and the PRC established diplomatic relations in 1972 before Taiwan and Japan could agree on this 'special arrangement', an unfinished task remained.

The following two decades saw alternating periods of little friction, when the two principles found each other in harmony, and periods of tension, when the two principles clashed.[4] International situations which surrounded the two countries were important in creating these shifts in the relationship.

(1) The first period of relative harmony lasted from 1952 to 1957. The period of thaw began after Stalin's death in March 1953, the end of the war in Korea in July 1953 and in Vietnam in July 1954 enhanced this direction in Asia. In September 1954 Zhou Enlai proposed to develop relations with Japan based on 'accumulating approach (*tsumiage-houshiki*)', which meant developing relations through the accumulation of a wide range of economic and cultural issues. In October 1954 the Soviet Union and the PRC issued a joint communiqué expressing their wish to normalize relations with Japan.

In Japan, Ichiro Hatoyama (Prime Minister from December 1954 to December 1956) tried to respond to these calls. His major emphasis became the Soviet Union, but at least he stayed away from 'provocative actions' toward the PRC.[5]

It was a period when trade developed steadily, based on a series of private sector trade agreements. The first agreement, to initiate barter trade, was concluded in June 1952; the second agreement, to establish trade representative offices in both countries was concluded in October 1953; and the third agreement, to hold commodity fairs, was concluded in May 1955.[6] The turnover of trade reached $151 million in 1956.[7] Cultural exchanges began to increase and the relationship proceeded harmoniously.

(2) The situation changed in 1957 and this second period, which lasted until 1962, was characterized by a definite chill.

Nobusuke Kishi took the office of Prime Minister in February 1957. As we have already seen in Chapter 2, he had a very clear orientation in his foreign policy, namely to bring the Japan-US relationship to an equal footing. In his China policy he was outspoken in his support of the RC. Thus in June 1957, during his visit to Taiwan, he made an open statement supporting Chiang Kai-shek's return to the mainland. Beijing reacted with furious comments.

---

[4] Tanaka, *op. cit.*, pp. 43–44.
[5] Ikei, *op. cit.*, p. 297.
[6] Hosoya, *op. cit.*, 1993, pp. 148–149.
[7] Ikei, *op. cit.*, p. 298.

This period coincided with a period of tension both domestically and externally for China: domestically, the 'ultra-romantic' period of economic expansion of 'the Great Leap Forward' under Mao Zedong's leadership had put society as a whole in turmoil; externally Mao and Khrushchev's approaches to communism began to show a clear discrepancy and the period of Sino-Soviet rivalry started.

The fourth private sector agreement signed in March 1958 brought about another complicated situation. The agreement included a new clause allowing each trade representative office to raise its own national flag. Since this implied giving mainland China a certain political and diplomatic status, it evoked a violent protest from Taiwan. The Japanese government conceded to this protest and denied the Trade Representative Office of the PRC the right to raise its national flag. The Chinese approach to politicize trade and economic relations and the Japanese approach to keep politics separate from trade and economic relations collided head on.

Communist China naturally responded with indignation and the final blow came in an incident on 2 May, when a right-wing Japanese youth pulled down a PRC national flag at a trade fair held in Nagasaki. He was detained but released on the same day and the Japanese government declared that his offence did not constitute that of 'damaging a national flag', because Japan had not recognised the PRC. Chinese anger with this logic showed no limits and on 11 May it declared that the cultural and economic relations between the two sides were terminated. In terms of the then existing Japan-PRC relationship this decision was equivalent to a breakdown in diplomatic relations.[8]

The turnover of trade in 1960 fell to $24 million.[9]

(3) The third period from 1962 to 1965 healed the rift.

Kishi retired in July 1960 and Prime Minister Hayato Ikeda, who replaced him, showed greater eagerness to expand economic relations with the PRC. In China 'the Great Leap Forward' had clearly proved to be an economic disaster and the exacerbating relations with the Soviet Union began to affect China's trade structure. Japan and the PRC started to find ways to revitalize economic relations.

In September 1962 Kenzo Matsumura, a senior LDP statesman, visited Beijing. He had talks with Zhou Enlai, and based on the

---

[8] Tanaka, *op. cit.*, p. 51.
[9] Hook, Gilson, Hughes, Dobson, *op. cit.*, p. 442.

political agreement reached between Matsumura and Zhou, a new framework agreement on trade relations to cover 1963 to 1967 was signed in November 1962.

China took a step forward in agreeing to the establishment of a liaison office without any diplomatic status, which it had originally called for in 1958.

In August 1963 the Japanese government in turn took a step forward by extending an Export-Import Bank loan to a top Japanese chemical fibre plant to be established in China. Since the Ex-Im Bank was a semi-governmental organization mobilizing public sector finances, that decision was taken as strong backing by the Japanese government to enhance economic relations.

(4) The fourth period began in 1965, bringing back another chill to the relationship. This situation continued until the establishment of diplomatic relations with the PRC at the beginning of the 1970's. Many political and economic elements, whether intentional or not, contributed to the chill in this fourth period.

Prime Minister Eisaku Sato took office in November 1964. At first Sato was considered to be a supporter of the 'principle of inseparability of political and economic relations', hence a supporter of Japan-PRC relations.[10] But in February 1965 he decided not to extend a new Ex-Im Bank loan to the establishment of a plant in the PRC. It is now believed that the decision to discontinue the Ex-Im Bank loan had already been taken during Prime Minister Ikeda's term of office and that Sato just implemented it. But because of this incident Sato inadvertently put himself into an anti-PRC position.

The Cultural Revolution which erupted in the spring of 1966 led China on a road to isolation. In 1967 China recalled a majority of ambassadors from abroad, two Indian diplomats were arrested in Beijing and the British Deputy Chief of the Mission's office was looted. The long-standing friendship between the Communist Party of Japan and the Communist Party of China was also broken off. In June 1967, China declared to Japan that "American Imperialism, the group of Soviet revisionists, Sato's reactionary cabinet and the revisionist faction of the Communist Party of Japan were all common enemies of both the people of Japan and China."[11]

---

[10] Tanaka, *op. cit.*, pp. 57–58.
[11] Tanaka, *op. cit.*, pp. 59–60.

Lastly, Prime Minister Sato's increasing assertiveness in consolidating Japan-US relations gave further pretexts for China to escalate the tension between the two countries. Prime Minister Sato visited Washington in November 1967 and issued a joint communiqué with President Lyndon B. Johnson referring to the "threat by the Chinese Communist Party". Furthermore, the Sato-Nixon Communiqué in November 1969 stating that "the maintenance of peace and security in the Taiwan area was also a most important factor for the security of Japan" acutely alerted the PRC. Thus heavy propaganda developed in the Chinese press against the revival of Japanese militarism.[12]

2. *Establishment of diplomatic relations with the People's Republic of China*

'Detente' and the changing international situation

At a time when Japan-China relations were characterized by mounting tension, critical changes were taking place quietly in the fundamental structure of international relations. The root of this change came from the United States.

Amidst the changing positions in the international arena politically (Chapter 2) and economically (Chapter 3), President Nixon, assisted by Henry Kissinger, envisaged the creation of external relationships better attuned to American interests.

In essence, President Nixon's new policy, which was later called the policy of 'Detente', was based on a clear understanding of the exacerbating relationship between the two communist giants: the Soviet Union and the PRC. China, which in the latter part of the Cultural Revolution was going through a difficult period, internally and externally, should have been seeking some fundamental needs for the improvement of the relationship with the US. The Soviet Union, under the collective leadership of Leonid Brezhnev, had a genuine need to expand consumer goods production at home and also had enormous difficulty in handling the situation in Eastern Europe. The Soviet invasion of Czechoslovakia in the summer of 1968 is fresh in

---

[12] Hosoya, 1993, *op. cit.*, pp. 154–155.

our memory. The communist giants each had a potential need for improved relations with the United States. Sino-Soviet relations were worse than ever as symbolized by the military collision at their eastern border in March 1969.

The strategic objective of 'Detente', as Japan understood retrospectively, took shape: the US grasped this opportunity of Sino-Soviet rivalry, with a view to 1) improving relations with one so that relations with the other would be positively influenced, 2) letting America withdraw from Vietnam with honour and thus, 3) creating an international environment with less tension and greater security for the United States.

At the end of the 1960's Japan was far from creating a new foreign policy initiative of that magnitude.

I joined the Ministry of Foreign Affairs in April 1968 and after spending three months in the Foreign Service Training Institute, worked for one year as a trainee in the East European Division covering the Soviet Union and all East-European countries.

As a trainee, things started very quietly and just in the middle of August I indulged myself by asking for a few days of summer vacation and went to a resort in the mountains. But on 20 August I was startled to hear on the radio that the Soviet Union and five Warsaw Pact countries had invaded Czechoslovakia. I cancelled my summer vacation and came back to the Ministry and tried to be of some use. The atmosphere in my division was very tense. Everyone was upset. The senior officers of the division drafted a strong statement protesting against this invasion to be pronounced at the highest level of the government.

The following year on 2 March, I faced another international crisis when Soviet and Chinese troops clashed near the Damansky Island on the river Amour at the eastern border between the Soviet Union and China. This time it was not so much anger but a sense of fear that permeated my division, not knowing exactly where this rivalry would lead. Again senior officers in my division drafted a strong statement condemning the use of force and calling for restraint on both sides.

Drafting strong statements was probably the most that Japanese foreign policy could have done then regarding these events in 1968 and 1969.

The basic attention of the government in the foreign policy arena was directed to the question of the reversion of Okinawa. But on 15 July 1971 President Nixon announced his plan to visit China. The fact that the announcement was made without any prior consultation shocked Japan. It was particularly shocking for many Japanese because the announcement came just after the signature of the Agreement on the reversion of Okinawa on 17 June, when a sense of mutual trust was heightened in the public opinion. 15 July 1971 has long been remembered in the mind of Japanese people as *Nixon-Shokku* (shock).[13]

In fact, there had already been signs of a rapprochement between the USA and the PRC, for example, the invitation of the American ping pong team to China in April 1971. The Japanese government itself was taking several measures to close the gap between Japan and mainland China. In January 1971 in his annual policy speech to the Diet, Prime Minister Sato used, for the first time the term 'the People's Republic of China'. In May the government hinted at granting a further Ex-Im Bank loan to the PRC. Nevertheless, the timing of President Nixon's announcement of his planned visit was completely unexpected in Japan.

President Nixon's announcement resulted in a dramatic change in the situation in the United Nations. By October 1971, allowing mainland China to join the UN was beginning to seem inevitable in the eyes of everyone. The remaining question was what to do with Taiwan. Should Taiwan go or could it stay, together with communist China?

Japan and the United States decided to make a last effort to keep Taiwan inside the United Nations. Analysts argue that Prime Minister Sato took this decision with a view to fulfilling his major agenda, the smooth ratification of the Agreement on the reversion of Okinawa. Pro-Taiwan congressmen both in Japan and America should not be given a pretext for a negative reaction against the Japanese government.[14] Here one might see an expression of gratitude on the

---

[13] Just less than one hour after Secretary of State Rogers informed the Japanese Ambassador, Nobuhiko Ushiba, President Nixon announced on television his intention to visit China. Prime Minister Sato was said to have been alerted only a few minutes before the TV announcement (Tanaka, *op. cit.*, p. 66).

[14] Tanaka, *op. cit.*, p. 72.

Japanese side to the generous attitude taken by Chiang Kai-shek at the time of the establishment of diplomatic relations.

Japan and the US proposed a procedural resolution to make the question of Taiwan's expulsion from the United Nations require a two-thirds majority. This procedural resolution was defeated by 55 to 59 with 2 abstentions. On 25 October 1971 the resolution to accept the People's Republic of China to replace the Republic of China was approved with a substantial majority of 76 to 35 and 17 abstentions.

President Nixon visited China in February 1972 and issued the Shanghai Communiqué. This visit changed the fundamental power structure in the Asian Pacific region. A new situation had arisen whereby no major foreign policy decision could ever be taken without affecting the interrelationship of America, China, and the Soviet Union. Japan also became a partner of these interrelations from the 70's, as we are going to see now, especially in Southeast Asia (Chapter 5) and Russia (Chapter 7).[15]

Tanaka's visit to China

Prime Minister Sato resigned and on 7 July 1972 Kakuei Tanaka was elected as the new Prime Minister. In Japan Tanaka is remembered as the initiator of the policy of 'Reconstruction of the Japanese Archipelago' (Chapter 3). He was a statesman of strong character, leading a very powerful faction of the LDP, fully capable of mobilizing the financial mechanism of the party, but whose political career was later severely damaged as a result of a bribery scandal.

By then public opinion in Japan had drifted strongly in favour of the establishment of diplomatic relations with the PRC. Except for pro-Taiwan political groups, the result at the UN voting in October 1971 was generally considered as Prime Minister Sato's political downfall. Prime Minister Tanaka was fast in grasping this opportunity.[16]

---

[15] Ibid., p. 73.

[16] Prime Minister Tanaka himself stated three reasons why he decided to resume diplomatic relations with the PRC: (1) Japan-China relations are a highly emotional issue which has a strong domestic connotation in Japan. Two-thirds of the domestic troubles could be resolved in solving this issue. (2) The total Japan-China population was one fourth of the world population. There would be no stability in Japan without resolving an issue of this importance. (3) Adequate proximity between Japan, America and China would create a stable security basis in the Far East (Ibid., pp. 75–76).

In fact, important negotiations through unofficial channels were already proceeding at the time Tanaka became Prime Minister. The most important approach was made by China to the Komei Party[17] delegation in June 1971, concerning the three basic principles for the resumption of relations:[18]

1) China is one entity. The People's Republic of China is the sole legitimate government that represents the Chinese people.

2) Taiwan is a part of China. It is an inalienable part of the territory of China. The Taiwan issue is a domestic issue for China.

3) The Treaty between Japan and Taiwan of 1952 is unlawful and invalid.

The three principles became the crux of the negotiations. By the summer of 1972 Japan had no difficulty with the first principle, had reservations on the second, and could not accept the third. The underlying thinking was that Japan was ready to go ahead with diplomatic relations with the PRC, was prepared for a breakdown in diplomatic relations with Taiwan, but wanted to do so with dignity, in a manner honourable to Taiwan and as consistent as possible with past Japanese policies.

On 29 July another important proposal was transmitted to the Japanese government through Yoshikatsu Takeiri, Chairman of the Komei Party. The proposal made it clear that China was not going to ask for war reparations nor object to the Japan-US Security Treaty.

Prime Minister Tanaka decided that the time was ripe to move quickly to achieve the objective of the normalization of the relationship. The differing position on the three basic principles was unresolved and he decided to go to China and settle the outstanding issues on the spot. From August to September Tanaka rapidly gained consensus within the LDP, with the United States and sent a special envoy to Taiwan.

Thus Prime Minister Tanaka and Foreign Minister Masayoshi Ohira together with Foreign Ministry officials visited Beijing from 25 to 30 September. It was probably one of the most dramatic nego-

---

[17] The Komei Party is a political party closely associated with a Buddhist sect called 'Sokagakkai'. The Komei Party sought to play the role of mediator in the process leading to the diplomatic recognition of the PRC. It was in opposition for many years but after the demise of 'the 1955 system' in 1993, it became part of the ruling coalition.

[18] Tanaka, *op. cit.*, p. 70.

tiations held in postwar Japanese diplomacy. The Joint Communiqué establishing diplomatic relations between Japan and the People's Republic of China was issued on 29 September 1972.

The main points of the communiqué are the following:

The most important point included in the preamble was the following passage to express Japan's apology for the deeds she had committed during the war: "The Japanese side is keenly conscious of the responsibility for the serious damage that Japan caused in the past to the Chinese people through war, and expresses its deep remorse."[19] The question of Japan's war responsibility is an issue we are going to discuss several times in this book. It is an issue which is still debated in Japan. Whatever the polemics around this issue, this expression 'express deep remorse', together with the same expression used toward South Korea in 1965 became a key expression representing Japan's position for many years to follow.

Let us now look at the three initial paragraphs which resolve the most difficult issue related to the three principles of June 1971:

> 1. The abnormal state of affairs that has hitherto existed between Japan and the People's Republic of China is terminated on the date on which this Joint Communiqué is issued.
> 2. The Government of Japan recognizes (the) Government of the People's Republic of China as the sole legal Government of China.
> 3. The Government of the People's Republic of China reiterates that Taiwan is an inalienable part of the territory of the People's Republic of China. The Government of Japan fully understands and respects this stand of the Government of the People's Republic of China, and it firmly maintains its stand under Article 8 of the Potsdam Proclamation.

Paragraph 1, dealing with the third principle was probably the one which required the toughest negotiations between the two sides.

China proposed to write here that "the state of war is terminated————." But Japan could not accept this proposal because the state of war had already been terminated under Article 1 of the Peace Treaty with the Republic of China (Taiwan). Japan's position

---

[19] The English text of the Joint Communiqué is a MOFA translation from the MOFA homepage (http://www.mofa.go.jp/region/asia-paci/china/joint72.html 2002-12-22). The last portion of the quoted Preamble "and expresses its deep remorse" was translated by the author, with a view to maintaining consistency with other documents which we are going to see in Chapter 5. The original translation by MOFA is "and deeply reproaches itself." The word used in Japanese is *hansei*.

could not be accepted by China, because they claimed that the Treaty with Taiwan was unlawful and invalid as was expressed by the third principle for the normalization. That was totally unacceptable for Japan because, although she was prepared to discontinue the Treaty with Taiwan, to label it unlawful and invalid was to deny the whole history of the past two decades and the honour of Japan-Taiwan relations. This deadlock was overcome by Zhou Enlai's compromise wording of "the abnormal state of affairs". With this expression, each side could interpret it as they wished to. After the adoption of the Joint Communiqué therefore, Foreign Minister Ohira could and did make a press conference to state that the Treaty with Taiwan was terminated.

Paragraph 2 dealing with the first principle was the easiest one and invited no objection from either side.

Paragraph 3 dealing with the second principle was difficult to handle.

The first half was obvious. It was the Chinese position on Taiwan as was expressed in the second principle. But the second half describing Japan's position on Taiwan was less obvious. "Fully understands and respects" usually implies 'in principle agree' or 'basically concur' or 'on the basic approach no objection'. Why couldn't Japan use the same expression used by the Chinese? The official reason went back to the San Francisco Peace Treaty of 1951, in which Japan renounced all rights to Taiwan. The Japanese delegation explained that it could not acknowledge, in full, China's right over Taiwan because it had "renounced all rights" over Taiwan, and thereby lost the legal grounds to determine the fate of Taiwan.

China finally agreed to include a compromise expression in this paragraph that "Japan maintains its stand under Article 8 of the Potsdam declaration". Article 8 states "The terms of the Cairo Declaration shall be carried out."[20] The Cairo Declaration of 1943 states "all the territories Japan has stolen from the Chinese, such as—Formosa (Taiwan)—shall be restored to the Republic of China."[21] In this context 'the Republic of China' should be understood to be the sole representative of China, which was now the PRC.

---

[20] MOFA, *op. cit.*, p. 1831.
[21] Ibid., p. 1823.

In this complicated round of arguments Japan expressed its basic consent to the fact that Taiwan is a part of China without committing itself to the 'legal' recognition of the PRC's rights over the island. To what extent this legalistic argument may have been motivated by the desire to preserve some of the honour in Japan-Taiwan relations is an interesting subject for future study.

Since then, Paragraph 3 has played an important role in explaining the Japanese government's position on Taiwan. Whenever a politically tense situation emerged regarding this question in the context of Japan's security issues, or in the context of Japan-China relations, the Japanese government tenaciously repeated this paragraph and refrained from any deeper interpretation. This strategy has subsequently protected its position quite successfully.

In addition to those three paragraphs, Paragraph 5 merits additional attention. It states that "The government of the PRC—renounces its demand for war reparations from Japan." One point in the negotiations was the use of the word 'demand'. Whereas the Chinese original version was said to have been 'the right to demand war reparations', Japan maintained that it could not agree to this because the 'right of demand' had already been renounced by the Treaty with Taiwan and that 'right' could not be renounced twice. As a compromise the word 'right' was omitted and the simple word 'demand' remained in the communiqué.[22]

3. *The conclusion of the Treaty of Peace and Friendship*

Unexpected difficulties surrounding the hegemony clause

After the establishment of diplomatic relations, the two countries steadily began developing their ties through the 70's. In the course of 1974 to 1975 four treaties, as outlined in Paragraph 9 of the Joint Communiqué, namely trade, aviation, shipping, and fisheries, were concluded. The amount of total trade increased from $1.1 billion in 1972 to $6.7 billion in 1979.[23]

However, in the middle of the 1970's this smooth process of development was unexpectedly interrupted. It was the international

---

[22] Tanaka, *op. cit.*, p. 81.
[23] JETRO figures (http://www.jetro.go.jp/ec/j/trade/excel/40w02.xls 2003–07–19).

situation which surrounded the two countries which inevitably influenced the bilateral relationship. Between 1972 and 1974 the international situation changed rapidly. Soviet expansionist moves in
Indochina and Africa were increasingly irritating the Western community (Chapter 2), and China, in particular, was becoming increasingly vocal in criticizing the expansionist trend of the Soviet Union.

The key issue which emerged was the question of a treaty of peace
and friendship. Such a treaty was foreshadowed in Paragraph 8 of
the Joint Communiqué: "The Government of Japan and the Government of the PRC have agreed that, with a view to solidifying and
developing the relations of peace and friendship between the two
countries, the two Governments will enter into negotiations for the
purpose of concluding a treaty of peace and friendship."

The negotiations started in November 1974 in Tokyo and at first
they seemed to be normal, non-polemical negotiations. But soon the
negotiations entered into a very difficult phase surrounding the question of a 'hegemony' clause.

In fact, a 'hegemony' clause had already been included in Paragraph
7 of the Joint Communiqué: "The normalization of relations between
Japan and China is not directed against any third country. Neither
of the two countries should seek hegemony in the Asia-Pacific region
and each is opposed to efforts by any other country or group of
countries to establish such hegemony."

In October 1972 when the Nixon-Kissinger Detente diplomacy
was in full swing, this clause did not invite particular anxiety for
Japan. A similar clause had already been included in the America-
China Shanghai Communiqué issued in February. In retrospect the
anti-hegemony clause in the Shanghai Communiqué was an important signal that no super power could expand its influence without
seriously affecting the relationship with other major powers in the
region. However, in 1972 it did not attract particular attention on
the part of the Asia-Pacific community.

But in 1974, after China intensified its criticism against the Soviet
Union as a 'hegemonic' power, whether or not to include an anti-
hegemony clause in a treaty of peace and friendship became a yard-
stick to judge Japan's proximity with the Soviet Union and China,
respectively. In this delicate political situation, increasing international media attention aggravated the difficulty.

It is interesting to note that despite the rapidly improving relations with China and the deteriorating relations with the Soviet

Union, the Japanese government was determined not to enter into an anti-Soviet alliance with China. The basic foreign policy for Japan was to improve bilateral-based respective relationships with the two socialist giants, while firmly maintaining its core relations with America.

By April 1975 the negotiations went into a deadlock.[24]

In 1976, after a stalemate of almost two years, it was primarily the domestic situation in each country that led to the breakthrough in the negotiations.

In Japan, Tanaka had to resign at the end of 1974 because of a bribery scandal involving the Lockheed company. Takeo Miki succeeded him, but the political turmoil continued with Tanaka's ultimate arrest in December 1975. The period of political volatility ended when Takeo Fukuda became the Prime Minister in December 1976. A bright former Ministry of Finance official and the political heir to Eisaku Sato, Fukuda expressed his foreign policy as 'omnidirectional diplomacy for peace (*zenhoui heiwa gaiko*)'.[25] His intention was to improve relations with both China and the Soviet Union: a second round of Japan's Detente policy. But as the period of Detente went by, Japan's policy of improving relations with both countries did not work: in the latter part of the 1970's Japan-China relations moved with dynamism, but relations with the Soviet Union stagnated (Chapter 7).

At any rate with China, Fukuda decided to resume the negotiations to fulfil what had been agreed in the 1972 Joint Communiqué and move the relationship on to a different phase.

In China, the two founders of the modern nation passed away in 1976: Zhou Enlai in January followed by Mao Zedong in September. Following the turmoil incurred by Mao Zedong's death, Deng Xiaoping consolidated his power and reappeared at the centre of power as the vice-chairman of the Communist Party of China in July 1977.

---

[24] F. Togo, who led the negotiations as Vice Minister for Foreign Affairs, wrote in his memoirs that the Japanese Foreign Ministry was not particularly concerned about the inclusion of the hegemony clause in the Joint Communiqué (F. Togo, *op. cit.*, p. 206). But Tanaka suggests that certain concern already existed during the normalization negotiations (Tanaka, *op. cit.*, p. 83).

[25] Bert Edstrom, *Japan's Evolving Foreign Policy Doctrine*, Palgrave, 1999, p. 96.

Making a breakthrough in the negotiations

Thus the two sides began informal contacts from autumn 1977 on-wards with a view to resuming negotiations or a treaty of peace and friendship.

By the spring of 1978 the Japanese position had already shifted to agree to the inclusion of the anti-hegemonic clause provided that another clause to mitigate the impression of 'alliance creation' would also be included. Already in September 1975 at the instruction of Prime Minister Miki, Foreign Minister Miyazawa was said to have expressed readiness to accept the hegemony clause with certain provisos.[26]

The negotiations were officially resumed this time in Beijing in July 1978. Several drafts were exchanged between the two sides to determine an adequate expression of the 'mitigation clause', but no agreement was reached. And yet there emerged a general feeling that China was preparing for a breakthrough. In early August Prime Minister Fukuda decided that the time was ripe to send Foreign Minister Sunao Sonoda to resolve the outstanding issues including the 'mitigating clause' and to conclude the treaty. As analysts observed, at the time Foreign Minister Sonoda was going to Beijing two draft proposals on the 'mitigating clause' were on the table, Japan's preferred version and a less preferred version.[27]

In 1978 I was working as the Deputy Director of the Treaties Division of the Treaties Bureau and had worked on this treaty from late spring to summer. Coming from a Russian background it was extremely interesting to observe that the whole Ministry was so sincere in seeking a reasonable mitigating clause on the basis of which we could clearly tell the Soviets that "Look, our treaty is not directed against you. The Chinese, knowing Japan's intention to defuse the hegemony clause by way of including a mitigating clause, have accepted this clause. So you need not to worry. Please work hard to improve Japan-Soviet relations and resolve the territorial issue."

I accompanied Foreign Minister Sonoda to Beijing together with the Director General of the Treaties Bureau, Mr. Seiichi

---

[26] Tanaka, *op. cit.*, p. 95.
[27] Ibid., p. 105.

> Omori. The Chinese government gave us the impression of a political decision, but we did not know until the actual meeting between the two Foreign Ministers how China would react in real terms. Would they agree to our preferred version? Would they agree to our less preferred version? Would they come up with a new alternative draft? Thus, when the Chinese Foreign Minister Huang Hua said that China would accept the Japanese preferred version at the ministerial meeting, we were so happy that under the table I shook hands firmly with my boss, Mr. Omori.

On 12 August 1978 the Treaty of Peace and Friendship was signed by the two Foreign Ministers: Article II, the anti-hegemony clause, and Article IV, the mitigating clause, read as follows:

> Article II: The Contracting Parties declare that neither of them should seek hegemony in the Asia-Pacific region or in any other region and that each is opposed to efforts by any other country or group of countries to establish such hegemony.
> Article IV: The present Treaty shall not affect the position of either Contracting Party regarding its relations with third countries.[28]

Article IV represented Japan's best efforts to dissociate herself from China's wish to create a united front against Soviet hegemony. The Soviet reaction, however, was tough. Sincere efforts on the Japanese side were not taken into account at all. Towards the end of August the Soviet Union made an official *démarche* in Tokyo to protest against the conclusion of the Treaty of Peace and Friendship. In the summer the first deployment of the Soviet army took place on the disputed 'four islands' (Chapter 7), an action which caused considerable anger on the Japanese side.

One may hypothesize that the formal establishment of diplomatic relations between America and China in January 1979, combined with the conclusion of the Japan-China Treaty of Peace and Friendship, created the impression in the Soviet Union that it was being surrounded by America, China and Japan. This fear of encirclement may have spurred the Soviet Union to adopt such an aggressive policy.[29]

---

[28] http://www.mofa.go.jp/region/asia-paci/china/traty78.html 2002–12–22.
[29] Hosoya, 1993, *op. cit.*, p. 161.

The Senkaku Islands

There was one more issue which had weighed heavily in the process of concluding this Treaty. That was the territorial dispute over the islands of Senkaku.

Let me go back to the history and give a basic account of this issue from the Japanese perspective:

– The Senkaku Islands are a group of eight very small islands situated west of Okinawa. They are located in the border regions of Japan and China.

– After the Meiji Restoration, Japan realized that there were fishery activities around the islands, and in 1895 the Japanese government officially included them as a part of the Okinawa Prefecture. After the San Francisco Peace Treaty the islands were governed by the American administration and were returned to Japan in May 1972 under the Agreement on the reversion of Okinawa.

– In 1968, however, the United Nations ECAFE conducted an exploration and stated that oil reserves could be found around the islands. Just before the reversion of those islands from America to Japan, on 11 June 1971, Taiwan claimed their territorial jurisdiction. On 30 December 1971 China also stated a claim.

– During the period of the resumption of diplomatic relations, China carefully stayed away from this issue. Above all, Japan had no reason to touch this issue, because from the point of view of the Japanese government there was no territorial issue which required resolution between Japan and China.

Against this background, on 12 April 1978, just as the atmosphere was becoming favourable for the resumption of the negotiations on the Treaty of Peace and Friendship between Japan and China, more than 100 Chinese vessels gathered around the islands and 40 of them entered into the territorial waters. Faced with strong protest from Japan, three days later the Chinese government stated that the whole incident was "accidental". All vessels withdrew by 18 April.

Following this incident, when Foreign Minister Sonoda went to Beijing just four months later, the Senkaku Islands had become a very sensitive issue.

> The entire delegation was very nervous. The Senkaku issue was left to the meeting between Deng Xiaoping and Foreign Minister Sonoda. Even if the mitigating clause was incorporated to the total satisfaction of the Japanese delegation in the meeting between the two Foreign Ministers, had Deng Xiaoping said something unacceptable on the territorial issue, the signing of the Treaty would have become extremely difficult.
>
> I remember a great sigh of relief in the Japanese delegation when Deng Xiaoping stated, as was reported after the meeting, that "China will not repeat such an incident". Chinese sources suggest that Deng stated to the Japanese delegation that the handling of this issue could be left to later generations.[30]

However, as we will see below, in the latter part of the 1990's the Senkaku Islands issue was again a source of contention between Japan and China.

4. *Relationships over the 1980's*

The 1980's became an important period of economic and political development for China. At the end of 1978 the Chinese Communist Party adopted a new policy of 'Reform and Opening'. The gist of the new policy was the strengthening of the Chinese economy through the market mechanism and cooperation with outside economies, while preserving strict control by the Communist Party. In the positive climate after the conclusion of the Treaty of Peace and Friendship, Japan welcomed this new economic policy.[31]

Thus economic relations developed fast, at the beginning with ups and downs, followed by a period of steady development. Political relations, however, due to many complex reasons, went through periods of harmony and tension which alternated quite regularly.

---

[30] A. Ishii, K. Shu, Y. Soeya, Lin Xiao Guang, *Nichuu Kokkouseijyouka, Nicchuu Heiwa Yuukoujyouyaku Teiketsu Koushou (Normalization of Japan-China diplomatic relations, Negotiations of Japan-China Peace and Friendship Treaty)*, Iwanami, 2003, p. 180. *See also* Ikei, *op. cit.*, p. 312.

[31] Y. Onishi, *Chuugokuha Dokoni Mukau (Where does China go?)* Chapter 2, I. Kayahara ed., Sousousha, 2001, p. 109.

Economic relations, bumpy at the beginning, and then steady development

In February 1978, six months before the conclusion of the Treaty of Peace and Friendship, a long-term private sector trade agreement was signed. In the course of eight years, from 1978 to 1985, each side committed itself to exporting about $10 billion: from China to Japan crude oil and coal, from Japan to China technology, construction materials and production plants. An economic boom exploded and contracts of $5 billion in total were rapidly agreed upon by August, and another $5 billion was in progress towards the end of the year.

But it still required some time before this newborn economic policy would develop in a stable manner. Thus amidst this economic euphoria, China suddenly reviewed the projects and in February 1979 decided to suspend 22 projects valued at a total of $2.7 billion.

The psychological shocks incurred in the minds of many Japanese businessmen were profound. In order to overcome this shock and sustain economic relations between the two countries, the Japanese government decided to mobilize its powerful instrument of economic cooperation. The emerging trend in China towards a market-oriented, stable, and strong economy shown in the policy of 'Reform and Opening' was in the interest of Japan, not only from an economic but also from a political point of view. A stable and rational China was in the interest of the security and prosperity of the entire Far East region.

In December 1979 Prime Minister Ohira visited China and announced his decision to extend the first package of Official Development Assistance in the form of yen loans to seven projects totalling 330.9 billion yen in the area of port, railroad and hydroelectric power stations for a period between 1979 and 1983. Since this decision could have deep political implications, Ohira made a simultaneous announcement of three principles of ODA to China: 1) coordination with America and Europe, 2) due balance with other Asian countries, particularly ASEAN, 3) no military cooperation. This decision broke the ice and another round of China fever started.[32]

But it still took some time for stable economic development. The Chinese authorities made another review of the projects in gigantic

---

[32] Tanaka, *op. cit.*, pp. 108–113, 133.

plants. In January 1981 a unilateral decision was made to cancel an important part of the contracts on these gigantic plants. The total amount of cancellation reached $3 billion, out of which the Japanese contracts occupied half, $1.6 billion.

Notwithstanding this second wave of shocks, the Japanese government's determination to stabilize the situation both from economic and political considerations stayed very firm. After complex negotiations with the Chinese authorities, a new assistance framework was formulated in December 1981, on the occasion of a ministerial meeting between the two governments.[33]

After the agreement on the new framework had been established, economic relations calmed down and from then on began to develop steadily.

In March 1984 the second yen loan package was announced covering the period 1984–1989 to implement in total 16 projects worth 470 billion yen, approximately in the same area of port, railroad, hydro power station and communications contained in the first package.[34]

In August 1988 the third yen loan package to cover the period 1990–1995, 42 projects and 810 billion yen was announced. It had increased considerably both in the number of projects as well as in the overall amount of yen loans. Regional development, agriculture and chemical plant were added as an object of cooperation.[35]

In 1983 the amount of total trade reached almost $10 billion. It expanded to $19.3 billion in 1988 and reached $22.3 billion in 1991.[36]

Japan's yearly Foreign Direct Investment (FDI) to China saw a sharp increase from 1984 to a level over $100 million and gradually increased since then.[37]

Political relations, harmonious periods and continued tensions

While economic relations became stabilized, political relations continued to float with a regular alternating of periods of ebb and tide

---

[33] Ibid., pp. 113–115.
[34] Ibid., pp. 133, 171.
[35] Ibid., p. 171.
[36] JETRO figures (http://www.jetro.go.jp/ec/j/trade/excel/40w02.xls 2003–07–19).
[37] Japan's yearly FDI to China in million dollars from 1984 to 1991 was 114, 100, 226, 1,226, 296, 438, 349, 579 (JETRO figures).

or harmony and tension. Four events symbolize the friendly relations in the 1980's: Zhao Ziyang's visit in '82, Hu Yaobang's visit
in '83, Nakasone's visit in '86, and Takeshita's visit in '88. Four
issues could be singled out as causing serious tensions during the
1980's: textbooks, the Yasukuni Shrine, Koukaryou (a Taiwan related
issue) and the Tiananmen Square incident.

Some background analysis may be useful in relation to issues
related to the 'recognition of history (*rekishi ninshiki*)', i.e. textbooks
and Yasukuni. It is my conviction that amongst the Japanese people a general feeling of remorse and apology grew as to what had
been committed in Asia. At the same time there remained some
undeniable feeling that not all that Japan did before the war was
wrong, that many of the Japanese who died during the war sacrificed
their lives for the country and that their honour had to be preserved.
The key question of what was wrong and what was right remains
unanswered to this day, and the 1980's probably added more confusion than resolution.

Some politicians naively expressed their own thinking about Japanese
righteousness, and through strong objection from neighbouring countries, emotional media reports in and outside Japan, their statements
soon became political scandals and these politicians often had to
resign from their official posts. If they knew what fate awaited them
in making these statements, why would responsible and able politicians, some of whom I know well, make them in the first place?

The role of the Ministry of Foreign Affairs tended to emphasize
conveying the feelings and messages from abroad. MOFA was sometimes criticized for failing to accurately present the feeling of the
Japanese people to those countries which were objecting. But what
kind of message could MOFA deliver when there was no real consensus in the nation to answer the question of what was wrong and
what was right?

On the other hand, there are now increasingly analysts in Japan
who argue that China was raising tension with Japan for its own
'motives'. These 'motives' varied from "turning the attention of the
population away from internal economic difficulty or from domestic
political tension" to "making pre-emptive propaganda against Japan
to strengthen China's position in international politics". But these
analyses have thus far found little resonance in the international
community.

(1) Zhao Ziyang's visit to Japan in the spring of 1982
In the spring of 1982 Prime Minister Zhao Ziyang visited Japan and
proposed that the relations of the two countries should be governed
by three principles: 'peace and friendship', which had been applied
to the political relations of the past ten years, 'equality and mutual
benefit', which had been applied to the economic relations of the
past ten years, and 'long-term stability' to be applied to the future
relations. Political analysts in Japan maintained that the third principle implied an important Chinese message, namely that Japan
should not waver from her friendly policy toward China, when a
slight cooling-off in Chinese-American relations or a warming up of
Soviet-Chinese relations were taking place.[38]

(2) The textbook issue in the summer of 1982
The harmonious environment created by Zhao Ziyang's visit to Japan
was swept away from July to September 1982 by the 'textbook issue'.
China and South Korea filed a strong protest against the content of
some textbooks which were under review by the Japanese authorities before their publication. There are at least three aspects to consider in this issue:
(a) The first aspect is the question of the 'recognition of history
(rekishi ninshiki)'. Whenever polemics on textbooks have arisen, there
have always been conflicting views in Japan about its own views on
history.
China's view is that Japan was guilty of aggression in China; the
aggression caused tremendous suffering; Japan should recognize these
historical facts; and should apologize for these wrongdoings and never
repeat them.
In Japan, the general feeling of remorse and apology, which the
Japanese people came to share, had been expressed in Foreign
Minister Shiina's statement addressed to South Korea in 1965 and
in the preamble of the Japan-China Joint Communiqué of 1972. But
the unanswered question of what was wrong and what was right is
still a painful wound. Even after the 1995 Murayama Statement

---

[38] General Secretary Brezhnev made a warm speech to China in Tashkent in
1982. American arms sales to Taiwan made US-China relations sour. Tanaka, *op. cit.*,
pp. 115–120.

which clearly determined the government position (Chapter 5) and the 1997 Supreme Court ruling in the Ienaga lawsuit,[39] this issue continues to be debated. Textbook publications cause inevitable controversy in Japan's sincere search for national and international consensus.

(b) Secondly, the Japanese system of textbook approval has added to the confusion. In Japan, as in many democratic countries, textbooks are, in principle, prepared by independent scholars. Then each completed version is reviewed and screened by a responsible council under the Ministry of Education. This review is done based on criteria, which were established beforehand. Finally, each school has the right to choose a textbook from those screened by the council.

The Japanese government standpoint was that the criteria for the review should be sufficiently flexible so as to allow adequate freedom of expression to independent scholars. But this view was attacked from various corners. Saburo Ienaga argued for a long time that any screening was a disguised form of censorship and therefore unconstitutional.[40]

On the other hand, from the standpoint of a criticizing country, if inadequate textbooks were being produced, then the criteria on the basis of which the government had given its approval must have been wrong. Asian countries have long maintained that the Japanese government must act responsibly, banning textbooks which distort history.

(c) Against this background, conflicting views on history have been expressed in conjunction with concrete descriptions of historical facts and analysis, as incorporated in 'problematic' textbooks. In June 1982 a Japanese newspaper reported that in some of the newly prepared textbooks the word 'advance' was used instead of 'aggression', in describing Japanese military activities in China. Another report indicated that these new textbooks described the Nanjing Massacre in terms which weakened Japan's responsibility for the massacre. These

---

[39] A lawsuit lodged by Ienaga Saburo, a professor of history, against the government of Japan in 1965 lasted for 32 years. It challenged the State that the true description of history was obstructed in the postwar publication of textbooks. The 1997 Supreme Court ruling opened a way for the inclusion of some of the descriptions Ienaga insisted be incorporated in his textbook.

[40] In the 1997 Supreme Court ruling the unconstitutionality of the screening system was not accepted.

reports had particularly infuriated China and the Chinese government made stern protests, which were then followed by protests from the South Korean government.

The Japanese government sent several missions to Beijing, gave many explanations, complicated exchanges took place between the two governments and, in essence, Japan accepted China's protests and agreed to introduce necessary changes in due course. A new criterion to pay due attention to the feelings of adjacent countries was introduced as one of the basic principles for textbook review.[41] China accepted the policy announced by the Japanese government and for the moment the heat was off.

(3) *Hu Yaobang's visit to Japan in 1983*

From autumn 1982 onwards, after the commotion surrounding the textbooks issue subsided, Japan and China entered into the next phase of harmonious relations. In November 1983 the General Secretary of the Communist Party Hu Yaobang visited Japan. Prime Minister Nakasone proposed to add a fourth principle, namely, 'mutual trust' to Zhao Ziyang's three guiding principles, which Hu Yaobang gladly accepted. They agreed also to establish a 'wise men' committee for Japan-China friendship toward the 21st century.

Nakasone visited China in March 1984 and inaugurated the 'wise men' committee. He also announced Japan's second yen loan package of 470 billion yen. Thus the period between 1983 and 1984 was sometimes referred to as "the best period in 2000 years of Japan-China relations".[42]

(4) *Nakasone's visit to the Yasukuni Shrine in 1985*

After this period, however, more political tension exploded, this time concerning the issue of the Prime Minister's visit to the Yasukuni Shrine.

The Yasukuni Shrine is one of the key shrines of the traditional Japanese Shinto religion, and is located in the centre of Tokyo. From the Meiji era until 15 August 1945, Yasukuni was the shrine where the spirits of all who fought and died in war for Japan were enshrined.

---

[41] Ikei, *op. cit.*, pp. 317–322. Tanaka, *op. cit.*, pp. 120–125.
[42] Tanaka, *op. cit.*, p. 132.

In this sense, it is similar to the many graveyards and monuments in other countries for soldiers who died in the service of their country.

After the end of World War II, successive Prime Ministers visited the Yasukuni Shrine, without creating any particular political problems.

In 1978 Yasukuni collectively enshrined the spirits of class A war criminals of the IMTFE, who had been sentenced to death or who had died in prison, including Shigenori Togo.

Since then, Prime Ministers continued to visit Yasukuni from time to time, but the key day for the commemoration of those who died during World War II, namely 15 August, was avoided.

It was against this background that Prime Minister Nakasone visited the Yasukuni Shrine on 15 August 1985. His intention was to draw a line in the political controversy surrounding postwar recrimination. His decision was reported widely before and on 15 August.

The Chinese government protested that his action could only be interpreted as legitimizing class A war criminals and so hurt the feelings of many Chinese. The Chinese government's protest was followed by violent student demonstrations, not only at the University in Beijing, but also in many universities throughout China from September to October.

(5) *Nakasone's visit to China in 1986*
But in November 1985, the Japanese government clarified its position and stated that Prime Minister Nakasone's visit to the Yasukuni Shrine did not imply the legitimization of class A war criminals, and that his visit was not made on a structural basis. It hinted that the visit would not be repeated in the following year and the Chinese protest died down. On 15 August 1986, upon reflection on the events of the previous year, Prime Minister Nakasone decided not to visit the Yasukuni Shrine.

Despite the calming of the situation, to this day the issue remains unresolved. Japan surely has the right to mourn those who died for her country. But Japan has failed to to communicate to the neighbouring countries that her mourning does not detract from a genuine sense of apology.

At any rate, in November 1986 Nakasone made a short visit to China and announced a programme to invite 500 Chinese youths over a period of five years. His proposal was well appreciated by the Chinese leadership.

(6) *Koukaryou verdict in 1987 (a Taiwan related issue)*
The relatively harmonious period of 1986 was again interrupted by another political issue, related to a legal dispute concerning ownership of a Chinese dormitory, called Koukaryou.

Koukaryou was a dormitory in Kyoto originally under the control of Kyoto University. After the war it was placed under the ownership of the Republic of China (RC), but was actually controlled by resident Chinese students, some supporting the RC and others the People's Republic of China (PRC).

In this complicated situation the RC officially filed a case with a Japanese court to claim ownership. The first verdict in 1977 was in favour of the PRC but the second and the third were all in favour of the RC. The Osaka district high court tribunal in February 1987 also brought in a verdict in support of the RC's ownership.

The Chinese government took this verdict very seriously. A series of criticisms in diplomatic channels as well as through the media continued until June. On this issue, however, the Japanese government explained, with patience, that within the democratic system of the division of responsibility between the judiciary, the legislature and the executive, the government had no real room for action.

The aftermath of this debate resulted in a statement made by a high-level Japanese Foreign Ministry official that even Deng Xiaoping, who did not understand the essence of the matter, has become 'a figure above the clouds'. The statement was met with indignation in the Chinese leadership. The Japanese leadership did not sympathize either. The Vice-Minister for Foreign Affairs Kensuke Yanagiya had to make an official apology, which was followed by his resignation at the end of June. Though the essential aspect of the democratic structure in Japan was blurred amidst this row on 'a figure above the clouds' Japan took a clear and determined position on this issue. Since then this issue has been kept outside the realm of political attention.

(7) *Takeshita's visit to China in 1988*
1988 became the 10th commemorative year of the signing of the Treaty of Peace and Friendship. Prime Minister Noboru Takeshita visited China in August and announced Japan's intention to extend the third package of yen loan projects of 810 billion yen.

(8) *Tiananmen Square incident in 1989*

After a relative lull in the Japan-China bilateral relations, 1989 saw real turmoil in the postwar Chinese domestic situation. After Hu Yaobang died in April a wave of demonstrations exploded, most notably in Beijing, led by students who were frustrated at the dragging economy and lingering political reform. The Chinese leadership suppressed it through the use of military force at Tiananmen Square on the morning of 6 June 1989.

Vivid television images of China's actions gave rise to sharp global criticism of this blatant suppression of freedom. Fierce debates took place at the G7 Summit in Paris in July 1989 to send a clear message to China, that such actions were not acceptable. The Japanese delegation headed by Prime Minister Sosuke Uno maintained that, while it was indispensable to state that things were not acceptable for the G7, it was also essential to send a message to China that the G7 did not intend to isolate China. As a result of Japan's efforts, an expression was included in the Communiqué that "China should create conditions which enable them to avoid isolation".[43]

Japan's position was not based on a disregard of human rights. Rather it was based on Japan's experience in dealing with China and her conviction that the continuation of the 'Reform and Opening' policy and the move toward democracy, however slow it might be, would be conducive to the interests of China and the countries in the Asia-Pacific region. To achieve this objective, avoiding too much pressure and instead using persuasion toward engagement should bear greater fruits. This was the prevailing thought amongst my colleagues with whom I spoke at the time.[44]

5. *Relationships from the 1990's onwards*

The Tiananmen Square incident was certainly a serious blow to the Chinese leadership. The image of China suppressing human rights was not easily erased from the minds of the democratic Western countries.

---

[43] Tanaka, *op. cit.*, p. 178.

[44] Japan continued to argue for stronger economic ties and increased engagement with China at the Houston Summit in 1990. This is well described in Wolf Mendl, *Japan's Asia policy*, Routledge, 1995, pp. 83–84.

But at the same time, from the 1980's to the 1990's the world attention was directed to China's outstanding economic success. With its massive population of 1,266 million[45] China has developed enormously economically since the adoption of the 'Reform and Opening' policy in 1978. The annual GDP growth rate reached around 10% through the 80's and in the 90's it even reached the apex of 14.1% in 1992 and thence onwards has remained at a level of around 7–8%.[46] China is said to have become the world market and world factory.[47]

The post-Cold War political environment in the 1990's first brought about some zigzags in Chinese foreign policy, but it has gradually affected China's policy toward a greater harmonization, in particular with the countries in East Asia. Politically friendly relations in East Asia were also conducive to China's economic interests.

Japan also has gone into a search for more self-assertive but harmonized relations with China. This was a very difficult process, but it proceeded with a sense of direction.

Toward the beginning of the 21st century the image of admiration and awe inspired by China's economic success and political power increased. But these feelings were also accompanied with a greater expectation for the emergence of a harmonized China in East Asia.

Relative harmony during the first half of the 1990's

The first half of the 1990's can be summarized as a period of relative harmony.

For China it was a period of harmonization with outside countries after the bloodshed at Tiananmen Square. It was also a period when economic reconstruction became so important to them that close Japanese cooperation was viewed as useful.

For Japan the stable development of relations with China had already been an important objective of its foreign policy. It was conducive to Japan's own economic development and to the stability of the Far Eastern region. Furthermore, it was a period in the last

---

[45] At the end of 2000. Shen Caibin, *The China Shock (in Japanese)*, Nihon Nouritsukyoukai Manejimento Centre, 2002, p. 19.
[46] Onishi, *op. cit.*, p. 109.
[47] Shen Caibin, *op. cit.*, pp. 16–27.

phase of the trade conflicts with America, 'the defeat' of the Gulf War and serious, but bumpy efforts to improve relations with Russia. From all these perspectives, a stable development in the relations with China was much desired.

In August 1991 Prime Minister Kaifu was the first G7 leader to visit China after the Tiananmen Square incident. He emphasized the importance of the Japan-China relationship in the context of global relations.

In October 1992 the Emperor Akihito and Empress Michiko visited China for the first time since World War II. In Japan, huge attention was focussed on the visit and the words the Emperor would pronounce on the war issue. The Emperor expressed his deep sorrow for the tremendous suffering which Japan had inflicted on the Chinese people and Japanese people's deep remorse that such a war had ever happened.[48] To the relief of all who spent so much energy in implementing this visit, both sides took it as a historic event towards the reconciliation of the two countries.

In March 1994 the newly elected Prime Minister from the (non-LDP) Japan New Party, Morihiro Hosokawa, visited China and spoke of "future-oriented and matured relations".

In May 1995 Prime Minister Murayama visited China and underlined two aspects of the relationship: 'future-oriented relations towards the 21st century' and 'relations aiming to peace and prosperity for the Asia-Pacific region and the world'.

The amount of total trade increased steadily and rapidly. In five years, from 1992 to 1996, it doubled from around $30 billion to $60 billion.[49] By this time Japan had become the No. 1 trade partner for China and China was the No. 2 trade partner for Japan, after America.

As if to symbolize this harmonious development, the 'first three years' of the fourth round of yen loan assistance was announced in 1994 for the period of 1996 to 1998 of an amount of 580 billion yen for 40 projects.

---

[48] W. Mendel, *op. cit.*, p. 91.

[49] The yearly total trade between Japan and China from 1992 to 1996 in $billion was 28.9, 37.8, 46.2, 57.9, 62.4 (from JETRO figures: http://www.jetro.go.jp/ec/j/trade/excel/40w02.xls 2003–07–19).

Expanding economic relations with new issues from the latter half of the 1990's

Japanese economic assistance continued and in 1998 Japan announced the 'latter two years' of the fourth round of yen loan assistance for the period of 1999 to 2000, amounting to 390 billion yen for 28 projects. More emphasis was given to environment, agriculture, and the development of the inner part of the continent.

During the latter half of the 1990's, the total amount of trade continued to rise constantly year by year, so that from $60 billion in 1997 it reached $100 billion in 2002.[50] The fact that Japan was the No. 1 trade partner for China and that China was the No. 2 partner for Japan seemed to be firmly grounded.[51]

In addition, China became a central point of investment for Japanese companies. A seemingly unlimited number of cheap and skilled labourers encouraged many Japanese companies to shift their production bases from Japan to China. Japanese direct investment in China kept a steady record of 1 to 2 billion dollars annually from 1992 to 2001.[52] Japanese electric and electronic factories in China increased sixfold from 42 companies in 1992 to 264 companies in 1999.[53] This new trend, however, threatened to increase unemployment in Japan. Renewed economic relations based on interdependence have since become a major topic for discussion.

Commensurate with her economic strength and backed by Japan's strong encouragement, China joined the WTO in November 2001 (Chapter 11).

In April 2002, as a result of participation in the WTO, when Japan introduced safeguard measures on relatively small-scale agricultural products such as Welsh onions and *shiitake* mushrooms, China immediately reacted in June by introducing retaliatory custom duties on Japanese automobiles, mobile telephones and air-conditioning coolers. After serious negotiations, the two governments agreed in

---

[50] The yearly total trade between Japan and China from 1997 to 2002 in $billion was 63.8, 56.9, 66.2, 85.7, 89.1, 101.5 (Ibid.).

[51] In fact, in 2002 China's export to Japan, $61.7 billion, exceeded US export to Japan, $57.6 billion. (JETRO figures, Ibid.)

[52] The yearly direct investment figure to China from 1992 to 2001 in $billion was 1.0, 1.6, 2.5, 4.4, 2.5, 1.9, 1.0, 0.7, 0.9, 1.4 (JETRO figures, www.jetro.go.jp/ec/ j/trade/ FDI to, country data 2003–08–04).

[53] Shen Caibin, *op. cit.*, p. 24.

December to resolve the issues through consultation, but clearly a new type of economic relations which needed careful analysis had emerged.[54]

Another issue which came under severe scrutiny in Japan was the issue of ODA to China. Against the background of the souring domestic economic situation, strong criticism emerged from the Diet, media and the people. In the media the expression 'hate Chinese' rose.[55] They asked:

– Why should Japan aid China when it is enjoying a tremendous economic boom and seems to be performing much better than Japan?
– Why should Japan aid China when China itself is engaged in substantial aid activities to poorer developing countries?
– Why should Japan aid China when Chinese 'militaristic tendencies' are clear and go directly against the Japanese aid philosophy (Chapter 10)?
– Why should Japan continue to aid China when it has wrongly been criticized for its misrepresentation of history?
– Why should Japan, in particular, pour so much money into railroads, ports, and other infra-structure, that obviously strengthen China's economic power, possibly to the detriment of Japanese economic development?

In 2000, a special advisory committee for MOFA chaired by the well-respected economist I. Miyazaki was established and published a report in December.

In October 2001 the Japanese government adopted a new ODA programme for China, based on the recommendations of the Miyazaki Advisory Committee. Japan decided to abolish the system of multiyear rounds of assistance, leave the gigantic infrastructure construction on the coastal area in the hands of China itself and to shift the emphasis of assistance to such projects as the environment, inner-continental development, and the enhancement of a market economy.

Political relations with greater tension from the latter part of the 1990's

(1) The first tension emerged surrounding the issue of the 'recognition of history'. "The goodwill that had developed during the Imperial

---

[54] Ibid.
[55] *Kenchuu* was the wording for that.

visit did not last for three years. In 1995 a huge campaign began all over China displaying pictures of the Nanjing Massacre in all primary schools. Even pro-Chinese MOFA officials were in a desperate mood."[56]

But the real tension over China was revealed in relation to another hot point in the Far East, the Taiwan Strait. From July to August 1995 and March 1996 China conducted a series of missile launching exercises over the Taiwan Strait. It was said that these exercises were performed because of China's increased anxiety over the internal situation in Taiwan. A presidential election was due in March 1996, where Lee Deng-hui's[57] victory was said to be sure. China probably wanted to state, through these missile launching exercises, its determination to prevent Taiwan's independence, regardless of the outcome of the election.

America reacted in March 1996 by sending two aircraft carriers to the Taiwan Strait. That was probably a gesture to show that America would not allow the military unification of Taiwan by China.

It was probably a display of force by each side to underline their respective policies over Taiwan; so much so that the situation was, though threatening, under control.[58]

But Taiwan's process toward democratization, its strategic importance for Japan, the affirmation of its national identity manifested by Lee Deng-hui and then by Chen Shui-bian and Taiwanese praise of Japanese colonial governance increasingly found echoes among some Japanese politicians and intellectuals, whose views were often combined with strong anti-Chinese feelings.

China's missile launching exercises were accompanied by nuclear tests in May, August and September 1995 and July 1996.

Against this background of mounting criticism of China's 'militaristic' tendencies, in July 1996 several right-wing Japanese organizations went ashore on the Senkaku Islands and constructed a lighthouse. The Chinese, in particular from Hong Kong and Taiwan, waged strong anti-Japanese demonstrations, and vessels from those areas exerted pressure on the shores of the islands. Japanese Maritime

---

[56] Y. Funabashi, in "How to end the issue of war responsibility", *Chuuoukouron*, Feb. 2003, p. 59.

[57] A Taiwan born leader of the Nationalist Party in Taiwan.

[58] Iokibe, *op. cit.*, pp. 241–243.

Agency vessels in the area had great difficulty in maintaining order without causing physical collision.

Finally Ryutaro Hashimoto, who became Prime Minister at the beginning of 1996, visited the Yasukuni Shrine on his birthday on 29 July, as the first Prime Minister to do so since Nakasone's visit on 15 August 1985. China reacted with strong indignation.

(2) Towards the latter half of 1996, the tension began to ease slightly. The Chinese missile launching exercises were terminated after America's decisive move to dispatch their aircraft carriers; the worst case scenario, a physical collision at the Senkaku Islands was avoided; at the end of July China announced a moratorium on its nuclear testing and in September the Comprehensive Test Ban Treaty (CTBT) was signed.

It is also interesting to note that after July 1996 China's policy on regional security cooperation became much more positive than before (Chapter 6).

Following this development to ease the tension in the latter half of 1996, 1997 became a year of the thawing of the relationship. For Japan, a series of important bilateral dialogues took place in the Asia-Pacific region, including China.

In March Japan announced the resumption of its Grant Assistance to China, which it had suspended in protest against China's nuclear testing.

In July, Hashimoto, given the reaction in 1996 from neighbouring Asian countries, decided against another visit to the Yasukuni Shrine on the day of his birthday.[59]

In September Hashimoto visited China, had substantial talks with the Chinese leadership and visited Southern Manchuria as the first postwar Prime Minister. It was another symbolic step towards reconciliation.

From 25–30 November 1998, Jiang Zemin visited Japan, the first Chinese Head of State after World War II to do so. A Joint Declaration entitled 'Building a Partnership of Friendship and Cooperation for Peace and Development' was adopted on this occasion.

---

[59] Families of the deceased and the political supporters of the PM's visit to Yasukuni, are angered at Hashimoto to this day, but relations with China calmed down.

This document is said to be the third key document in the relationship, after the 1972 Joint Communiqué and the 1978 Peace and Friendship Treaty. In terms of its approach to the past it contained the following delicate passages, which reflected the continuing tension between the two countries:

> The Japanese side observes the 1972 Joint Communiqué of the Government of Japan and the Government of the People's Republic of China and the 15 August 1995 Statement by former Prime Minister Tomiichi Murayama. The Japanese side is keenly conscious of the responsibility for the serious distress and damage that Japan caused to the Chinese people through its aggression against China during a certain period in the past and expressed deep remorse for this.
>
> The Chinese side hopes that the Japanese side will learn lessons from the history and adhere to the path of peace and development.
>
> Based on this, both sides will develop long-standing relations of friendship.[60]

We see here a clear recognition on the Chinese side that they are still not happy about Japan's approach to the past. In fact, during his visit to Japan, Jiang Zemin quite straightforwardly stated this point in many instances.

We also see that, while confirming Japan's observance of the Murayama Statement of 1995 (Chapter 5), the Japanese side carefully omitted the key wording of 'heartfelt apology' in the Japanese statement. In fact, a part of Japanese public opinion became frustrated by Jiang Zemin's blunt approach and applauded Prime Minister Obuchi's toughness shown in the language of the Communiqué.

Thus the visit proved to be a mixture of deep underlying tension regarding the past and a positive outlook embodied in the Declaration regarding future-oriented relations between the two countries. A Joint Press Statement was announced, based on the Declaration, covering 33 items for cooperation, such as the construction of a high-speed railway between Beijing and Shanghai, the preservation of cultural heritages in the Silk Road area, human rights, non-proliferation, and exchanges on security and police activities.

Jiang Zemin's visit was an important visit, with some complexity, but not without a forward-looking orientation. In July 1999 Prime Minister Obuchi visited China and discussed the concrete implementation of the 33 items for cooperation.

---

[60] Hook, Gilson, Hughes, Dobson, *op. cit.*, p. 488.

(3) In 2000 new items of friction appeared. From the spring to summer, Chinese maritime investigation vessels appeared frequently in the Japanese Exclusive Economic Zone without prior consent from the Japanese authorities. In May and July, Chinese navy vessels were said to have joined in these maritime investigation activities around Japan. The Japanese government strongly protested and an agreement was reached in principle in August 2000 to create a mechanism of prior notification.

The Chinese Prime Minister Zhu Rongi visited Japan in October and the two sides further agreed on the enhancement of the security dialogue and defence exchanges such as port visits. The mechanism of prior notification on maritime investigation was agreed upon by both sides in February 2001.

(4) Thus when Prime Minister Junichiro Koizumi came to power in April 2001, overall relations between Japan and China stood on a seemingly quiet, but in reality, a very precarious ground. In fact, two underlying difficulties re-emerged: textbooks and Yasukuni.

Already at the beginning of 2001 it became known through the media that one company called *Fusousha* was preparing a textbook attempting to describe history more 'objectively' and avoid descriptions where Japan's prewar activities were portrayed 'too apologetically'. Before any conclusion was drawn by the Council under the Ministry of Education, this textbook was already under the severe scrutiny of the media and adjacent countries.

On 3 April, after substantial revision of the text in 137 places based on comments by the council, the textbook was approved.

In May, China and South Korea made their démarche with requests to introduce further changes. In July the Japanese government replied to the Chinese government that eight items which they requested could not be subjected to changes. The Chinese government requested once again that "Japan should take effective measures and resolve the issue in an appropriate manner."[61]

At this time another issue emerged to attract political attention, and the textbook issue was put aside without resolution. The issue was the question of Prime Minister Koizumi's visit to the Yasukuni Shrine on 15 August.

---

[61] *Gaikou Seisho (Diplomatic Bluebook) 2002*, Chapter 1>5> (2) (http://www.mofa.go.jp/mofaj/gaiko/bluebook/2002/gaikou/html 2002–10–10).

During the campaign to elect the new Prime Minister, Koizumi repeatedly made it clear that to pray for the souls of those who died for their country in Yasukuni on 15 August is an action which a Japanese Prime Minister must not avoid.

However, after being elected Prime Minister in April, from May to August, he faced stern warnings from China and Korea as well as advice from within the country. He gradually changed his initial position and finally visited the Yasukuni Shrine on 13 August, two days before the commemorative day of 15 August.

China expressed "strong dissatisfaction and indignation", while taking note that Prime Minister Koizumi had chosen a date other than 15 August. On 15 August some demonstrations took place in China to protest against Koizumi's visit to Yasukuni, but it did not develop into an uncontrollable situation.

Prime Minister Koizumi visited China in October. His meeting with the Chinese leadership saved the relations from plunging into further tension. Jiang Zemin stated that "There are good periods and bad periods in Japan-China relations, and when relations are not good the textbooks and Yasukuni issues rise to the surface."[62]

Koizumi visited the Yasukuni Shrine again in April 2002 and January 2003. China and South Korea reacted angrily.

This issue is revisited in the Korean context in the next Chapter.

6. *Ways ahead*

In November 2002 the Communist Party introduced a major generational change in its leadership under the newly elected General Secretary Hu Jintao. The Party is said to represent more clearly the interests of private enterprises and the capitalists.

Problems may be numerous, ranging from corruption, gaps between the 'haves' and 'have-nots', gaps between the prosperous sea coast and the poor inner continent, growing military power, human rights and so on. But looking ahead to the initial decades of the 21st century, there is no doubt that the impact of China's role, economically, politically and militarily in the Northeast and Asia-Pacific region would become greater.

---

[62] www.mofa.go.jp/mofaj/kaidan/s_koi/china0110/gh.html, 2002-10-08.

In 2003 China moved further toward a more harmonized approach with its neighbouring countries, particularly in Southeast Asia (Chapter 6).

In Japan-China relations, 2002 marked the 30th year of the establishment of diplomatic relations between the PRC and Japan. Of great significance is that the exchange of people, which did not amount to even 10,000 in 1972, has now reached around two million.[63] Economic relations are growing unequivocally as stated above. Even on the the difficult issue of the 'recognition of history', an interesting article appeared in one of the central bimonthly journals in China at the end of 2002, criticizing China's policy toward Japan for its rigidity and lack of objectivity.[64]

And yet, issues related to the 'recognition of history' are far from being resolved. There were several incidents which added frictions in the bilateral relationship in 2003: in June Chinese activists approached the Senkaku Island; in August the remainder of the chemical weapons left by the former Japanese army contaminated local inhabitants, including one death, in Northeast China; in September Japanese businessmen were engaged in an organized mass prostitution in the Southeast coastal region and received wide newspaper coverage.

Prime Minister Koizumi's insistence on continuing his visit to the Yasuki Shrine might be interpreted as Japan's endeavour to adopt a more self-assertive policy *vis-à-vis* her neighbouring Asian countries. The post-Cold War political environment perhaps unleashed energy in Japan toward that direction. But Japan has not yet found the discourse of reconciliation and harmonization with these neighbouring Asian countries in implementing this policy of greater self-assertiveness.

Thus the nature of the Japan-China relations can be summarized as 'full of potential'. It remains in the wisdom, courage, and endeavours of those people in both sides in implementing both self-assertive but harmonized policies each other.

---

[63] *Asahi Shinbun*, 29 September 2002.

[64] Ma Licheng, 'New thinking in China-Japan Relations', in *Strategy and Control*, translated and published in Chuuoukouron, March 2003, pp. 164–180. Another article appeared in 2003 in *Strategy and Control*, by Shi Yin-Hong, entitled 'China-Japan Rapprochement and Diplomatic Revolution'.

CHAPTER FIVE

KOREA: SOUTH KOREAN RELATIONS DEVELOP WITH COMPLEXITY, WILL NORTH KOREAN RELATIONS START?

1. *Establishment of diplomatic relations with South Korea*

Fourteen years of negotiations

Diplomatic relations between Japan and South Korea were established in 1965—20 years after the Pacific War ended. This fact alone suggests the complexity of Japan-Korea relations. Although Korea is geographically the closest country to Japan, historically relations with Korea have been amongst the most complex and sensitive.

The first factor which complicated the path towards normalization was the division of Korea into North and South Korea after Japan's capitulation in 1945. Historically, Korea had been a part of Imperial Japan since 1910. In 1943 the Cairo Declaration stated that "in due course Korea shall become free and independent."[1] After WW II, Korea was occupied by the Soviet Union in the north to the 38th parallel and by the USA in the south.

That was the beginning of the tragedy of the division of Korea, as a result of which the Soviet Union recognized the North in October 1948 and the United States the South in January 1949. In June 1950 war broke out in Korea (Chapter 12). Immediately after the San Francisco Peace Conference in September 1951, to which neither North nor South Korea (who were then at war) was invited, preliminary negotiations started in Tokyo to establish diplomatic relations between Japan and South Korea. It was America's intention that the negotiations be successfully concluded by the spring of 1952, before the San Francisco Peace Treaty came into force.

And yet, it took another 14 years, seven rounds of negotiations and some 1500 official meetings to reach the final agreement in

---

[1] MOFA, *op. cit.*, p. 1824.

1965! The fundamental reason for this lengthy process was 36 years of Japanese occupation of Korea, from 1910 to 1945, and the emotion and sense of distrust which had built up in Korea against Japan. The sensitivity in the relationship is illustrated by the following incident. One of the Japanese chief negotiators made the statement that "there had been some positive aspects in the Japanese governance of Korea".[2] This remark brought the negotiations to a halt for almost five years, from 1953 to 1958.

It is probably fair to observe that another reason which made the whole process so difficult was some of the policy introduced from the Korean side. For example, fisheries became a contentious issue. In 1952 President Rhee Syng-Man of South Korea unilaterally established an exclusive fishery zone on the high seas adjacent to South Korean territorial waters, prohibiting Japanese fishermen from engaging in any fishing operations. This angered Japanese fishermen, who continued fishing inside what came to be known as the 'Rhee Syng-Man Line' in Japanese terminology and the 'Peace Line' in Korean terminology. Japanese vessels were regularly detained by the Korean authorities and tension naturally heightened.

From the end of the 1950's to the beginning of the 1960's the South Korean internal political situation experienced a turning point; waves of student demonstrations against the autocratic regime of Rhee Syng-Man succeeded in ousting the President in April 1960; his successors' government was ousted by a military coup in May 1961; the chief general who led the coup, Park Chung-Hee, was elected as President in October 1963 and he created a civil government.

Under the leadership of President Park and Prime Minister Eisaku Sato, who assumed the post in November 1964, the two governments finally decided to concentrate their efforts on overcoming the heavy burden of the past. Thus, on 22 June 1965 in Tokyo, a comprehensive agreement on all issues was achieved and the relevant treaties and agreements were signed. Some issues had a breakthrough a few years before the final agreement in 1965, but waited for the comprehensive agreement to be reached. Let us have a quick review of the five major issues of the negotiations.

---

[2] Ikei., *op. cit.*, p. 278. Sakamoto, *op. cit.*, p. 94.

Five major issues of the negotiations

(1) *Treaty on Basic Relations between Japan and the Republic of Korea*
The first issue was how to reach a moral, legal and political reconciliation with the past, as well as how to reconcile the Cold War
reality of the division between the North and the South. The breakthrough was made at literally the last moment of the negotiations
in 1965.

The key statement of apology was expressed by Foreign Minister
Etsusaburo Shiina on 17 February upon his arrival in Seoul:

> It was truly regrettable that an unfortunate period existed within the
> long history of Japan-Korea relations and I express deep remorse.[3]

Together with the Japan-China Joint Communiqué of 1972, the
expression of 'deep remorse' became the key expression of Japan's
apology for more than a quarter of a century. An official expression
of remorse was widely reported in Korea and contributed to creating a positive environment for the negotiations.[4]

Another issue from the past caused considerable difficulty. That
was related to the treaties which Japan and Korea had concluded
before the annexation of 1910. The Korean position was that these
treaties were not valid from the time of their conclusion, whereas
the Japanese position was that, however much the Korean side
resented these treaties, they were lawful and were concluded in accordance with the then existing international law. The two sides found a
compromise in the language of Article II of the Treaty on Basic
Relations that all past treaties before 1910 "are already null and void".[5]

Regarding the reconciliation with Cold War reality, Japan wanted
to allow for a possible development of relations with North Korea
in the future and therefore wanted to limit the relations now being
established to the area where South Korea had real governance.
However, it was essential to South Korea that the wording of the
treaty show that it established diplomatic relations on behalf of Korea
as a whole. Both sides agreed to resolve the issue by citing in Article
III of the Treaty on Basic Relations, a UN resolution that "the
Government of the Republic of Korea is the only lawful Government

---

[3] Ikei, *op. cit.*, p. 282.
[4] Tadokoro, *op. cit.*, p. 127.
[5] MOFA, *op. cit.*, p. 54.

in Korea as specified in the Resolution 195(III) of the UN General Assembly."[6]

This is another example of the art of diplomacy: each side interpreted this article in its own way and ultimately both sides succeeded in achieving a common objective, which was to establish diplomatic relations.

(2) *Agreement between Japan and the Republic of Korea concerning the Settlement of Problems in regard to Property and Claims and Economic Cooperation*

The second issue was related to the question of reparations. Japan rejected South Korea's strong demand for reparations, arguing that Japan and Korea had not been at war as they had constituted a single country. Japan did, however, renounce all her claims against Japanese property left in Korea. A significant breakthrough was achieved after the military coup led by Park Chung-Hee in 1961. A 'special arrangement' to be applied to Korea as an area previously occupied by Japan, based on the San Francisco Peace Treaty Article 4 (a), could not be agreed because of legal, political and pragmatic reasons. The final form of the agreement was that Japan would pay $0.8 billion through economic cooperation: $0.3b of grant assistance from the government, $0.2b in low interest loans from the government, and $0.3b in private sector loans.

(3) *Agreement between Japan and the Republic of Korea concerning Fisheries*

The third issue was the conclusion of the Agreement on Fisheries. Some rapprochement was made during the negotiations of the early 60's, but the breakthrough came in the course of 1965. The basic principle was that outside the 12 nautical mile zone, areas of joint control would be established with respective jurisdiction implemented by the country to which each ship belonged. Thus the 'Rhee Syng-Man Line' ceased to exist.

---

[6] The UN Resolution 195 (III) 2 reads as follows: "The General Assembly declares that there has been established a lawful government (the Government of the ROK) having effective control and jurisdiction over that part of Korea where the Temporary Commission was able to observe and consult and in which the great majority of the people of all Korea reside; that this Government is based on election which were valid expression of the free will of the electorate of the part of Korea and which were observed by the Temporary Commission; and that this is the only such Government in Korea". (Ibid., p. 60).

(4) *Agreement between Japan and the Republic of Korea concerning the Legal Status and Treatment of the People of the Republic of Korea Residing in Japan*

The fourth issue was the status of Koreans resident in Japan. When the war ended in 1945 there were about two million Koreans resident in Japan. A torrent of 'home returns' began, but when war broke out in the peninsula in 1950, around 600 thousand Koreans decided to remain in Japan. What would be the legal and substantive status of these Koreans? The issue was real and serious. A breakthrough agreement was made in March 1965 to give permanent right of residence to all Koreans who were living in Japan in August 1945 and to any children born in Japan up until five years after the 1965 Agreement entered into force. The fate of those excluded by this definition would be a subject for future negotiation.

(5) *Exchange of Notes concerning the Resolution of Conflict between Japan and the Republic of Korea*

Then, last but not least there was the territorial issue regarding Takeshima, as we call it in Japan, and Dokdo as it is called in Korea. That was a difficult issue, where no clear answer has yet been found.

Takeshima is located to the northwest of the Shimane Prefecture, between Japan and Korea. It consists of two small islands and is surrounded by rocks.

(a) The way this issue is perceived in Japan is as follows:

– For centuries, Takeshima—has been under the effective governance of Japan, as many documents show. For example, one document shows that in the middle of the 17th century the Tokugawa Shogunate allowed two families of the Tottori clan to govern Takeshima.

– On the other hand, Korea maintained sovereignty over another island named 'Ullungdo' in Korean or 'Utsuryoto' in Japanese (or 'Dagelet'), located between Korea and Takeshima.

– In fact, from 1438 to 1883 Korea conducted an 'empty island policy' with regard to Ullungdo.

– After Korea began its 'empty island policy' Japanese nationals began to commute to Ullungdo through Takeshima. In 1618 the Tokugawa Shogunate gave special licenses to Japanese nationals allowing them to travel to Ullungdo. Japanese fishermen continued to travel to Ullungdo through Takeshima and engaged in fishing around Takeshima as well.

— In 1696 the Tokugawa Shogunate decided to withdraw from Ullungdo, but not from Takeshima.

— In 1905 Takeshima became officially incorporated as part of the Shimane Prefecture.

(b) Korea maintained that Japanese claims to Takeshima were unfounded:

— There was sufficient documentation to show that not only Ullungdo but also Takeshima was under effective reign of the Korean dynasty from ancient times.

— In 1696 a Korean national hero forced Japan out of both Ullungdo and Takeshima.

— Japan's incorporation of Takeshima in 1905 could not be accepted.

— Takeshima therefore was a part of the territories Japan had "taken by violence and greed" as defined by the Cairo Declaration of 1943.

— Memoranda issued by the General Head Quarters (GHQ) during the occupation period excluded Takeshima from the territory of the occupying forces.

— Rightly Takeshima was regarded as Korean territory when the Rhee Syng-Man Line was drawn in 1952, and rightly South Korean forces were permanently stationed on the islands since July 1954.

(c) Japan counterargued that the island claimed from ancient times by Korea was not Takeshima but rather Ullungdo; Takeshima was not a territory which Japan obtained by 'violence and greed'; the GHQ memoranda were not meant to prejudge any territorial demarcation of Japan; and Korean occupation of the islands was unlawful.

To resolve this impasse the two sides agreed to conclude an Exchange of Notes stating that "conflicts between the two countries shall be primarily resolved through diplomatic channels."[7] Japan understood that based on this Exchange of Notes the territorial issue pertaining to Takeshima would be resolved through negotiations. The Korean position was that Takeshima did not constitute a 'conflict' as defined in this Exchange of Notes. Thus the two governments

---

[7] Translated into English by the author. MOFA, *op. cit.*, p. 59.

found a way to deal with Takeshima, so that it would not hamper the overall agreement to be made in 1965, but the issue continued to haunt the relationship ever since.

Whatever the difficulty pertaining to Takeshima, on 22 June 1965, all documents mentioned above were simultaneously signed in Tokyo and a new era was opened between Japan and South Korea.

2. *The first 30 years: economic relations developed but political relations were troubled*

Rapid economic development

After the signing of the treaties and agreements in 1965, relations between South Korea and Japan developed rapidly, particularly the economic relations.

Total trade, limited to $221 million in 1965, amounted to $48,559 million in 1995, a 219-fold increase in 30 years.[8]

Japanese investment in South Korea, starting slowly and limited to $17 million dollars in 1970,[9] reached the level of over $100 million in 1982, $400 million in 1986, and after some scaling down to the level of $200 million in the early 1990's, came back to $400 million in 1994.[10]

As for exchanges, whereas only 10,000 people travelled across the channel in 1965, this figure was 2.6 million in 1995. Japan became the most popular destination for South Koreans and South Korea was the second most popular country for the Japanese after the United States.

In contrast to this sound economic development, political relations remained uneven, with certain ebb and flow characteristics similar to the situation between Japan and China. But in the case of South Korea, big waves occurred once each decade during the 30 years after the establishment of relations.

---

[8] JETRO figures.

[9] Hook, Gilson, Hughes, Dobson, *op. cit.*, p. 451.

[10] Yearly FDI to South Korea from 1986 to 1994 in million dollars are as follows: 436, 647, 483, 606, 284, 260, 225, 246, 400 (JETRO figures, 1990–1994: www.jetro.go.jp/ec/j/trade/FDI to, country data 2003–08–04).

Abduction of Kim Dae-Jung

Under President Park Chung-Hee the bilateral political relationship developed as well. President Park sought a rapid industrialization of Korea; Japan was in search of a stable neighbour offering greater trade and investment opportunities. Japan's ODA played an important role in enhancing these two objectives. Both countries found interests in having solid relations with the United States: Prime Minister Sato directed his major policy objective to the reversion of Okinawa, and the Korean Clause in the 1969 Sato-Nixon Communiqué reflected the importance he attached to Korea in that context. President Park sent Korean troops to Vietnam to back up the Americans.

But President Park's regime began to display increasingly autocratic characteristics and this aspect brought about the political crisis of the 1970's. On 8 August 1973, Kim Dae-Jung, then an influential opposition party leader who happened to be staying in Tokyo, was abducted and taken to South Korea. Five days later he was found safe at his home in Seoul, but when strong suspicion emerged that Kim had been abducted by a first secretary of the Korean Embassy in Tokyo, the issue became a serious diplomatic issue between Japan and South Korea, with possible infringement of Japanese sovereign rights by Korean authorities.

As a result of strong Japanese protest and a request for a fair investigation, in November Prime Minister Kim Jong-Pil came to Tokyo and expressed regret for the incident, promising that the investigation would be continued, and that such an incident would not happen again. The first round of a diplomatic settlement had been achieved.

In the spring of 1974 however, two Japanese were arrested for subversive activities in South Korea. On 14 August the Korean government reported that the investigation had found insufficient evidence to prove that the first secretary at the Korean Embassy in Tokyo was involved in the abduction of Kim. It was totally unsatisfactory to the Japanese authorities. On the following day, 15 August 1974 a Korean national with Japanese citizenship shot President Park and killed his wife in Seoul.

Emotion flared on both sides. It took a whole year to heal the wound. The second round in the diplomatic settlement took place in July 1975, when Korea informed Japan that, although insufficient evidence was found to prosecute the first secretary concerned, his conduct in Tokyo was unbecoming and therefore he was removed from his post as a civil servant.

The recognition of history

President Park was assassinated in October 1979 and in September 1980 Chun Doo-Hwan was elected as President. His 'high-handed' approach to require $6 billion assistance, taking into account the crucial security role South Korea was playing for the security of the Far East, created diplomatic tension with the Japanese Prime Minister Zenko Suzuki.

Yasuhiro Nakasone became Prime Minister in November 1982 and he made a spectacular debut in foreign policy by visiting South Korea on 11 January 1983. I was then following Japan's Asia policy in the political section of the Japanese Embassy in Moscow, and the confusion of the Japan-Korea relations in 1982 was sad to observe. Nakasone's determination, swiftness and concrete action, which resulted in an agreement of $4 billion assistance for seven years, was breathtaking. It became all the more so, when we learned that his visit to South Korea paved the way for his next visit to Washington of 17 January (Chapter 2).

Despite this initial success, the Japan-Korea relations under Nakasone had gone through a turbulent period regarding the issues of war responsibility.

Prime Minister Nakasone's visit to Yasukuni in 1985 evoked equal emotions in South Korea as in China.

In 1986 another incident occurred, which probably became the most critical issue of the 1980's in the Japan-Korea relations. It all started again when in May 1986 another textbook was approved. The textbook came for approval before the Screening Council under the auspices of the Ministry of Education and Culture. The view of some members of the Council that this textbook could be problematic from the point of view of adjacent countries was reported in the media. Naturally China and South Korea reacted with strong criticism. Due to Prime Minister Nakasone's personal intervention the Council took extraordinary procedures to revise the textbook 'after' its approval, so as to reflect, more adequately, the feelings of the adjacent countries.

The action taken by Nakasone was well appreciated by China and South Korea, but there was some feeling in Japan that the extraordinary step taken by the government was too much of a concession to external pressure.

Seiko Fujio, who was appointed as Minister of Education and Culture in July 1986 in the third Nakasone cabinet, shared this dissatisfaction. But when asked about the question of the textbook revision at a press conference after his appointment, Fujio answered: "It is an issue resolved by the previous cabinet, so no further follow-up is needed. But those (in foreign countries) who are protesting should think twice whether they themselves would not have done the same."[11]

Fujio's statement invited considerable anger from China and South Korea, but since he had not named any specific country, Nakasone's personal apology calmed down the situation.

Then, in early September, Fujio gave an interview in one of the leading monthly magazines and stated that "there was some responsibility on the Korean side for Japan's annexation of Korea."

> The Ministry of Foreign Affairs knew about Fujio's statement a few days before publication. It was the moment of truth for the newly appointed Minister for Foreign Affairs Tadashi Kuranari. As his personal secretary, I still remember very well the evening the responsible Director General rushed into the Minister's room with the advance copy of the monthly magazine, *Bungei Shunjyu*, in his hand and explained to the Minister those parts which would inevitably invite strong anger from South Korea. For the Minister, and for me, it was obvious that Fujio's statement went directly against the wounded feelings of the Korean people. Everything became public on 6 September and, as foreseen, South Korea reacted in the strongest terms that Minister Fujio's article was the most serious incident since the establishment of diplomatic relations in 1965.

Minister Kuranari did his best to save the situation. What could be done? Clearly, Minister Fujio's statement was outside the accepted scope of governmental dialogue between South Korea and Japan. Theoretically, Minister Fujio could apologize but given the fact that his words were based on his convictions, that possibility was excluded. The next possibility was Minister Fujio's resignation, but how could

---

[11] Ikei, *op. cit.*, p. 322.

someone explain to Minister Fujio that his article warranted a voluntary resignation? After a traumatic few days of highly delicate
political contacts, on 8 September, instead of Minister Fujio's resignation, Prime Minister Nakasone, based on his constitutional power,
relieved Minister Fujio from his post as Minister for Education and
Culture.[12]

Comfort women

The 1980's were a period of rapid economic development for South
Korea, and the 1988 Seoul Olympic Games, where all major countries of the world (except North Korea) gathered, were a symbol of
their achievement.[13] South Korean external relations during the first
half of the 1990's were also heavily influenced by the major event
of the era: Gorbachev's *perestroika* and the end of the Cold War.
President Roh Tae-Woo swiftly grasped this opportunity and established diplomatic relations with the Soviet Union on 30 September
1990 and with China on 24 August 1992.

In the post-Cold War political climate and with this sweeping
diplomatic success for South Korea, relations between North and
South Korea were activated as well (Section 4 below). Japan and
North Korea also held their first round of negotiations toward the
establishment of diplomatic relations from January 1991 to January
1992. Japan's insistence that "this negotiation should also contribute
to the peace and stability of Northeast Asia"[14] must have reassured
South Korea that Japan was not just selfishly pursuing its objective
of normalization (Section 5 below).

After Kim Young-Sam was elected President in February 1993,
the nuclear crisis in North Korea became a vital common concern
for Japan and South Korea.

Thus, security relations between Japan and South Korea strengthened over these years, but in the bilateral relationship the issue of

---

[12] Ikei, *op. cit.*, pp. 322–323.

[13] It is noted that the 1980 Moscow Olympic Games were boycotted by the
Western countries as a protest to the Soviet invasion to Afghanistan and that 1984
Los Angeles Olympic Games were boycotted by the Soviet Union as a counter-
measure.

[14] K. Odagawa, *Kitachousen-Sono Jitsuzouto Kiseki- (North Korea-reality and traces-)*,
Chapter 12, Kobunken,1998, *op. cit.*, p. 256.

'comfort women' became the focal point during the first half of the 1990's.

At a time when prostitution was an accepted practice of society in Japan, the Japanese army in the prewar period had customarily provided 'comfort women' to accompany the troops, except for those places where brothels already existed. The women were recruited from the then Japanese territory, that is, from the Japanese homeland, Korea and Taiwan and from the occupied territories as well.

The true state of affairs about those women from Korea, Taiwan and the occupied territories was not spoken about for a long time after the end of the war. As the years passed and the women who had suffered reached old age, towards the end of the 1980's pressure emerged from various sources, including from within Japan, that things could not just be left as they were.

Thus in December 1991 the Miyazawa government decided to embark on a full-scale investigation of the matter.

In August 1993 the Japanese government published the results of the investigation and acknowledged that "there have been many instances where women were gathered against their own wishes" and that "honour and respect of many women were deeply injured under the participation of the military". The Japanese government expressed "heartfelt apology and remorse" to everyone who suffered from that experience.[15]

To reflect this apology and remorse, in August 1994 Prime Minister Murayama, the socialist Prime Minister of the coalition government that had been formed in June, declared a 'Peace, Friendship and Exchange Initiative'. The two pillars of this initiative were collecting information on past history, and exchanges among intellectuals, youth, and others. He also indicated his intention to find another wider avenue to let the Japanese people join in this expression of apology and remorse regarding the issue of comfort women.

Prime Minister Murayama's intention was realized in July 1995 by the establishment of the Asian Women's Fund, that was to be privately funded by the Japanese people who could thereby join the government in their common efforts for reconciliation. From this fund each comfort woman was to receive 2 million yen as atonement.

---

[15] Statement by the Chief Cabinet Secretary Kono on 4 August 1984. Translated by the author.

The whole process was given heavy media attention in Japan and the countries concerned. The human suffering disclosed naturally invited further emotions of anger and sorrow. The way the issue was dealt with by the Japanese government met with criticism from different perspectives. But I see here a genuine effort by the Japanese people to face up to the reality of the past combined with concrete action, which, at least among some people who had suffered, had some positive results.

By September 2002, altogether 285 women in Korea, Taiwan and The Philippines had received atonement money.[16]

3. *The turn of the century: from the Murayama Statement to Prime Minister Koizumi*

The Murayama Statement of 1995

As the years passed, the impression held by the international community that there was a persistent lack of clarity in Japan's position on World War II did not diminish.

The textbook and Yasukuni issues, combined with repeated statements by leading individual politicians during the 1980's, confused the voice from the government that Japan's position was consistent, Japan was firmly on the road to peace, and that it had no intention to justify deeds which needed an apology. Occasionally criticisms also emerged from Asian and European observers that the key expression, 'deep remorse', based on the 1965 Shiina Statement and the 1972 Japan-China Joint Communiqué was not clear enough.

With this criticism in mind, successive Prime Ministers in the first half of the 1990's began to use the equivalent and more straightforward word 'apology' in their official statements in relation to Korea:

Prime Minister Kaifu in May 1990: "humble (*kenkyo*) remorse and sincere (*sotchoku*) apology".[17]

Prime Minister Kaifu in October 1990: "deep remorse and apology (*ikan*)".[18]

---

[16] http://www.awf.or.jp/ Q&A, No.5, 2003-07-09.
[17] Kaifu's speech on the occasion of President Roh Tae Woo's visit to Japan.
[18] Kaifu's policy speech at the Diet.

Prime Minister Miyazawa in January 1992: "heartfelt remorse and apology (*owabi*)".[19]

Prime Minister Hosokawa in November 1993: "deep remorse and heartfelt apology (*chinsha*)".[20]

And yet even these expressions did not have the desired impact in clearing the cloud of uncertainty.

On 15 August 1995 at the 50th commemoration of the end of World War II, Prime Minister Murayama decided to make a statement once and for all. The key section of his statement reads as follows:

> During a certain period in the not too distant past, Japan, following a mistaken national policy, advanced along the road to war, only to ensnare the Japanese people in a fateful crisis, and, through its colonial rule and aggression, caused tremendous damage and suffering to the people of many countries, particularly to those of Asian nations. In the hope that no such mistake be made in the future, I regard, in a spirit of humility, these irrefutable facts of history, and express here once again my feelings of deep remorse and state my heartfelt apology.[21] Allow me also to express my feelings of profound mourning for all victims, both at home and abroad, of that history.[22]

When this statement was announced in August 1995 I was the Deputy Chief of the Mission in our Embassy in Moscow. I was impressed by the clarity, strength, and courage of this statement. I thought that there was something I needed to convey to the Russian people about Japan's courage in overcoming the past. I wrote in one the most popular Moscow weekly '*Moskovskie Novostji* (Moscow News)', dated 24 September 1995, an article which starts with the following sentences:

"It has become almost an axiom that, as a final resort, relations between states converge to relations among the people. Therefore, if there is no trust among the people, there is no trust among states. 50 years have passed since the end of the war, but Japan still has complex issues related to the past war with the people of Asian countries. Many people in Asia have feelings of distrust and antipathy against Japan, so that to this date they can-

---

[19] Miyazawa's policy speech during his visit to South Korea.
[20] Hosokawa's statement at the joint press conference during his visit to South Korea.
[21] The word used in Japanese was *owabi*.
[22] Translation by MOFA.

not be convinced of the sincerity of the Japanese people in their apology for their deeds in the past."

And then I introduced the key expression of the Murayama Statement, referring to his 'apology' toward the colonial rule and aggression and stated that: "Of course one statement does not solve all problems and we need further steps but on the whole the people of Asia dealt positively with the Murayama Statement." (After that my observations regarding Japan-Russia relations followed.)

After the Murayama Statement, all subsequent expressions of apology which Japan has since made were based on this statement, and in general, they were well received by other countries.

Developments in the Japan-Korea Relations

After the pronouncement of this historic statement, the bilateral relations between South Korea and Japan developed rather smoothly for many years.

In 1996 two significant steps were taken in the area of fisheries and soccer.

On fisheries, the United Nations Convention on the Law of the Sea was being ratified in both countries. The two governments agreed in June to expedite the negotiations on a new fisheries agreement based on the concept of the new convention. The issue of Takeshima was in essence dissociated from the negotiations.

On soccer, the World Soccer League decided at the end of May that the 2002 World Cup Competition would be jointly hosted by Japan and South Korea. A unique opportunity for the two countries to implement a joint project of worldwide significance emerged. Expectation rose that this event could significantly narrow the gap between the two countries.

In 1997 the Asian financial crisis erupted and South Korea became one of the countries seriously affected. IMF led with a package of $58 billion of financial assistance for South Korea and Japan decided to bear the biggest share of $10 billion.

1998 became a great year for Japan-Korea relations, culminating in President Kim Dae-Jung's visit to Japan from 7 to 10 October.

Kim Dae-Jung was inaugurated as President in February of that year and his 'sunshine policy' towards North Korea had already sent some fresh air to the atmosphere on the peninsula.

His visit to Japan in October was a long awaited breakthrough visit. The key paragraph of the Joint Declaration 'A new Japan-Republic of Korea Partnership towards the Twenty-first Century', adopted on 8 October, reads as follows:

> Looking back on the relations between Japan and the Republic of Korea during this century, Prime Minister Obuchi regarded in a spirit of humility the fact of history that Japan caused, during a certain period in the past, tremendous damage and suffering to the people of the Republic of Korea through its colonial rule, and expressed his deep remorse and heartfelt apology for this fact.
>
> President Kim accepted with sincerity this statement of Prime Minister Obuchi's recognition of history and expressed his appreciation for it. He also expressed his view that the present calls upon both countries to overcome their unfortunate history and to build a future-oriented relationship based on reconciliation as well as good-neighbourly and friendly cooperation.
>
> Further, both leaders shared the view that it was important that the peoples of both countries, the young generation in particular, deepen their understanding of history, and stressed the need to devote much attention and effort to that end.[23]

Perfect! The tone and content of the Joint Declaration were different from the Partnership for Friendship and Cooperation adopted with China two months later (Chapter 4). The 'heartfelt apology' was stated by Prime Minister Obuchi together with the future oriented expression by President Kim "to overcome their unfortunate history". Many people thought that with these statements the two countries finally crossed the Rubicon from the past to the future.

President Kim's determination to overcome the past was not only in word, but also in deed. Korea thus far had maintained a strict policy of not allowing Japanese culture to penetrate Korean society, but at the end of October the first round of liberalization of Japanese culture took place in the area of selective films and videos and cartoon books.

These positive actions were well reflected in the economic area as well. Japan further implemented its assistance amidst the continuing economic difficulty in Korea, and extended an Ex-Im Bank loan of $1 billion in May, and another $3 billion in October 1998.

In the area of fisheries, hard negotiations lasted for well over two years. A basic agreement was reached in September and the new

---

[23] http://www.mofa.go.jp/region/asia-paci/korea/joint9810.html 2003–07–09.

Agreement which replaced the entire structure of the 1965 Fisheries Agreement was signed in November 1998. A mutually acceptable solution was introduced to handle the issue of Takeshima.

In November 1998 a unique encounter took place in a small village called Miyama,[24] at the outskirts of Kagoshima City on the southern edge of Kyushu, as if to symbolize the glorious year of the relationship. At the end of the 16th century, when Hideyoshi Toyotomi, the leading warlord who preceded the Tokugawa Shoguns invaded Korea, a group of Korean pottery makers were deported to Japan and allowed to live in this village. For centuries they continued to live there, where green bamboo and rice paddies grew gently under the quiet southern breeze, looking over the serene ocean which separates them from their homeland. They preserved their highly developed skills of pottery making and began to produce beautiful Korean pottery.

1998 happened to coincide with the 400th anniversary of the commemoration of the arrival of these Korean pottery makers to Japan. Many festivities were conducted through the year, and the concluding event was the visit of the two Prime Ministers and other cabinet members on 29 November, after a ministerial meeting between Japan and South Korea was conducted on the preceding day in the town of Kagoshima.

Since Shigenori Togo was born in the village of Miyama in the period of Meiji, I happened to have been kindly included as one of the members of the Japanese delegation which visited the village of Miyama.

It was a beautiful autumn day. Villagers laughed, smiled, and were excited about this rare opportunity to receive so many dignitaries from both countries. Leaders of the village and their Korean counterparts were sometimes in tears, while attending this unique and historic occasion of reconciliation and harmonization.

After this commemorative year, everything looked even smoother.

Prime Minister Obuchi visited Korea in March 1999 and the 'Japan-Korea Economic Agenda 21' was adopted so as to implement the Joint Declaration in concrete terms and to further boost

---

[24] Miyama means 'beautiful mountain' in Japanese.

Fig. 1. Prime Minister Obuchi, Prime Minister Kim Jong-Pil and the author at Miyama, Kagoshima, in front of the statue of Shigenori Togo (29 November 1998)

the economic relations. Within this Agenda, both sides decided to conclude an agreement to protect and encourage investment, and negotiations began with vigour.

The total trade stayed at the level of $30 to $50 billion in the latter part of the 1990's.[25] The FDI to South Korea marked a historical record of $980 million in 1999 and $810 million in 2000.[26]

The gradual liberalization policy of Japanese culture developed steadily, to include a wide range of films and videos, Japanese folk songs, and TV and radio broadcasts in the area of sports, documentaries and news reports.

Preparations towards cohosting the World Cup in 2002 proceeded with enthusiasm.

Reviving tension under the Koizumi cabinet

And yet in 2001 both the textbooks and the Yasukuni issues reopened tension in the bilateral relationship.

Regarding the textbooks, the one presented by *Fusousha* was the focal point (Chapter 4). Korea requested Japan in May to make a series of modification. The two factual changes Japan agreed to introduce in July were far from satisfactory to the Koreans. In retaliation Korea decided to suspend its liberalization policy towards Japanese culture.

As for Prime Minister Koizumi's visit to the Yasukuni Shrine on 13 August, both the Chinese government (Chapter 4), and the Korean government expressed their anger and regret.

Since President Kim's visit to Japan in October 1998 had created a genuine impression of crossing the Rubicon, what happened in the course of 2001 was truly regrettable. After President Kim's visit, Japan lost a significant opportunity to pro-actively address issues related to the past, and to enter into a deeper dialogue with Korea. The importance underlined in the Obuchi-Kim Communiqué that particularly the young generation should deepen their understanding of history, should have been taken into account much more

---

[25] The total trade between Japan and Korea from 1996 to 2002 was in billion dollars 45.4, 40.8, 27.3, 39.0, 51.3, 42.7, 44.0 (JETRO figures).

[26] The yearly FDI to Korea from 1995 to 2001 was in million dollars 445, 416, 442, 303, 980, 813, and 543 (JETRO figures: http://www.jetro.go.jp/ec/j/trade/ FDI to, country data 2003–08–04).

seriously. Independent historians and scholars could have played an important role. Some of the views expressed by the authors of the *Fusousha* textbook could have been useful in discussions amongst these groups.

Nonetheless, after the turmoil, Prime Minister Koizumi visited Korea in October 2001 and an agreement was reached that Japan and Korea would cooperate to set up a joint commission of historians from both countries. That was a step in the right direction. It was a little belated perhaps, but the deepening of mutual understanding through these processes was probably the only way to overcome this issue. It would require many more years of mutual effort.

Prime Minister Koizumi made yet another proposal during this Korean visit, namely, to set up a commission to consider a memorial to pray for peace and to commemorate those who died at war, where everybody, Japanese and foreigners alike, would come. The commission was soon established and in December of 2002, after a whole year, a report was formulated, stating in principle, the necessity of constructing a memorial for all war victims.[27] Several voices, however, had already been raised against the establishment of such a new institution. To what extent this new idea would resolve the complex issue of the Yasukuni Shrine was yet unclear. But at least one idea to overcome a difficult issue from the past is under consideration.

So in total, though very much different from the period of relaxed optimism of 1998–2000, the year 2002 proceeded with reasonable harmony. In the economic arena, an Investment Agreement was signed in March 2002 and a new agenda of a Free Trade Agreement which could benefit future economic relations between the two countries has emerged. The cohosting of the world soccer turned out to be a successful example of cooperation. Prime Minister Koizumi and President Kim issued a powerful statement for future cooperation upon the conclusion of the soccer game on 1 July 2002.

President Roh Moo-Hyum, elected in February 2003, also maintains a policy of dialogue with Japan and does not put the issue from the past to the forefront of the relationship. Economic relations developed, so that at the APEC Bangkok meeting in October 2003 both agreed to start the negotiations on FTA before the end

---

[27] *Asahi Shinbun*, 14 December 2002.

of the year and conclude it by 2005 (Chapter 6). South Korea intends to resume its cultural opening policy from January 2004 onwards.

In these circumstances, when overall relations were moving ahead between Japan and South Korea, while textbook and Yasukuni issues still caused a considerable tension, the relationship with North Korea surfaced as a critical issue both for Japan and South Korea.

4. *The North Korean situation (until 2001)*

North Korea became probably one of the most militaristic, totalitarian and oppressive regimes in the post-WW II era. Under the leadership of Kim Il-Sung it became a strange country "composed of a unique trilogy: a fundamentalist dogma called 'Ju Che', a dictatorship led by a charismatic fatherly figure, and a paternalist Confucian tradition".[28] At the same time the postwar history of North Korea may be seen as a passage from a euphoric outcry for regime development to a desperate effort for regime survival.

The North Korean situation during the Cold War and its aftermath

The peculiarity of North Korea was not so obvious during the Cold War, particularly when the country was founded and when it began to construct a socialist country after the end of the Korean War in 1953. In fact, until the end of the 1960's North Korea was perceived as being equally successful in its economic and social development as South Korea.

During the 1970's and 1980's South Korea had undergone a period of rapid economic development under the quasi-militarist government of President Park Chung-Hee, Chun Doo-Hwan and Roh Tae-Woo. North Korea stagnated, with its concentration of economic resources on military production and its ill management of the economy. The economic gap grew and the end result was the symbolic South Korean success of the 1988 Seoul Olympic Games without North Korean participation.

During these two decades North Korea had pursued a strange policy-mix of the worst kind of terrorist activities and an occasional soft-handed and friendly diplomacy, particularly to South Korea.

---

[28] Fuji Kamiya, State Crime Exposed, *Asahi Shinbun*, 22 September 2002.

In July 1972 the two Koreas announced a joint declaration, which to this day forms the basis of unification, probably strongly influenced by the overriding political climate under the Detente.[29] However in the post-Detente era of the latter part of the 1970's, North Korea abducted a number of Japanese (from 1979 to 1983), and in October 1983 an assassination attempt on the major South Korean leadership took place in Burma. The preceding years leading to the Seoul Olympic Games were years of contacts and dialogue between North and South, including the first family reunion in September 1985. But the friendly policy came to an end when in a terrorist attack a South Korean airliner exploded over the Indian Ocean in November 1987.

Thus, as the years passed, towards the end of the 1980's North Korea became a country heavily reliant on military power, very much isolated from the outside world, and miserably impoverished. By that time South Korea had developed an unequivocally stronger economy.

In such a difficult situation the end of he Cold War probably came as the most critical blow for the regime survival of North Korea. The fall of the Soviet Union and the East-European states, as well as the changes occurring in the rapid economic development in China under the policy of 'Reform and Opening' should have put North Korea in real isolation. Economically North Korea should have suffered a lot by losing its traditional trading ties with the Soviet Union and China. Politically President Roh Tae-Woo's startling success in establishing diplomatic relations with the Soviet Union in September 1990 and with China in August 1992 must have exacerbated North Korea's sense of isolation.

North Korea had to act. North-South Prime Ministers talks in September 1990, the Agreement on Reconciliation, Non-aggression, Exchange and Cooperation between North and South signed in December 1991 and the Joint Declaration on a Nuclear-free Korean Peninsula signed in January 1992 are probably the results of North Korea's effort to keep in step with the major trend in history. North

---

[29] The declaration includes the three principles of unification: independent resolution without outside intervention; peaceful measures without resorting to the force of arms; and unity as one nation overcoming the differences in thoughts and system (K. Kobayashi, *Kitachou sen—Sono Jitsuzouto Kiseki (North Korea, its Reality and Locus)*, Chapter 8, Kobunken, 1998, p. 170).

and South Korea simultaneously acceded to the United Nations in 17 September 1991. But all these achievements probably did not mitigate North Korea's fundamental sense of isolation.

During the 1990's: the relationship with America

In addition to the diplomatic failure in the aftermath of the Cold War, the economic situation in North Korea disintegrated throughout the 1990's. A Korean bank analysis indicates that the North Korean GNP showed a minus growth of 2 to 8% from 1990 to 1995.[30] The agricultural situation, particularly the floods in 1995 and 1996 as well as the droughts in 1997, created a real economic crisis. At the same time a crisis in the energy situation was also widely reported.

In this dangerously difficult situation North Korea began on a new path: nuclear harassment. The suspicion emerged that North Korea was producing plutonium necessary for the production of nuclear weapons in its nuclear plant at Yongbyon, north of Pyongyang.

Was it because North Korea was so desperate in securing at least her military superiority in Northeast Asia in its increasing sense of isolation? Or was it because it had calculated that the harassment would result in economic benefits, which it greatly needed to overcome its economic difficulty? Or was it just a not well thought out exercise to demonstrate her power to the outside world?

Whatever the answer to these questions is, in February 1993 North Korea refused to allow an IAEA's special inspection and in March it announced its intention to withdraw from the NPT.[31] In June 1993 it softened its position but in June 1994 it again declared withdrawal from the NPT. America could not let the situation proceed further. An extremely dangerous situation took shape, possibly close to war. In June, against the background of this tension, former President Jimmy Carter visited Pyongyang to remedy the situation, and this visit probably saved the Far East from one of the worst catastrophes after WW II.

After Kim Il-Sung's death in July a so-called 'Agreed Framework' was reached between the two countries in October: North Korea

---

[30] Kobayashi, *op. cit.*, p. 181.
[31] North Korea was a member of the NPT from 1985.

would stay inside the Non Proliferation Treaty (NPT) but two light water nuclear reactors would be provided by the international community to North Korea.

The nature of the 1993–94 nuclear crisis in North Korea still needs considerable analysis, but one may conclude that by way of utilizing nuclear harassment, North Korea gained two things: financial benefit for constructing light water reactors and full-scale bilateral negotiations with the United States. From the point of view of the international community it also achieved (or it was perceived so) two things: a nuclear-free Korean peninsula and greater stability in the Northeast Asia. There have been criticisms against this arrangement, but if the objectives thus envisaged would have been truly realized, it would not have been a bad bargain for all participants.

In fact, up until the end of 2002 America, South Korea, and Japan basically continued to work diligently to realize the Agreed Framework. Japan took an active part in enhancing the construction of the light water nuclear reactor project:

– In March 1995 America, South Korea and Japan signed an agreement on the Korean Peninsula Energy Development Organization (KEDO), which was joined later by the European Union in September 1997.[32]

– In December 1995 North Korea formally joined KEDO.

– In August 1997 the construction of KEDO began.

– In July 1998 a basic agreement on cost sharing was reached: out of the total amount of $4.6 billion, South Korea would bear 70%, Japan $1 billion, and the United States the cost of heavy oil, which would be provided to North Korea until KEDO began functioning.

– In 1999 respective agreements were reached between KEDO and Korean and Japanese financial institutions for the implementation of the project.

Meanwhile, in April 1996 President Clinton and Korean President Kim Young-Sam had a meeting at Cheju Island and agreed to propose Four-Party Talks, consisting of North and South Korea, the

---

[32] As of August 2002 in addition to these three counties and the EU there are 9 countries which are members of KEDO (http://www.mofa.go.jp/mofaj/gaiko/kaku/kedo/index.html 2003–07–10).

United States and China, the four parties that had taken part in the Korean War. North Korea accepted this proposal and a preparatory meeting began in August 1997. The first meeting took place in December 1997 and series of meetings have taken place since then. It was another step towards pulling North Korea out of its isolation, through a neighbouring country. Japan supported this initiative from the very beginning when it was proposed.

In 2000, after relative stalemate years of 1998 and 1999, Secretary of State M. Albright visited North Korea in October to discuss issues of common concern and see whether there was a sufficient basis to prepare President Clinton's visit to North Korea before the expiry of his term. That visit did not take place.

When President Bush came to office at the beginning of 2001, he took time to revise his North Korean policy during the first half year of his presidency. The conclusion which he drew in June 2001 to initiate a dialogue without any preconditions was rebuffed by the North Koreans on the grounds that it could imply the question of reduction of conventional forces. President Bush's State of the Union speech in January 2002 characterizing North Korea as constituting an 'Axis of Evil' was seen by North Korea as being "tantamount to a Declaration of War".[33]

During the 1990's: relations with South Korea

Kim Il-Sung's decision to hold a summit meeting with President Kim Young-Sam on 25 July 1994 was never realized because of Kim Il-Sung's death on 8 July. After his death South Korea continued to seek opportunities for cooperation. In North Korea, Kim Jong-Il, Kim Il-Sung's son, who had already been known to be the heir, rose to power. Under the continuous difficulty in economy and sense of isolation, North Korean policy toward South Korea fluctuated regularly between warming-up and provocative incidents:

 – In June 1995 South Korea decided to send 150,000 tons of rice in humanitarian aid to North Korea.
 – In September 1996 a North Korean submarine ran aground on the northeast coast of South Korea, and after heavy firing,

---

[33] *Gaikou Seisho (Diplomatic Bluebook)* 2003, Chapter2>1>1.

South Korea confirmed that of the 25 North Korean agents, 11 had been found dead, 13 had been shot down and 1 had been taken captive.

– In May 1997 an agreement was reached by the North-South Red Cross that 50,000 tons of corn in humanitarian assistance would be provided by South Korea.

– In February 1998 Kim Dae-Jung was elected President of South Korea. He announced the three 'Sunshine Policy' principles: that South Korea rejected any provocation by force, but it would not unify Korea by way of absorbing the North into the South, and that it intended to enhance reconciliation and cooperation, wherever they were deemed to be possible.

– From June to July and from November to December 1998, however, a series of provocations occurred on the eastern coast of South Korea and near Seoul.

– In February 1999 North Korea made a proposal to conduct official high-level talks, combined with some concrete measures to be taken within North Korea to alleviate social, military, and security tension in the peninsula. That proposal was welcomed by the South Korean government.

– From 13 to 15 June 2000, the historic North-South Summit took place in Pyongyang. Waves of emotions flooded over the peninsula, in favour of reconciliation and future unification of the homeland. As symbolic measures to incarnate this process, 'family reunions' were implemented in August and in November. A series of dialogues was initiated at various levels. This North-South Summit gave a spectacular impression to the world. An important part of it was due to President Kim Dae-Jung's Sunshine Policy but Kim Jong-Il was also an effective player.

In contrast to the overwhelming emotions that prevailed in June 2000, little has happened to reduce military tension since then.

At the beginning of the 2000's: relations with other countries

At the beginning of the 21st century Kim Jong-Il conducted a rather successful policy of rapprochement with other countries. The North-South Summit in June 2000 created a favourable political climate for breaking North Korean isolation, and Kim Jong-Il quickly seized the opportunity.

First there was China. Relations between China and Korea date back to the days of the feudal dynasties and have in principle been close but complex. During the Cold War, China's intervention on the North Korean side in October 1950 brought the two countries very close. But when tension mounted surrounding the Sino-Soviet rivalry, North Korea's 'equal distance' policy towards China and the Soviet Union irritated the Chinese leadership, which naturally expected close North Korean support of China. During the 1980's the relationship improved, but after the end of the Cold War delicate points of contention have remained: China's recognition of South Korea in 1992 brought a chill to the North Koreans; North Korea's adventurism with nuclear activities in 1993–94 could not have pleased the Chinese leadership.[34]

In the critical year of 2000, Kim Jong-Il moved. In May 2000 he visited Beijing, and further in January 2001 visited Shanghai. Jiang Zemin reciprocated with his official visit in September 2001. Those visits naturally helped in warming up the relationship between the two countries.

Then with Russia, partly thanks to the actions by President Putin, the relationship has been constantly warming. Putin visited North Korea in July 2000, just before the Okinawa Summit. Kim Jong-Il visited Russia from July to August 2001 travelling on the Siberian railroad, and they had their third round of talks in Vladivostok in August 2002.

With European countries, North Korea made substantial progress in opening up diplomatic relations with major countries in 2000 and 2001. It started with Italy and Great Britain in 2000, followed by the Netherlands, Belgium, Spain, Germany, Luxembourg, Greece and the European Union in 2001. France is the only major European country which had not established diplomatic relations with North Korea as of the end of the year 2002.

In July 2000 North Korea sent its Foreign Minister to the ASEAN Regional Forum (ARF) Meeting for the first time (Chapter 6), a step long awaited by other member countries.

---

[34] K. Yokobori, *Kitachousen—Sono Jitsuzouto Kiseki (North Korea, its reality and traces)*, Chapter 11, Koubunken, 1998, pp. 237–239.

5. *Japan-North Korea relations (until 2001)*

Japan-North Korea relations during the Cold War and its aftermath

Before 1965, when Japan's major aim was the establishment of diplomatic relations with South Korea, Korean nationals, resident in Japan continued to return home in the euphoric expectation of socialist success in North Korea. Based on information from the Red Cross, between 1959 and 1984, 93,000 Koreans returned to North Korea, including 1,831 Japanese-born spouses.[35]

After the establishment of diplomatic relations with South Korea the Japanese leadership intended to maintain practical relations with North Korea. That basic position was already reflected in the way the Basic Treaty with South Korea was negotiated (Section 1) and Prime Minister Sato made this position clear as well.[36]

During the 1970's and the 1980's moderate steps were taken in the economic and cultural spheres. A private sector agreement was concluded on trade (1972) and fishery (1977), a North Korean team participated in a youth sport festival (1985). Party-to-party exchanges also developed at a moderate pace. But at the same time, the North Korean arrest of two crew members of the *Fujisanmaru*-18 in 1983, as well as terrorist activities in Burma (1983) and on the Indian Ocean (1987) attracted huge media attention and it cooled down these exchanges, which had only been moderate in scale.

But all these 'non-developments' were shaken when the whole world began to move dramatically to the post-Cold War era. Prime Minister Takeshita probably made Japan's first initiative toward North Korea in the post-Cold War era in his statement at the Diet on 30 March 1989. He expressed "deep remorse and apology (*ikan*) to all people in this area" with a clear implication of addressing both South and North Korea and expressed his willingness to "improve relations" with the North. Later, when a Japanese socialist parliamentarian was

---

[35] Hook, Gilson, Hughes, Dobson, *op. cit.*, p. 177.

[36] On 29 October 1965, Prime Minister Sato made a statement at the Special Committee for Japan-South Korea Treaties in the House of Representatives, stating that "Japan is not going to maintain diplomatic relations with the North. We have talked with the South but we have not talked on anything with the North. Therefore relations with the North are *hakushi* (a blank paper). We are going to deal with it as *practical problems*." (Odagawa, *op. cit.*, p. 271).

visiting North Korea, Kim Il-Sung expressed his appreciation of Takeshita's expression of apology addressed to North Korea.[37]

In September 1990, just one week before Gorbachev recognized South Korea, Shin Kanemaru, who was known as 'the Godfather of the LDP', visited North Korea heading a LDP-Japan Socialist Party (JSP) delegation and met with Kim Il-Sung. The three parties, LDP-JSP-Korean Workers Party (KWP), agreed on the conditions to begin negotiations to establish diplomatic relations. As if to symbolize this positive development, North Korea released the two captive crew of the *Fujisanmaru*-18.

Though some of the conditions agreed to by Kanemaru were highly problematic, such as the acknowledgement of Japan's responsibility for postwar North Korean damages, the negotiations nevertheless started and the first eight rounds took place from January 1991 to February 1992. The talks were divided into four agendas:

(1) Basic issues including jurisdiction, past treaties, apology;

(2) Economic issues implying reparations or economic cooperation, depending on the way one looked at this issue;

(3) International issues including North-South dialogue and nuclear development;

(4) Other issues including humanitarian issues.

Regarding (1) and (2) Japan maintained the same position displayed in its negotiations with South Korea, namely that there cannot be war reparations, that prior-1910 treaties were not unlawful, but that Japan was prepared to consider economic cooperation. As for the postwar compensation agreed to by Kanemaru, the delegation took a clear position that it would not be bound by a party agreement. North Korea, as expected, insisted on war reparations, condemned the pre-1910 treaties as unlawful, and urged the implementation of the three party agreement.

Regarding (3) Japan insisted that North Korea should clear doubts regarding nuclear weapons and allow IAEA inspection and indicated that if this aspect was not met to the satisfaction of the international community, the establishment of diplomatic relations was difficult. North Korea objected that these issues had nothing to do with the normalization negotiations.

---

[37] Ibid., p. 250.

Regarding (4) Japan requested the home-return of Japanese-born spouses whose destiny had become unknown. In relation to the abduction issue (Section 6) the Japanese delegation had persistently claimed information concerning a mysterious Japanese woman, who had apparently taught Japanese language and customs to a North Korean agent, Kim Hyeon-Hui, who blew up the South Korean airliner in November 1987. At the eighth round of the talks, the North Korean delegation stated that it was no longer necessary to listen to the Japanese allegations and walked away.[38]

Japan-North Korea relations during the 1990's

Thus the first eight rounds of negotiations ended without achieving tangible results. After this initial endeavour for rapprochement, relations between Japan and North Korea went through a regular fluctuation between tension and relaxation, in close conjunction with the relationship between the US and North Korea.

(1) Relations between Japan and North Korea cooled off for three years from 1992 to 1994. Japan was left on the edge of a nuclear crisis from March 1993 to June 1994.

(2) In 1995, when the nuclear crisis was under control and the Framework Agreement and KEDO were in place, relations between Japan and North Korea were also revitalised and lasted for about two years.

– In March 1995 a delegation led by Michio Watanabe, an influential LDP party leader visited North Korea and agreed that "there wasn't any precondition to resume the negotiations for the normalization of the relationship."

– In June Japan decided to grant 150,000 tons of rice through the Red Cross and provide another 150,000 tons through deferred payment. Another contract was additionally agreed upon in October in which 200,000 tons were provided by deferred payment.

– Humanitarian assistance was given from Japan through international organizations as well:

a) $500,000 through UN organizations in September 1995
b) $6 million through UNDHA in June 1996

---

[38] Ibid., pp. 256–266.

c) $27 million in response to a special UN appeal in October 1997

d) 1.1 million Swiss francs through the International Red Cross and related organizations in October 1997

Preliminary talks were conducted between the two sides to resume negotiations for normalization in August 1997. The return home of a number of Japanese-born spouses took place in November 1997 (15 spouses) and in January to February 1998 (12 spouses). With sensational media coverage the Japanese people welcomed it.

The change in the international climate, brought about by the US-North Korea Agreed Framework talks, Four-Party Talks, KEDO and so on were conducive to the limited progress in the Japan-North Korea relations of that period.

(3) And yet, relations saw a downturn from 1998 to 1999.

First, there was the abduction issue. It was becoming public knowledge that at the end of the 1970's at least about a dozen Japanese citizens had been abducted by North Korea. Already "in March 1988 the Japanese government made an historic announcement in the Diet that there were enough doubts to suspect that three couples had been abducted by North Korea".[39] The families of those abducted began to contact each other and established a Families Union in 1997. The Union strongly influenced public opinion, so much so that "it gained the strength to confront Kim Jung-Il".[40]

It was then followed by a Taepodong missile testing over the Japanese islands in August 1998. This became another tangible sign of the North Korean threat.

In March 1999 'unidentified vessels' appeared inside Japanese territorial waters and a Maritime Safety Agency gunboat pursued and fired on these vessels. Though it was not legally proven, evidence indicated that the vessels came from North Korea. The incident became another vivid example of the threat from North Korea, brought into the homes of millions of television viewers.

---

[39] Tsutomu Nishioka, Vice-President of the Organization for the Rescue of the Abducted, *Asahi Shinbun*, 8 December, 2002.

[40] Teruaki Masumoto, Deputy Director General of the Families Union, *Asahi Shinbun*, 10 November, 2002.

In August 1998 I became the Director General of Treaties Bureau and had the opportunity to participate in and observe tense parliamentary debates in the 1998 autumn session regarding Taepodong and in the 1999 spring session regarding unidentified vessels. In both cases all parliamentarians seemed to share two common concerns: that Japanese sovereignty had been infringed upon and that Japanese security might be seriously threatened. There were differences in nuance and emotion, depending on the political positions taken by each party, but everyone was seeking more effective measures to stop this type of activity. Right-wing or left-wing, conservative or liberal, all keenly felt a deep frustration over Japan's inability to prevent these incidents from happening. This no doubt created a favourable environment for the smooth parliamentary debate on Defence Guidelines (Chapter 2) and subsequently underpinned Prime Minister Koizumi's decision for Japan's active participation in the cause of international peace and security.

(4) That cooling off period, however, was followed by a period of warming up from the end of 1999. It was exactly in line with the general 'relaxation of tension' policy then adopted by North Korea. In December 1999 former Prime Minister Murayama led a multiparty delegation to North Korea and this visit became an icebreaker in the relationship.

In March 2000 the Japanese government announced that 100,000 tons of food aid would be provided and that the suspended negotiations on the normalization of the relationship would be resumed.

The ninth round of the negotiations took place in Pyongyang in April, immediately after this announcement, and continued through August (10th round) and October (11th round). North Korea put great emphasis on the question of apology and reparations whereas Japan pounded North Korea with the humanitarian (above all, abduction) and security (nuclear and missiles) issues. The positions of the two sides remained opposed and the 12th round of the normalization talks quietly disappeared from the agenda of the two governments.

Notwithstanding this unsatisfactory development, in October 2000 the Japanese government announced its intention to supply another 500,000 tons of rice aid through the World Food Programme and implemented it in the course of 2001.

The relative calmness of the relationship was shaken again on 22 December 2001 when an 'unidentified vessel' was detected by the Japanese coastal guard off the Amami Islands. Unlike the incident in March 1999, the coastal guard fired four times at this vessel, and the vessel finally exploded and sank.[41]

Throughout 2002 the relationship, though tense, remained quiet.

6. *Prime Minister Koizumi's visit to North Korea and rising tension*

Initial success

Prime Minister Koizumi's visit to Pyongyang on 17 September 2002 and the adoption of the Japan-DPRK Pyongyang Declaration were first perceived by the international community as a shining example of the success of Japan's recent foreign policy. In Japan as well, despite the outburst of emotions and anger against North Korean abductions, the overall evaluation was positive. It was felt that Koizumi had taken the right decision to normalize the relationship.

The task of opening diplomatic relations and normalizing the relationship with North Korea has long been a priority of Japan's foreign policy. For Japan, unless it could achieve normal relations with North Korea, which Japan annexed in 1910 and ruled for 35 years, an important agenda remaining from the time of World War II was left unresolved. Sometime, somehow it had to be done. Normalization also should have brought to Japan a greater diplomatic leverage in her foreign policy in the Far Eastern region.

From the point of view of North Korea, probably because the economic situation facing the country had become so bad and its sense of alienation from the real power basis of the world, the United States, so imminent, a dire need for normalizing relations with Japan emerged. President Bush's tough policy against North Korea could have played an important role as a catalyst for warming up North Korean policy toward Japan.

But in Japan emotions were piling up against North Korea, particularly around the abduction issue. The shadows of Taepodong and the unidentified vessels had not disappeared either. Thus in

---

[41] *Asahi Shinbun*, 24 December 2001.

Pyongyang, Koizumi had to obtain assurances on three agendas before he could decide to go ahead with full-scale negotiations for normalization: abduction, security and WWII related issues.

The abduction of Japanese citizens took place from 1979 to 1983, mainly from the eastern coast of the main island of Japan, Honshu. Police investigations suggested that altogether eleven citizens were abducted in eight cases.

On 17 September in Pyongyang, North Korea conveyed to the Japanese delegation a list of thirteen abducted individuals out of which eight were dead and only five were alive. Kim Jong-Il acknowledged the fact, apologized and promised that it would never happen again. It was a concessionary gesture that no-one had predicted before the visit. But the Japanese people were deeply shocked and overwhelmed with anger that eight of the thirteen had died, most of them under mysterious circumstances.

The five survivors made a temporary return visit to Japan from 15 October and were given a warm welcome by the people of Japan under full-scale media attention. Despite the tragedy of the eight deceased, this 'coming home' brought bright news to the Japanese people.

On security, North Korea agreed to comply with all the relevant international agreements regarding the nuclear issue, as stated in the Japan-DPRK Pyongyang Declaration. But the concrete modality of North Korea's commitment was unclear. Koizumi knew very well that he had to get an unambiguous assurance from North Korea that it would not go nuclear before Japan could enter full-scale negotiations for normalization.

On missiles, North Korea agreed to extend the moratorium of missile test launches in and after 2003, but no progress was apparently made on the sale of missiles.

Concerning the entry of unidentified vessels into Japanese territorial waters, Kim Jong-Il again showed surprising frankness and stated that he had not known that such events had taken place, that it would never happen again, and that an investigation had already started.

With a view to follow up these issues, a special group was established to discuss security matters between Japan and North Korea.

As if to follow up Japan-North Korea exchanges a high-ranking US special envoy, Assistant Secretary of State Jim Kelly, visited North Korea from 3 to 5 October, after an interval of almost two years.

On World War II related issues, North Korea seemed to have accepted the apology based on Prime Minister Murayama's Statement on 15 August 1995, as well as the basic structure of economic cooperation instead of reparations. Those issues which had been fundamental obstacles in the 1965 negotiations with South Korea and in subsequent rounds of negotiations with the North, such as jurisdiction and past treaties, do not seem to have created fundamental difficulties. The outstanding issue was the amount of assistance. Analysts indicated $5 billion[42] and a media report suggested $8 to $10 billion.[43]

Breakdown of the negotiations

In all respects substantial achievements were made and a real opportunity for intensive negotiations seemed to have been opened. Alas, history will record it otherwise.

On 24 October 2002, under strong pressure from some family members of the abductees, the Japanese government decided not to return the five survivors to North Korea.[44] The decision was received with a positive reaction which rapidly developed into overall praise and support by the Japanese public opinion. After a while the five agreed and followed the government decision.

North Korea observed this development. At the next round of the talks on normalization on 29 and 30 October held in Malaysia, it denounced the Japanese government for betraying an agreement. The talks did not bear any fruit. Security dialogue did not take place. North Korea went back to its original tough position that these matters could only be discussed with America.

Thus, toward the end of 2002 normalization talks between Japan and North Korea broke down completely. The confidential channel between the North Korean authorities and the Japanese Foreign Ministry seemed to have stopped functioning. The five abductees probably lost opportunities to see their children for a considerable length of time.

Meanwhile, another blow changed the entire course of negotiations. On 16 October the State Department revealed that during

---

[42] Hook, Gilson, Hughes, Dobson, *op. cit.*, p. 182.
[43] *International Herald Tribune*, 18 September 2002.
[44] *Asahi Shinbun*, 25 October 2002.

the visit of US special envoy Jim Kelly in early October, North Korea admitted that it had continued its uranium enrichment programme even after the Framework Agreement of 1994. The Bush administration announced that the only solution for the North was to abandon this programme as agreed in the Framework Agreement.

But North Korea continued its collision course. By the end of 2002 North Korea declared that it would resume the construction of nuclear facilities and commence operations, and IAEA inspectors were asked to leave the country.

In the first half of 2003 while the eyes of the world were on Iraq, the situation in North Korea was very tense. North Korea, while expressing readiness to negotiate with the US, also held its position to continue its nuclear weapons programme. The Bush administration was very firm in maintaining that before any negotiations could start, North Korea had to abandon its nuclear programme in a verifiable manner.

Emergence of the Six-party Talks

The chance of resolving the impasse arose in August 2003 when China, Japan, North Korea, South Korea, Russia and the US gathered in Beijing for what became known as the 'Six-party Talks'. The second round of talks was planned, first for December, and then at the beginning of 2004, where North Korea's ending of its nuclear weapons programme and a US 'written security assurance' of North Korea might be discussed. Meanwhile pressure was also rising: KEDO decided to suspend its activities in November 2003.

From Kim Jong-Il's point of view, the roughly drafted scenario of normalization which started at the end of the 1990's and which developed through the North-South Summit in 2000, rapprochement with China and Russia from 2000 to 2002, European recognition in 2000 and 2001, and a breakthrough with Japan in 2002, and which naturally should have enhanced its ultimate goal for normalization with the US, failed entirely. Had this scenario succeeded, it would have brought everything he sought: regime preservation, economic development and an end of isolation. What went wrong?

Probably Kim Jong-Il underestimated the nature of the Bush administration and totally misplayed the nuclear card. His experience in 1994 might have taught him the wrong lesson, namely that nuclear harassment could bring about a better bargain. Kim Jong-

Il also could not predict the emotional nationalism in Japan, which swept away the initial success of Koizumi's visit to Pyongyang.

The Six-party Talks have emerged as a mechanism which might provide a breakthrough. Each party is seeking a solution to resolve its own dilemma:

– North Korea is wary of a multilateral forum in which other parties might 'gang up' against it. But, if it can get what it wants, which is the guarantee of regime preservation, it may find some use in the forum. And if four parties would act as mediators between the US and North Korea, incentives for the North Korean participation would increase.

– The US primary objective is to have a WMD-free Korean peninsula. President Bush is not prepared to negotiate bilaterally with North Korea, before it assures the ending of its nuclear weapons programme. But Bush also knows that waging war against North Korea to achieve this objective is not realistic. The forum might offer an opportunity to resolve this dilemma.

– China, on one hand, has historically played the role of the 'guardian' of the Korean peninsula, but on the other hand, is opposed to a nuclear capability in North Korea. Through this forum, China might be able to achieve its objective of nuclear-free North Korea, while keeping a guardian role in the peninsula. China's strategic position in the region would also be strengthened through its leadership in the Six-party Talks.

– South Korea strongly advocates a peaceful solution of the nuclear issue, but has little leverage to achieve this objective. The forum could be a better framework to influence North Korea than just North-South bilateral talks.

– Russia does not want North Korea holding nuclear weapons, but is interested in maintaining deeper and wider relations with North Korea. The forum gives greater opportunity for Russia to achieve these objectives. It may also allow Russia to improve its strategic role in Northeast Asia.

– Japan is the party most threatened by North Korean nuclear weapons. Japan's own ability to influence North Korea is very limited, particularly after the collapse of the bilateral negotiations at the end of 2002. The Six-party Talks may offer a role for Japan to influence the whole process of normalization in the Korean peninsula.

Thus Northeast Asia has entered an interesting stage in history. For the first time in post-WWII history, an opportunity has emerged to a strategic multilateral dialogue to resolve a fundamental issue of peace and security of the region.

Whatever the outcome of the current crisis, normalization of relations between the South and the North must take place sometime; Japan and North Korea must also settle the issues from the time of the Pacific War; and North Korea has to become a normal member of the international community.

Japan's new defence-security policy

It is important to note that Japan's relations with North Korea from the end of the 1990's have created an impression of a genuine security threat in the minds of many ordinary Japanese. Abduction was the most shocking example of that threat. The intrusion of unidentified vessels increased that impression. The possibility of being exposed to North Korean nuclear weapons seems the ultimate risk.

Nearly a decade has passed from the end of the Cold War, and Japan's exposure to the North Korean threat erased another vestige of Japan's postwar passive pacifism. In 2003 the JDA presented a new budget proposal which incorporated the deployment of a missile defence system of 142.3 billion yen for one Patriot Advanced Capabilities-3 missile around Tokyo and one Standard Missile-3 on an Aegis destroyer. The JDA is planning to deploy four PAC3 and four SM3 in four years. Another 116.4 billion yen is directed to purchase a gigantic helicopter carrier.

The strengthening of the SDF capabilities will constitute an important background in the debates related to the revision of Article 9 of the Constitution in the coming years (Chapter 2).

CHAPTER SIX

ASIA AND THE PACIFIC: EXPANDING RELATIONS FROM BILATERAL TO MULTILATERAL

The previous two chapters explored Japan's relationship with China and Korea. This chapter deals primarily with Southeast Asia supplemented by some other parts of the Eurasian continent and Pacific region.

1. *Beginning of relations: war reparations and early policy initiatives*

The period of reparations

Postwar Japanese foreign policy toward Southeast Asia started with reparations. Some negotiations were concluded reasonably fast, others took time to come to an agreement. After the signing of the San Francisco Peace Treaty in 1951 major negotiations were concluded by the end of the 50's and all outstanding talks by the end of the 60's. Reparations and grants amounted to about $1.68 billion. An additional $0.95 billion in reparations-related loans brought the aggregate figure to approximately $2.63 billion (Chapter 10).[1] The last reparations payment terminated with a payment to the Philippines as late as 1976.[2] Apart from a relatively small amount of reparations which went primarily to the Europeans who were prisoners of war and internees (Chapter 8), the overwhelming amount went to Asian countries.

It is difficult to appreciate the size of these amounts in the context of the economic conditions then existing in Japan. But the Japanese

---

[1] Yen value is: aggregate 945.53 billion yen, reparations and grants 604.75 billion yen and loans 340.78 billion yen. Dollar value is calculated with the exchange rate of $1 = 360yen (MOFA calculation based on public figures, May 2000). The figures include South Korea, but do not include North Vietnam.

[2] ODA Summary 1994 (www.mofa.go.jp/policy/oda/summary/1994/1.html 2002–11–22).

Ministry of Foreign Affairs (MOFA) has made a comparative calculation to illustrate the weight of reparations for postwar Japan. As an example, if one calculates each year's reparations value in relation to the national budget and recalculates the proportionate value with 1998 national budget figures, the overall amount would be $232.4 billion in 1998 year value.[3]

In addition to these reparations Japan also relinquished its external assets with an estimated 1945 value of $28.014 billion.[4]

Let us list the major negotiations and their end results:

With Burma, a Reparations and Economic Cooperation Agreement was concluded in November 1954, amounting to $200 million with 10 years deferred payment. The Peace Treaty was simultaneously concluded, because Burma did not participate in the San Francisco Conference. In 1964 grant assistance of $140 million was added.

With the Philippines, a reparations agreement was concluded in May 1956, of $550 million for reparations with 20 years of deferred payment. The San Francisco Peace Treaty was then ratified.

With Indonesia, a reparations agreement of $223 million was signed in January 1958, with 12 years of deferred payment. Indonesia signed the San Francisco Peace Treaty but did not ratify it and finally concluded a separate peace treaty.

Both Laos and Cambodia renounced their rights for reparations. An Economic and Technical Cooperation Agreement was signed with Laos in 1958 of 1 billion yen (about $2.78 million) in grants and with Cambodia in 1959 of 1.5 billion yen (about $4.17 million) in grants.

With Vietnam a reparations agreement was signed in May 1959, for an amount of 39 million dollars with 5 years of deferred payment.

With Thailand, Malaysia, and Singapore the question of compensation was subsequently settled during the 60's.[5] A 'Special Yen Agreement' was concluded with Thailand in 1962.[6] Both Malaysia and Singapore were paid 2.94 billion yen (= about 8.17 million dollars) in grants in 1968.[7]

---

[3] MOFA internal calculation based on public figures, May 2000.

[4] Calculated by the Inspection Commission on Japanese Assets Abroad, established under the auspices of MOFA and MOF (Ministry of Finance) by a GHQ memorandum.

[5] Sakamoto, *op. cit.*, pp. 90–91.

[6] Hosoya, 1993, *op. cit.*, p. 165.

[7] MOFA calculation based on public figures, May 2000.

These reparations played a very important role in strengthening the economic ties between Japan and Southeast Asian countries. As we will see in Chapter 10, all postwar reparations and economic cooperation related to reparations directed to Asian countries was done in the form of purchases by the Japanese government of goods and services supplied by Japanese companies. In other words the Japanese government paid its yen to Japanese companies and purchased the goods and services to be supplied to each country to which Japan owed reparations and payment. Thus, the reparations also played an important role in stimulating production and exports for Japanese business.[8]

Early policy initiatives towards Southeast Asia

The first Prime Minister who consciously tried to strengthen Japanese policy towards Southeast Asia was Nobusuke Kishi. On February 4, 1957, just before becoming Prime Minister, Foreign Minister Kishi outlined in his speech at the Diet the three pillars of postwar Japanese foreign policy: 'United Nations-centred diplomacy', 'Cooperation with the free world', and 'Maintaining the position as a member of Asia'.[9] These three pillars were incorporated into the first edition of the Japanese Foreign Ministry 'Diplomatic Bluebook' published in September of that year (Chapter 12).

Foreign Minister Kishi also outlined in his speech the following three principles to govern Japan's relations with Asian countries: improvement of the status of Japan through the consolidation of neighbourly relations; improvement of welfare in Asia through development cooperation; and the development of the Japanese economy through reparations and economic cooperation (Chapter 10).

He visited six Asia-Pacific countries from May to June[10] and a further nine countries in the area from November to December.[11]

In this postwar period when Japan's economic relations with Korea and China, the two countries which had been very important to the

---

[8] Sakamoto, *op. cit.*, p. 91. Tadokoro, *op. cit.*, pp. 130–31.

[9] Akihiko Tanaka, database, *Sekaito Nihon (World and Japan)*.

[10] Burma, India, Pakistan, Sri Lanka, Thailand and Taiwan. C. Hosoya, 1993, p. 165.

[11] South Vietnam, Cambodia, Laos, Malaysia, Indonesia, Singapore, Australia, New Zealand and the Philippines. Ibid.

prewar Japanese economic development, were not in harmony, Southeast Asia was perceived as the primary area for Japanese trade, investment, and procurement of energy resources. During his trip to the Asia-Pacific countries as well as to America in 1957, Prime Minister Kishi introduced the first Japanese concept to establish a 'Southeast Asian Development Fund' based on financial resources from the US, Japanese technology and know-how and Southeast Asian labour forces. Partly because of the fear in Southeast Asian countries of a strong Japanese role in the region and partly because of American unwillingness to bear financial responsibility for the region, this idea did not immediately fly.[12] But Prime Minister Kishi had clearly articulated that Japan was willing to play a creative and effective role in Southeast Asia.

During the 60's countries in Southeast Asia also saw some substantial economic and political development. The Association of Southeast Asian Nations (ASEAN) was created in August 1967. It was first comprised of Indonesia, Malaysia, the Philippines, Singapore, and Thailand. ASEAN was destined to play a key role in the economic and political development of the region.

Relations between Japan and Southeast Asia developed steadily. Two projects of importance led to the consolidation of economic cooperation between Japan and the region.

The first was the establishment of the Asian Development Bank (ADB) in 1966. Japan played a major role in establishing this bank and sought to locate the bank in Japan. The countries of the region, however, chose Manila.

The second initiative was a Ministerial Conference for the Economic Development of Southeast Asia first convened in 1966 in Tokyo. Nine countries in the region, excluding North Vietnam, were invited, but Burma did not participate due to its policy of neutrality. Indonesia and Cambodia sent observers only, in accordance with their non-alignment policy.[13]

In both projects Japan's initiatives were not met with full support by the Southeast Asian countries. There was a certain reluctance on the part of the Southeast Asian countries to let Japan play too conspicuous a role in regional leadership, due to their wartime memo-

---

[12] Sakamoto, *op. cit.* p. 92.
[13] Tadokoro, *op. cit.* pp. 132, 134.

ries. In the prevailing Cold War climate and particularly with the ongoing war in Vietnam, a dominant role for Japan, a clear ally of the United States, also created uneasiness on the part of the Southeast Asian countries.

The war in Vietnam was indeed becoming an increasingly dominant factor for the peace and security of the region. After the French withdrawal from Vietnam in 1954, a pro-democratic and pro-American regime was established in Saigon. Armed resistance against the South Vietnamese government began in 1959. American intervention began in 1961, a US Command was established in Saigon in 1962, followed by the bombardment of North Vietnam in 1964, and in 1965, 200,000 US ground troops were deployed. The military situation began to deteriorate substantially after January 1968 for the Saigon government and America, but US troops in Vietnam reached 540,000 in 1969. The Japanese government recognized the expansive nature of the communist powers and supported the US policy to combat the 'threat' of communism from North Vietnam.[14] But Japanese public opinion saw this war more in the context of the fight for independence by the Vietnamese people against French and American 'imperialist power'. Political tension permeated Japan throughout the 60's.

2. *Strengthening the relationship: the Fukuda Doctrine and the establishment of PECC*

For Japan the 1970's became an interesting period in the Asia-Pacific region where several important international events as well as changes in Japan's policy toward the region gradually converged into the creation of the first regional multilateral cooperation structure.

The end of the Vietnam War

First there was the end of the Vietnam War. For President Nixon, who assumed the presidency in 1969, a priority foreign policy objective

---

[14] F. Togo wrote in his memoirs (1982, p. 201): "The war in Vietnam ended in tragedy, but so long as one acknowledges the existence of South Vietnam, which claimed its survival under freedom and without intervention from the North, the American position to assist it has to be commended within the power politics of the world."

was to put an end to the American involvement in Vietnam. Henry Kissinger negotiated hard with his North Vietnam counterpart, and the Peace Accord on Vietnam was signed in Paris in January 1973. Despite the outward assurance for the preservation of the Saigon government the Peace Accord led to the eventual fall of Saigon in April 1975.

Japan acted quickly and by September 1973 had established diplomatic relations with North Vietnam. It took a while to resolve the question of reparations, but the two sides eventually agreed that Japan would extend 13.5 billion yen of grant aid to North Vietnam. At the beginning of 1976 the two countries exchanged ambassadors.[15]

Thus the major threat to the peace and security in the region was overcome, but the situation in Indochina remained in turmoil. The massacre by the Khmer Rouge in Cambodia through 1975–1978, Vietnam's invasion of Cambodia in 1978, and clashes between Vietnam and China in 1979 left Indochina outside the scope of the mainstay of regional socio-economic development.

Japan's changing policy toward Southeast Asia (Tanaka's visit and the Fukuda Doctrine)

While the war in Vietnam was drawing to a close Japan's policy toward Southeast Asia had undergone important changes.

The booming Japanese economy of the 60's led to an expanded presence of Japanese business in the economies of its Southeast Asian neighbours. While these countries benefitted from the expanded economic relations with Japan, this sudden and significant economic presence invited antipathy as well.

During Prime Minister Tanaka's visit to Thailand and Indonesia in January 1974 riots erupted. Analysts say that the riots were caused by the frustration of the people against the strong Japanese economic presence, combined with dissatisfaction with their own authorities, who could not solve their domestic economic difficulties. The riots shocked the Japanese delegation and gave food for thought to the significance of Japanese economic activities and the overall approach Japan should take to enhance good neighbourly and friendly relations with the countries of Southeast Asia.[16]

---

[15] Nakanishi, *op. cit.*, p. 166.
[16] Ibid., p. 167.

Having taken account of the experience of this visit, by the time Prime Minister Fukuda visited Southeast Asia in August 1977, Japanese foreign policy bore more depth, breadth and subtlety to respond to the thinking of the people of the region. While attending the second round of the ASEAN Summit Meeting in Manila he outlined three principles of his Asian policy:

– Japan would not become a strong military power;
– Japan would establish relations of 'heart to heart' and not concentrate only on economic or political relations, but also emphasize social and cultural relations;
– Japan would make positive contributions towards strengthening the ASEAN intraregional process and enhancing its own relations based on mutual confidence with the countries of Indochina.

Japanese efforts to establish more harmonious overall relations with the countries of the region as embodied in Prime Minister Fukuda's approach had some positive outcomes.

In 1978 Japan was accepted as a dialogue partner at the ASEAN Foreign Ministers Meeting. In 1979 the ASEAN-Japan Meeting was expanded to include the Foreign Ministers of America, Australia, New Zealand, and the EC. Canada joined in 1980 and Korea in 1991. The meetings came to be called the ASEAN Post-Ministerial Conference (PMC).[17]

As for the last point of the Fukuda Doctrine, to establish "relations based on mutual confidence with the countries of Indochina", ongoing instability in the region prevented Japan from taking meaningful initiatives. Japan's positive involvement in the Cambodian issue had to wait until the end of the 1980's (Chapter 12).

Some comments need to be made here regarding another aspect of Japan's policy on Indochina. One consequence of the social and political upheaval in Indochina was the number of refugees seeking asylum. Traditionally Japan's policy was, in principle, not to accept refugees, but that situation began to change after 1975 with the emergence of Indochinese refugees, the so-called 'boat people', on Japan's shores. Financially, Japan offered $90 million in assistance to the UNHCR in 1979.[18] But more importantly, in 1978 Japan

---

[17] Nakanishi, *op. cit.*, pp. 173–174. India, China and Russia joined the ASEAN-PMC in 1996 (www.mofa.go.jp/mofaj/area/asean/gaiyo.html 2003–07–16).

[18] Ikei, *op. cit.*, p. 325.

decided to open its doors to Indochinese refugees. The number of 'boat people', or refugees, who fled to Japan, peaked from 1979 to 1982, each year exceeding 1,000 people, eventually reaching a total of 10,666 by the end of 2000.[19]

So as to better cope with the refugee problem, Japan joined the Convention Relating to the Status of Refugees in October 1981 and up to the end of 2000 had admitted 265 refugees, excluding the refugees from Indochina.[20]

The question of refugees is a difficult issue where all political, social, economic and cultural elements are intertwined. But whether from Indochina or elsewhere, there is no doubt that it is an important issue which Japan will have to face more squarely in the 21st century, together with the issue of foreign workers.

Efforts by scholars and business people toward regional cooperation

From the end of the 1960's Japanese scholars and business people have exerted some leadership in creating a multilateral forum for exchanges and cooperation.

The Pacific Basin Economic Conference (PBEC) was created in 1967 by a joint initiative of Japan and Australia, with a view to enhancing exchanges and contacts among the business people. Noboru Goto, President of the Japan Chamber of Commerce and Industry, nicknamed 'Mr. Pacific', developed a strong leadership.

In academia, the Japanese scholar Kiyoshi Kojima proposed the creation of a forum of major advanced countries in the Pacific community. In 1968 the Pacific Trade and Development Conference (PAFTAD) was formed, to discuss the establishment of an OECD type of organization in the Asia-Pacific region.

In 1976 Saburo Okita, another well-known scholar and economist, proposed the creation of the Organization for Pacific, Trade, Aid and Development (OPTAD) to include both developed and developing countries in the region to discuss regional trade and investment.[21]

---

[19] www.mofa.go.jp/mofaj/gaiko/nanmin/main3.html 2003–01–03.
[20] Ibid.
[21] A. Fukushima, *Japanese Foreign Policy, The Emerging Logic of Multilateralism*, Macmillan, 1999, pp. 167–168.

Relations with ASEAN countries under Prime Minister Ohira and the establishment of PECC

Under Prime Minister Ohira, who replaced Prime Minister Fukuda in December 1978, a new initiative towards a regional, multilateral and structural dialogue started. It was the beginning of a process which would develop over time into a new structure in the Asia-Pacific region.

In contrast to Europe, where regional multilateralism played a very important role in foreign policy after WWII, the clearest examples being the establishment of the North Atlantic Treaty Organization (NATO) in 1949, the European Economic Community (EEC) in 1958, the European Community (EC) in 1967, and the Conference on Security and Cooperation in Europe (CSCE) in 1975, regional multilateralism was almost mute in the Asia-Pacific region.

Analysts give many reasons for this and I might summarize them in the three following points:

First, the basic security structure which evolved in the region was a bilateral security arrangement between the country concerned and the United States. This structure became known as the 'Hub (US) and Spoke (each contracting party)' relationship. Each security conflict in Asia arose from a specific issue and was considered to be best dealt with through the bilateral security arrangement such as US-Korea or US-Taiwan.

Second, the diversity of the countries of the region in history, ethnicity, religion, population, size of the territory, per capita GDP, economic system, and political structure, or, in other words, the lack of common ground and experience in Asia, formed a psychological and substantive obstacle to the creation of a regional and multilateral institution.

Third, historical and geopolitical circumstances dictated that it was the Southeast Asian countries that were to set the tone and pace of this process towards multilateralism. The Southeast Asian countries took a very cautious approach, partly because of the history of Chinese imperialism, European colonialism and Japanese occupation. In addition, there was the inherent fear that an institution led by the major powers of the region might not allow their independent voices to be heard.[22]

---

[22] Fukushima, *op. cit.*, pp. 131–132.

Despite this traditional cautiousness, Prime Minister Masayoshi Ohira began to take leadership in enhancing multilateral cooperation in the Asia-Pacific region. Strengthened relations with Australia (Section 7), the normalization of relations with Vietnam mentioned above, the improved relations with China (Chapter 4), and concrete ideas from scholars and business people, all these elements created the basis of his leadership.

Just after he assumed the role of Prime Minister, Ohira established a committee to study cooperation among the Pacific Rim countries. The committee was chaired by Saburo Okita, a respected scholar and well-known advocate for Asia-Pacific cooperation. Things then began to move fast. An interim report by the Okita Committee was adopted in November 1979; Okita was then chosen as Foreign Minister; Ohira visited Australia in January 1980 and agreed with Prime Minister Malcolm Fraser to cohost an international seminar on pan-Pacific cooperation in Australia; and the final report of the Okita Committee on the concept of a pan-Pacific association was published in May 1980. Sadly, Ohira passed away in June 1980 but the international seminar went ahead, hosted by Prime Minister Fraser in September in Canberra. Academics, business people and government officials from Australia, the US, New Zealand, Japan, ASEAN, Korea, Papua New Guinea, Fiji and Tonga participated. This was the beginning of what became known as the Pacific Economic Cooperation Conference (PECC).

The following observations can be made on the establishment and development of PECC.

– The initiative for such a scheme of cooperation came from Japan and Australia;

– Japan agreed to let Australia play a leading role. Japan's cautious approach could be explained by the recognition that its initiative to establish the Great East Asia Co-prosperity Sphere during the Pacific War was still a source of resentment in other Asian nations.

– The step-by-step and non-governmental approach and the structure of PECC as a forum for exchanges of views precisely met the requirements of ASEAN representatives;

– The United States, the strongest Pacific power, was also represented.[23]

---

[23] Nakanishi, *op. cit.*, pp. 174–175. Fukushima, *op. cit.*, p. 168.

PECC thus became the most effective organ of multilateral exchange and cooperation over the 1980's. It succeeded in accumulating a common experience, gradually creating common ground, and cooperation matured in an Asian way based on consensus.

3. Development of the Asian economies and the creation of APEC

Enhanced economic cooperation in the Asia-Pacific region

In the course of the 1980's Southeast Asia became a focal point of economic development among all the developing countries in the world. An enhanced regional multilateralism began to take shape, led by this economic success.

The economic development of the Asia-Pacific region was primarily the result of internal efforts made by the respective countries in the region. Among the 'Newly Industrialized Economies (NIEs)' Korea, Singapore, Taiwan and Hong Kong, the 'Four Asian Dragons', attracted worldwide attention with their economic dynamism. Other ASEAN countries followed the lead of these dragons in their economic development.

At the same time, the power of the economic giants of the region became another engine of economic development. Together with the United States, Japan, with its strengthened yen, particularly after the Plaza Accord of 1985, absorbed a substantial share of the exports from the Southeast Asian countries.[24] China, with its vast economic potential and a new market-oriented economic policy of 'Reform and Opening', boosted economic activity in the region. Intraregional trade became a real salient factor for enhanced cooperation among the countries of the region.

Another element, which worked as an 'awakening factor' for enhanced regional cooperation, was several sharp moves in other major economic entities of the world. Clear examples were heightened discussions on the creation of the US-Canada Free Trade Agreement (entered into force in January 1989) and strengthened cooperation in the European Community directed towards a single

---

[24] Murata, *op. cit.*, pp. 210–212.

market and currency through the Single European Act (adopted in February 1986).

The emergence of APEC

Thus, towards the end of the 1980's conditions became ripe for the Asia-Pacific region to establish an enhanced mechanism of regional cooperation. Symbolically enough, in November 1989 when the Berlin wall fell, the Asia-Pacific Economic Cooperation (APEC) was launched.

Japan did not stay silent. The country was in the midst of an economic boom commonly referred to as the 'bubble economy'. The Ministry of International Trade and Industry had taken a substantial initiative in launching a regional organisation comparable to the EC and US-Canada FTA. But again, the leading role was wisely offered to Australia and the first meeting was held in Canberra. It took six years before Japan hosted the APEC Leaders Meeting in Osaka in 1995.[25] Japan's cautiousness was again attributed to the memory of the Pacific War.

APEC started as a gathering of 12 regional countries, 6 ASEAN countries including Brunei,[26] which joined the organization in 1984, and 6 non-ASEAN countries, which were Japan, Korea, Australia, New Zealand, America and Canada.

ASEAN determined the key directions of APEC activities, likewise in the case of PECC. ASEAN leadership became strengthened by the economic success through the 1980's and the diplomatic experience gained through regular dialogue with larger countries of the region. ASEAN adopted an approach of consensus, non-binding, and 'step by step', in true Asian fashion. It was cautious to avoid establishing a structural, organizational and rigid institution. APEC therefore started as an ad hoc meeting of trade and foreign ministers and grew steadily through the 1990's:

- Regular yearly ministerial meetings were agreed (1990, Singapore).
- Goals and scope of activities were agreed (1991, Seoul).
- The Secretariat was established in Singapore (1992, Bangkok).
- The first APEC Leaders Meeting was held (1993, Seattle).

---

[25] Iokibe, *op. cit.*, pp. 231–233.
[26] Brunei joined ASEAN in January 1984.

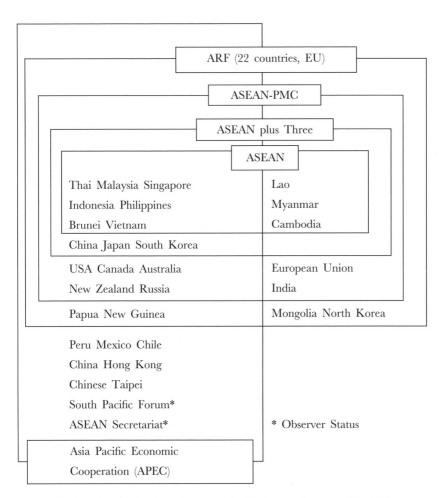

Regional organizations in the Asia-Pacific region as of 2003[27]

---

[27] www.mofa.go.jp/mofaj/area/asem/arf/gaiyo.html 2003–03–18.

– A declaration was adopted to achieve free trade and investment in the region by 2010 for advanced countries and by 2020 for developing economies (1994, Bogor).

– The Action Agenda based on the Bogor Declaration was agreed (1995, Osaka).

– The Manila Action Plan for APEC (MAPA) was adopted to expedite the liberalization process voluntarily (1996, Manila).

– Nine sectors for Early Voluntary Sectoral Liberalization (EVSL) were proposed (1997, Vancouver).

– The EVSL was discussed (1998, Kuala Lumpur).[28]

Kuala Lumpur became an important meeting that brought the member countries to 21. The new members were China, Taiwan, and Hong Kong (1991), Mexico and Papua New Guinea (1993), Chile (1994), Vietnam, Peru, and Russia (1998).

The Kuala Lumpur Meeting may also be considered a turning point for APEC development, because for the first time in its history it faced serious difficulties on the nature of the agreement it wanted to reach.

APEC's dilemma

The Asian way of gradual consensus building began to irritate some participants of APEC, notably the United States. The United States under the Clinton administration first played a very positive role in initiating a leaders meeting in Seattle. But the US administration became increasingly frustrated that the non-binding Asian way did not produce concrete and measurable results in enhancing free trade and investment. The American delegation began to request concrete and binding decisions, which were not met with warm support by the Asian countries.

The differing approaches of the two groups were reflected in the discussion concerning the objectives and methods of APEC. America argued that the "liberalization" of the market should be the key policy to enhance free trade and investment. The Asian countries preferred the 'facilitation' of trade and investment, implying a soft and

---

[28] Fukushima, *op. cit.*, pp. 134–138.

gradual approach of enhancing and encouraging a free flow of trade and investment.

In June 1998, at the Trade Ministers Meeting, Japan clashed sharply with the US. Debates between the two groups were heated on the nine sectors for Early Voluntary Sectoral Liberalization (EVSL). Japan maintained that it could not take a decision on fish and fish products and forestry products because of internal constituencies. It was the position of the Japanese government that any decision which would apply greater pressure toward liberalization other than the WTO process was simply unacceptable. America argued forcefully that APEC should take concrete decisions towards further liberalization and that Japan should join others. From June to November both sides tried to persuade other member countries to follow its course. At the Kuala Lumpur Meeting, several Asian countries including China, Indonesia, Thailand, and Malaysia did not support the implementation of the EVSL programme. Consequently APEC could not come to an agreement and a face-saving measure to send it to the WTO was taken. The inability of APEC to reach a concrete decision thoroughly disappointed the US and other like-minded countries.[29] In the immediate short-term objective, Japan succeeded in achieving its goal. But in the long run, Japan continued to be caught in a basic contradiction that as a free-trading nation she nonetheless required the 'definite' protection of agricultural and fishery products.

After the Kuala Lumpur Meeting APEC deliverability on concrete economic matters became obscured. But after 9/11 at the 2001 Shanghai meeting and the 2002 Mexico Meeting,[30] international terrorism became one of the central issues for discussion among the top leaders of the region. Political matters cannot be outside the scope of the interests of world leaders, therefore, like the G7/G8, APEC might play a useful role in the systematic approach to political issues.

---

[29] J. Ravenhill, *APEC and the construction of Pacific rim regionalism*, Cambridge University press, 2001, pp. 183–184. Ravenhill analyses that Japan's assistance of $30 billion in helping the Asian financial crisis "may not have been a coincidence" for gaining support by some Asian countries.

[30] The 1999 meeting was held in Auckland and the 2000 meeting in Brunei.

4. *Security cooperation after the Cold War: ARF and NEACD*

ARF: Emerging interests in security cooperation

From the beginning of the 1990's, after the end of the Cold War, the Asia-Pacific countries began to bear a more positive attitude towards multilateral security cooperation. The disappearance of US-Soviet rivalry brought about a climate more conducive to a multilateral security dialogue. The rigid structure of 'Hub and Spoke' had softened, allowing for a broader type of multilateral security forum. Rapid economic development of the NIEs and ASEAN created a wider ground for deliberating regional security matters. Above all ASEAN had become more willing to take some initiatives. The envisaged dialogue was, in the European context, nothing similar to NATO, which constituted a military alliance against a common enemy, but a CSCE type of cooperation, which aimed at enhanced security dialogue towards confidence building.

The first initiative was taken by the Australian Foreign Minister Gareth Evans who, in July 1990 proposed a Conference on Security and Cooperation in Asia (CSCA), an Asian version of CSCE.[31]

But Japan was not silent either. A year later, in July 1991 at the ASEAN-PMC meeting, the Japanese Foreign Minister Taro Nakayama proposed the establishment of an Asia-Pacific regional security dialogue within the framework of ASEAN-PMC, combined with the creation of a Senior Officials Meeting. This proposal was based on Japan's recognition that multilateral security dialogue could play a useful role to enhance confidence building in the post-Cold War environment.

Traditionally Japan had always been cautious in Asia-Pacific multilateral dialogue, because of the Soviet Union. Soviet interest in enhanced regional cooperation had always been interpreted as putting a wedge between the Japan-US security alliance and weakening US naval presence in the Pacific. Gorbachev's visit to Japan in April 1991 introduced some relaxation in this traditional cautiousness and Japan welcomed Soviet participation in PECC.[32] But in the area of

---

[31] Fukushima, *op. cit.*, p. 139.
[32] Paragraph 24 of the Japan-Soviet Joint Communiqué of 18 April 1991 stated that "Japan welcomes the Soviet Union's intention to join PECC, sharing the prin-

security, Japan's initiative was kept halfway, because Japan, on the one hand, proposed a multilateral dialogue framework but, on the other, the Soviet Union was not included in this proposed framework.

These proposals were not warmly welcomed by ASEAN and other regional countries. This was probably due to the lack of prior consensus building efforts.

It was finally based on an ASEAN initiative that a new regional security forum was established. At the 1993 Meeting of ASEAN-PMC in Singapore, an agreement was reached to establish a security forum of foreign ministers of ASEAN, PMC and some major outside countries. Since then Japan has been an active participant.

In 1994 in Bangkok the first meeting of the ASEAN Regional Forum (ARF) was held and in 1995 at the second meeting in Brunei the future direction of ARF was agreed.

ARF was to conduct discussions in an Asian way, based on consensus and with a step by step approach. In fact, the agreement reached at the second meeting that ARF would "move at a pace comfortable to all participants" came to be called the 'ASEAN way'.

The future work outlined in the 1995 Brunei Meeting was composed of "three phases of development: promotion of confidence building measures, preventive diplomacy, and development of approaches to conflict, which meant conflict resolution".[33]

ARF started in 1994 with 18 members. The six existing ASEAN countries, the two future ASEAN members (Vietnam and Laos),[34] the seven PMC members (Japan, Korea, Australia, New Zealand, America, Canada and the EU) and in addition Russia, China, and Papua New Guinea were also included.

By 2002, two had joined from ASEAN (Myanmar and Cambodia) and India, Mongolia and DPRK[35] joined from non-ASEAN countries, bringing the total membership to 23. The inclusion of DPRK in the ARF completed the picture and contained all members necessary for the security of the region.

---

ciples of freedom and openness." (MOFA, *Warerano Hoppyouryoudo (Our Northern Territories)*, 2001, Materials, p. 41).

[33] Ibid., p. 147.

[34] Vietnam joined ASEAN in July 1995, and Laos in July 1997.

[35] These countries joined ARF as follows: Cambodia (1995), Myanmar and India (1996), Mongolia (1998) and North Korea (2000). Myanmar joined ASEAN in July 1997 and Cambodia in April 1999, both after joining ARF.

The first phase of confidence building has proceeded with certain success as exemplified by the publication of defence 'White Papers' by each of the member countries. Through accumulated dialogue in the ARF framework, member countries have probably less misgivings and suspicions when facing the security issues of other countries in the region. China began to participate more actively in the dialogue.[36] The mere fact that the DPRK joined the forum at the July 2000 meeting is another small step forward for enhanced confidence building.

As to the second stage of preventive diplomacy, the discussion was strained. It was partly because of China, who maintained that the discussion concerning preventive diplomacy could lead to a possible intervention in domestic affairs. Some countries became frustrated by the slow pace of the discussion. Other sceptics criticized ARF for being unable to play any effective role in the East Timor crisis in 1999. Voices were heard from ASEAN think tanks that "ARF had reached a watershed".

In June 2002, the Japanese State Minister for Defence, Gen Nakatani, proposed at the Asia Pacific Defence Ministers Meeting in Singapore (also referred to as the Shangri-La Meeting, named after the hotel where the meeting took place) to formalize and regularize the Asia-Pacific Defence Ministers Meeting. Details of his proposal were unclear but it was a proposal from Japan that had not been heard since Nakayama's ill-fated initiative in 1991.[37]

Northeast Asia Cooperation Dialogue (NEACD) and the Six-party Talks

Under ASEAN leadership, ARF became the most successful security framework developed in the Asia-Pacific region over the 1990's. Meanwhile, there were some attempts to create a security framework exclusively covering Northeast Asia, such as NPCSD and NEACD. Their development was slow and stayed at the level of track II at best. Japan has not taken a notable leadership role, but continued to be a stable supporter for these moves.

---

[36] China was very cautious first for fear that ARF might intrude in its domestic affairs, but its position began to change after the July 1996 ARF Jakarta meeting, when China volunteered to co-chair a 'Confidence Building' group in ARF along with the Philippines (Fukushima, *op. cit.*, p. 146).

[37] Saga Shinbun, *Kyodo*, 2 June 2002.

In the northern part of East Asia, the first initiative to establish a multilateral security dialogue came from Canada, at the time of the demise of the Soviet Union. In July 1990, the Canadian Foreign Minister, Joe Clark, proposed the North Pacific Cooperative Security Dialogue (NPCSD). Seven conferences and workshops were held between April 1991 and March 1993 on topics such as unconventional security issues, regional confidence building measures, and the interrelationship between history, culture and regional security cooperation. Participants in NPCSD included academics and officials in their private capacities from Canada, China, the DPRK, Japan, Mongolia, the ROK, Russia and the United States.

In March 1993, however, these far-sighted initiatives by Canada came to an end due to funding problems in Ottawa. Professor Susan Shirk, Director of the University of California's Institute on Global Conflict and Cooperation (IGCC) proposed to follow up this type of gathering. At the planning conference in July 1993 'the Northeast Asia Cooperation Dialogue (NEACD)' was established with the participation of government officials and academics from China, Japan, Russia, the United States, the ROK and the DPRK (Canada and Mongolia were excluded). The first meeting of the NEACD was held in October 1993 in La Jolla, California, and since then the subregion has witnessed more frequent exchanges among defence and security personnel, both bilaterally and multilaterally.[38]

The DPRK participated in the planning session but did not attend any meetings after the first session in October 1993, only to reappear in October 2002 in Moscow. The North Korean change of position could have been a byproduct of Koizumi's successful visit to North Korea in September (Chapter 5).[39]

Against this background, the Six-party Talks (Chapter 5), which emerged in summer 2003 out of the North Korean nuclear crisis, may become an important multilateral organization in dealing with key security matters in Northeast Asia.

The future structure of security dialogue in the Asia-Pacific region is not quite clear. Nor is the concrete role of Japan's participation clear. And yet it seems to me that this is an area where Japan could take positive initiatives for a strengthened framework for cooperation.

---

[38] Fukushima, *op. cit.*, pp. 155–158.
[39] Fukuhsima, 2001, *op. cit.*, p. 34.

5. *In search of new cooperation: ASEAN plus Three and FTA*

ASEAN plus Three

From the 1980's to the 1990's Asian economies continued to develop
with dynamism. But this remarkable development led to an over-
heated economic situation. In 1997 a currency crisis erupted in
Thailand. The Thai economy had enjoyed a 9% economic growth
for 10 years until 1995. Investment boomed in asset markets and
the Thai currency continued to rise against the dollar. But the downfall in exports, the uncertainty over future economic development,
and the abrupt movement of speculative money resulted in a sudden downfall of the Thai currency in the middle of 1997, affecting
many ASEAN countries and Korea.

In August an international conference was held in Tokyo and
$17.2 billion of assistance to Thailand was agreed upon. International
assistance to Indonesia amounted to $39 billion in October and to
Korea $57 billion in November.[40]

Meanwhile, Japan, particularly the Ministry of Finance, proposed
the creation of a new Asian Monetary Fund (AMF) to supplement
the existing International Monetary Fund (IMF). The United States
did not agree. The US official position was that it was more a fundamental structural reform than financial assistance that was necessary. Japan had to resort to the traditional networking of a bilateral
assistance scheme.

Thus by the end of 1998 Japan's assistance reached around $80
billion:

– From July 1997 to November 1998, Japan announced assistance
of $44 billion, including $10 billion to South Korea, $5 billion to
Indonesia and $4 billion to Thailand.[41]

– In October 1998 Japan announced another scheme of $30 bil-
lion, half of which was for the medium to long-term financial needs
and half of which was for the short-term capital needs; this was
known as the 'New Miyazawa Initiative'.

– At the ASEAN plus Three Summit Meeting in December 1998,

---

[40] "Ajiano Tsukakiki (Financial Cricis in Asia)" *Gendaiyogono Kisochishiki* (*Basic
Knowledge of Contemporary Vocabulary*), 2002, *op. cit.*

[41] Iokibe, *op. cit.*, pp. 250–253.

Japan announced a special loan facility scheme in the amount of $5 billion.[42]

Amidst this monetary and financial crisis, the ASEAN Leaders Meeting was held in December 1997 in Kuala Lumpur commemorating the 30th anniversary of ASEAN. The ASEAN leaders invited leaders from China, Korea and Japan. All of them accepted. This was the beginning of what we now call 'ASEAN plus Three'.[43]

Cooperation in this structure developed fast.

In the 1998 Hanoi ASEAN plus Three Leaders Meeting, an agreement was reached to hold meetings regularly once a year, in conjunction with the ASEAN Leaders Meeting.

At the 1999 ASEAN plus Three Leaders Meeting in Manila, Japan surprised everyone by inviting leaders from China and Korea for a breakfast meeting. Given the complexity of the relations with these two countries, as we have seen in the two previous chapters, for many Japanese, the harmonious images which were televised from Manila, at the heart of ASEAN, on the morning of 28 November 1999 evoked a great sigh of relief. The ingenuity displayed in holding the breakfast meeting at a triangular table was also warmly received by the Japanese television audience.[44]

The gathering of three Northeast Asian leaders immediately became a regular event at the fringe of ASEAN plus Three meetings. Tripartite cooperation started at government level. 2002 became the year of tripartite exchanges and many cultural events took place in each of the three countries.

At the Bali Meeting in October 2003 a Joint Declaration on the Promotion of Tripartite Cooperation among the three countries was adopted. It set a clear course of "across-the-board and future-oriented cooperation in a variety of areas" and defined the tripartite

---

[42] *Asian Economic Crisis and Japan's Contribution*, October 2000 (http://www.mofa.go.jp/policy/economy/asia/crisis0010.html 2002–11–26).

[43] After Cambodia joined ASEAN in 1999 and made the participant countries of ASEAN 10, this meeting is occasionally called 10 + 3.

[44] Vice-Minister for Foreign Affairs, Yutaka Kawashima, stated at the press conference: "There was an attempt to hold a Japan-China-Korea leaders meeting at the time of President Kim Young Sam. He proposed to discuss the three *kans*, *Kanji* (Chinese character), *kanpou* (Chinese medicine), *kankyou* (environment). Time was not ripe then. I think it is quite meaningful that three countries which have common historic and cultural background gather together." (11 November 1999, http://www.mofa.go.jp/mofaj/press/kaiken/jikan/j_9911.html 2002–11–03).

cooperation as "an essential part of East Asian cooperation".[45] In my view this declaration may have a historical significance in determining Japan's strategic position in East Asia.

At the ASEAN plus Three structure, regular meetings of Ministers of Finance started in 1999, Ministers of Foreign Affairs and Ministers of Economic Affairs in 2000, and Ministers of Labour and Ministers of Agriculture in 2001, Ministers of Tourism, Energy and Environment in 2002.

Tangible results had already emerged at the second meeting of Ministers of Finance at Chiang Mai, Thailand in May 2000. A proposal to create a network of bilateral emergency currency swap accords was received positively by the countries in the region. This proposal could be interpreted as an ASEAN version of the failed AMF initiatives put forth by Japan at the time of the Asian financial crisis. Japan took a positive lead in establishing this framework,[46] and by early 2003 concluded such accords with Korea, Thailand, the Philippines, Malaysia, China and Indonesia. Negotiations are proceeding with Singapore.[47]

Free Trade Agreement

From the end of the 1990's countries in the region began to show interest in concluding Free Trade Agreements (FTA). Internally, the growing economic power of the NIES and ASEAN, common experience in overcoming the Asian financial crisis, and China's rapid economic development combined with her keen interests in enhancing regional cooperation, all contributed to the development of the Free Trade Agreement. Externally, rapid regional integration in Europe and America gave further impetus for strengthened regional cooperation in Asia-Pacific countries.[48]

---

[45] http://www.mofa.go.jp/region/Asia-Pacific/asean/conference/asean3/joint0310. html 2003–10–27.

[46] Saga Shinbun, *Kyodo*, 7 May 2000.

[47] http://www.mofa.go.jp/mofaj/area/asiakeizai/asean_3ci.html 2003–07–18.

[48] In Europe, the Treaty of Maastricht was agreed in 1991, signed in 1992, and went into force in 1993. The European Union fixed its definite course of economic integration, including the introduction of a common monetary unit, the 'euro', implemented in January 2002, as well as a path towards gradual political integration. In America, NAFTA, adding Mexico to America and Canada, was signed in 1992 and entered into force in 1994 and headed towards a totally free trade area,

It was probably China that took the most dynamic initiative in concluding an FTA with ASEAN. This policy was in line with China's enhanced policy toward greater harmonization, both economically and politically with the countries of the Asia-Pacific region. In autumn 2001 China and ASEAN reached a basic agreement to conclude an FTA in ten years time, that is before 2010.

In Japan, it started with the conclusion of the Free Trade Agreement with Singapore. In December 1999 Prime Minister Obuchi and Singapore Premier Goh Chok Tong agreed to begin an experts' deliberation. Upon the submission of the experts' report a year later, the two countries agreed to enter into formal negotiations, and the FTA was signed in Singapore between Prime Minister Koizumi and Premier Goh Chok Tong in January 2002.[49]

In October 2002 the Japanese Foreign Ministry made a policy statement to signal that FTA in the Asia-Pacific region is a natural response to the emergence of a powerful EU and NAFTA, that the WTO will still be an important overall organization to govern world trade and investment, and that the WTO will be usefully supplemented by regional organizations such as the FTA. The next priority countries for Japan to conclude an FTA with will be Korea, ASEAN and Mexico.[50]

In October 2002 at the APEC Leaders Meeting held in Mexico, Japan and Mexico reached a basic agreement to begin the study of concluding an FTA. The two countries failed to reach an agreement in October 2003, but are continuing to make efforts toward a breakthrough.

In November 2002 at the ASEAN plus Three Meeting in Cambodia, Japan and ASEAN adopted the Declaration for a Comprehensive Economic Partnership (CEP). This notion includes not only 'liberalization' but also 'facilitation' of trade and investment, as well as cooperation in a wide range of areas, including finance, information

---

to be realized in 15 years time (http://www.customsbrokerage.com/japanese/naftaj/naftaj.html 2002–10–20).

[49] http://www.mofa.go.jp/mofaj/area/singapore/kyotei/kyotei.html 2002–10–20
Precisely 10 years had passed since February 1992 when the Treaty of Maastricht was signed in Europe, and December of the same year when the NAFTA was signed by America, Canada and Mexico.

[50] MOFA, *Nihonno FTA Senryaku (Japan's FTA Strategy)*, October 2002 (http://www.mofa.go.jp/mofaj/gaiko/fta/summary.html 2002–10–20).

technology, science, education, small to middle-scale enterprises, tourism, transport, energy, food security.[51] Prime Minister Koizumi explained at the meeting with the ASEAN leaders that Japan is taking a double track approach of concluding bilateral free trade agreements with those countries which are ready, while pursuing an overall framework of Comprehensive Economic Partnership with ASEAN.[52]

But the process toward a CEP with ASEAN moved fast. On 8 October 2003 in Bali the Framework for CEP between Japan and ASEAN was signed.[53] Consultation on CEP will begin from the beginning of 2004, negotiation from the beginning of 2005 to be terminated before 2012, for the newer four ASEAN member states before 2017.

At the fringe of APEC meeting in Bangkok in October 2003 an agreement was also reached between Japan and Korea to conclude an FTA before 2005 (Chapter 5).

In fact, India joined this process in Bali and agreed to conclude with ASEAN a Framework Agreement on Comprehensive Economic Cooperation before 2011, for the newer four ASEAN Member States before 2016.

Enhanced regional cooperation around ASEAN

2003 experienced waves of enhanced regional cooperation between ASEAN and other major regional powers.

At the ASEAN Leaders Meeting in Bali China and India took a positive approach in enhancing overall relations with ASEAN. China acceded to the Treaty of Amity and Cooperation (TAC), an important founding document for ASEAN, and also signed a Joint Declaration on Strategic Partnership for Peace and Prosperity. India also acceded to TAC.

Japan and ASEAN leaders met in December in Tokyo. It was the first meeting where all ASEAN leaders meet with a leader outside the organization. They commemorated 30 years of relationships and

---

[51] http://www.mofa.go.jp/mofaj/gaiko/fta/j_asean/kouso.html 2003–07–19.

[52] MOFA, *Nichi-ASEAN Shyunoukaigino Gaiyou (Summary of Japan-ASEAN leaders meeting)*, 5 November 2002, http://www.mofa.go.jp/mofaj/kaidan/s_koi/asean_02/ j_asean_gai/html 2003–01–03.

[53] http://www.mofa.go.jp/region/asia/-paci/asean/pmv0310/framework.html 2003–10–31.

adopted a basis document to guide future relationships in all spheres with a view to build an East Asian community: 'Tokyo Declaration for the Dynamic and Enduring Japan-ASEAN Partnership in the New Millenium'.

6. *In the Eurasian continent: India and Silk Road countries*

India, a giant Asian country with great potential

India is a huge country with a population of 1.03 billion, the second largest population in the world after China's 1.27 billion.[54]

India is strategically located at the sea passage from Japan to the Middle East, or as we sometimes say, 'Japan's oil line'.

During the Cold War, India was one of the key figures in the developing countries or the Third World or non-aligned countries, while maintaining solid relations with her neighbour to the north, the Soviet Union. India, having gone through a long period of economic stagnation due to the ill functioning of a planned economy, changed the fundamental course of its economic policy after the demise of the Soviet Union towards market oriented liberalization, including that of foreign investment.

The new economic policy in India was a conspicuous success. In the mid-90's it marked three years of consecutive growth of 7%, and during the latter part of the 90's kept the level at 6%.[55]

On bilateral relations, trade between Japan and India was only at the $5 billion level during the latter half of the 1990's. In the area of ODA however, Japan has almost always been the uncontested No. 1 donor from the mid-80's, at times providing half of the bilateral assistance to India.

India's underground nuclear testing, together with Pakistan, in May 1998 created a serious problem in Japan-India relations. So as to express strong objection, Japan suspended new yen loans and grant assistance with a few exceptions in humanitarian and other restricted areas. In October 2001, however, taking into account that

---

[54] Indian figure: 2001, Chinese figure: November 2000 http://www.mofa.go.jp/mofaj/area/india(or china)/data.html 2003–07–19.

[55] http://www.mofa.go.jp/mofaj/area/india/kankei.html 2002–10–20.

India introduced a unilateral moratorium on testing and a positive approach to its eventual participation in the Comprehensive Test Ban Treaty (CTBT), Japan waived the suspension of its economic assistance.

In August 2000 Prime Minister Mori visited India and agreed that Japan and India will develop a 'Global Partnership in the 21st century'. Based on this concept, in December 2001 the Japan-India Joint Declaration was adopted in Tokyo between Prime Minister Atal Bihari Vajpayee and Prime Minister Koizumi.[56] In bilateral areas, the two countries acknowledged the importance of "broad as well as deepened economic relations", with a strong accent on information and communication technology, and also agreed to promote exchanges in "culture, education and science and technology". On global issues, cooperation will be enlarged in such areas as anti-terrorism, CTBT, peace and stability in Afghanistan, the United Nations, safe and secure maritime traffic, WTO, globalization, and COP 7.[57] Thus, in the first decades of the 21st century Japan-India relations are destined to develop with greater dynamism.

With Pakistan, given its important geopolitical location and traditional friendly relations, Japan had implemented an active policy of assistance, and from 1990 Japan became the No. 1 donor to Pakistan. Pakistan's nuclear testing in May 1998 forced Japan to take similar measures of protest as those taken against India. After 9/11, taking into account the critical position Pakistan has occupied in the war against terrorism, Japan announced in November 2001 a two year assistance programme of $300 million.[58]

Japan is also developing constructive relations with other countries in the region, Bangladesh, Sri Lanka, Nepal and Bhutan.

Silk Road countries, a new strategic area for Japan

Another group of countries constitutes a new area in Japan's foreign policy. They are the eight countries of the Community of Independent States (CIS), which gained independence in early 1992

---

[56] http://www.mofa.go.jp/region/asia-paci/india/joint0112.html 2003–03–09.
[57] The 7th Session of the Conference of Parties to the United Nations Framework Convention on Climate Change.
[58] http://www.mofa.go.jp/mofaj/area/pakistan/kankei.html 2003–03–02.

after the demise of the Soviet Union—five in Central Asia: Kazakhstan, Uzbekistan, Turkmenistan, Kyrgyzstan, and Tajikistan; three in the Caucasus: Azerbaijan, Georgia, and Armenia.

After the fall of the Soviet Union, Japan was reasonably fast in developing her relations with the Central Asian countries. Foreign Minister Watanabe visited Kazakhstan and Kyrgyzstan in 1992; a Japanese Embassy was opened in Kazakhstan and Uzbekistan in 1993; a Japan Centre for Economic Cooperation opened in Kyrgyzstan in 1995; and substantial ODA started to flow, particularly to these three countries.

In the summer of 1996, having served for two years and a half in the Japanese Embassy in Moscow, I came back to Tokyo and became one of two Deputy-Director Generals of the European Affairs Department. My area of responsibility was Russia and the CIS.

Although relations between Japan and the CIS were developing, I strongly felt that a substantial vacuum still existed, particularly in relation to Central Asia and the Caucasus. I tried hard to gather my thoughts to find a way to conceptualize more clearly the importance of these countries and explain it to Japanese leaders, both inside and outside MOFA.

On an autumn day in 1996 I happened to be sitting in my office, looking at the map of the Eurasian continent on the wall. Suddenly, looking at the map, the geopolitical location of these countries struck me: five of the eight countries stretch to the east of the Caspian Sea, and three lie west of that sea and are met by the Black Sea; north of this belt region Russia looms heavily; east they face China; south of this region three Islamic countries are lined up, Afghanistan, Iran and Turkey. Clearly, the stability, peace, and security of the eight countries at the centre of the Eurasian belt would directly affect the security and stability of Russia, China and the three Islamic countries. For Japan's security interests, a destabilized Russia, China or major Islamic countries would have critical implications. The strategic implications of these eight countries seemed obvious.

After this first *strategic* point had been firmly established, it was not too difficult to introduce the second *economic* point on abundant energy resources in and around the Caspian Sea, and the third *psychological* point, related to cultural exchanges through the Silk Road and to

warm memories in the region associated with Japan's victory over
Russia in 1905.

In July 1997, when Prime Minister Hashimoto made his historic
speech on Japan's new Eurasian policy, a new concept of 'Silk Road
Diplomacy' was also happily included (Chapter 7).

Probably thus far the dynamo of the Japanese 'Silk Road Diplomacy'
has been economic assistance. Towards the end of the 1990's, in the
three countries mentioned above, Kazakhstan, Uzbekistan, and
Kyrgyzstan, likewise in Turkmenistan, Japan held the No. 1 donor
position.

Japanese ODA to Central Asia, Comparative DAC Statistics[59]			
	1996	1997	1998
Kazakhstan	3rd	1st	1st
Uzbekistan	2nd	1st	1st
Kyrgyzstan	1st	1st	2nd
Turkmenistan	2nd	1st	1st

For the Caucasus, substantial ODA started in 1997 and continues
to grow.

In Tajikistan the demise of the Soviet Union engendered a civil
war which continued longer than in any other CIS country. In 1994
the first provisional armistice was signed, after which the United
Nations became closely involved. The final agreement for peace was
made in 1997, at which time a Japanese scholar whose vitality and
creativity was well-known amongst his friends, Yutaka Akino, joined
the UN Office. This ended tragically when he was assassinated by
anti-government rebels in July 1998.[60]

Nevertheless, thanks to these dedicated efforts, the situation continued to calm down; the presidential election at the end of 1999
and the parliamentary election in early 2000 were successfully implemented.[61] Akino's successor arrived from Japan in October 2000, a

---

[59] DAC statistics, MOFA homepage, country analysis, development assistance.

[60] Akino worked at the Japanese Embassy in Moscow as a research scholar from
1983 to 1985. He was my colleague in the political section and since then we maintained a friendship.

[61] http://www.mofa.go.jp/mofaj/area/tajikistan/data.html 2002-10-20.

Japanese diplomatic mission opened there in early 2002, economic assistance began to grow substantially and bilateral assistance amounted to 4.64 billion yen by the end of 2001.[62]

After 9/11, the strategic importance of this region came to be appreciated more acutely by world observers. Japanese foreign policy toward the Silk Road countries could certainly be more energetic and dynamic, and I do hope that today's embryonic form will someday bloom into beautiful flowers of cooperation.

7. To the Pacific: Australia and the Pacific Island countries

Australia, a search for creative partnership

Australia has played a vital role in postwar Japanese economic development. It did not necessarily occupy front page headlines in major newspapers, but it has always been an important underlying factor.

The key element was the mutually beneficial, complementary trade structure. Japan steadily imported such raw materials as coal, iron ore, natural gas, and aluminium ingots and alumina as well as beef. Australia imported Japanese industrial products, items of which changed over the years. Those which appear prominently now are automobiles, office equipment, electrical machinery, tires, and chemicals, etc.[63]

The volume of trade is very significant for both sides, reaching $21.01 billion in 1998, with a substantial surplus on the Australian side.[64]

At the same time there has always been a mutual desire to extend the relationship beyond trade.

The first attempt to give emphasis to the political relations began during the early 70's when the Detente climate created new opportunities in international relations. In 1971 Prime Minister Sato and Prime Minister E.G. Whitlam agreed to establish a Regular Meeting of Cabinet Ministers. The Basic Treaty of Friendship and Cooperation concluded in 1976 symbolized the endeavours of this period.[65] The

---

[62] http://www.mofa.go.jp/mofaj/area/tajikistan/kankei.html 2003–07–19.
[63] http://www.mofa.go.jp/region/asia-paci/australia/index.html 2003–07–19.
[64] Japanese export $8.02 billion and Japanese import $13.00 billion.
[65] Nakanishi, op. cit., p. 168.

spirit of cooperation between the governments developed into joint efforts in contemplating forums for regional cooperation, as we have seen in PECC in 1980, APEC in 1989, and ARF in 1994.

Towards the end of the 1990's, both Australia and Japan began to seek a more dynamic relationship to explore potential cooperation in a wide range of areas.

The prime motivation was economic: global economic changes dictated that the traditional structure of trade in raw materials and industrial products was simply too narrow to fully absorb the economic potential. Both countries had to become more creative to open up new areas of trade and investment.

A second reason was related to social issues shared by the two countries. After a half century of post-Pacific War development, Japan and Australia realized that mutual exchanges and cooperation could play an important role for the solution of common problems. One may add here that both Australia and Japan have developed historical, philosophical and cultural issues of identity between East and West.

Another motivating factor was regional security. Both Australia and Japan were extremely concerned by the eruptions of political violence in Cambodia and East Timor.

In April 2001, with strong support from the two governments, a group of 'wise men' from the two countries gathered in Australia and had inspiring talks on the future course of the Japan-Australia relationship for the 21st century. The Sydney Declaration for Japan-Australia Creative Partnership was adopted. Let me point out some of the salient points of this declaration:[66]

On economic relations, such sectors as "IT, telecommunications, biotechnology, capital market linkages, as well as health care and health care for the elderly" were outlined as future areas for cooperation.

On cooperation in the cultural, social, science and technological issues, "more media exchanges—print and electronic media—and more educational exchanges, especially in the IT area" were emphasized.

On security and political cooperation fresh ideas "to improve the capacity to respond to crises, e.g. peacekeeping training, new transnational security issues" appeared in the adopted document.

---

[66] Quotations are from the Sydney Declaration (www.mofa.go.jp/region/asia-paci/australia/conf0104/joint.html 2002–10–21).

Prime Minister Koizumi visited Australia in May 2002 and with Prime Minister John Howard adopted a joint press statement entitled 'Japan-Australia Creative Partnership', the spirit and content of which reflected the forward-looking approach of the Declaration of the previous year.

Pacific island countries, Pacific frontier diplomacy

When we discuss the Pacific as an object of Japanese foreign policy, due attention has to be paid to the island countries in the Pacific Ocean.

New Zealand is an island country, but is usually perceived as an important Japanese partner together with Australia. What I mean here are the 14 countries and areas, such as Papua New Guinea, Fiji, Samoa, Solomon Islands, which are scattered around the vast ocean leading to the west coast of the United States.

These 14 countries and areas, together with Australia and New Zealand, formed the South Pacific Forum (SPF) in 1971, renamed the Pacific Islands Forum (PIF) from the year 2000.

Geographically the location of these island countries gives rise to a variety of issues related to the ocean:

– They are located at important points of passage, as exemplified when the question of nuclear waste transport occurs.
– Being so small, some of the countries now run the risk of annihilation by global warming and the resulting sea water level upsurge. They could have important voices in the Conference of Partners (COP) discussion (Chapter 11).
– Fisheries are often the key industry for their economic survival.

Historically, one can not forget that precisely a half century ago Japan and the United States fought a war in the Pacific over these islands. Many islands were occupied by the Japanese for a certain period and memories of those days remain.

Postwar relations with those island countries started with Japanese economic cooperation. The aggregate sum of the cooperation started with $40 million in the 1970's, increased to $430 million in the 1980's, and eventually totalled more than $1,750 million dollars in the 1990's.[67]

---

[67] The figures for the 1990's are only available up to 1998 (K. Togo, in *Taiheiyouwo Kangaeru (Thinking the Pacific)*, Gaiko Forum, May 2000, pp. 19–21).

From the mid-1980's, for the first time after WW II, Japan approached these islands with some strategic thinking. It was the last years of Cold War tension before Gorbachev changed the entire context of international relations. Soviet research vessels appeared in the region and there were talks of Soviet Aeroflot coming to the Pacific islands. Prime Minister Nakasone visited the islands in 1985 and Foreign Minister Kuranari in 1987. The important mission of Kuranari's trip was to show Japanese presence in the region against the backdrop of Soviet moves. He was tremendously impressed by the enthusiasm and warmth of the people who received him.

The end of the Cold War, however, subdued Japan's political interest in the region for a while.

In 1997, after an interval of 10 years, Prime Minister Hashimoto invited all SPF leaders to Japan to hold a joint Japan-SPF Summit Dialogue. The SPF had been meeting annually at the leaders' level since 1971, but Hashimoto's initiative was the first attempt for any outside country to create a political impetus with the countries of the SPF.

At the beginning of April 2000 Prime Minister Obuchi had a sudden stroke and Prime Minister Yoshiro Mori replaced him from his post as LDP General Secretary. Later in April, as his first foreign policy agenda, Prime Minister Mori held the second Japan-SPF Summit at Miyazaki, a prosperous town in the southern part of the island of Kyushu.

Prime Minister Mori at his inaugural welcome speech declared that Japan was now ready to open a new 'Pacific Frontier Diplomacy' to strengthen its relations with SPF island countries in three areas:

1) To support sustainable economic growth of the island countries, where people, particularly the *youth*, will play a key role;

2) To squarely face all major common issues, particularly those centred around the *sea*; and

3) To strengthen the Japan-SPF partnership, where a *future*-oriented approach will play a key role.

With these three key words, *youth*, *sea*, and *future*, Japan thus launched a new 'Pacific Frontier Diplomacy' directed at the heart of the Pacific Ocean, comparable to the 'Silk Road Diplomacy' directed at the centre of the Eurasian continent.

The Oceanian Division was then a part of the European Department in the Japanese Ministry of Foreign Affairs. It resembled a vestige of the British Commonwealth.[68] Akio Miyajima, Director of the Oceanian Division and his staff worked diligently to welcome these heads of states from the Pacific island countries.

How to organize an enjoyable programme, how to structure an interesting discussion, and what kind of economic cooperation could Japan specifically announce during the Summit Meeting? These were the issues we faced. In addition, during the preparations, Miyajima and I became increasingly convinced that the history and geopolitics of these islands showed that they had a certain strategic importance for Japan and that this importance should be better conveyed to the outside world.

Thus we became determined to find an attractive label to cover Japan's new initiative toward this region. Miyajima insisted that the initiative had to be formulated in a way to attract the young and future generation. Dry and stereotyped phraseology had to be avoided. Nor would an eccentric and provocative call be effective. We had spent several evenings together discussing various options. Finally we agreed on one label, 'Pacific Frontier Diplomacy' for the new initiative and three key words, 'youth, sea and future' to describe the contents of this initiative.

---

[68] From the beginning of 2001, the Oceanian Division of MOFA became a part of the Asian Department and that Department has now been renamed 'Asia and Oceanian Department'.

CHAPTER SEVEN

RUSSIA: TERRITORIAL DISPUTES AND STRENGTHENING THE RELATIONSHIP

1. *The end of the Pacific War: beginning of the disconnection*

Japan-Russia relations before the Pacific War were full of ups and downs. Periods of relative warmth and friendship were juxtaposed with direct military confrontations.

The ups and downs in postwar Japan-Russia relations were modest in scale, however, the relationship continued to be difficult and complex. The more I ponder the more I feel that the roots of the difficulty between the two countries lie in the events, which took place from spring to summer 1945—the concluding year of the Pacific War.

First of all, there was the Yalta Agreement. On 11 February 1945, the leaders of the Soviet Union, the US and Great Britain signed an agreement in Yalta. They agreed that "in two or three months after Germany has surrendered"[1] the Soviet Union would enter into war against Japan. The conditions of this entry into war were that the southern half of Sakhalin Island would be returned and that the Kurile Islands would be handed over to the Soviet Union.

This confidential agreement was concluded at a time when Germany was close to its final surrender and the overall objective of the agreement was to defeat Japan quickly and effectively.

Naturally, Japan was not aware of these developments. Japan was in its last stage of war and capitulation when on 8 August, to Japan's total surprise, the Soviet Union declared war.

Japan took it as a serious breach of the Pact of Neutrality the two countries had signed on 13 April 1941. The Soviet attack violated its obligation to maintain neutrality at a time when Japan was at war with any third country. Admittedly, the Soviet Union officially informed Japan on 5 April 1945 that it did not intend to extend

---

[1] MOFA, *Principal Treaties, op. cit.*, p. 1825.

the Pact after its expiry in April 1946. But until April 1946, the Pact of Neutrality legally bound the Soviet Union.

The shock was even greater because, precisely during the months which preceded the attack, the Japanese government was seeking mediation through the Soviet Union, as we saw in the Prologue.

Perhaps from the Soviet point of view, the attack was a reflection of the reality of war, and legitimate because it was based on the Yalta Agreement signed by Roosevelt, Churchill and Stalin. But from Japan's point of view concluding a new agreement which contravened a previously existing agreement was a violation of international law.

By early September 1945, the Soviet Union completed the occupation of Manchuria, the whole of Sakhalin, the Kurile Islands, and the islands of Etorofu, Kunashiri, Shikotan, and Habomai.

From the Soviet point of view the occupation of Sakhalin and the Kurile Islands was justified by the Yalta Agreement.

From Japan's point of view the situation was not clear at all. For Japan the Yalta Agreement could not become the basis of its territorial demarcation, because Japan was not a signatory, nor even knew of its existence when it was signed. For Japan the Potsdam Declaration was the most relevant document. It prescribed that "The terms of the Cairo Declaration shall be carried out and Japanese sovereignty shall be limited to the islands of Honshu, Hokkaido, Kyushu, Shikoku, and such minor islands as we determine."[2] The Cairo Declaration stated that Japan should be punished and expelled from "territories which she has taken by violence and greed", but the three allies "have no thought of territorial expansion".[3]

The language of the Potsdam Declaration implies, with reason, that Japan would be reduced, in principle, to the size of Japan at the beginning of the Meiji Restoration. At the same time it posed the question of how to harmonize this reality with the Cairo Declaration. Should the Kurile Islands, which Japan acquired in exchange for Sakhalin, be considered as "territories which Japan has taken by violence and greed", and from which Japan should be expelled? Should South Sakhalin be returned to the Soviet Union,

---

[2] Paragraph 8 of the Potsdam Declaration (Ibid., p. 1831).
[3] Ibid., pp. 1823–1824. The Soviet Union joined the Cairo Declaration on 8 August 1945.

because Japan acquired it as a result of her "treacherous attack of Japan in 1904", as prescribed by the Yalta Agreement?

While Japan was reeling from the capitulation and the losses of South Sakhalin and the Kurile Islands, the Soviet Union delivered the critical blow of including the 'four islands' into Soviet territory. Etorofu, Kunashiri, Shikotan, and Habomai islands had never been contested either by Tsarist Russia or by the Soviet Union, since the border between the two countries was demarcated for the first time in 1855, 13 years before the Meiji Restoration. And yet the Soviet Union officially declared those 'four islands' to be a part of their territory by internal legislation in February 1946.[4]

It gradually became known that the Soviet Union had taken captive approximately 600,000 Japanese soldiers who had been stationed in the area of Soviet occupation, and had transported them to concentration camps.[5] Roughly 60,000–70,000 internees died and the last detainee was returned home 10 years later, after the conclusion of the Joint Declaration in 1956. The misery experienced by those interned in the Soviet camps and other tragedies under Soviet occupation were burned into Japan's national consciousness.

In fact, the critical point of postwar Japan-Russia relations was that at the end of the Pacific War Japan was left with an entirely different memory of the Soviet Union *vis-à-vis* other nations.

After the deep abyss through which the nation had gone following the capitulation, Japan gradually developed a general feeling of remorse and apology, in particular towards Korea, China and other Asian countries which it had occupied. These feelings applied in general to the European countries, like Great Britain and the Netherlands, whose soldiers and citizens Japan had imprisoned or detained. Even towards the United States, which was responsible for the deaths of 500,000 civilians[6] in indiscriminate city bombing, including the two atomic bombs which annihilated Hiroshima and Nagasaki, the Japanese

---

[4] The Ministry of Foreign Affairs, Japan and Russia, *Nichiroryoudomondaino Rekishinikansuru Kyoudousakuseishiryoushuu (Joint Compendium of Documents on the history of Japan-Russia Territorial Problem)*, 1992, 2nd page of Japanese preface.

[5] Accurate numbers of Japanese detainees in the Soviet Union are not identified, but statistics from the Ministry of Health indicate 574,530. (Microsoft Encarta Reference Library 2003).

[6] Aggregate death tolls of American carpet-bombing and Hiroshima and Nagasaki bombing is calculated at 479,324, based on the footnotes 3 and 4 of Chapter 1.

people in general, did not harbour such a strong sense of injustice and wounded feelings as was the case with the Soviet Union.

2. *The San Francisco Peace Treaty of 1951*

The second crucial factor which determined postwar Japan-Russia relations was the Cold War. Under the Allied occupation, Japan committed itself to join the democratic countries and concentrate its energy on peaceful economic development, while developing firm 'security ties with the US' and 'minimum forces for self-defence'. For the Soviet Union, Japan's decision to side with America and other democracies meant putting Japan in the basket of 'adversarial' countries.

Because the San Francisco Peace Treaty was concluded based on 'partial peace', the Cold War antagonism between Japan and the Soviet Union was aggravated. During the negotiations leading up to the Peace Treaty Conference the Soviet Union expressed strong objections to the 'partial peace' approach. Soviet participation in the San Francisco Peace Conference was therefore received with surprise. At the conference, the Soviet delegation denounced the text prepared for signing as encouraging Japanese militarism and proposed a revised text. When it became clear that this revised proposal would not even be discussed, the Soviet delegation abstained from signing the treaty.[7]

While the San Francisco Peace Treaty was, for the Soviet Union, an unacceptable product of the adversarial camp under American leadership, for Japan it meant an acceptance of the reality of war. Japan legally and formally renounced all right, title and claim to the Kurile Islands and South Sakhalin.

But in doing so, Prime Minister Yoshida, the Japanese plenipotentiary to this conference, gave an honest and general account of the Japanese government's perspective on this issue:

> With respect to the Kuriles and South Sakhalin, I cannot yield to the claim of the Soviet Delegate that Japan had grabbed them by aggression.
> At the time of the opening of Japan, her ownership of two islands of Etorofu and Kunashiri of the South Kuriles was not questioned at

---

[7] Hosoya, 1984, *op. cit.*, pp. 265–266.

all by the Czarist government. But the North Kuriles north of Urruppu and the southern half of Sakhalin were areas open to both Japanese and Russian settlers. On May 7, 1875 the Japanese and Russian Governments effected through peaceful negotiations an arrangement under which South Sakhalin was made Russian territory, and the North Kuriles were in exchange made Japanese territory. But really, under the name of "exchange" Japan simply ceded South Sakhalin to Russia in order to settle the territorial dispute. It was under the Treaty of Portsmouth of September 5, 1905 concluded through the intermediary of President Theodore Roosevelt of the United States that South Sakhalin became also Japanese territory.

Both the Kuriles and South Sakhalin were taken unilaterally by the Soviet Union as of September 20, 1945, shortly after Japan's surrender.

Even the islands of Habomai and Shikotan, constituting part of Hokkaido, one of Japan's four main islands, are still being occupied by Soviet forces simply because they happened to be garrisoned by Japanese troops at the time when the war ended."[8]

The San Francisco Peace Treaty did not specify the territorial definition of the Kurile Islands which Japan had renounced, and therefore lacked a certain precision with regard to the precise extent of the area it relinquished.

On 19 October 1951, Kumao Nishimura, Director General of the Treaties Bureau, stated at a parliamentary hearing that "the scope of the Kurile Islands as stipulated in the Treaty covers North Kurile and South Kurile." Director General Nishimura immediately added in his statement that the Japanese government would firmly maintain the statement made by Prime Minister Yoshida in San Francisco.[9]

Because the Soviet Union did not sign the San Francisco Peace Treaty, the question of the restoration of peace and resolution of all related problems, including the territorial problem, was left open to bilateral negotiations between the two countries.[10]

---

[8] Joint Compendium, *Prime Minister Yoshida's Statement at the San Francisco Peace Conference.* Japanese version, p. 32. English translation is from the MOFA homepage
(http://www.mofa.go.jp/region/europe/russia/territory/edition92/period4.html 2003-07-12).

[9] Director General Nishimura's statement is referred to in the Joint Compendium between the two Foreign Ministries of 1992, Japanese preface, page 3. Actual quotation of his statement is from H. Kimura, *Nichirokokkyoukoushoushi (History of Border Negotiations between Japan and Russia)*, Chuukou Shinsho, 1993, pp. 122–123.

[10] Prime Minister Yoshida later explained the Japanese government position in San Francisco as follows: "Japan as a defeated country simply could not have made a clear reservation on an interpretation of the Treaty. Taking into consideration

3. The Khrushchev period: the Joint Declaration of 1956 and the Memorandum of 1960

Despite the difficult and complex situation which surrounded the two countries, several conditions emerged towards the middle of the 1950's to make Japan-Soviet rapprochement a viable foreign policy agenda.

Stalin died in 1953 and Nikita Khrushchev took over the leadership of the country. Khrushchev began a new policy of strengthening socialism inside the country and establishing a peaceful coexistence in external relations. A new policy of 'de-Stalinization' and a policy of 'thawing' began. Japan became one of the objectives of this policy of 'thawing'.

In Japan, Ichiro Hatoyama succeeded Prime Minister Yoshida at the end of 1954. Mamoru Shigemitsu was chosen as his Foreign Minister. Though Shigemitsu had some interests in revising the Security Treaty with America (Chapter 2), the single major interest of the Hatoyama cabinet in foreign policy became the normalization of relations with the Soviet Union.

Thus at the beginning of 1955 conditions seemed to ripe for negotiations to re-establish diplomatic relations between Japan and the Soviet Union.

Apart from the territorial problem there were three concrete issues Japan needed to resolve with urgency: the immediate return of the remaining Japanese detainees in Soviet camps; the establishment of fishery regulations; and Soviet agreement to Japan's accession to the United Nations.

Negotiations started in London in June 1955, between Japanese plenipotentiary Shunichi Matsumoto and Soviet Ambassador Yakov Malik. The three issues mentioned above did not pose fundamental obstacles. The most difficult point soon proved to be the territorial problem. Scholarly works on these negotiations indicate that the Japanese government maintained the perspective expressed by Prime Minister Yoshida in San Francisco, but did not have a predetermined fixed position.[11]

---

that the boundary of the Kurile Islands was not made clear in the Treaty, the best approach was to state Japanese thinking on the record and leave the issue for the future." (Shigeru Yoshida, "The road to the resolution of the Northern Territory", Sankeishinbun, 11 October 1961, quoted from H. Wada, *Hoppouryoudomondai (Northern Territorial Problem)*, Asahi Sensho, 1999, p. 274).

[11] The initial proposal, with which Matsumoto came to London, was said to state

The initial Soviet stance was uncompromising: South Sakhalin and the Kurile Islands, inclusive of Habomai and Shikotan, were Russian territory. At the beginning of August, however, Malik reversed his position and proposed to settle the territorial issue by returning the Shikotan and Habomai islands. It was a concessionary gesture beyond Japan's expectations.[12] But Tokyo's response to Malik's 'two' islands proposal was "the reversion of 'four' islands and that an international conference should be convened to determine the fate of South Sakhalin and the Northern Kurile Islands."[13]

The negotiations came to a deadlock. From January to March 1956 the second round of the London negotiations was held, but it did not produce any results. Meanwhile, the Japanese government clarified some ambiguity related to the Nishimura Statement of October 1951 and announced that 'the Kurile Islands' did not include the islands of Kunashiri and Etorofu.[14]

The Soviets pressured Japan into utilizing their negotiating power over salmon fisheries in the high seas. Ichiro Kono, Minister for Agriculture, visited Moscow and signed an agreement on the fisheries issue in May, but its entry into force depended on the conclusion of the peace treaty.

The first round of the Moscow negotiations, at which Foreign Minister Mamoru Shigemitsu represented Japan, started at the end of July. The Soviet Union firmly maintained that the two smaller islands could be transferred, but that would be their final position.

---

that the islands of "Habomai, Shikotan, Kuriles and Southern Sakhalin are historically Japanese territory. When peace is being resurrected we need a frank exchange of views regarding ownership of these areas." (Ikei, *op. cit.*, p. 252). Matsumoto described the nature of this proposal as "approaching the matter with flexibility, not insisting on the return of all the territories mentioned above." (Shunichi Matsumoto, *Mosukuwani Kakeru Niji* (*The Rainbow to Moscow*); quoted from Ikei, *op. cit.*, p. 253).

[12] Matsumoto was said to have "led the negotiations based on his understanding that Japan should come to an agreement with the Soviet Union with the reversion of the two islands." (Ikei, *op. cit.*, p. 254).

[13] Quoted from Ikei, *op. cit.*, p. 254. Same description in N. Shimotomai, *Hoppouryoudo Q&A 80 (80 Q&A on Northern Territory)*, Shougakkan, 2000, p. 92.

[14] At the Parliamentary hearing on 11 February 1956, Vice-Minister Morishita made a statement reflecting a "unified government view" that "the Japanese Government viewed that the Kurile Islands, as referred to in the San Francisco Peace Treaty, does not include the islands of Kunashiri and Etorofu." (H. Kimura, G.T. Alison, K. Sarkisov, *Nichibeiro Shinjidaiheno Shinario (A Scenario of New Era between Japan, US, and Russia)*, Dayamondosha, 1993, p. 251).

To the surprise of many of his colleagues both in Moscow and in Tokyo, Shigemitsu was said to have inclined towards agreeing to settle the territorial issue with the reversion of two smaller islands. Last minute instructions from Tokyo prevented Shigemitsu's move.[15]

After the negotiations again entered an impasse, Shigemitsu went to London and met John F. Dulles, the US Secretary of State. J.F. Dulles gave a clear message that the United States did not welcome Japan siding with the Soviet Union in the return of two smaller islands.[16]

Prime Minister Hatoyama decided to go to Moscow in person to attempt a breakthrough. By that time it became clear that there was no possibility of an agreement on the territorial issue. Therefore, before Hatoyama's visit the two sides had agreed in the Exchange of Notes between Matsumoto and Gromyko of 29 September that "the Japanese Government assumes that negotiations on the conclusion of a peace treaty including the territorial issue will continue after the reestablishment of normal diplomatic relations between the two countries."[17]

Prime Minister Hatoyama arrived in Moscow and on 19 October a Joint Declaration between Japan and the Soviet Union was signed. Paragraph 9 deals with the question of the Peace Treaty:

> 9. Japan and the Union of Soviet Socialist Republics agree to continue, after the restoration of normal diplomatic relations between Japan and the Union of Soviet Socialist Republics, negotiations for the conclusion of a peace treaty.
> The Union of Soviet Socialist Republics, desiring to meet the wishes of Japan and taking into consideration the interests of Japan, agrees to hand over to Japan the Habomai Islands and the island of Shikotan. However, the actual handing over (of) these islands to Japan shall take

---

[15] Ikei, *op. cit.*, p. 258.

[16] Ibid. After this talk, on 7 September 1956 the United States issued a Memorandum to Japan indicating that "the United States, after careful consideration reached the conclusion that the islands of Etorofu and Kunashiri, together with the islands of Habomai and Shikotan, which are a part of Hokkaido, have always been an integral part of Japanese territory, and that they should justifiably be recognized as being under Japanese sovereignty." (MOFA, *Our Northern Territories*, 2001, *op. cit.*, US Memorandum on Japan-Soviet negotiation, Materials, p. 19. Translated by the author).

[17] Joint Compendium, Japanese version, pp. 36–37.
(http://www.mofa.go.jp/region/europe/russia/territory/edition92/period5.html 2003-07-12).

place after the conclusion of a peace treaty between Japan and the Union of Soviet Socialist Republics.[18]

A few observations are required here:

First, throughout the negotiations the Soviets agreed only to the return of the 'two' smaller islands. This applies to the Matsumoto-Gromyko Exchange of Notes and the Joint Declaration as well.

Second, there was serious internal deliberation in Japan. In the end it converged into a single position requesting the reversion of the 'four' islands. The territorial problem for Japan as prescribed in the Matsumoto-Gromyko Exchange of Notes was nothing other than the 'four' islands issue. The objective of the peace treaty negotiations under Paragraph 9 of the Joint Declaration was the 'four' islands issue as well.

Third, Japan's request was never accepted by the Soviets. Nor did Japan agree to the Soviet proposal. Thus within the common language of Paragraph 9 of the Joint Declaration, two totally different and non-converging positions were incorporated: The Soviets closing the issue with the 'two', and Japan insisting on the reversion of the 'four'.

Apart from the territorial issue all issues were in fact resolved: a state of war was terminated and diplomatic relations re-established; the Soviets agreed to free all detainees upon the entrance into force of the Declaration; the Fisheries Agreement would also become a fact upon the entrance into force of the Declaration; the Soviets agreed to support Japan's membership of the United Nations; and the Soviets relinquished all rights to reparations.

The Gromyko Memorandum and economic relations

Political relations between Japan and the Soviet Union warmed up for a while after the Joint Declaration of 1956. However, it soon suffered yet another blow.

In 1960 the Soviet Union responded fiercely to the conclusion of the new Japan-US Security Treaty. On 27 January the Soviet government issued a memorandum stating that the islands of Habomai and Shikotan would only be transferred to Japan when all foreign

---

[18] Ibid., p. 38.

troops had been withdrawn from Japan and the Peace Treaty concluded between the two countries.[19]

The Soviet response was met with surprise and anger in Japan and the Japanese government rejected it immediately. The Security Treaty was revised primarily to bring Japan-US security relations on an equal basis (Chapter 2). The Soviets apparently wanted to drive a wedge between Japan-America relations, but in Japan the link between the Security Treaty and the territorial problem received no sympathy.

In 1962 the Cuban missile crisis shook the world and two years later Khrushchev was dismissed by his colleagues for his 'adventurism' in his domestic and external policy. Leonid Brezhnev replaced him as the Party General Secretary and began his era with the cautious approach of collective leadership.

While nothing spectacular took place in the political arena, the 60's saw a certain development in economic relations. After the conclusion of the Fisheries Agreement in 1956, Japan maintained stable relations with the Soviet Union on salmon fishing in the Pacific. But trade figures began to grow. Total trade was almost nil when the relationship began in 1956, but soon it overtook America. By the middle of the 1960's, Japan had become an influential trade partner of the Soviet Union together with Italy, France, and Germany. In the second half of the 60's Japan became one of the leading trade partners with the Soviet Union, this time together with Finland and Great Britain and in 1970 and 1971 Japan became the Soviet Union's No. 1 trade partner amongst all Western nations.

Japan almost exclusively imported such raw materials as timber, iron ore, coal, and oil. The Soviet Union imported machinery and equipment, pipes, textiles and household appliances. The total trade in 1970 was not gigantic, just over 650 million roubles (the official rate of a Russian rouble was usually fixed at just 10–20% higher than a dollar), but the trade structure was mutually complementary and trade relations with a central planned economy were stable and predictable.[20]

---

[19] This memorandum is usually referred to in Japan as the 'Gromyko memorandum'.

[20] Trade figures from the statistics of *Planovo-ekonomicheskoe upravlenie SSSR (Economic Planning Agency USSR)*, various years.

4. *The Brezhnev period: Detente and thereafter*

Prime Minister Tanaka's visit to the Soviet Union

At the beginning of the 1970's Japan-Soviet relations began to warm up.

Detente was probably the first element which affected this change. In America Richard Nixon became President in January 1969. His task was to restructure relations among the major powers—the Soviet Union and the PRC—and create such relations that would better suit the American position in the world. The honourable withdrawal of America from Vietnam was one of his major objectives as well. In the Soviet Union Brezhnev was accumulating power. Stable relations with America well suited his objectives to create a strong and prosperous country. US-Soviet agreements in Moscow on SALTI and the ABM Treaty in May 1972 were the first landmark of Detente.

> When President Nixon came to the Soviet Union at the end of May 1972 I was in Moscow studying the Russian language with a private instructor. I was instructed by the Embassy to go to Leningrad where Nixon made a one day trip and help members of the newly established Consul-Geneal's office to observe the mood of the city.
>
> So I saw Leningrad for the first time in my life. The beauty of this city, constructed by Peter the Great in the image of European civilization at the beginning of the 18th century, overwhelmed me. It was just before the 'white night'. At night I went out to the promenade along the river Neva, where people of the city quietly gathered here and there. The beauty of the black silhouettes of the silent palaces overlooking the river and the amazing deep and lucid blue sky which never darkened left an unforgettable impression.
>
> On the following morning, I went to the corner of one of the major streets and mingled with the crowds of poorly dressed people, mostly of elderly, smiling and welcoming President Nixon's long motorcade—.

But it was probably China which became the key element in the process of Detente. The Sino-Soviet rivalry, ranging from ideology, geopolitical hegemony, border disputes, security and trade, swept from the end of the 50's through to the 60's. In the spring of 1969 several military clashes took place along the river Amur on the eastern border between the two countries.

President Nixon's visit to China in February 1972 was a well-calculated gesture to incite Soviet fear of a US-China rapprochement. Prime Minister Tanaka's visit to Beijing in October had the same impact (Chapter 4). Prime Minister Tanaka played Japan's version of Detente, i.e. utilizing his policy of rapprochement to China for the betterment of the relationship with the Soviet Union.

The Soviet Union, with its historic 'siege mentality', i.e. fear of encirclement, began to feel a sense of isolation at an impending US-China-Japan re-alignment.

The economy was another reason why the Soviet Union became more interested in Japan. Brezhnev began a massive programme to develop Siberian resources and Japan's economic, financial and technological power witnessed during the 60's, became a genuine source of attraction.

In January 1972 Foreign Minister Andrei Gromyko visited Japan after a six year interval. In October Foreign Minister Ohira visited Moscow. In March 1973 Tanaka and Brezhnev exchanged letters. All these paved the way for Prime Minister Tanaka's visit to Moscow from 7 to 10 October 1973.

After tense negotiations between the two leaders on the territorial issue a key expression 'the settlement of unresolved problems left over from WWII' was included in the Joint Communiqué adopted on 10 October.[21]

At the last meeting between Prime Minister Tanaka and General Secretary Brezhnev, Tanaka confirmed twice, that "unresolved problems" included the issue of the 'four' islands and Brezhnev answered affirmatively twice by saying, first, "I know" and second, "Yes".[22]

> In October 1973 I was working at the Japanese Embassy as a young third secretary, serving as the Ambassador's Secretary. My responsibility was to organize a return banquet held by Prime Minister Tanaka in honour of Brezhnev and other Kremlin

---

[21] Joint Compendium, p. 41 (www.mofa.go.jp/region/europe/russia/territory/edition92/period5.html 2003–07–12).
[22] Kimura, *op. cit.*, pp. 152–153.

dignitaries. In compiling an accurate guest list of the Soviet leadership, I was excited to see names which I would otherwise only see in official Soviet newspapers, such as *Pravda* and *Izvestiya*. It was all the more exciting to think that my Prime Minister would engage in a serious *tête-à-tête* dialogue with General Secretary Brezhnev.

Makiko Tanaka, daughter of Prime Minister Tanaka, was also accompanying her father and charmed the Kremlin leaders with her buoyant energy.[23]

When the Joint Communiqué was finally issued the Director of the division in charge of the Soviet Union, Mr. Arai, had tears in his eyes when he briefed the press about this breakthrough. For me, it was a nostalgic reminder of the days I had spent as a young diplomat in Moscow under the Soviet regime.

Unfortunately, the momentum gained by Tanaka's visit to Moscow did not last for long. Japan plunged into the oil crisis of 1973 and economic indicators hit rock bottom in 1974 in growth, inflation and trade balance (Chapter 9). The Soviet Union, on the other hand, as one of the major oil producers and exporters of the world saw a substantial increase in its trade balance. Thus Japan, at least temporarily, lost its relative economic charm in the eyes of the Soviets. Prime Minister Tanaka was hit by a bribery scandal and was forced to resign at the end of 1974.

As for the political environment created by Detente, President Nixon resigned in 1974 and the Soviet Union expanded its activities in Indochina and Africa substantially in 1975 and '76 (Chapter 2). A very different international climate of tension and misgivings was created in the middle of the 1970's.

Political tension followed by an economic downturn from the middle of the 1970's

From the middle of the 1970's political relations between Japan and the Soviet Union also returned to confrontation and complacency.

In September 1976 a Soviet Air Force MIG-25 defected to Hokkaido. The Soviet government, embarrassed by this unexpected

---

[23] Makiko Tanaka later became Minister for Foreign Affairs in 2001–2002.

incident, had made several protests against the Japanese government for mishandling the matter, which in turn offended the Japanese authorities, because they felt they were handling the matter as best they could.

In February 1977 the Soviet Union enacted a new demarcation line establishing a 200 mile maritime fishery zone. A part of the new zone was demarcated from waters surrounding the 'four' islands. Japan could not allow its vessels to continue fishery there, because it would be tantamount to the acknowledgement of Soviet jurisdiction over the 'four' islands. It took a full half year of fierce negotiations, withdrawal of the Japanese fishing vessels from the newly established 200 mile zone, as well as the establishment of a Japanese 200 mile fishery zone, before a compromise agreement was reached in May 1977.

In August 1978 Japan concluded the Treaty of Peace and Friendship with China. Japan exerted great efforts to include an adequate mitigating clause against the hegemony clause. But the Soviet Union reacted by deploying military forces on the disputed four islands in the summer of that year (Chapter 4).

In December 1979 the Soviet Union invaded Afghanistan and Japan, together with other 'Western' nations imposed sanctions, including the boycott of the 1980 Olympic Games.

In November 1982 Brezhnev died and was succeeded by Yuri Andropov. His attempt to achieve a fresh and dynamic reform was prevented by his ailing health.

In September 1983 the Soviet Union shot down a South Korean airliner (KAL-007) flying from New York to Seoul and 269 people including 28 Japanese were killed. Japan acted decisively to bring this case out into the open and condemn the Soviet Union (Chapter 2).

The peace treaty negotiations were making little progress. The oral agreement that the four islands were the object of negotiations disappeared. The Soviet Union began to announce publicly that "an understanding that an 'unresolved territorial problem' exists between the two countries is one-sided and inaccurate."[24] In January 1978 Foreign Minister Sonoda visited Moscow to conduct regular foreign ministerial talks with his counterpart A. Gromyko. But after Sonoda's

---

[24] Kimura, *op. cit.*, p. 154.

visit to Moscow Gromyko never visited Japan, due to his reluctance
to face Japanese claims over the four islands. Consequently no peace
treaty negotiations were held for eight years from 1978 till 1986.

On the economic front, after the Tanaka-Brezhnev Joint Communiqué things seemed to move a little more smoothly. During the
Summit Meeting in October 1973 Brezhnev made a passionate statement on the future of Siberian development. Taking into account
the progress achieved in the political arena, the Japanese government decided to give greater support to economic participation in
developing Siberia. Three conditions—mutual benefit, protection of
private business interests, and due attention to third country interests (particularly that of America)—were the underlying motives in
Japan.

Japanese involvement in Siberian resource projects in the form of
suppliers' credit (SC) or bank loans (BL) is shown below:

Japanese involvement in Siberian resource projects[25] (million dollars if not otherwise indicated)		
Kawai-Sedov Timber & Machinery No. 1 (SC)	1968	163
Port of Urangelj (SC)	1970	80
Pulp & Chip No. 1 (SC)	1971	45
South Yakut Coal (BL)	1974	450
Yakut Gas (BL)	1974	50
Kawai-Sedov Timber & Machinery No. 2 (BL)	1974	500
Sakhalin Continental Shelf: SODECO No. 1–3	1975	237.5
South Yakut Coal addendum (BL)	1981	40
Kawai-Sedov Timber & Machinery No. 3 (BL)	1981	200 billion yen

As we see in the list shown above, the most active period for Japan's
participation in Siberian resource projects was 1974 and 1975, in
the form of bank loans. From then onwards, the transformation of
Japan's economy to a less energy-intensive industry and a cold and
complacent political climate towards the Soviet Union made further
participation of Japanese industry in the Siberian development
subdued.

---

[25] K. Ogawa, *Saigono Nyuufurontia (The last new frontier)*, Daiichi-Insatsu, 1993, pp.
172–174.

Trade figures from 1970 to 1985 are also an interesting reflection of that tendency. Soviet-German trade developed rapidly through the 70's and Germany became the No. 1 trade partner, reaching seven billion roubles by 1984. Japan, after having occupied the position of No. 1 trade partner in 1970 and 1971, kept the No. 2 partner position in principle until 1978, and then joined the second largest group consisting of Finland, Italy, and France. By 1983 and 1984 Japan's position was placed in the third group with America and Great Britain, with a trade volume of around three billion roubles. As a result of changes in the industrial structure, electronics became the leading item for Japanese exports, instead of textiles and household appliances. The downturn of Japan-Soviet trade relations ran parallel to the growing political impasse which the two countries entered into from the mid-70's to the mid-80's.[26]

5. Gorbachev's Perestroika: a new overture

Early Gorbachev years

Mikhail Gorbachev came to power after Konstantin Chernyenko died in March 1985. Gorbachev's policy of *perestroika* completely changed the Soviet Union, including its external relations. *Perestroika* was aimed at pulling the Soviet Union out from the long period of stagnation (*zastoi*). It shook society with *glasnostj*, which meant access to information and freedom of expression. It sought an efficient, motivated, and powerful economy within the broad framework of socialism. *Perestroika* meant reconstruction. In foreign policy, it embarked on a new way of thinking (*novoe myshlenie*), which emphasized dialogue and mutual trust, instead of force and suspicion.

The impact of *glasnostj* was breathtaking. The Soviets began to speak like people in other civilized nations, expressing independent and personal views, sometimes even being critical of the Soviet authorities. Foreign policy suddenly became active. In July 1985 Eduard Shevardnadze, First Party Secretary of the Georgian Republic, replaced Gromyko as Foreign Minister. Settling the war in Afghanistan and

---

[26] Trade figures from the statistics of *Planovo-ekonomicheskoe upravlenie SSSR (Economic Planning Agency USSR)*, various years.

resolving the issue of Intermediate-Range Nuclear Forces (INF) were priorities for the new Soviet leadership. In the economy, numerous ideas for 'reconstruction' began flooding the media. Some of them were boldly implemented.

In the beginning the Soviet-Japanese relations began to move in line with these changes. Shevardnadze visited Japan in January 1986, after an eight year interval. It was an ice-breaking visit. Shevardnadze did not object to Japan stating views it thought important, including those on the territorial issue. This did not mean that the Soviets gave an inch of their own position, but their readiness to talk was a warm breeze in the frozen relationship which had existed for nearly a decade.

Japanese Foreign Minister Shintaro Abe immediately made a return visit to Moscow in May and agreed, in principle, to resume visits by former islanders to the graveyards of their ancestors on the four islands and also concluded a cultural agreement. When Kuranari became Foreign Minister in July 1986, the possibility of a visit by Gorbachev to Japan in January 1987 was being discussed through diplomatic channels.

But the situation changed in the autumn of 1986. Japan's decision to join the American SDI research programme in September brought about a negative reaction from the Soviet side. In April 1987 a scandal surfaced in which a company affiliated with Toshiba leaked special technology on submarine interception to the Soviet Union. It developed into serious Japan-bashing by America. Bilateral Japanese-Soviet relations cooled down fast, entailing even some of the worst incidents in postwar Soviet Japanese relations, including the expulsion of diplomats on charges of alleged spying activities.[27]

Latter Gorbachev years: careful preparation for the first presidential visit

In 1988 tensions began to subside. In July, former Prime Minister Nakasone visited Moscow and had a meeting with Gorbachev.

---

[27] On 20 August the Soviet Union expelled a Japanese military attaché and a member of the Mitsubishi Trading Firm. Japan in turn expelled a representative of the Soviet Trade Representative Office. Another round of expulsions took place in September (T. Hasegawa, *Hoppouryoudomondaito Nichirokankei (Northern Territorial Issue and Japan-Russia Relations)* Chikuma, 2000, p. 111).

> Having just been appointed as the new Director of the Soviet Union Division of MOFA, I was fortunate in being able to attend this meeting to record notes. Gorbachev was lively, full of energy, eloquent, particularly on *perestroika* and on Soviet security, interested in listening to Nakasone's views, but obviously at an early stage of learning on Japan. He was clearly very different from any other Soviet leader that the world had ever known. It was indeed impressive to see a man with such power speaking and behaving like an ordinary human being. Nakasone succeeded in directing Gorbachev's attention further towards Japan.

I became firmly convinced that the time had come for Japan to take initiatives to search for a breakthrough in our relations. There were only two issues which merited the attention of a top leader of the Soviet Union regarding Japan: to create mutually beneficial economic relations through which Japan's huge economic potential could be mobilized for the development of their economy, and to develop strong politico-security relations with Japan, which would strengthen the Soviet strategic position in the Far East. On the other hand, Japan wanted to resolve the territorial problem. The breakthrough was possible only by way of creating a common vision on mutual cooperation comprising these three agendas.[28]

In December 1988 Shevardnadze made his second visit to Japan. After serious talks the two sides agreed to establish a new framework of dialogue consisting of three working groups: the peace treaty (to deal with the territorial issue), bilateral relations (to deal with economic and other relationships) and international matters (to discuss issues where Japan and the Soviet Union might find common interests, particularly in the Asia-Pacific region).

At the beginning of 1989, however, when Shevardnadze met Japanese Foreign Minister Sousuke Uno in Paris at the fringe of the Chemical Weapons Destruction Conference, traditional disconnection regarding the question of 'what comes first' re-emerged. During the Cold War, Japan basically maintained that the "Territorial problem needed to be resolved first, so as to create positive overall relations between the two countries." The Soviets maintained that "Overall

---

[28] K. Togo, *Nichiroshinnjidaiheno Jyosou (Japan and Russia, in Search of Breakthrough)*, Simulshuppankai, 1993, pp. 81–83.

relations needed to be improved first and on that basis difficult issues such as the territorial problem, if any, could be resolved." The same type of polemics was exchanged between the two ministers.

The discrepancy in Paris was overcome reasonably well in May, when in Moscow Uno proposed a new concept of 'development in equilibrium'. With this concept Japan meant to overcome the theological debate of 'what comes first', and concentrate on what each side could do to improve the relationship.

From then on the preparation of Gorbachev's visit proceeded reasonably smoothly.

The peace treaty working group gathered all together seven times. All historical and legal aspects of the issue were discussed thoroughly. The discussion was straightforward, tense, occasionally emotional, but sincere. By the time Gorbachev's visit was to take place, there emerged a shared feeling among the participants that the time was ripe for some kind of political decision.

In the area of economic cooperation, the Japanese government began to take unprecedented initiatives. On two occasions, in November 1989 and April 1990, it invited high-level missions from Soviet central ministries in charge of *perestroika*. The missions were particularly impressed by the 'planned' aspect of the Japanese economy and the socialist 'welfare' system of Japan's society. The missions went back with enriched knowledge on Japan to use it a study case for Soviet *perestroika*. The Japanese government also decided to extend the first package of humanitarian assistance of food and medical equipment in December 1990. Grant assistance to those who suffered from the Chernobyl nuclear disaster was supplied to the World Health Organization (WHO) in February 1991.

Trade figures began to recover from 1985 onwards. Germany kept its place as the first trading partner to the Soviet Union, but Japan became a leading member of the second group, together with Finland and Italy, with around $5 billion of total trade, and reached a historic figure of $6 billion in 1989, with a reasonable balance between exports and imports.[29]

Even in the area of security and defence, after thorough preparation on the Japanese side, a cautious dialogue on security in the

---

[29] IMF, Direction of trade statistics, 1992.

Asia-Pacific region began between the two Foreign Ministries at the end of 1990.

After all these preparations President Gorbachev came to Japan in April 1991. It was the first visit made by a leader of this neighbouring country since the time of Czarist Russia.

The centre of attention for both countries was the issue of the 'four' islands.

Japan had, in essence, two objectives: first, to reconfirm in writing what Prime Minister Tanaka had verbally achieved in 1973, namely that the object of the negotiations was the issue of the 'four' islands, second, to let Gorbachev withdraw the 1960 Gromyko Memorandum and acknowledge the international obligation of the 1956 Joint Declaration including Paragraph 9. If these two objectives were achieved, then, conditions to focus the negotiations on the core issue, the sovereignty of Kunashiri and Etorofu, would emerge.[30]

Gorbachev basically agreed on the first, but persistently rejected the second. Even after six rounds of prolonged and fierce debates with Prime Minister Kaifu, he made it clear that a part of the 1956 Joint Declaration could not be restored in full.[31]

The Joint Communiqué which was adopted on 18 April reflected exactly the content of the negotiations: the importance of concluding a peace treaty, which included the resolution of the territorial issue, whereby the positions of the two sides differed on the 'four' islands (with concrete names), and all these points were clearly documented. For the first time in an agreed official document between the Soviet Union and Japan the names of Kunashiri and Etorofu appeared. On the 1956 Joint Declaration, however, lengthy explanatory texts were included, but it was clear that the Japanese objective to confirm this declaration in full had not been met.

It was also agreed to enhance exchanges between Japan and the 'four' islands, including an establishment of a framework of non-visa exchanges.

Thus on the territorial problem an important step was made, but not to the extent of making a breakthrough.

Other than the territorial issue, the Joint Communiqué incorporated positive clauses on all aspects of bilateral relations, including economic

---

[30] K. Togo, *op. cit.*, pp. 159–168.
[31] A. Panov, *Fushinkara Shinraihe (Beyond Distrust to Trust)*, Simulshuppankai, 1992, pp. 134–140.

relations and Japan-Soviet cooperation on key international affairs. In addition to the Joint Communiqué, 15 documents were signed. All of these reflected the concept of 'development in equilibrium'.

On the whole the visit, the first by a top Soviet leader, should be considered to have been a reasonable success. But as the result of six years of efforts after *perestroika* had started, it was a humble step forwards.

Gorbachev came to Japan after all major East-West agendas were accomplished, such as the agreement to dismantle INF (1987), the Soviet withdrawal from Afghanistan (1989), the fall of the Berlin wall (1989), and the unification of Germany (1990; Chapter 2).

By that time, domestically, Gorbachev's *perestroika* was in crisis. Economic reform to create a 'market-oriented economy based on socialism' was in sheer confusion. The economy became a monstrous and uncontrollable animal. The republics constituting the Soviet Union, particularly the Baltic, revolted in search of independence. Blood was shed in January 1991 in Lithuania. Ethnic collisions swept the Caucasus from the end of the 1980's. Opposition both from the conservative communist old guard to revolutionary democrats lined up in criticism of Gorbachev. He was not in a position to take strong decisions on such a delicate issue as the territorial problem.

6. *Yeltsin's Russia: emergence of a new world*

Yeltsin's dramatic years

On 19 August 1991, four months after Gorbachev's visit to Japan, the Soviet old guard waged a coup against Gorbachev. But in three days the coup was suppressed and one of the most spectacular dramas of the 20th century began: the demise of the Soviet Union. Power shifted almost instantaneously to Boris Yeltsin, President of the Russian Federation. Among the three Soviet ruling organizations, the army had barely survived, but the Communist Party had virtually ceased to exist and the KGB was split and substantially weakened. The three Baltic states gained almost immediate independence and the entire Soviet Union was dissolved by the end of the year. The Russian Federation, led by Boris Yeltsin with his refreshing 'reform policy' towards democracy and market economy replaced the Soviet Union. It was a rare moment in history, in which a nation and the values it had embodied for 70 years disintegrated in just four months.

In Japan-Soviet relations, after a four-month lull since Gorbachev's visit, a historic opportunity emerged. Ruslan Khasbulatov, acting Chairman of the Supreme Council of the Russian Federation, visited Japan in September 1991. He brought a presidential message which stated that the winner and victor divide from WWII must be relinquished; that the peace treaty between the two countries must be concluded urgently; and that the territorial issue should be resolved based on the principles of 'law and justice'.[32]

Japan reacted and on 24 September at the United Nations General Assembly, Foreign Minister Nakayama declared, in his foreign policy speech, five new principles to govern Japanese policy towards the Soviet Union/Russian Federation:

1) To express support and solidarity to Soviet internal and external reforms and to increase effective assistance;

2) To strengthen relations with the Russian Federation;

3) To expand cooperation, so that the Soviet Union would become a constructive partner in the Asia-Pacific region;

4) To support cooperation between the Soviet Union and IMF, the World Bank, and other international economic organizations;

5) To drastically improve bilateral relations by way of concluding the peace treaty based on the principle of law and justice, as a most important issue.[33]

On 8 October Japan announced a new assistance package of $2.5 billion of Ex-Im Bank credits and MITI (Ministry of International Trade and Industry) trade insurance.

Nakayama visited Moscow from 12 to 17 October and had talks with President Gorbachev and President Yeltsin, respectively. A concrete framework of non-visa exchanges with the four islands was agreed upon.

And yet again nothing happened. I left the post of Director of the Soviet Union Division in early December, when waves of expectation on both sides were still in full swing. From the beginning of 1992, however, President Yeltsin introduced, in a drastic manner,

---

[32] Kimura, *op. cit.*, p. 188.
[33] K. Togo, *op. cit.*, pp. 214–215.

market mechanisms into Russian society. It succeeded in unleashing consumer goods in markets, but entailed a hyperinflation of a 27-fold price hike through 1992. The early euphoria for reforms rapidly waned and already in the spring of 1992 resentments toward President Yeltsin's reform policy were manifest in many areas.

The underlying desire to achieve a substantial breakthrough in Japan-Russia relations seemed to have waned as well. President Yeltsin had abruptly cancelled his visit to Tokyo in September 1992, just four days before it was scheduled to take place. In Russia, Japanese stubbornness and their self-righteous approach to the territorial issue was rapidly reported as the main reason for cancelling the visit. In Japan, impressions of Russian rudeness and lack of respect spread widely. Whatever the real reasons for the cancellation, relations suffered a severe blow and probably the most promising window of opportunity that had opened during the 1990's was shut.

As the economic situation continued to worsen, President Yeltsin's internal position became increasingly fragile. The US and other European countries decided to assist Yeltsin, so that his reform policy towards democracy and a market economy would be upheld. They asked Japan to cooperate. Inside Japan, however, politicians and public opinion voiced strong views against helping Russia, since Russia did not display even minimal respect to Japan. The Japanese government was put in an extremely difficult position, but took a careful and well-balanced decision, and in the spring of 1993 announced a $1.5 billion assistance of Ex-Im Bank credits and MITI trade insurance and $0.32 billion of technical and other assistance towards Russia. Japan also agreed to invite President Yeltsin to the Tokyo Summit in July 1993.

Despite these efforts by the 'West', the political situation in Russia worsened. In September members of parliament objecting to Yeltsin's reforms had occupied the Duma[34] and an insurrection flared up on 3–4 October. Yeltsin ordered the military to crush the revolt, the result of which was a bloody encounter. Amidst this extremely difficult domestic situation, preparations for a renewed presidential visit to Japan proceeded carefully, and when in mid-October the internal situation began to calm down, President Yeltsin finally visited Japan.

---

[34] The lower chamber of Russian parliament.

On 13 October the Tokyo Declaration was adopted. The key paragraph related to the territorial issue reads as follows:

> 2. The Prime Minister of Japan and the President of the Russian Federation, sharing the recognition that the difficult legacies of the past in the relations between the two countries must be overcome, have undertaken serious negotiations on the issue of where Etorofu, Kunashiri, Shikotan and the Habomai Islands belong. They agree that negotiations towards an early conclusion of a Peace Treaty through the solution of this issue on the basis of historical and legal facts and based on the documents produced with the two countries' agreement as well as on the principles of law and justice should continue, and that the relations between the two countries should thus be fully normalized. In this regard, the Government of Japan and the Government of the Russian Federation confirm that the Russian Federation is the State retaining continuing identity with the Soviet Union and that all treaties and other international agreements between Japan and the Soviet Union continue to be applied between Japan and the Russian Federation.[35]

The three principles to guide the peace treaty negotiations, 'historical and legal facts', 'the principles of law and justice' and 'the documents produced with the two countries' agreement' were clearly defined.[36] Japan welcomed these principles.

The understanding that all "international agreements between Japan and the Soviet Union continue to be applied" between the two countries seems to indicate that the 1956 Joint Declaration is one of such documents to be applied to Russia.[37] That expression was indirect and somewhat vague, but certainly better than the text agreed upon in the Kaifu-Gorbachev Communiqué of 1991.

A four-year pause

On the whole Yeltsin's visit in October 2003 brought Japan-Russia relations back to the level they were at in the autumn of the pre-

---

[35] www.mofa.go.jp/region/n-america/us/q&a/declaration.html 2003–07–14.

[36] The Joint Compendium of Documents on the History of Territorial Problems between Japan and Russia, compiled by the two Foreign Ministries based on the debates at the Peace Treaty Working Group and published in 1992, just after the cancellation of President Yeltsin's visit, is included in these documents.

[37] President Yeltsin, asked at the final press conference whether the 1956 Joint Declaration is included in the agreements to be applied to Russia, answered affirmatively. He had apparently not done so during his meeting with Prime Minister Hosokawa (T. Hasegawa, op. cit., pp. 316–319).

vious year. But in December 2003 a Duma election was held, where former communist and nationalist forces gained an unexpected victory. President Yeltsin's reform policy was again doomed.

> I arrived in Moscow in February 1994 to assume the post of Deputy Chief of the Mission of the Japanese Embassy. It was probably one of the darkest Russian winters the Russian people had ever experienced:
> – "Where is Russia going," I asked.
> – "I don't know, please tell me," answered my Russian friends.

For two and a half years, Yeltsin's presidency had the difficult task of overcoming inflation and achieving economic recovery, maintaining a basic policy of political reforms, and winning the presidential election in the summer of 1996. Meanwhile, since the end of 1994, the fighting in Chechnya had become an issue of national importance. Under these circumstances the immediate implementation of the Tokyo Declaration and the resolution of the territorial issue ceased to be a viable political agenda.

Thus, from the end of 1993 to November 1997, when re-elected President Yeltsin and Prime Minister Hashimoto met at Krasnoyarsk, the territorial negotiations on the sovereignty of the four islands had not shown any momentum.

Several achievements had nevertheless been made during these four years to enlarge and deepen the scope of relations:

First, there was an issue which by this time needed a solution. Since the Soviet occupation Japanese fishermen in Hokkaido had continued fishing around the four islands. Soviet border patrols arrested them whenever they found these 'illegal' catches. Particularly after the collapse of the Soviet Union, Japanese fishing activities increased. With the return to law and order, the Russian border guards became impatient. An arrangement was needed quickly, so as to avoid further incidents and bloodshed. Preliminary negotiations started as early as autumn 1994; a breakthrough was made in the spring of 1997; and an agreement was finally made in the spring of 1998. I was lucky to head the Japanese team as Deputy Director General of European Affairs for one year from autumn 1996 to summer 1997 and go through this formidable process of negotiations, a theme which may merit another book to be written someday.

Second, on economic relations, the initial expectation that a new democratic and market-oriented Russia would create bigger business opportunities soon proved to be an illusion. While Japanese imports remained at about the same level as before, Japanese exports began to decline sharply. This kept the total trade at a $4 to $5 billion level[38] until the end of the 1990's.

At the end of 1994 the Japanese government initiated a regular trade and economic committee at the ministerial level so as to encourage President Yeltsin's reform policy, to give a stimulus to Japan-Russia trade relations, to help Japanese companies which were in difficulty under the confusing economic and social situation in Russia and to facilitate the implementation of Japanese assistance, which totalled more than $4 billion.

Third, a substantial change occurred in the security area. After the embryonic dialogue on security between the two Foreign Ministries at the end of 1990, the first security and defence talks[39] began in June 1992. Watershed events were the first visit by the Japanese State Minister for Defence in April 1996 and an epoch-making visit to Vladivostok by a Maritime Defence Force vessel in July that year. Both ministerial and maritime visits were soon reciprocated by Russia. They have since become regular events between the two countries.

But in the summer of 1996 Yeltsin was re-elected for a second four-year term as president and relations began to warm up. Yeltsin's health, however, was seriously limited by a heart attack during the election campaign, and it was only in the spring of 1997 that he came back to the Kremlin. From March 1997 he reshuffled top level appointments to activate economic reforms and took a critical decision on an issue which haunted Russia after the demise of the Soviet Union: NATO's expansion to the east. From April to May, Yeltsin decided to accept former East-European countries joining NATO. The NATO Summit in Madrid in July 1997 signalled that one of the most important post-Cold War security issues had finally been resolved.

In Japan Ryuutaro Hashimoto, who became Prime Minister in January 1996, saw a historic opportunity. Now that a major issue

---

[38] Ministry of Finance Statistics.
[39] It involved the Russian Defence Ministry, the Japanese Defence Agency, and two Ministries of Foreign Affairs at Director General level.

at the western part of the Eurasian continent had been resolved, the
tide of the history might move to the eastern part of that continent.
Hashimoto contemplated allowing Japan to play a more substantial
role in this respect, including a possible breakthrough with Russia.
He took a series of initiatives to stimulate the relationship: exchang-
ing letters with President Yeltsin, accepting Russia in principle as a
member of the G8 in March, and making a historic speech in July
on Japan's new Eurasian policy in which he emphasized the necessity of establishing enhanced strategic relations with Russia based on
three new principles: trust, mutual benefit, and long-term perspectives (Chapter 6 on Silk Road countries).[40] This went straight to the
hearts of many Russian leaders and intellectuals.

The Hashimoto-Yeltsin Krasnoyarsk meeting and its follow-up

On 1 and 2 November 1997 Hashimoto and Yeltsin met in Krasnoyarsk and held an informal summit meeting, called a 'no necktie
meeting'. To the surprise of many, Yeltsin proposed to conclude the
peace treaty by the end of 2000. His wish to do something on the
islands was clear, although no concrete idea was incorporated in his
proposal. Japan proposed the so-called 'Hashimoto-Yeltsin plan' to
boost economic relations in the seven following areas, which the
Russian side greatly appreciated: 1) investment cooperation initiative, 2) Russia's incorporation in the global economy, 3) enlargement
of reform assistance, 4) management training programme, 5) strengthening of the energy dialogue, 6) peaceful utilization of nuclear power,
7) and space cooperation.[41]

Faced with this new situation the Japanese government took a
series of substantial initiatives: in November at the APEC Meeting
in Vancouver, Japan took the lead to include Russia in APEC; in
February 1998 Foreign Minister Obuchi announced another $1.5
billion of untied loans assistance from the Japan Bank of International
Cooperation (JBIC), former Ex-Im Bank, during his visit to Moscow;
and in April 1998 at Kawana, where Yeltsin visited to hold the sec-

---

[40] The speech was made at the *Keizaidoyuukai* on 24 July 1997 (Wada, *Hoppouryoudo-
Mondai (Northern Territorial Issue)*, Asahi, 1999, p. 366).
[41] http://www.mofa.go.jp/mohaj/area/russia/shien/index.html 2002–10–25.
In Krasnoyarsk it was a six-point plan and the seventh cooperation over 'space'
was added later in Kawana in April 1998.

ond 'no necktie meeting' Hashimoto made a new proposal for the resolution of the territorial problem, the first and only concessionary proposal Japan had ever made since 1956, based on the concept of border demarcation between the islands of Etorofu and Uruppu.

And again, to my sadness that was the highest point the two countries ever reached under President Yeltsin.

In Russia, an Asian financial crisis ignited another economic crisis in May and August 1998. President Yeltsin's ailing health weakened his leadership position.

In Japan, the failure of its economic policy led to a significant defeat of the LDP in the parliamentary election of July 1998, and Prime Minister Hashimoto had to resign. The Hashimoto-Yeltsin personal friendship, which guided the relationship, faded to the background.

Nevertheless, the two governments continued to make efforts. Prime Minister Obuchi, who succeeded Hashimoto, visited Moscow in November 1998, hoping to obtain a positive reply to Hashimoto's Kawana proposal.

> I accompanied the delegation and attended the Summit Meeting in the Kremlin as Director General of the Treaties Bureau. The President Yeltsin I saw there was different from the Boris Yeltsin I had seen in October 1991 with Foreign Minister Nakayama. Then, he had been confident, determined and articulate. But now, ill health limited his endeavours. And yet, Yeltsin's spirit, filled with goodwill towards Japan, determined to improve the relationship and to do something about the peace treaty, radiated from his ailing body. That was a moving experience and one not easily forgotten.

As for the territorial issue, the Russian proposal was given in a written form. Several leaks to the press indicated that in essence it would conclude two agreements which would eventually lead to territorial demarcation. In other words, it was a procedural proposal, which Japan could not accept as the basis of further negotiations.

In 1999, with an ailing leader, the Russian domestic situation entered a period of stagnation. The peace treaty negotiations also came to a standstill. Neither the Kawana proposal nor the Moscow proposal could become the basis for further negotiations.

I was appointed as Director General of the European Department in August 1999, facing this difficult situation. On 31 December 1999

President Yeltsin announced his retirement and the appointment of Vladimir Putin, then Prime Minister, as his successor.

7. President Putin and future perspectives

Vladimir Putin was formally elected as President in March 2000. His task was to continue Yeltsin's reform policy with an emphasis on order and stability in domestic politics and active engagement in foreign policy. But during the first year of his tenure, relations with Clinton in his last year of presidency were not fruitful. His relations with Europe were somewhat constrained, for instance on Chechnya. Japan seemed to have appeared an interesting objective for his foreign policy. Was it because he saw unexploited potential on geopolitical proximity, or because of President Yeltsin's legacy, or due to Judo which he had practiced for 20 years, we do not know.

In Japan, Prime Minister Obuchi, who had been looking forward to having in-depth dialogues with Putin, suffered a stroke in April 2000 and was replaced by Yoshiro Mori, the LDP General Secretary. Mori was greatly interested in Russia and right from the beginning of his tenure began sending messages.

Mori chose St. Petersburg as his first place for a visit in April? 2000. From then onwards the two leaders met in Okinawa (July), Tokyo (September), Brunei at the fringe of APEC Meeting (November) and Irkutsk (March 2001). This unprecedented frequency, five times in a year, with solid discussions on all relevant issues between the two countries, including the territorial problem, shows the efforts on both sides to overcome the legacy of the past.

These talks started in St. Petersburg with overviews of the relationship: geopolitical-strategic cooperation, economic cooperation and the conclusion of the peace treaty.

For me, it was the third time I attended a meeting where President Putin spoke.

I met with him for the first time in Oakland at a bilateral meeting with Prime Minister Obuchi in September 1999 on the occasion of the APEC Leaders Meeting. Putin looked sharp, strong-willed but a little rough.

> The second time I saw him was in April 2000, when I was in Moscow with a special envoy of Prime Minister Muneo Suzuki to fix the date of the first meeting with Prime Minister Mori.
>
> Each time he seemed to be speaking with more confidence and determination, quickly mastering a presidential manner of discourse.
>
> Just an example: in Oakland he was using long briefing papers; in Moscow he had a few small cards which he occasionally glanced at; in St. Petersburg he spoke in detail on each complicated subject without referring to any notes. He was learning fast. That was quite impressive to watch.

After his 'debut' in July in a multilateral forum in Okinawa, where Prime Minister Mori greeted him with a real warmth and courtesy, Putin visited Tokyo in September. There Putin made a surprising statement, saying: "I consider the 1956 Joint Declaration effective." This statement triggered extremely serious and substantial negotiations on the question of sovereignty of the four islands for seven months, until the leaders meeting in Irkutsk on 25 March 2001.

The relevant paragraphs of the concluding Communiqué read as follows:

> "Both parties———
> – Confirmed that the 1956 Japan-Soviet Joint Declaration is a basic legal document that established the starting point in the negotiation process for the conclusion of a peace treaty subsequent to the restoration of diplomatic relations between both countries;
> – Based on this confirmation, agreed to promote future negotiations to accomplish complete normalization of Japan-Russia relations by means of concluding a peace treaty through the solution of issues concerning the attribution of the islands of Etorofu, Kunashiri, Shikotan and Habomai, on the basis of the 1993 Tokyo Declaration on Japan-Russia Relations;"[42]

Outwardly what was achieved might sound modest: the ambiguity around the 1956 Joint Declaration, which had haunted Japan-Russia relations since the Gromyko Memorandum of 1960, was simply eradicated. But what was critically important was that, based on this communiqué, negotiations were continuing with genuine momentum.

---

[42] www.mofa.go.jp/region/europe/russia/pmv0103/state.html 2003-07-14.

And yet again, seven months of negotiations ended when Makiko Tanaka, daughter of the late Prime Minister Kakuei Tanaka assumed the post of Minister for Foreign Affairs at the end of April 2001. The total confusion which occurred between the Foreign Minister and Foreign Ministry officials paralyzed many aspects of Japanese foreign policy, including its Russian policy. In addition, confusion around a parliamentarian Muneo Suzuki, who was known to be a close 'supporter' of the Ministry of Foreign Affairs, as well as an 'intruder' in various matters of several ministries including the Foreign Ministry, virtually halted the relationship for a while.

At the beginning of the 21st century, despite all the confusion as described above, Japan and Russia managed to find common interests in some geopolitical issues in the Asian Pacific region, such as the peace and stability of the Korean peninsula, as well as in developing economic relations of mutual benefit. On the most difficult issue of the territorial problem, there are several agreements such as the 1956 Joint Declaration, the Tokyo Declaration, and the Irkutsk Communiqué, which establish the common framework of negotiations. Prime Minister Koizumi's visit to Moscow in January 2003 and the establishment of an Action Plan is keeping the relationship at a moderate temperature.

How the relationship could develop so as to maximize the interests and foreign policy leverage of both countries is left in the hands of the leaders and those who will handle the relationship henceforth.

Fig. 2. With President Putin at St. Petersburg (29 April 2000).

CHAPTER EIGHT

EUROPE: STRUGGLE FOR RELEVANCE

The history of Japan and Europe could be characterized as a struggle for relevance.

As we have seen in the Prologue, from the Meiji Restoration to the Pacific War, Europe occupied an important place in many aspects of Japanese life, politics and international relations. Europe was intrinsically relevant for Japan.

Europe first of all was the centre of 'Western civilization'. Japan strived hard to catch up with the West. *Datsu-A-Nyu-Ou*[1] became the motto of the era. Europe became the model of many social and political structures, as well as the source of science and technology, which were critically important to build a 'prosperous country and strong military'.

Throughout this period the first area where Japan sought to establish its sphere of influence was the eastern part of the Eurasian continent, from the Korean peninsula through Manchuria to China. The Pacific Ocean was the second area of its geopolitical concern. Relations with the European powers had been a critical element for Japan in ensuring its position in these areas of primary interest.

For the European powers, as Japan gradually established its sphere of influence from the Korean peninsula to Manchuria, relations with Japan also became a critical element in ensuring their interests in the eastern part of Asia, namely to implement smoothly and effectively their colonial policy. Japan became relevant for Europe as well.

The European powers directly affected the development in international politics in the Far East. It started with the Triple Intervention by Russia, Germany and France in 1895, after the Japan-China War. Then Japan entered into an alliance with the United Kingdom in 1902. This became Japan's cornerstone to win the war with Russia

---

[1] Getting out (=*Datsu*) from Asia (=*A*) and entering into (=*Nyu*) Europe (=*Ou*); see Prologue.

in 1904–1905. The alliance lasted for two decades, until it was replaced by a quadrilateral treaty between Japan, the UK, France and the United States, signed in Washington in 1921.

After the Manchurian Incident in 1931, Japan went through a strenuous period of defining its course. While expanding its sphere of influence to mainland China and Indochina, this search resulted in an alliance with Germany and Italy, a neutrality pact with the Soviet Union and a disastrous war in the Pacific against the US.

1. A prolonged postwar period (1945–1969)

In 1945, when WWII ended, this picture substantially changed. Japan lost all its colonial territories and areas under its sphere of influence, and devastated by war, began concentrating its efforts on economic reconstruction and on re-establishing primarily economic relations with the Asian countries. Japan also came under the strong influence of the United States.

Europe, which in principle appeared as a victor, in reality lost its colonial possessions in Asia and many countries were subjected to devastation at home. Europe also had to concentrate its energies on postwar economic recovery. For the countries that had fought against Japan, especially Great Britain and the Netherlands, the war left them with memories of humiliation and atrocities.

Thus, postwar relations between Japan and Europe began with mutual disregard at best, with a slow and cautious effort toward reconciliation, or at worst with a sense of antipathy from Europe towards Japan. A quarter of century of 'irrelevance' began, in principle, between Japan and Europe.

But of course there were relevant elements as well.

Postwar reparations

The first aspect of relevance came from the necessity for both of resuming peace and normal diplomatic relations. The reconciliation between Europe and Japan started with the San Francisco Peace Treaty, signed in September 1951. From Europe, seven countries that had fought the war with Japan signed this treaty: Belgium, France, Greece, the Netherlands, Norway, Turkey and the United Kingdom.

But in addition, to a certain degree the score of war had to be settled for Europe. Based on Article 14 (b) of the San Francisco Peace Treaty,[2] these allied countries waived their rights for reparations. But based on Article 16 of this Treaty, Japan paid in 1955 to the International Committee of the Red Cross (ICRC) 4.5 million pounds "as an expression of its desire to indemnify those—who suffered undue hardships while prisoners of war of Japan."[3] In 1956 an additional 10 million dollars were "voluntarily tendered as a solatium" to the Netherlands "for the purpose of expressing sympathy and regret for the suffering inflicted during the Second World War by agencies of the Government of Japan upon Netherlands nationals,"[4] based on the Protocol concluded between the two countries.

Even after these basic decisions were made by the Japanese and European governments, war-related issues were not entirely settled (Section 5 below).

Normalization of economic relations

In general, from the middle of the 1950's onwards economic matters became the central issue between the two sides. In particular Japan placed high policy priority in resolving the question of whether and when membership to major international economic institutions such as GATT would be granted (Chapter 11).

Japan's first application for membership to GATT in 1952 was opposed by the UK. It was in 1955 that Japan was accepted as a

---

[2] Article 14 (b) of the San Francisco Peace Treaty reads as follows: "Except as otherwise provided in the present Treaty, the Allied Powers waive all reparations claims of the Allied Powers, other claims of the Allied Powers and their nationals arising out of any actions taken by Japan and its nationals in the course of the prosecution of the war, and claims of the Allied Powers for direct military costs of occupation." (MOFA, *Principal Treaties, op. cit.*, p. 19.)

[3] Quoted from Article 16 of the San Francisco Peace Treaty, MOFA, *Principal Treaties, op. cit.*, p. 22. In addition to the UK and the Netherlands, Australia, France, the Philippines, Vietnam, Cambodia and other countries submitted a list as recipient countries. The US renounced its right (MOFA documents).

[4] Quoted from Article I of the Protocol between the Government of Japan and the Government of The Kingdom of the Netherlands relating to the Settlement of the Problem concerning Certain Private Claims by Netherlands Nationals, signed in Tokyo, 3 March 1956, MOFA, Collection des Traites, 1956–XXXIV, No. 22 (No 1279), June 1956.

GATT member, with strong support from the United States. And yet, 14 countries, including the UK, France and the Netherlands did not agree to grant Japan a Most-Favoured-Nation status. These countries, urged by their textile industries, which feared fierce Japanese competition, refused to abolish discriminatory measures against Japan (Chapter 11). More generally, the Europeans feared that Japanese goods, produced by workers prepared to accept lower salaries and longer working hours, would be dumped on their market. Antipathy from wartime experiences continued to persist as well.[5]

After strenuous negotiations the Treaty of Commerce and Navigation between Japan and the UK was concluded in 1962 and finally Japan was granted Most-Favoured-Nation treatment. But the UK reserved the right to a 'safeguard clause,' which allowed her to introduce selective measures of import restriction in case of future emergencies.

In 1963 Japan concluded treaties of commerce with France and the Benelux, where the Most-Favoured-Nation status was granted but the 'safeguard clause' was equally preserved.

It is a well-remembered episode in Japan that when Prime Minister Ikeda visited Europe in 1962 and met with the French President Charles de Gaulle, the President later described him as a 'transistor radio salesman'. Humiliating as it may sound, this episode perhaps reflects Japan's efforts in these postwar years, seeking international recognition through success in economic development.

As we are going to see in Chapter 11, Japan's full-scale participation in the international economic community was achieved through three events: gaining Article 11 status in GATT in 1963, Article 8 status in IMF in 1964, and membership of OECD in 1964.[6] In the context of Japan-Europe relations it meant that Europe accepted Japan as its economic partner on an equal footing.

European culture during the difficult years

During this difficult period Europe stayed quite relevant for Japan with respect to how Japanese intellectuals and even ordinary people felt towards Europe as the birthplace of 'Western' civilization. Such great names in literature and philosophy as Plato, Aristotle, Shakespeare,

---

[5] Tadokoro, *op. cit.*, p. 113.
[6] Hosoya, 1993, *op. cit.*, pp. 195–199.

Goethe, Tolstoy, Dostoevsky, Racine, Stendhal, Kant, Hegel, Marx and many others, never ceased to evoke admiration. In the area of music, composers such as Bach, Mozart, Beethoven, Tchaikovsky and Puccini had a profound and lasting impact on music lovers of all generations. For many Japanese art lovers Rembrandt, the French impressionists, and Picasso were symbols of Western beauty.

In Europe, at least for a minority of specialists on Asia, Japanese tradition and culture, combined with its natural beauty, remained sources of wonder and admiration.

2. Trade conflicts with Europe (1969–1991)

1969 became an important dividing point in Japan's economic relations with Europe, just as this year became an important landmark in Japan-US relations. For the first time in trade history between Japan and EC trade deficits appeared on the European side.[7] In Europe, the emergence of trade deficits with Japan had a gloomy psychological impact. In addition, Japan's exports began to be concentrated in such industries as radio, television, electronics, ships, and automobiles. In each sector fears emerged for future European production.[8]

> From 1969 to 1972, I was sent from the Foreign Ministry to England to study the Russian language and Soviet affairs. Trade conflicts did not influence my daily academic life. But I remember very well an evening hosted by a senior Counsellor of the Japanese Embassy. He explained to us, young diplomats, each studying a foreign language in various parts of England, what kind of problems the Embassy had to deal with daily:
>
> "The fact that the Japanese are working hard, much longer hours than the Europeans, that we are living in such poor conditions, already often labelled as 'rabbits hutches', and that we are producing high quality attractive commodities is creating real anxieties among the Europeans. For us, nothing is wrong with hard work and living in confined quarters is not a crime. But

---

[7] Japanese exports totalled $968 million; EC exports totalled $821 million (JETRO statistics www.jetro.go.jp/ec/j/trade/excel/40w02.xls 2003–07–19).

[8] Ikei, *op. cit.*, p. 332.

> they are so greatly concerned that the European way of life could be threatened by Japanese 'torrential rains'. The Japanese themselves must now give thought to the need for harmonizing the Japanese way of life with the outside world. But many Japanese still lack an acute awareness. It is really worrisome. . . ."
>
> His mood was very serious, and for young diplomats enjoying their academic life, it was quite interesting and stimulating to hear his concerns.

The creation of the European Economic Community (EEC) in 1958 developed into the European Community (EC) in 1967. It introduced structural changes in Europe that shifted some power for trade negotiations to the European Commission in Brussels. In 1974 the Representative Office of the European Community opened in Tokyo.

Bilateral trade conflicts, however, still had to be settled primarily through negotiations in the capitals.

By 1973 EC trade deficits *vis-à-vis* Japan reached $1 billion.[9]

The first round of trade conflicts: 1976–1980

Increasing trade deficits and overwhelming exports from Japan heightened deep frustrations in Europe. In October 1976, a large-scale delegation of Japanese businessmen headed by Toshimitsu Doko, president of *Keidanren*[10] visited Europe. European interlocutors from various capitals, the European Community, and business sectors, all subjected this delegation to close scrutiny. The President of the European Commission, Mr. François-Xavier Ortoli, warned with an unprecedented harshness that "the EC countries were extremely annoyed by Japanese export offensives and the substantial increase of trade deficits. All levels of industries and trade unions requested the introduction of restrictive measures against Japanese exports. If current trade deficits were to continue between Japan and Europe, Japan would face grave consequences."[11]

---

[9] JETRO figures (http://www.jetro.go.jp/ec/j/trade/excel/40w02.xls 2003–07–19).

[10] This is a business association in which major Japanese companies and trade firms participate called *Keizai* (Economic) *dantai* (corporation) *rengoukai* (association), abbreviated as *Keidanren* or *Nippon Keidanren*.

[11] Hosoya, 1993, *op. cit.*, p. 202.

In 1976 Japan's exports to the EC were approximately double its imports from the EC, resulting in a trade deficit of $3.6 billion.[12] On a sectoral basis Japanese exports, referred to as 'torrential rain', moved from fear to reality in automobiles, electronics, ball bearings, steel and shipbuilding. The impression that the Japanese market was closed to European exporters exacerbated the tension.

The Japanese government and industries were shocked by the results of the Doko Mission in Europe.

The government took a series of measures: in November 1976 at the High Level Officials Group between Japan and the EC, Japan proposed three principles, consisting of free trade, dialogue with the EC, and consideration of third party interests. In May 1977 an EC-Japan Ministerial Meeting was held in Tokyo and in-depth discussions on trade imbalances were conducted. In March 1978 an EC-Japan joint communiqué was issued to underline Japanese efforts to decrease its trade surplus vis-à-vis Europe. In 1979 the Japanese government opened a Representative Office in Brussels.

The private sector joined this process as well. Japan-UK automobile sectors reached a Voluntary Export Restraint (VER) agreement to keep the Japanese market share in the UK at 11%. A similar agreement was reached in Japan-UK electronics industries. VER was a subject of discussion between Japan and many EC countries on a variety of topics and at various levels.[13]

These concerted efforts by the Japanese government and companies to solve the problems facing European industries succeeded in alleviating tension from trade disputes by the end of the 1970's.

The second round of trade conflicts: 1981-end of the 1980's

The actual amount of the trade deficit, however, did not decline significantly. As early as 1981 the EC deficit amounted to $10 billion.[14] Japan continued to expand its exports in Europe in such key industries as automobiles, colour televisions and high-tech products (VTRs, computers, semi-conductors). European discontent continued. The lull experienced in trade tensions at the end of the 1970's was shortlived.

---

[12] JETRO figures (http://www.jetro.go.jp/ec/j/trade/excel/40w02.xls 2003–07–19).
[13] Hosoya, 1993, *op. cit.*, pp. 203–204.
[14] JETRO figures (http://www.jetro.go.jp/ec/j/trade/excel/40w02.xls 2003–07–19).

As for the automobile sector, by 1981 France had introduced import restrictions to limit Japan's share to below 3% of newly-registered cars; Italy had placed a ceiling on annual imports from Japan of 3,300; and the UK had private sector VER agreements in operation. The European Commission wanted to expand these restrictive measures to include other major EC countries. Thus in 1981, Japan agreed to take VER measures with Germany to limit the yearly rate of increase in Japanese exports to under 10%; with the Netherlands to keep the exports at the same level as the previous year and with Belgium and Luxemburg to limit the amount of exports to 7% lower than the previous year.

As for colour televisions and VTRs, Japan agreed in 1983 to give an 'Export Forecast' for the following three years. That was another way of stating that Japan was prepared to implement VER measures to keep its exports below the level of that forecast.[15]

The third round of trade conflict: end of the 1980's-beginning of the 1990's

Despite these efforts during the first half of the 1980's trade deficits reached $20 billion in 1987. They continued to increase steadily and reached a historic record high of $31 billion in 1992.[16]

But this time the reaction on the part of Europe was different.

On the one hand, it was a time of historic integration for Europe. In June 1985 a White Paper from the Commission to the European Council, entitled 'Completing the Internal Market' was adopted. The agenda for European integration was clearly outlined: "to create an area for free movement of goods, services, capital and persons, a common market".[17] In February 1986 a Single European Act was adopted to formalize that agenda. The Treaty of Maastricht creating the European Union was agreed upon in December 1991, signed in 1992 and entered into force in 1993. European confidence grew stronger.

---

[15] Hosoya, 1993, *op. cit.*, pp. 205–206.

[16] The EC trade deficit with Japan from 1987 to 1992 in billion dollars is 20.0, 22.8, 19.7, 18.4, 27.3, 31.1 (from JETRO figures: http://www.jetro.go.jp/ec/j/trade/excel/40w02.xls 2003–07–19).

[17] T. Togo, *20seikino yoroppa (Europe in the 20th Century)*, Sekainougokisha, 1991, p. 164.

On the other hand, just as in the case of Japan-America trade conflicts in this period, Europe tried to overcome trade conflicts with Japan in an 'expansionist' manner, that is to say, rather than restricting Japanese exports to Europe, Europe began to take concrete measures to increase Japanese investment in Europe and expand its exports to Japan.

First, Japanese investment in Europe helped to create more jobs and give greater stimulus to European production. During the latter half of the 1980's, on a yearly basis, Japanese investment in the EC mounted. From only $600 million in 1970[18] it reached over $1 billion in 1984 and $14 billion in 1989.[19] The investments included a wide range of production and services, including electronics, electric equipment and automobiles. Great Britain led in receiving Japanese investment, followed by the Netherlands.

Second, from 1990 onwards a three year programme to enhance EC exports to Japan was implemented. European governments, together with their private sectors, also made efforts to enlarge business opportunities in Japan. European efforts did not bear immediate fruit during the first half of the 1990's, but began to have an impact on the trade situation from the latter part of the 1990's.

3. A wide range of cooperation between Japan and Europe during the 1990's

At the beginning of the 1990's the era of trade conflicts was gradually replaced by a new era of cooperation in a wide range of areas, including political relations.

From an economic point of view the growing economic power of the European Union, in contrast to Japan's failure to overcome non-performing loans and deflationary economy, took the heat off the trade disputes. This mirrored the changes occurring in the Japan-US trade relationship. Admittedly, these changes occurred gradually, because at the beginning of the 1990's there was only limited awareness of Japan's growing economic difficulties.

---

[18] Hosoya, 1993, *op. cit.*, p. 207.
[19] Japan's yearly direct investment in the EC from 1984 to 1992 in billion dollars was 1.4, 1.5, 3.0, 6.3, 8.3, 14.0, 13.3, 8.8, 6.6 (JETRO figures, 1990–1992 www.jetro.go.jp/ec/j/trade/ FDI to, country data 2003–08–04).

From a political point of view the end of the Cold War no doubt had an underlying impact. It was as if the countries of the world had embarked on a new voyage in uncharted waters, with Japan and Europe appearing as two regions with their common values of democracy, market economy and peace binding them close together. At least, this was the view of some of the Japanese leaders and top MOFA officials.

The Japan-EC Joint Declaration in 1991

On 18 July 1991 Prime Minister Kaifu held a Japan-EC Summit in The Hague with Prime Minister R.F.M. Lubbers of the Netherlands, the President of the European Council, and Mr. Jacques R. Delors, the President of the European Commission. The Joint Declaration on relations between the European Community and its member states and Japan was adopted.

The Declaration covers both the economic and political relationships between Japan and Europe, and it marked a turning point in the relations from economic conflicts to political cooperation.

In the economic relationship, the Declaration included an important principle to govern trade, investment and economic relations. The two parties announced in the Declaration that:

> They will endeavour to strengthen their cooperation in a fair and harmonious way in all areas of their relations taken as a whole, in particular with respect to the following (*inter alia*):
> – Pursuing their resolve for *equitable access* to their respective markets and removing obstacles, whether structural or other, impeding the expansion of trade and investment, on the basis of *comparable opportunities*.[20]

The focal point in preparing the draft of this Declaration was the nature of access and opportunities. The EC tried to ensure that the access or opportunities should basically be 'equal' or 'the same' in Europe and in Japan. Japan, while maintaining the principle of free trade, emphasized that inherent differences between the two markets had to be reflected in the nature of access and opportunities. After discussing numerous options the two sides agreed on the notion

---

[20] All quotations from the Joint Declaration, emphasis added by the author (http://www.mofa.go.jp/region/europe/eu/overview/declar.html 2003-07-20).

of *equitable access* and *comparable opportunities*. The language found was an adequate way of balancing the differences in approach and the need to expand trade and investment relations, between Europe and Japan.

In the political relationship, the Declaration emphasized such cooperation as:

> "Promoting negotiated solutions to international or regional tensions";
>   "Supporting social systems based on freedom, democracy, the rule of law, human rights and market economy";
>   "Enhancing policy consultations and, wherever possible, policy coordination on the international issues—such as the non-proliferation of nuclear, chemical and biological weapons, the non-proliferation of missile technology and the international transfer of conventional weapons."

The Declaration was the first major document after WWII to emphasize wide ranging cooperation, in particular, political cooperation between Japan and Europe. So as to give a further boost to this enhanced cooperation, annual consultations between the President of the EC, the Chairman of the Commission and the Japanese Prime Minister were agreed.

Economic issues during the 1990's

While the Joint Declaration in 1991 had already signalled the transition from economic conflicts to a wide range of cooperation between Japan and Europe, economic issues still weighed heavily in the first half of the 1990's in Japan-Europe relations.

After three years of an export expansion programme for 1990–92, the EU initiated another three year programme for 1994–96 called 'Gateway to Japan'. Information and financial assistance were given to European companies wishing to penetrate the Japanese market.

Many European countries launched special programmes, such as 'Le Japon c'est possible' by France for 1992–1997, 'Action-Japan Campaign' by the UK for 1994–1997, 'Three times Japan' by Germany from 1994, etc. All these programmes were designed to encourage European exports and investment in Japan and in some cases helped Japanese investment in Europe.

As a result of these efforts Japan's investment in the EU continued to grow, reaching $25 billion in 1999 and $23 billion in 2000. EC/EU investment in Japan was not of the same magnitude, but began to grow in strength as well. In 1990 it reached $1 billion and stayed at that level until 1996, but from 1997 it showed substantial momentum on a yearly basis: $12 billion in 1999 and $8 billion in 2001.[21]

As for the EU trade deficits *vis-à-vis* Japan, they began to decline steadily from $31 billion in 1992 and bottomed out with $13 billion in 1996. They began to increase again and exceeded $30 billion in 1998, 1999 and 2000, after which they dropped to below $20 billion.[22] Significantly, similar to the situation in America, three consecutive years of trade deficit over $30 billion, which had been cause for alarm in 1992, did not cause any political sensation. Strengthened economic power and confidence in Europe and economic stagnation in a deflationary Japan explained this change.

During the second half of the 1990's the economic relationship remained on the agenda, but with a greater sense of cooperation than confrontation. For instance, Japan and Europe shared common interests in agriculture in the WTO. Another instance of economic cooperation was the Regulatory Reform Dialogue between Japan and the EU.

Broader agenda for cooperation based on bilateral programmes

From the latter half of the 1990's Europe and Japan began to strengthen cooperation in a broader scope of relations. In particular, Japan and the three major European countries, the UK, France and Germany, launched bilateral cooperation programmes in a wide range of areas.

(1) With Great Britain it started with a *Japan-UK Action Agenda* in December 1995; it was revised as a new *Action Agenda for a Special Partnership* in September 1996. The promotion of global peace (cooperation on security and political issues) and prosperity (cooperation on economic issues), and promoting Asia-Europe regional cooperation were the three pillars of this revised agenda. Prime Minister

---

[21] The yearly FDI between Japan and EU from 1993 to 2001 in billion dollars is, from Japan to the EU 7.1, 6.0, 8.1, 7.1, 10.9, 13.8, 25.1, 23.9, 10.2; from the EU to Japan 0.8, 1.3, 1.1, 1.6, 2.3, 2.0, 12.3, 4.2, 8.5 (JETRO figures, www.jetro.go.jp/ec/j/trade/ FDI to and from, country data 2003–08–04).

[22] The EU trade deficit with Japan from 1993 to 2002 in billion dollars is 26.2, 22.0, 21.4, 13.6, 20.2, 32.2, 31.6, 31.5, 19.8, 17.3 (from JETRO figures: http://www.jetro.go.jp/ec/j/trade/excel/40w02.xls 2003–07–19).

Hashimoto and Prime Minister Tony Blair agreed on a *Common Vision to the 21st Century* in January 1998 and emphasized the importance of reform and investment, enhancing Asia-Europe relations, and cooperation towards a better global community. In September 1999 the *Action Agenda 21: the UK and Japan in the 21st Century* was adopted between the two governments and three areas of cooperation were identified: people-to-people links (exchanges and culture), mutual prosperity (economic relations), and a better world (foreign policy and security cooperation), each consisting of seven concrete points.

Having assumed the post of Director General for the European and Oceanian Department in August 1999, one of my first responsibilities was to prepare for the visit to Japan of Mr. Robin Cook, the British Foreign Minister. By the time I began the preparatory work the content of the new *Action Agenda 21* had already been finalized. The preparatory work was therefore not that difficult. But what Minister Cook said to Minister Masahiko Komura when they had finally and formally agreed on the new Action Agenda truly surprised me.

The British Foreign Minister said: "I wish that political relations between our two countries would become as strong as our economic relations."

Well, for a person whose memory was still heavily shadowed by the period of trade conflicts, and who instinctively thought that a political relationship might help in resolving economic difficulties, what he said turned my thinking on its head. With experience in my new role, I came to realize the truth behind Minister Cook's words.

(2) With Germany an *Action Agenda for the Japan-Germany Partnership* in five areas was agreed to in May 1996. They were revised in October 1997 as follows:

1) Promoting peace and stability of the international community
2) Cooperating in the international economic system
3) Cooperating in common tasks such as environment and development
4) Cooperating in Asia-Europe relations such as ASEM
5) Strengthening Japan-Germany bilateral relations

This Action Agenda developed into the *Seven Pillars of Cooperation for Japan-Germany Relations in the 21st Century* in October 2000. In essence, among the five areas mentioned in the 1997 Action Agenda, bilateral relations were divided into political, economic and cultural relationships, adding another two areas to make seven pillars, and Europe-Asia relations were transformed into 'Contribution to the stabilization of regional situation'.

(3) As for France, in November 1996 the *Japan-France 20 Actions for the Year 2000* were agreed upon between Prime Minister Hashimoto and President Jacques Chirac. The 20 Actions were divided into three categories: more regularized and intensive consultations, strengthened bilateral cooperation, and joint actions towards the 21st century.

Each Action Agenda had its specifics, emphasis and categorization. But in essence concrete items for cooperation with the UK, Germany and France bore more similarities than differences. These items ranged from multilayered consultations, human exchanges, cultural exchanges, economic cooperation, assistance to developing countries, the environment, globalization, Asia and Europe, regional instability, the United Nations, disarmament, non-proliferation and conflict prevention, etc.

Since economic relations had always been an important part of the bilateral relationship with each country, it was no surprise that they formed an integral part of this overall agenda.

But what was most conspicuous was the increasing emphasis on the political cooperation between Japan and Europe. This was a direct follow-up to the 1991 Joint Declaration.

The United Nations, disarmament, non-proliferation, conflict prevention and other issues of a global nature were the focal points in the political cooperation. Another focal point was political cooperation, which bore a regional character such as the OSCE, Yugoslavia or Asia-Europe Cooperation in the form of ASEM. We will see more in detail in the following section.

The special importance of cultural exchanges

These action agendas also had a strong emphasis on cultural exchanges and people-to-people exchanges.

A new type of exchange called 'working holidays' developed in designing these action agendas. This scheme gave the younger generation a greater opportunity to travel, live and work on the other side of the Eurasian continent.

Parallel to these action agendas, significant cultural events took place, particularly in the latter half of the 1990's. In 1997 an impressive Japanese Cultural Centre was opened in Paris, followed by spectacular cultural events such as the 'Japan Year' in France in 1997 and the 'France Year' in Japan in 1998. Another huge cultural event called the 'Japan Year in Germany' was held in 1999. In Great Britain, a huge cultural event known as 'Japan 2001' took place in 2001.

For many years, European interest in Japanese culture had been limited to traditional culture such as *ikebana* and *kabuki* amongst a select number of intellectuals and experts. Large-scale cultural events in the 1990's were an attempt to break these limitations. Daily life and culture in contemporary Japan, with its advanced technology, fashion, and music became subjects of cultural performances. For instance in 'Japan 2001' in Great Britain, conscious efforts were also made to reach out to a wider portion of the population through numerous performances in small towns and cities, seeking active local participation in these events. One may observe the interesting phenomenon of 'politicization' of culture in Japan-Europe relations.

4. *Asia-Europe cooperation*

The emphasis given to a broader scope of Asia-Europe cooperation and the attempt to locate Japan-Europe cooperation in this broader scope of cooperation was another characteristic of these action agendas. In fact, Japan became involved and contributed to some political and security agendas which could be conceived as strictly European. Vice versa, Europe became more concerned and began becoming involved in issues related to peace and security in the Asia-Pacific region.

Japanese cooperation with the OSCE and human rights issues

The first Japanese involvement in European politics and security was its acceptance as a non-member state in the Conference on Security and Cooperation in Europe (CSCE)—transformed to become the Organization for Security and Cooperation in Europe (OSCE) in 1994—in 1992 at their Helsinki Summit Meeting. Japan was accepted as a Partner for Cooperation, invited to major conferences with the right to speak, but without voting rights. Six Mediterranean states (Algeria, Egypt, Israel, Jordan, Morocco and Tunisia) as well as South Korea, Thailand and Afghanistan[23] now hold the position of Partner for Cooperation.

Since then, Japan has made some contributions to the OSCE, such as sending lecturers or making financial contributions for seminars.

In December 2000 in Tokyo, Japan and the OSCE held a Joint Conference on 'Comprehensive Security in Central Asia—Sharing OSCE and Asian Experiences'. The conference was based on three major themes of the OSCE: security, human rights, and economy. Five Central Asian states, very much Asian in their culture and tradition, but as full members of the OSCE, basically a European organization, sent their representatives from the capitals. The most interesting part of the discussion developed around the issue of 'human rights'. Central Asian countries did not hide the fact that they were perplexed at being overwhelmed by such 'Western' values as 'human rights' n the short period after their independence in 1992. Delegations from Europe, America, and international organizations pleaded for the necessity of protecting 'human rights', by each expressing its position with delicate and different nuances. Japan took a position somewhere in the middle, and worked hard to find a consensus based on equilibrium. History, tradition, geopolitical interests and human welfare all mingled in a lively, friendly and intense debate. It was indeed a pleasure and honour for me to have prepared and participated in this stimulating discussion as the Director General of MOFA in charge of both Central Asia and the OSCE.

Japan's position regarding human rights might be summarized as follows:

First, Japan believes that it has something to say regarding the importance of human rights, based on its own experience in postwar democracy and even on prewar Taisho democracy.

Second, Japan's position has always been accompanied by a certain humility, because Japan realized through her own experience

---

[23] http://www.osce.org/ec/partners/cooperation/partners/ 2003-07-20.

that protecting human rights is a difficult task and that each country must find its own way.

Third, Japan is aware of her lingering war responsibility issues and is reluctant to preach others about inadequate commitment to human rights issues.

These factors have led to a policy approach characterized by 'gradualism'. In this context, the Diplomatic Bluebook 2002 carried an interesting passage. At the UN Commission on Human Rights, where "an overtone of confrontation between the Western countries and the developing countries" was marked, "Japan continued to serve as a bridge between the countries of Asia and Africa and the other regions, based on its position that human rights are universal values in the international community."[24]

Japanese cooperation with former Yugoslavia

Another area where Japan was involved and made direct contributions was former Yugoslavia. Japanese contributions to Yugoslavia and European contributions to Korean Peninsula Energy Development Organization (KEDO) were sometimes perceived as parallel support, or cross support, regarding security matters of critical importance in each region (Chapter 5).

During the 1990's Japan made a total of approximately $1 billion in humanitarian and reconstruction assistance available to the former Yugoslavia:

– To Bosnia and Herzegovina: from the beginning of the conflicts until the Dayton Agreement in November 1995, Japan committed $180 million in humanitarian assistance. At the second round of the Bosnian Assistance Conference in April 1996 Japan committed $500 million for reconstruction assistance, to be implemented from 1996 to 1999.[25]

– To Macedonia and Albania: considering that stability in these areas were so important for peace and security in Yugoslavia, Japan pledged assistance to the amount of $62.63 million from 1999–2000.

---

[24] *Diplomatic Bluebook 2002*, section 4: Global Problems, subsection A: Human Rights, p. 133.

[25] www.mofa.go.jp/mofaj/gaiko/oda/00_hakusho/euc/euc_12.html 2002–11–07.

– To Yugoslavia: in the autumn of 2000, after the drastic change in the situation towards democracy, Japan first sent emergency humanitarian assistance amounting to $10 million in October 2000. Japan declared another package assistance of $60 million in June 2001.

– To Kosovo: Japan had already made humanitarian and reconstruction assistance amounting to $178.04 million.[26]

In total the above mentioned assistance came to $990.67 million.

In addition to economic assistance, Japan took the initiative to host a 'high-level officials conference on Southeastern Europe' in Tokyo in May 2000. The conference was designed to initiate a dialogue among all political forces, including those who were at war until quite recently, towards reconciliation and conflict prevention. As a follow-up to this conference a seminar on education and the protection of cultural heritage in Southeastern Europe was held in Tokyo in March 2001. It was a humble but concrete initiative to underline the importance of education and cultural heritage in the long process of reconciliation and conflict prevention.

Asia-Europe Meeting (ASEM)

In discussing closer exchanges between Asia and Europe and the notion of cross support between these two regions, mention should be made of ASEM.

The idea of holding a summit meeting between Asia and Europe was first proposed in October 1994 by Singapore to France. The primary purpose of this summit was to strengthen Asia-Europe relations, which were commonly recognized as a weaker aspect of the Asia-USA-Europe triangle.

The first Asia-Europe Meeting (ASEM) was held in March 1996 in Bangkok. Fifteen EU countries and the Commission attended from Europe and ten countries, seven from ASEAN (five founders plus Brunei and Vietnam) and three others (China, Japan and South Korea) attended from Asia. Under the rising economic power of the Asian NIEs and Southeast Asian countries, Europe had shown particular interest in starting this forum.

---

[26] The data for Macedonia, Albania, Yugoslavia and Kosovo are from www.mofa.go.jp/mofaj/area/yugoslavbia/kankei.html 2002–11–07.

The second meeting was held in April 1998 in London, when the Asian financial crisis was raging. European interest in Asia subsided. At the meeting more issues were discussed regarding political cooperation and long-term perspectives. A new framework for future ASEM activities, the *Asia-Europe Cooperation Framework (AECF)*, was adopted.

The third meeting in October 2000 in Seoul adopted a concrete direction for ASEM activities in the next decade, entitled *AECF 2000*. The meeting also adopted the *Seoul Declaration for peace on the Korean peninsula*, which supported the historic improvement in North-South relations.

The fourth meeting in September 2002 in Copenhagen adopted two declarations concerning *International terrorism* and *Peace on the Korean peninsula*. The meeting emphasized free exchanges of views among heads of states and the first 'retreat session'[27] was held, where a dialogue on cultures and civilizations was conducted.[28]

Since the establishment of ASEM in 1996, numerous meetings on a variety of subjects at various levels involving ministers, high-level officials and businessmen, were convened among the participant countries of Europe and Asia. The chairman's statement in Copenhagen expressed satisfaction at these expanding activities and underlined three areas of attention for future ASEM activities:

– the fight against international terrorism and organized crime;
– closer economic partnership, cooperation in the social, educational, and environmental fields;
– dialogue on cultures and civilizations.[29]

At present, Japan is striving to maintain the momentum of ASEM. Strengthening ASEM could result, in the mid to long-term perspective, in resolving important issues of globalization. At the same time, ASEM could also be an effective supplementary mechanism to strengthen Japan-Europe relations, not to mention Japan-Asia relations.

---

[27] A meeting where accompanying officials are not allowed to participate.
[28] http://www.mofa.gp/mofaj/area/asem/1.html 2002–11–02.
[29] Homepage of the Danish Foreign Ministry: www.um.dk/asem/erklaeringUK.asp 2002–11–10.

5. *Wounded feelings from the Pacific War:*
Great Britain and the Netherlands

Historical background of unresolved problems

As described in Chapter 6 and Section 1 of this Chapter, all claims and reparations, both from states and their nationals, in relation to World War II were settled by international agreements. These agreements included the San Francisco Peace Treaty in 1951, Japanese payment of 4.5 million pounds to the ICRC in 1955, and another payment of 10 million dollars to the Netherlands based on the Protocol in 1956. That was the position taken by the Japanese government, shared by the British and Dutch governments.

However, the sufferings inflicted by Japan on British and Dutch nationals have yet to be healed. Japan held 57,000 British and 50,000 Dutch Prisoners of War (PoWs).[30] 110,000 Dutch civilians were detained and 18,000 died in camps.[31] Victims of the war began to speak up about their wounded feelings in the first half of the 1990's. Several elements must have been contributing factors: prolonged indignation that their wounded feelings had not been adequately heard by their own society and Japan; a sense of urgency because those who directly suffered during the war had reached their 60's and 70's; and frustration due to repeated media reports from Japan that influential politicians continued to negate Japan's responsibility for the war. All these elements combined, former war victims in the UK and the Netherlands in January 1995 and April 1994, respectively, began to file lawsuits in Japanese courts seeking apologies and individual reparations.

The Japanese government maintained in these lawsuits that the obligation for reparations based on international law had already been met by the postwar settlement. At the same time the Japanese government, led by Tomiichi Murayama, in an unprecedented statement addressed these victims and their wounded feelings caused by the war, with sincerity. As we have already seen in Chapter 5, in

---

[30] Figures of PoWs are from the Japanese Information Bureau on Prisoners, established after the war (MOFA documents).
[31] These figures are from an Allied investigation committee on prisoners of wars (MOFA documents).

August 1994 the government decided to establish the 'Peace, Friendship and Exchange Initiative', with a view to deepen historical research and to enhance exchanges. In July 1995 the Asian Women's Fund was established to deal with the issue of the comfort women. On 15 August 1995 Prime Minister Murayama declared in his historic statement Japan's "deep remorse and heartfelt apology".

Although the Japanese government efforts seemed to be directed primarily towards Asian countries such as China and Korea, European countries such as the UK and the Netherlands were clearly included in the minds of those who prepared the scheme and articulated the words of apology and remorse.

Thus the UK and the Netherlands became serious potential participants of the 'Peace, Friendship and Exchange Initiative'. War victims, their families, and their grandchildren were regularly invited to Japan. Memorial visits by British and Japanese veterans to Southeast Asia where the two sides fought were implemented. Research on wartime history conducted by a Dutch research institute was funded by this initiative. In the case of ihe Netherlands the issue of comfort women was also a difficult, delicate and important task.

For the Japanese Embassies both in the UK and in the Netherlands the task of opening a sincere dialogue with those whose hearts were wounded became a priority task during the 1990's.

Against this background, historic visits by the Japanese Emperor Akihito were realized in the United Kingdom in May 1998 and in the Netherlands in May 2000.

For Japanese external relations the role which the Imperial family has played after the war must not be underestimated. Traditional Japanese values, the high esteem in which the people of Japan hold these traditions, and the genuine nobleness, warmth and sincerity of the Emperor and Empress have impressed many foreign dignitaries visiting Japan. One of the highlights of a state visit to Japan is the state banquet with the Emperor and the Imperial family. An Imperial visit abroad has also enormous significance for the relationship with that country. The visits often leave unforgettable memories for the receiving country and those who participated in it.

For the countries with which Japan fought, the situation surrounding an Imperial visit was more complicated. In some countries that suffered during the war, the Japanese Emperor was the symbol of that suffering. But for the overwhelming part of the Japanese people, Emperor Showa who passed away in 1989 was the person who took the decision to end the war and the Japanese people were genuinely grateful to him for that. The present Emperor Akihito is, as prescribed in the Constitution, the symbol of the state, accepted and esteemed by the majority of the people. Basic contradictions cannot be avoided.

Therefore a successful Imperial visit could become a tremendous occasion for reconciliation. At the same time, should any incident happen to spoil the dignity of the Emperor during that visit, it could have grave consequences for Japan's relationship with that country.

The Imperial visit to the United Kingdom in May 1998

In the case of the United Kingdom, it was, more than anyone else, Prime Minister Blair and Prime Minister Hashimoto who paved the way to a successful Imperial visit. Prime Minister Blair visited Japan and had an in-depth and straightforward discussion on 12 January 1998 with Prime Minister Hashimoto. Based on Blair's advice Hashimoto sent a letter to a popular English Newspaper The Sun on 14 January which included the following paragraph:

> Recalling what my predecessor said in 1995, I made a formal statement to Tony expressing our feelings of deep remorse and heartfelt apology for the tremendous damage and suffering of that time.

Just before the Imperial visit, on 26 May Blair sent a reply letter to The Sun with the following paragraph:

> As Japanese Prime Minister Ryu Hashimoto wrote in his groundbreaking article in The Sun earlier this year, relations between our two countries have never been better. It is against this background that the Emperor and Empress will make their visit. And it was also against this background that Ryu expressed his sorrow and regret for the suffering inflicted by his countryman during the Second World War. In his Sun article, he spoke directly to the British public of his "deep remorse and heartfelt apology" for the tremendous damage and suffering caused. That took courage.—The Emperor, like our Queen, is above the political fray. He is bound by protocol over what he can say. But this month he told the British media himself of personal sadness at past events and also referred specifically to Mr. Hashimoto's apology.

The Emperor Akihito and Empress Michiko arrived in Britain on 25 May. On 26 May the Emperor and the Queen rode in a royal carriage down the Mall to Buckingham Palace, greeted cheerfully by a crowd of 25,000. A group of about 500 former PoWs, however, gathered at one spot to utter protests at the royal carriage, turning their backs as the two sovereigns rode past and one person burned a Japanese flag. That particular aspect received a huge amount of media attention. But a substantial change in the tone in media reporting began and surfaced in the latter part of the visit from the 29th to the 31st. They highlighted the warmth and dignity of the Emperor and Empress and the positive aspects of Japan-UK relations, which were symbolized by this visit.

The change of tone of the media reports was due to the fundamental soundness of Japan-UK relations, combined with the personalities of the Emperor and Empress. The endeavours of so many people on both sides to try to make this visit a success was no doubt a major contributing factor. Thus the PoWs issue will continue to be addressed sincerely within the basic relations of mutual confidence and friendship between the UK and Japan.

The Imperial visit to the Netherlands in May 2000

In the case of the Netherlands it was Prime Minister Keizo Obuchi and Prime Minister Willem Kok who were responsible for preparing a successful Imperial visit. Prime Minister Kok visited Japan in February 2000, but before then thorough negotiations had taken place for several months between the two governments.

As the Director General in charge of the Netherlands I headed the Japanese delegation, which negotiated the statements to be exchanged by the two leaders. Ambassador H. Wijnaendts, a wise and experienced diplomat from the Dutch Foreign Service, headed the Dutch delegation.

> I realized that it was going to become an important negotiation and began my home work in autumn 1999. One day, while reading a thick file which was prepared by my colleagues in the Department, I found a confidential paper which was a translation of the testimonies made by Dutch 'comfort women'. Until then I had only been vaguely aware of this issue. The brutality of the facts and the extent of human suffering crushed me. Here was something which required a clear, unambiguous, and straightforward apology from Japan. This inner conviction helped a great deal in structuring Japan's position in the negotiations.

> The negotiations were difficult and did not go smoothly. There were two constituencies we needed to address. One was the wounded feelings of the Dutch war victims, including the 'comfort women'. The other was the political feelings in Japan which had become very sensitive to an excessive apology the government might make to foreign countries. It was not easy to find an answer which would satisfy both the two constituencies.
>
> But finally, Ambassador Wijnaendts and I found a mutually acceptable version. In Prime Minister Obuchi's statement the key wordings of "deep remorse and heartfelt apology" and "Dutch war victims" were finally included.
>
> In Prime Minister Kok's statement, Ambassador Wijnaendts' ingenuity allowed the inclusion of the same expression "to overcome the unfortunate past", as was used in President Kim Dae Jung's historic statement in the autumn of 1998.

On 21 February 2000 in Tokyo the following exchanges were made between the two Prime Ministers and were released to the press immediately after the meeting:

> Prime Minister Obuchi: "As Prime Minister, I reaffirm the position of the Government of Japan already expressed by the then Prime Minister Murayama in 1995 when he, on behalf of the Government of Japan, renewed the feelings of deep remorse and heartfelt apology for the tremendous damage and suffering caused by Japan to many people including Dutch War Victims."
>
> Prime Minister Kok: "I would also like to express my sincere appreciation for the views that you have expressed on the issue of Dutch War Victims.—I believe that, with our discussions today and what you have said about the period during the war, we should be able to overcome the unfortunate past and build an even closer, future-oriented relationship between the Netherlands and Japan."[32]

Emperor Akihito and Empress Michiko arrived in the Netherlands on 23 May 2000. The Emperor and Empress, together with Queen Beatrix, walked in solemn dignity from the Royal Palace on the Dam Square to the National Monument for the War Dead to lay a wreath in their honour. The Emperor and Empress, accompanied by the

---

[32] Press release by the Dutch delegation on 21 February 2000.

Fig. 3. With Yorkshire terrier Jenny at the residence of the Japanese Ambassador in The Hague, the Netherlands (12 September 2001).

Queen, bowed deeply and prayed in silence for a long, long time. It was an unforgettable and moving experience which symbolized spiritual reconciliation.

Demonstrations were conducted at various places where the Emperor visited. But all demonstrations were conducted with restraint. The media coverage was overwhelmingly positive and television broadcasts which presented pleasing and candid images of a smiling Emperor conversing with female students from Leiden University, while strolling down the Rapenburg, and the Empress caressing a young child in a clinic, established the basic tone of the visit.

So many people had worked towards the common end of making this visit a success. The warmth, wisdom and determination of Queen Beatrix to make this visit a fundamental success, were felt everywhere the Emperor and Empress went. The Emperor and Empress shared this determination. It was the result of a friendship which has lasted for 40 years between the Emperor and the Queen.[33]

In July 2001, the Asian Women's Fund announced the conclusion of its work in the Netherlands, having presented financial atonement to 78 former Dutch comfort women.

In May that year I left the post of Director General and was appointed as Ambassador of Japan to the Netherlands. In August I presented my credentials to Queen Beatrix. The first message with which I arrived in the Netherlands was that Japan would not be oblivious to the past and that it would remain highly sensitive to the wounded feelings stemming from World War II. This message was of course compatible with my efforts to create a forward-looking relationship with the Netherlands and the nine months of my tenure were truly rewarding and enjoyable.

6. *An action plan for EU-Japan cooperation*

Foreign Minister Kono's initiative for Japan-Europe cooperation

On 13 January 2000 Foreign Minister Yohei Kono, during his European tour, stopped in Paris and made a policy speech on Japan-

---

[33] M. Watanabe, Grand Chamberlain of the Emperor, *Koushitsuto Orandaoukeno 50nen (Fifty years between the Imperial family and the Dutch Royal family)*, Chuoukoron 2003.

Europe relations entitled 'Seeking a Millennium Partnership: New Dimensions in Japan-Europe Cooperation'. Kono intended to show Japan's reaction to the tremendous dynamism of European integration, that had been particularly strengthened in security and foreign policy in the preceding years.

The underlying thinking in drafting this speech to emphasize political cooperation between Japan and Europe could be summarized as follows:

(1) Japan and Europe in the post-WWII era each developed its own society based on *common values*: democracy, market economy and peace. Of course there were differences due to history, tradition, and culture; Japanese democracy was a consensus democracy, where individuals could be subordinated under the general trend of the society; but still they were heading in the same direction.

(2) At the same time, after a half century of postwar development Japan and Europe had *common problems* internally (such as social welfare, aging and women's rights), externally (such as the United Nations, disarmament, non-proliferation and conflict prevention), and globally (such as development, the environment, population growth and globalization). Again the way these problems were handled differed, but it was precisely for this reason that Japan felt that there was benefit in mutual exploration of the issues.

(3) These common grounds brought Japan and Europe to share a *common responsibility* in resolving these problems. In doing so, Japan and Europe were situated in a complementary geopolitical position in the East and the West of the Eurasian continent.

Based on this thinking Kono proposed to make the first decade of the 21st century (2001–2010) as 'The Decade of Japan-Europe Cooperation' and outlined three pillars of cooperation:

    – realizing shared values while respecting diversity;
    – strengthening Japan-Europe political cooperation, in particular, the prevention of conflicts, disarmament and non-proliferation, reform of the United Nations; and
    – sharing the benefits of globalization.

EU-Japan Action Plan of 2001

The EU-Japan Summit in July 2000 in Tokyo, held just before the Okinawa G8 Summit, accepted the Kono proposal and agreed to name the first decade of the 21st century 'The Decade of Japan-Europe Cooperation'.

The EU-Japan Summit in December 2001 in Brussels adopted a new Action Plan for EU-Japan Cooperation entitled 'Shaping our Common Future' based on the recommendation made at the Tokyo EU-Japan Summit. After analyzing briefly the evolution since the Joint Declaration of 1991, the changes in Europe and the Asia-Pacific region, the status of enhanced EU-Japan cooperation in the age of globalization, the new Action Plan proposed four major objectives for cooperation:

1) Promoting Peace and Security;
2) Strengthening the Economic and Trade Partnership;
3) Coping with Global and Societal Challenges, and
4) Bringing together Peoples and Cultures.

The detailed and concrete items of the Action Plan will be periodically reviewed by the governments of the EU and Japan.

After the cool, if not cold, relations of the postwar period and heated relations during the trade conflicts, Japan and Europe have reached a stage of seeking conditions to live in a mutually comfortable climate where mutual relevance can be explored in full.

Japan feels that Europe and Japan have come to share common values, common problems, and common responsibilities to tackle the agenda of the 21st century. Recent trends emphasizing political cooperation between Europe and Japan are certainly aimed in the right direction.

The way ahead

From the end of 2002 the international community entered a serious crisis surrounding the situation in Iraq. The international community developed a unanimous view that Saddam Hussein was a dangerous figure, that Iraq should be disarmed, and that threats of weapons of mass destruction should be eliminated. President Bush was determined that America was going to disarm him, if necessary, unilaterally. In Europe, the UK, Spain, Italy, many former East European countries and the Baltics sided with President Bush. But France and Germany, and the mass of public opinion in Europe were against a premature decision for war and insisted that all outstanding measures of UN inspection be implemented first and that decisions regarding military action had to be taken at the United Nations.

As we will see in more detail in Chapter 9, Japan's position was somewhere in between America and France. It could be described as a position close to "Blair without armed forces". This Japanese position may be criticized, accepted or praised. Whatever position observers might take *vis-à-vis* Japan's approach towards Iraq, one thing is certain. There was no issue more important than this one for Japan and Europe to engage seriously in an exchange of views. The issue of war in Iraq presented a unique and unprecedented opportunity to deepen dialogue and mutual understanding between Japan and Europe.

Conversely, if little of that nature had actually taken place between Japan and Europe, it means that both Japan and Europe have missed a historic opportunity to strengthen their relationship through an enhanced political dialogue. It also shows that the struggle for relevance and enhanced political cooperation so earnestly sought during the 1990's is still a distant objective.

CHAPTER NINE

THE MIDDLE EAST:
OIL DIPLOMACY AND ISSUES OF WAR AND PEACE

1. *Energy and oil diplomacy in Japan*

From the postwar situation to the oil crisis

Japan is almost entirely dependent on imported energy resources. In 1998 Japan's dependence on imported oil, coal and natural gas, sometimes called the fossil fuel resources, was 98.8%. In other words, Japan's indigenous resources produce only 1.2% of its total fossil fuel supply.

Oil, coal, and natural gas constitute 81% of Japan's primary energy supply. Nuclear resources take up 14%. If nuclear energy is viewed as imported energy, because it is produced from imported uranium, Japan's import dependence for the primary energy supply becomes 93.82%. The indigenous energy sources consist of hydroelectricity, geothermal electricity, and new energy.[1] If nuclear energy is viewed as indigenous, import dependence for the primary energy supply is still at 80.1% as calculated in Table 1 below.

Table 1 Japan's dependence on the import of primary energy[2] (Million ton, oil equivalent, 1998)		
	primary energy supply	indigenous supply	dependence on import
Oil	285.2(53%)	0.7(0.3%)	284.5(99.7%)
Coal	89.3(16%)	2.1(2.4%)	87.2(97.6%)
Natural gas	67(12%)	2.3(3.4%)	64.7(96.6%)
(Aggregate)	*441.5(81%)*	*5.1(1.2%)*	*436.4(98.8%)*
Nuclear	74.8(14%)	74.8(100%)	0%
Hydro	21.5(4%)	21.5(100%)	0%
Geothermal	1(0%)	1(100%)	0%
New energy	6.1(1%)	6.1(100%)	0%
(Aggregate)	*103.4(19%)*	*103.4(100%)*	*0%*
Total aggregat	544.9(100%)	108.5(19.9%)	436.4(80.1%)

[1] 436.4 Mton (fossil fuel) + 74.8 Mton (nuclear) = 511.2 Mton; 511.2 Mton divided by 544.9 Mton = 0.9382 = 93.82%.

[2] N. Tanaka, *Enerugiimondai Nyuumon (Introduction to Energy Issues)*, Nihon Keizaisha, 2000, p. 47.

In the postwar reconstruction period Japan had one strong indigenous energy production: coal. In 1961, the apex year in postwar
Japanese coal production, there were 622 coal mines, approximately
300,000 workers, producing more than 55.40 million tons. However,
the industry has gradually declined and in 2000 there were only 13
coal mines, 2,672 workers and a production of just 2.97 million tons.[3]

As indigenous coal production declined, crude oil became the
incontestable leader of primary energy. In 1973, 77.4% of Japan's
primary energy requirement was supplied by crude oil, virtually all
of it from imported sources. Of this imported crude oil, an outstanding portion, 78.1% in 1973, came from the Middle East (Table
2 below).

The Japanese government was aware of the danger in being overwhelmingly dependent on imported resources. While continuing efforts
to maintain indigenous coal production, the government encouraged
private sector engagement in oil excavation abroad. The Arabian
Oil Company was established in 1958 with Japanese capital and
acquired the right of excavation to an offshore oil field at the sea
border between Saudi Arabia and Kuwait. In 1960 the first drop of
oil was produced by this Japanese company. The Japanese people
were fascinated. It was almost a symbolic event, signalling the advent
of the 'period of high growth'.

By far the majority of the oil supply, however, continued to be
channelled through the Seven Sisters.[4] The Organization of Petrolium
Exporting Countries (OPEC) played a limited role.[5] Japan's energy
requirements continued to grow and its total energy consumption
reached 280 million kL of crude oil equivalent in 1973.

---

[3] Ministry of Economic Affairs, Trade and Industry (http://www.enecho.meti.go.jp/
policy/coal/coal01.htm 2002-11-14).

[4] The Seven Sisters consisted of Texaco, Gulf, Exxon, Mobil, Socal, Royal Dutch
Shell and British Petroleum. Socal and Gulf merged as Chevron in 1984. It has
now developed into four groups: BP Amoco, ExxonMobil, Chevron Texaco and
Royal Dutch Shell (Microsoft Encarta 1993–2002).

[5] OPEC was founded in 1960 by Saudi Arabia, Kuwait, Iran, Iraq and Venezuela.
It now consists of 11 countries including Libya, Algeria, the United Arab Emirates,
Qatar, Indonesia and Nigeria (Microsoft Encarta 1993–2002).

Table 2 Japan's energy consumption and dependence on oil[6]				
	1973	1979	1985	2000
Final energy consumption (mil. kL)	280	301	below 300	405
Oil% in primary energy supply	77.4%	71.5%	56.3%	51.8%
Middle Eastern oil% of oil imports	78.1%	76.3%	70.4%	(88.4%)[7]

The first oil crisis in 1973–1974

On 6 October 1973, Egypt and Syria attacked Israel and the Yom Kippur War (the fourth Middle East War) began. After the initial victories on the Arabian side, Israel fought back and based on UN Resolution 338 of 22 October, a ceasefire took place.

The Yom Kippur War is remembered as the first war where oil was used as a real strategic weapon in a Middle East conflict. On 17 October the Organization of Arab Petroleum Exporting Countries (OAPEC)[8] announced a 5% production cut of crude oil, and in early November a further production cut, up to 25%, was introduced. Furthermore, an oil embargo against pro-Israel countries, such as the US, the Netherlands and Japan, was declared.

Japan, overwhelmingly dependent on Middle East oil, was hard hit by this first oil embargo. On 22 November, the Chief Cabinet Secretary of the Tanaka cabinet, Susumu Nikaido, issued a statement stressing the need for Israel's full withdrawal from the 'occupied territories', which had been gained as a result of the 1967 Six Day War (the third Middle East War)? based on UN Resolution 242, and recognized the legitimate rights of the Palestinians in the course of establishing a fair and lasting peace in the Middle East. In

---

[6] Ministry of Economic Affairs, Trade and Industry: Comprehensive Energy Statistics: Final energy consumption: www.enecho.meti.go.jp/policy/energy/ene01.htm 2002-11–04. Oil statistics: www.enecho.meti.go.jp/policy/oil/oil01.htm 2002-11–14.

[7] Data for 2000 were not applicable. In 2001, the oil from the Middle East formed 88.4% of total oil imports.

[8] Created by Saudi Arabia, Kuwait and Libya in 1968. Algeria, United Arab Emirates, Qatar, Bahrain, Iraq, Egypt and Syria joined by 1973.

December the OAPEC Oil Ministers Conference redefined Japan as a friendly country *vis-à-vis* the Arab nations and lifted the oil embargo.[9]

The oil crisis did not end there. Already on 16 October 1973 a price increase of 70% (from $3.01 per barrel to $5.12 per barrel) was announced. In January 1974 OAPEC doubled the price of crude oil, bringing the price of Arabian Light, the market leading brand, to $11.65 per barrel. In simple terms this meant that a barrel of crude oil which cost $3 in January 1973 rose to $12 by January 1974. The world economy had to face a four-fold price hike in one year.[10]

The quadrupling of oil prices had a dramatic impact on the already inflationary Japanese economy (Chapter 3). The inflation rate for 1974 reached 20.9%. Anti-inflationary fiscal measures resulted in a sharp decline in the growth rate, to record an unprecedented −0.5% in 1974.[11] The Japanese trade surplus of $5.1 billion in 1972 fell to deficit of $1.4 billion in 1973 and plunged into a historic deficit of $6.6 billion in 1974.[12]

Thus in 1974, Japan experienced a triple crisis in inflation, a negative growth rate and a trade deficit. If 1960 brought Japan its first postwar political crisis, 1974 saw the first social and economic crisis. The fear of inflation and a shortage of consumer goods threatened the tranquil lives of housewives throughout Japan. They began to form long queues at nearby supermarkets to seek household commodities. The oil crisis turned into a toilet paper crisis in many cities.

Great efforts were exerted by the government to overcome the oil crisis. The Ministry of International Trade and Industry introduced a new policy to ensure energy 'security' consisting of the following five pillars:

1) Conservation: a national campaign to consume less electricity and gasoline was started; together with far-reaching parallel efforts by industry to restructure for increased energy efficiency;

---

[9] T. Sudo, *Darenidemowakaru Chuutoufunsou (Middle East Conflict for everyones' understanding)*, Chuutou Chousakai, 1995, pp. 43–44. T. Kagami, *Chuutoufunsou Sonohyakunenno Soukoku (100 Years of Middle East Conflict)*, Yuuhikaku Sensho, 2001, pp. 114–116.
[10] S. Koyama, *Saudiarabia (Saudi Arabia)*, Chuukousensho, 1994, p. 128, p. 132. Suzuta, *op. cit.*, p. 192.
[11] Suzuta, *op. cit.*, p. 194.
[12] JETRO statistics.

2) Alternative energy: alternative energy resources replacing oil were given a new stimulus; non-oil energy sources were explored in electricity production, industrial consumption and household utilities;

3) Diversification of oil sources: government and industry began efforts to increase oil imports from non-Middle East areas such as Indonesia, Alaska, Russia and Mexico;

4) Oil Reserve: national efforts started to increase oil reserves to cope with a sudden shortage of oil;

5) Cooperation with oil-consuming countries: under Secretary of State Henry Kissinger's initiative, the International Energy Agency (IEA) was established in Paris in November 1974 as a key organization for cooperation among oil-consuming countries. Japan strongly supported this organization and implemented the abovementioned energy initiatives in coordination and cooperation with the IEA (Chapter 11).

In macroeconomic terms the 'period of high growth' envisaging a GDP growth of 10% was over and a period of stable growth of approximately 5% began. Even after the 'bottoming' in 1974, the GDP growth saw a sharp upturn in 1975 of 4% and 6.3% in 1976.[13] The 1976 trade balance saw a surplus of $5.8 billion.[14] Inflation began to calm down as well.

In oil-producing countries state revenues suddenly quadrupled. This revenue soon appeared as oil dollars in international financial markets and was invested in middle-income developing countries such as South America. However, in many cases these investments were not directed into credible industry and infrastructure. They engendered colossal accumulated debts and the global economy later had to tackle this painful problem.[15]

The second oil crisis of 1978–1979

From the end of 1978 till the beginning of 1979 an Islamic revolution swept through Iran; the Shah was ousted in January 1979,

---

[13] 6.3% is a GNP figure quoted from Nakanishi, *op. cit.*, p. 176. GNP (Gross National Product) is the production made by nationals, including those temporarily staying abroad, whereas GDP (Gross Domestic Product) is the production inside the country. Before the 1970's GNP was used more often than GDP, whereas thereafter GDP is used more frequently.

[14] JETRO statistics.

[15] Kagami, *op. cit.*, p. 117.

and Islamic revolutionaries took over the country in February under the leadership of a radical Islamic fundamentalist, Ayatollah Khomeini. Iran's oil production, 5.49 million barrels per day (B/D) in October 1978, was halted from November 1978 till March 1979.[16]

Saudi Arabia, faced with the emergence of Islamic fundamentalism in its neighbouring country and a new destabilization of the oil market, drastically increased its production to 10 million B/D from October 1978 till June 1981.[17] The International Energy Agency also monitored the situation closely and prevented the outbreak of panic in the member countries. Oil shortages did not occur, but the oil price shot up again from $13.9 to $34.6 per barrel[18] from the autumn of 1978 till the spring of 1979.[19]

Japan, under Prime Minister Ohira, was chairing the G7 Economic Summit held in Tokyo in June 1979. Energy and oil became the most important agenda of this Summit. The G7 countries agreed to establish common goals for restricting oil imports.

I worked as a member of the Japanese delegation at OECD in charge of IEA from spring 1979 till summer 1980. The IEA held three ministerial meetings during this period. It was certainly a dramatic year to work as an 'energy advisor' in Paris. Dr. Ulf Lantske, the Executive Director of the IEA, urgently needed to know the results of the Tokyo Summit. I made a special arrangement with Tokyo to have the agreed Declaration sent immediately by fax, which was then cutting edge technology, and together with Bill Martin, Dr. Lantske's Executive Assistant, waited for the fax to arrive at the communication room of the Japanese delegation. This is another pleasant memory of a diplomatic life 25 years ago.

The impact of the second oil crisis was serious for Japan, as in all major advanced industrialized countries.

Although Japan had been implementing an energy security policy for six years, the basic structure of energy consumption was not that

---

[16] Koyama, *op. cit.*, p. 160, p. 133.
[17] Ibid., p. 160.
[18] Suzuta, *op. cit.*, p. 195.
[19] Koyama, *op. cit.*, p. 160.

different from the situation in 1973. Final energy consumption declined for two years, then bounced back a little, but was still a 301 million kL of crude oil equivalent. Dependence on crude oil within the primary energy supply fell 5.9%, from 77.4% in 1973 to 71.5% in 1979. But Japan's dependence on the Middle East for imported crude oil fell only 1.8%, from 78.1% in 1973 to 76.3% in 1979 (Table 2).

The rise in oil prices hit Japan's trade balance hard and in 1979 a $7.64 billion deficit was recorded, which rose higher in 1980 to $10.72 billion.[20]

Japan's GDP growth was also seriously affected and three years of recession followed from 1980 to 1982. However, the minus growth experienced during the first oil crisis did not eventuate and the growth was maintained between 2 and 3%.[21]

The government and private sectors enhanced their endeavours to reduce energy consumption in Japanese industry. MITI added a second element, which was 'cost', to Japan's energy policy, on top of the first element, 'security'.

Collapse of oil prices in 1985–1986

After the price hike at the end of the 1970's, the international energy situation saw a drastic change. Global demand for oil began to decline sharply, due to the recession in the major industrialized economies. Global oil consumption, 64.5 million barrels per day (B/D) in 1979, declined to 58 million B/D in 1983, with a net decline of 6.5 million B/D in four years. A slowdown in economic development, as well as some results achieved in conservation and the development of alternative energy contributed to this reduced demand for oil. Non-OPEC oil production, for instance in the North Sea, sharply increased by four million B/D during the first half of the 1980's. Thus, had the level of production by the established oil suppliers continued, the world oil market would have faced an over-supply of 10.5 million B/D by the middle of the 1980's.[22]

Saudi Arabia acted as a 'swing' producer, reducing its production so that demand and supply would meet in the changing market.

---

[20] JETRO statistics.
[21] GDP growth for 1980 to 1983 was 2.6%, 3.0%, 3.1%, and 2.5% (JETRO statistics).
[22] Koyama, op. cit., p. 156.

From 10 million B/D at its peak, Saudi Arabia's production dropped to 2.35 million B/D in August 1985.[23]

Sharp reduction of oil production resulted in sharp reduction of oil revenues in Saudi Arabia. Saudi Arabia began to increase its production from the autumn of 1985. The global oil price which was kept at a level of $27–28 dollars in 1985 fell further to $10 in 1986.[24] For oil-producing countries it was a 'reverse oil shock', but for the economies of oil-consuming countries it was the best news in a long time.

Japan's reaction to this 'good' news was perhaps surprising. As the Director of the International Energy Division in the Economic Affairs Department of MOFA from the summer of 1984 to the summer of 1986, I was aware of at least three issues which had to be considered.

The first issue was related to the essence of energy policy. From the macroeconomic point of view, the sharp decline of oil prices meant a sharp decline of costs and that really helped in curbing inflation and enhancing economic growth. But from the point of view of the domestic energy policy, cheaper oil threatened to reverse progress in conservation and the development of alternative energy.

Since 1979 Japan's final energy consumption had declined for three years and had bounced back a little, but was kept at a level just below 300 million kL of crude oil equivalent by 1985. Dependence on crude oil within the primary energy supply was the area of greatest achievement and saw substantial drops from 71.5% in 1979 to 56.3% in 1985, that is, a 15.2% decline in six years. Japan's dependence on the Middle East for imported crude oil also fell 5.9%, from 76.3% in 1979 to 70.4% in 1985 (see Table 2).

These achievements had to be preserved and consolidated. At the IEA Council Meeting in April 1986 Japan made a clear statement that "the long-term stability of the oil market is desirable." MITI and MOFA, the two ministries in charge of energy policy in Japan,

---

[23] Ibid., p. 161.

[24] OPEC made efforts to control the price and in December 1986 agreed to adopt an $18 system. This system continued until July 1990, when OPEC decided to aim for a $21 system. The Gulf War resulted in a temporary price hike, but Saudi Arabia's drastic increase in production stabilized the market. Since then, the $21 system has continued with downward pressure of oil prices in the market (Ibid., pp. 157–158).

were in full agreement. After some debates the IEA adopted this view and a tight energy policy was recommended to member countries. But in many countries, including Japan, tightening the energy policy in an oil glut situation was indeed a difficult political task.

A relatively relaxed situation in the energy market enabled policy-makers to take a fresh look at environmental factors, which from this period onwards increasingly attracted the attention of energy specialists and policymakers. Hence MITI added a third element to energy policy, the element of 'quality'.

The second issue I had to face was more complicated. After the first and second oil shocks, many oil-producing Gulf countries began developing their own internal industries. Oil-related industries were a natural choice for their investment, for instance, the refinery industry, producing various oil products such as gasoline, light oil or heavy oil. Oil experts were estimating that from the summer of 1984 to 1985–86 about 1 million B/D of oil products would appear on the global market. Oil-producing countries were concerned with the amount of oil revenues which this new type of oil commodities might engender.

Against this background Japan's system of oil products imports suddenly caught the attention of world energy and trade experts. Japan had developed a firm practice of importing crude oil and producing oil products in refineries located inside Japan. That policy, guided by MITI, was called 'the principle of refining at the place of consumption'.[25] A finely structured system of MITI administrative guidance ensured that gasoline in particular, the most lucrative oil product, was not allowed to be imported. International observers, who were severely criticising inaccessible Japanese markets (Chapter 3), began to focus on the closure of the Japanese gasoline market.

At the end of 1984, the issue was brought to a head by a single businessman from a tiny self-made oil company, Mr. Sato of *Laionsu Sekiyu* Company, who decided to import a symbolic amount of gasoline from a Singapore refinery. MITI was not prepared to concede to the pressure from this single businessman.

The importance of oil as the driving force in a wide range of industries was sometimes compared to the crucial significance that rice occupied in Japanese agriculture. We became deeply concerned

---

[25] In Japanese it was called *Shohichi Seiseishugi*.

for the international image of the Japanese oil industry, and indeed, of Japan as a trading nation. The invisible trade barrier created by MITI for the total ban on gasoline imports was incompatible with GATT and in the long run would not serve to ensure a stable oil supply to Japan. We had to move quickly to rectify the situation.

In January 1985, I formulated a short MOFA policy paper and brought it to my MITI counterpart. MOFA emphasized such principles as adherence to international obligations and the opening up of the market, while it also acknowledged the importance of developing a sound refinery industry in Japan. But even that was too radical for the then existing oil industry policy. The debates between the two ministries were leaked to the press. Influential politicians representing the interests of the oil industries became involved. What followed were six months of harsh interministerial debates between MOFA and MITI.

It was a fascinating experience for me and for those working in my division. After the initial difficult discourse with MITI, I gradually began to feel that MITI understood the necessity of changing the system. But because of the strong pressure group in the industry and among politicians, the crucial aspect was how to do it. The well-known system of *shingikai*[26] (advisory council) played an important role. For a MOFA official it was a very fortunate occasion to establish solid contacts with key members of *shingikai* and grasp the essence of consensus building in a traditionally Japanese way.

By the summer of 1985 MITI probably had established a blueprint for opening up the gasoline market. But the mood of the refinery industry and politicians was so tense that before the IEA Ministerial Meeting in July 1985 nothing concrete could be revealed. Japan first needed adequate pressure from the IEA Ministerial. A message to emphasize the importance of opening up the market would be helpful, but a too strongly critical tone regarding the Japanese market would be counterproductive. All my friends in

---

[26] *Shingikai* is an organ attached to a respective ministry. Representatives of industries concerned and some 'wise men' are assembled. Through discussions consensus is built. The basic line of the discussions is usually preconceived by the respective ministry, but discussions have to be carried out very carefully so as not to miss the opportunity for consensus building.

> Paris and Washington from the IEA days, including Bill Martin who was then Deputy Secretary for the Energy Department, were very helpful in finding that delicate balance.

The IEA Ministerial ended successfully, underlining the importance of IEA solidarity and market mechanism. In autumn a new law called 'The Provisional Measures Law concerning the Import of Specified Oil Products' was adopted by the Diet, allowing 'orderly' gasoline imports. The key concept was 'gasoline will be imported, but it will be done in an orderly manner by designated importers'. Japan's decision was welcomed by the international economic community.

The third issue was the most complicated and went beyond the scope of the energy policy. The sharp decline in oil prices engendered an unexpected windfall of 'oil yen'. One expert calculated this amount as nine trillion yen for 1986.[27] This 'oil yen' fuelled the Japanese bubble economy throughout the second half of the 1980's (Chapter 3). In retrospect the 1986 oil price collapse that freed up so much cash in Japan was a very mixed blessing. The aftermath of the bubble economy still haunts the Japanese economy today. In hindsight, what appeared to be the gospel was nothing more but a disguised form of Satan's sweet whispering.

Present situation

Since the oil price collapse of the mid-1980's the price of oil has fluctuated occasionally and the average price for the latter part of the 1980's over the 1990's fell below \$18.[28] In Japan, dependence on crude oil in the primary energy supply continued to decline from 56.3% in 1985 to 51.8% in 2000. But dependence on Middle East oil was at its lowest in 1985 at 70.4% and since then continued to rise, up to 88.4% in 2001. Total energy consumption also drastically increased from just below 300 million kL of crude oil equivalent in the mid-1980's to 405 million kL crude oil equivalent in 2000 (see Table 2).

Japan's energy policy maintained the same thrust: "Realization of a stable energy supply while paying due attention to such elements

[27] N. Tanaka, *op. cit.*, p. 53.
[28] N. Tanaka, *op. cit.*, p. 141.

as enhanced efficiency and environmental protection". This is, in principle, the confirmation of 'security, cost and quality', the three principles developed during the 70's and the 80's.[29]

Several points need to be highlighted:

(1) So as to fill in the gap between the growing energy consumption and the declining oil supply, nuclear energy became a major means of electricity generation. In 2002 it occupied 34.3% of electricity production. After the United States and France, Japan is the world's third largest producer of nuclear electricity.[30] Recent domestic situations, such as troubles in nuclear electricity generation and increasingly resistant public opinion, may be creating a serious problem for Japan's future electricity production.

(2) Deregulation of the oil industry continued. The Provisional Measures Law adopted in the autumn of 1985 was finally abrogated in the spring of 1996,[31] bringing a complete liberalization of the gasoline market. The process of internal deregulation of the gasoline market, not as a direct response to external pressure, is a success story in achieving a gradual but significant structural change in an important part of Japanese industry.

(3) The increasing dependence on Middle East oil is still a serious matter for consideration. In August 2001 MOFA produced a document entitled 'Tasks of Energy Diplomacy' in which it gave high priority to the establishment of a strategic partnership with Middle East countries and other energy producing countries.[32]

2. Relations with the Gulf countries and wars in the Persian Gulf

Japan's basic policy towards the Persian Gulf countries

The first priority of Japanese foreign policy in the Middle East is the Persian Gulf region. This includes the six countries from OAPEC (Saudi Arabia, Kuwait, the United Arab Emirates, Qatar, Bahrain and Iraq), Iran and Oman.

---

[29] http://www.enecho.meti.go.jp/policy/energy/ene02.htm 2002–11–14.
[30] http://www.enecho.meti.go.jp/policy/nuclear/nuclear01.htm 2002–11–14.
[31] http://www.enecho.meti.go.jp/policy/oil/oil02.htm 2002–11–14.
[32] http://www.mofa.go.jp/mofaj/gaiko/energy/policy.html 2002–11–14.

It is these Persian Gulf countries that supply the majority of Middle Eastern oil to Japan. Ensuring a stable oil supply from these countries and establishing stable and friendly relations with these countries have become priorities in Japan's foreign policy.

From the 1970's the Japanese government began conscious efforts to enhance bilateral relations with these countries. Diplomatic relations were established with Qatar, the UAE and Oman, so that by the mid-1970's Japan had relations with all Persian Gulf countries. The Japanese government also sought to enhance economic relations through technical cooperation to the Gulf countries, including technical training in Japan.

Japanese private companies enhanced their activities as well. Following the success of oil excavation by the Arabian Oil Company in 1960, they put particular efforts into developing—sometimes in joint venture—oil in the Gulf region such as in Kuwait, Qatar and the UAE.

One of the sad developments which attracted a lot of media attention was the closure of the Arabian Oil Company by the Saudi authorities in February 2000.[33]

Prime Minister Hashimoto visited Saudi Arabia in November 1997 and proposed a 'Japan-Saudi Comprehensive Partnership for the 21st Century'. It resulted in the 'Japan-Saudi Cooperation Agenda' in October 1998,[34] but all these efforts could not change the fate of the Arabian Oil Company.

The Arabian Oil Company had maintained its outstanding half of oil mining rights in Kuwait until January 2003 and an agreement was reached to conclude a new contract, which would allow the

---

[33] The press outlined several reasons for this:

– Saudi Arabia's financial difficulty from the time of the oil price fall in the middle of the 1980's and Japan's alleged slow reaction to this difficulty.

– Failure to agree on a $10 billion joint Japan-Saudi refinery project in 1992. Saudi Arabia, planning to strengthen its downstream operation through powerful Japanese finance, was disappointed. But Japanese companies, facing the collapse of the bubble economy, could not participate in such a gigantic and possibly risky project.

– Saudi's disappointment was said to be worsened when Japanese companies backed away from a railroad construction project in Saudi Arabia, negotiated during the latter part of the 1990's. Again, Japanese companies judged the risks too high (Asahi Shinbun, February 29, 2000).

[34] http://www.mofa.go.jp/gaiko/oda/00_hakusho/ckt/ckt_12.html 2002–11–13.

company to purchase crude oil for 20 years, while supplying technical cooperation to Kuwait.[35]

Parallel to these economic efforts in strengthening relations between Japan and the Persian Gulf countries, Japan also made efforts to contribute to the stability of the region through diplomatic efforts, when faced with political crises and wars. Japan's efforts brought about some success, but some failures too. Japan's relations with Iran and Iraq are outlined below.

Iran

Historically, Japan had close and mutually beneficial relations with Iran under the Shah's regime. For Japan, Iran was a stable crude oil supplier, and for Iran, Japan was an important country, offering substantial investment and economic assistance.

The Islamic revolution in Iran in February 1979 shook the Gulf world. Kingdom states such as Saudi Arabia, Kuwait, and the United Arab Emirates were concerned about the emergence of a radical fundamentalist state in their neighbourhood. The breakdown of diplomatic relations between Iran and Israel further fuelled tension.[36] Above all, the occupation of the American Embassy by radical students in November 1979 exacerbated the relations between Iran and America.

However, Japan maintained diplomatic relations after the revolution and the seizure of the American Embassy in Teheran. The United States introduced an embargo on Iranian oil imports. Japan, whose oil imports from Iran took up 15% of its total oil imports, continued importing oil from Iran. For about six months a tense situation persisted between Japan and America, but in May 1980 Japan joined other countries in an oil embargo against Iran.[37]

In September 1980 Iraq's Saddam Hussein attacked Iran, resulting in an eight year war between the two countries. During this eight year war, when the international community was more sympathetic to Iraq because of Iran's hostile attitude to the West, Japan maintained a relationship with both Iran and Iraq. Particularly in

---

[35] *Asahi Shinbun*, 28 March, 2002.
[36] Kagami, *op. cit.*, p. 145.
[37] Nakanishi, *op. cit.*, pp. 179–180.

1984 and 1985 Foreign Minister Shintaro Abe of the Nakasone cabinet became well-known for his enthusiasm in conducting Iran-Iraq diplomacy, abbreviated in Japanese as 'Ira-Ira Gaikou'.[38] Japan's efforts in becoming a window for exchanges between the opposing parties and between Iran and the United States might not have achieved direct results, but they were appreciated by the international community.

Ayatollah Khomeini died in 1989, Akbar Hashimi Rafsanjani assumed the presidency, and Saddam Hussein invaded Kuwait in 1991. Mohammad Khatami was elected president of Iran in May 1997 and declared a new reform policy based on the rule of law and the creation of a civil society.

Japan-Iran relations became active. The Iranian Foreign Minister visited Japan in 1998, the Japanese Foreign Minister Masahiko Komura visited Iran in 1999 and President Khatami visited Japan in October 2000. It was the first visit of an Iranian leader for 42 years.[39] Together with Germany and France, Japan is one of the three major donors to Iran. Currently, Iran is Japan's third largest supplier of crude oil, after the United Arab Emirates and Saudi Arabia.[40]

In 2003 Iran is still in a difficult and delicate position, both internally and externally. Constant strife between the reformists and the conservatives continues. The relationship between Iran and the US has stayed extremely tense.

The US continues to maintain strong concerns on the Iranian position *vis-à-vis* the peace process in the Middle East, on weapons of mass destruction, and human rights. In January 2002 President George W. Bush declared Iran to be one of the 'axes of evil' together with Iraq and North Korea and condemned her as a country which supports terrorism.

In Japan's view the policy of dialogue and engagement *vis-à-vis* Iran encourages moderate forces in Iran and helps this country become a more harmonious member of the international community.

After the War in Iraq in 2003, the US continued to warn the world about Iran's weapons of mass destruction. Japan was moving

---

[38] 'Gaikou' means 'foreign policy'; 'Ira-Ira' means 'Iran-Iraq', but it is also a play on words as there is a Japanese word 'ira ira', meaning 'an irritated state of mind'.

[39] http://www.mofa.go.jp/mofaj/area/iran/kankei.html 2002–11–13.

[40] http://oil-info.ieej.or.jp/static/oil/2–2a.html 2003–07–25.

ahead to participate in oil development in Iran in search of long-term oil import contracts. The credibility of Japan's policy toward Iran in the context of its alliance with the United States is being tested.

The Gulf War in 1991

On 2 August 1990 Iraq invaded Kuwait. The international community was totally shocked by this invasion and unanimously condemned it.

On 5 August, based on a UN resolution condemning Iraq, the Japanese government headed by Prime Minister Toshiki Kaifu imposed concrete economic sanctions, banning oil imports from Iraq and Kuwait and exports to Iraq and Kuwait. Investment in both Iraq and Kuwait was suspended and economic assistance to Iraq was halted as well. On 10 August Iraqi and Kuwaiti assets were frozen. Thus, initial Japanese economic measures were taken with impressive speed.[41]

The Bush administration was moving fast to deploy American forces in and around the Persian Gulf, particularly so as to pre-empt a possible Iraqi attack against Saudi Arabia.[42] Multinational forces were also quickly building up to fight back if Iraq did not withdraw from the occupied territory. Given Japan's heavy dependence on Middle Eastern oil, visible Japanese financial and physical contributions to this joint exercise of likeminded democratic countries became an urgent requirement from the international community, particularly from the US.

> I was in Tokyo working as the head of the Soviet Union Division preparing for Gorbachev's visit scheduled for spring 1991. I could feel that an electric shock had run through the entire Ministry, including the Prime Minister's office. There was a clear awareness in Tokyo that Saddam Hussein's act fundamentally destroyed the order in the Persian Gulf and that this would impact on Japan's crucial interests of securing its oil supply.

---

[41] R. Teshima, *1991 Nihonno Haiboku (Japan's Defeat in 1991)*, Shinchousha, 1993, p. 109.
[42] Ibid., p. 111.

> But after the initial commendable step of economic sanctions, Japan began to lag behind. Japan was simply not prepared to cope with an international crisis of such magnitude taking place in the Middle East, where the peace and security of the world and Japan's vital interests were at stake. MOFA was plunged into a state of emergency and many able colleagues were temporarily recalled from foreign assignments to join numerous task forces created inside the ministry. Staff members were also conscripted from various MOFA divisions judged to have excess capacity (The Soviet Union Division was, fortunately, exempted). After enormous efforts, decisions were taken, but belatedly, discordantly and unsuccessfully.

Financial assistance was still the main area of Japan's contribution. After Japan's prolonged silence, toward the end of August international expectations were high regarding the amount of contributions Japan would make. As a result of an extremely unfortunate disconnection among the Prime Minister's office, MOFA and the Ministry of Finance (MOF), on 29 August a general statement on Japan's contribution was issued devoid of any figures. A strong sense of disappointment permeated the media. A coincidental telephone call from President Bush on that day further complicated the situation. On 30 August Japan announced a $1 billion contribution to the Gulf operation, but media reports suggested that Japan took this unwillingly under US pressure.[43]

America's frustration regarding Japan's slow decision-making mounted during September. Then a newspaper leak was published, reporting a possible second round of contributions of another $1 billion to the Gulf operation, combined with $2 billion of assistance to the surrounding countries of Jordan, Turkey and Egypt. Again, as if forced by these media leaks and American pressure, Japan took the decision to extend a $3 billion contribution on 14 September.[44]

There was awareness, however, in the Japanese government that financial assistance alone was not sufficient and that some physical Japanese participation was absolutely needed. Because of Article 9

---

[43] Ibid., pp. 235–237.
[44] Ibid., pp. 239–242.

of the Constitution the Japanese Self-Defence Forces could not participate in any combat activities, but there was also no legal basis
within the Constitution, which allowed them to participate in logistic support activities.

The government first began to explore voluntary civilian participation: civilian flights and ships were asked to transport goods and
medical doctors. But public opinion was critical of the government
for transferring the burden to civilians. The civilians concerned were
not enthusiastic either.[45]

The government finally decided to enact a new law within Article
9 of the Constitution, to create a basis for the participation of the
Self-Defence Forces in logistic support activities. A new bill was presented to the Diet in October, but it was so ill-prepared that the
government had to withdraw it from parliamentary approval in
November (Chapter 12).

Meanwhile, on 29 November the Security Council of the UN
adopted Resolution 678, which authorized member countries to take
"all necessary measures" to restore international peace and security.
The time limit for the Iraqi withdrawal was set for 15 January 1991.
On 17 January the multinational forces began bombing Iraq and on
24 February they attacked Iraq on land.

The demise of the new bill on contributions by the Self-Defence
Forces in November left no perspectives for Japan to make substantial 'human' or 'physical' contributions. Small civilian participation left little impression on the international community. Enhanced
financial contributions were the only additional measures Japan could
take. On 24 January, the day the attack on land began, Japan took
the third decision in the form of a $9 billion financial contribution.[46]
The news was overshadowed by the resounding victory of the multinational forces on land, and Japan was left with an image of 'too
little and too late'.

Finally, a regrettable lack of precision in the negotiating process
surfaced. Whether the $9 billion was committed in dollar terms or
in its yen equivalent was left ambiguous. Faced with a sharp rise of
the dollar after the war, Japan maintained that she committed to
the yen equivalent of $9 billion. The US rejected this view unequiv-

---

[45] Ikei, *op. cit.*, p. 340.
[46] Ibid., p. 342.

ocally. Japan was forced to concede and made an additional fourth contribution of $0.5 billion in July. This incident further increased the frustration of the American administration and, through repeated press leaks, inflated the image of a Japan unwilling to adhere to its financial commitments.[47]

In total Japan's contribution to the Gulf war amounted to $14 billion, including its assistance of $0.5 billion to Syria committed in March.

On 11 March 1991 the Embassy of Kuwait in America issued a one page announcement to major American newspapers such as the Washington Post and the New York Times, to express its gratitude towards America and other nations of the world community for helping the Kuwaiti liberation. The name of Japan was omitted.[48] That experience was later referred to in Japan as 'Japan's defeat in 1991'.

The virtual absence of human participation in the common efforts of the community of nations was the primary reason for this defeat. Another reason for this defeat was the miscommunication and mishandling which occurred in the decision-making processes regarding the $14 billion financial contribution. The impression of 'too little and too late' could not be eradicated from the beginning till the end.

The War in Iraq in 2003

After the 'defeat in 1991' Japan's position was well attuned to the common actions of the international community against Saddam Hussein. At the United Nations Security Council Japan made a positive contribution in leading the debates requesting Iraq to implement its obligations, based on the Security Council Resolution 687 of 3 April 1991, to dismantle all weapons of mass destruction.[49]

In March to April 2003, twelve years after the 'defeat of 1991', the United States, the United Kingdom and other coalition forces attacked Iraq and implemented, through force, the regime change of Saddam Hussein. Japan's reaction was different from its reaction

---

[47] Teshima, *op. cit.*, pp. 283–319.
[48] Ibid., p. 337.
[49] Even the Japanese Communist Party recognized that Japan and the UK took a leading role in adopting the Resolution 1154 as of 2 March 1998 which warned Iraq of 'grave consequences' for non-compliance of obligations to dismantle weapons of mass destruction (*Akahata*, 18 December 1998).

in 1990 to 1991. Japan became much more forthcoming in supporting President Bush and, though in its own way, participated in Iraqi operations in the reconstruction phase. Several reasons may be given for Japan's changing policy.

First, a full decade had passed since 1991 and several major decisions had been taken: a new International Peace Cooperation Law in 1992 (Chapter 12), the Japan-US Guidelines for Defence Cooperation in 1997 and the Surrounding Situations Law in 1998 (Chapter 2), and the Anti-Terrorism Special Measures Law in 2001 (Chapter 12). All these new decisions were taken as a result of the agonizing defeat Japan had to suffer from the summer of 1990 to the spring of 1991. There was clearly a greater acceptance in Japanese public opinion for Japan to play an active role in the area of international peace and security.

Second, Japan's alertness on national security matters became considerably more acute because of North Korea. The North Korean security threat became more and more real as a result of numerous incidents, including its nuclear weapons programme (1993–1994), the Taepodong missile launching (1998), the infiltration of 'unidentified vessels' (1999) and so forth. However, for the Japanese people in particular, the hard reality of the abduction of Japanese nationals, which came to the foreground of national attention, accelerated the image of a North Korean threat. For the politicians, bureaucrats and intellectuals the disclosure of a renewed nuclear weapons programme came as the final blow (2002). The realization that the Japanese security structure was solely dependent upon the United States in a time of a national security emergency, based on the asymmetry of security relations, became increasingly convincing to many Japanese. Thus Japan's support of President Bush's policy gained much stronger political ground.

Third, Japan's position was not a simple and unconditional support of President Bush's policy. It endeavoured to weigh carefully its national interest, public opinion and relations with other regions and countries. In my view, there were several areas where Japan's breadth and depth of foreign policy based on national interests were tested, but one cannot deny that Koizumi strived hard to identify an effective and meaningful policy.

When in the summer of 2002 President Bush decided to disarm Saddam Hussein, public opinion in Japan, as in many countries in Europe and in other parts of the world, was against a premature attack on Iraq. Judging from all media reports Prime Minister Koizumi seems to have been determined right from the beginning that ultimately Japan was going to support the US decision to disarm Saddam Hussein. But then the key question was 'how' to disarm him. Koizumi thought that disarming Saddam would be most effectively carried out if Saddam was declared to be not only the enemy of the United States but also the enemy of the community of nations. Thus, from the summer of 2002 to the winter of 2003 Japan advised the United States, in a discreet manner, that it should utilize channels in the United Nations.

The United States did go through the United Nations, but from February to March 2003 failed to command the support of the Security Council. At this moment when a deep rift appeared in the longstanding transatlantic alliance, Japan emerged as a clear supporter of President Bush's position. On 18 March 2003, only hours after President Bush sent the ultimatum to Saddam Hussein, Prime Minister Koizumi declared his open support for President Bush's decision.

Within a few days after the war broke out, Japan announced a humanitarian aid commitment of $5.03 million through UNHCR, WFP, and UNICEF, and another $3.3 million through Japanese NGOs.[50] These amounts increased after the war ended, reaching $32 million in total by 21 May 2003, when the government announced a further $42 million of humanitarian and reconstruction aid through international organizations and NGOs. The areas envisaged included electricity, water, hospitals, education and reconstruction of demolished buildings.[51]

At the October Madrid Conference, Japan committed $5 billion of reconstruction assistance from 2004 to 2007. It was the second largest commitment after the $20 billion of US commitment.

Japan's position regarding 'human participation' was basically to limit itself to verbal support during the war. Pacifism inside the country did not allow Koizumi to take part in the war, even to the same extent that Japan participated in the joint operations against international terrorism after 9/11. Koizumi's position then could be summarized as 'Blair without armed forces'.

---

[50] http://www.mofa.go.jp/mofaj/area/iraq/jsf.html 2003-04-08.
[51] http://www.mofa.go.jp/mofaj/area/iraq/f_shien.html 2003-08-06.

On 13 June 2003 the Koizumi government presented a bill Concerning the Special Measures on Humanitarian and Reconstruction Assistance in Iraq. The bill was approved by the House of Representatives on 3 July and then by the House of Councillors on 26 July. Notwithstanding mounting problems and casualties in Iraq, Koizumi started sending SDF units to Iraq in December 2003.[52]

Koizumi's decision to support President Bush and send the SDF with this timing has been widely discussed in Japan. Given the general security concern of the Japanese people as described above, there was general understanding and support for Koizumi's response to President Bush. But many intellectuals raised serious questions (1) in relation to the United States, while recognizing that there was no better option for Japan than ultimately to support President Bush, whether Japan had developed the best possible dialogue faced with the new American unilateralism (Chapter 2);

(2) in relation to the United Nations, whether Japan had made maximum efforts to preserve the authenticity of that organization (Chapter 12);

(3) in relation to Europe, whether Japan and Europe had profited from this unprecedented opportunity for an in-depth political dialogue (Chapter 8);

(4) and in relation to the Middle East, whether Japan's position in sending the SDF in autumn would best serve Japan's Middle East policy.

It is still difficult to draw a clear conclusion to this fourth question, the implications for Japan's Middle East policy. The government clearly maintained that Japan's decision was taken independently, without American pressure.[53] Some argued that the major issue here was how to develop Japan's policy in the Middle East; the decision might have been taken too late and without a clear vision, but it was much better than doing nothing. Others maintained that at a time so much criticism was raised regarding the War in Iraq from the Islamic world in the Middle East and Asia, not to mention from Europe, Koizumi's decision did not help in enhancing Japan's posi-

---

[52] *Asahi Shinbun*, 27 January 2004.
[53] A special reference is made in the law that Japan's decision is taken 'independently and positively' (Article 1).

tion in the Middle East at all. There were also people who thought that Japan's policy toward the Middle East was less relevant, because Koizumi's decision was made in reality primarily from the point of view of strengthening the Japan-US alliance.

3. *Relations with the countries involved in the Middle Eastern peace process*

Relations with the countries involved in the Middle Eastern peace process are the second pillar of the Japanese foreign policy toward the Middle East. These countries include Egypt, Jordan, Syria, Lebanon, Israel and the PLO.

There is a clear awareness in the Japanese government that peace and stability in the Middle East cannot be achieved without resolving this complex and difficult issue, which has already lasted for more than a century. Japan is also aware that its objective in keeping stable relations with the Gulf countries is also severely constrained by the peace process. The oil embargo in 1973 made Japan acutely feel the link between the Middle Eastern peace process and the stability in the Persian Gulf region. When Saddam Hussein launched missiles against Israel during the Gulf War in 1991 Japan once again felt a serious interconnection between the two issues.

At the same time, there has been a clear limitation on Japan's ability to act usefully to resolve this complex issue. Japan, unlike Europe, has no historic and geographic proximity with this region. Japan, unlike the US, has no Jewish population. Japan's political manoeuvrability in this region has therefore been greatly limited.

Consequently, Japan has made its contribution to the Middle Eastern peace process in a different area. Japan focussed its policy upon economic factors, namely, without economic stability it would be difficult to foresee smooth progress in the peace process. There are such issues as poverty and economic disarray beneath the violence and terrorism exploding in that region. Japan therefore conducted a policy of assistance in order to remedy the economic issues underpinning the political goals.

In August 1993 the whole world was amazed to learn that Israel and the Palestine Liberation Organization (PLO) successfully concluded in Oslo confidential negotiations that had been ongoing for about a year. On 13 September 1993 a historic agreement was signed in Washington between Israel and the PLO.

> Working in the Japanese Embassy in Washington I happened to
> be invited to the ceremony following the signing of the agree-
> ments. 3,000 guests were invited to the Capitol garden. It was
> one of the most beautiful autumn days in Washington. Prime
> Minister Yitzhak Rabin and Chairman Yasser Arafat, accompa-
> nied by President Clinton and other dignitaries, appeared on a
> central stage. Encouraged by President Clinton, Chairman Arafat
> slowly stretched his right hand and after a moment of hesitation,
> Prime Minister Rabin accepted and the two leaders shook hands.
> We were all filled with hope that after a century of war a last-
> ing peace in the Middle East had finally been achieved.

After this historic occasion Japan substantially increased its assistance
to the Palestinians. Japan pledged $200 million for the year 1999–2000
at the Washington Conference to Support Middle East Peace and
Development in October 1993. Since then, Japan has implemented
a series of assistance programmes covering such areas as infrastructure, schools, hospitals and job opportunities. By 2002 the accumulative amount of assistance amounts to $630 million. In October
1999 Japan organized the Palestine Assistance Coordination Conference
in Tokyo. After the tragic re-emergence of tension between Israel
and the Palestinians in September 2000, Japan has continued its
emergency aid of $50 million in the area of medicine, foods, and
job opportunities.[54]

In June 2002 Foreign Minister Noriko Kawaguchi paid a visit to
Israel and Palestine and declared a "road map of Japanese assistance in accordance with the progress in the peace process."[55] This
proposal was an effort by Japan to mobilize its economic assistance
from a passive reconstruction contribution to a useful incentive for
enhancing the peace process.

Japan has also extended its assistance to other key countries involved
in the Middle Eastern peace process. Japan became in principle the
No. 1 donor country in the second half of the 1990's in Syria and
Jordan, the No. 4 country in Egypt (after the US, Germany and
France) and is enhancing its assistance in Lebanon after the peace
process began in that country.

---

[54] MOFA, *Present Situation of Middle Eastern Peace Process and Future Perspectives*, 15
November 2002 (www.mofa.go.jp/mofaj/area/chuto/genjo_04.html 2003–03–22).
[55] Ibid.

Japan also became an active participant in the multilateral assistance processes which began at the Moscow Meeting for Multilateral Negotiations on the Middle East in January 1992 and became the chair country of the Environmental Working Group, the leading country (the so-called 'Shepherd') on tourism within the Economic Development Working Group, and promoted a project to expand fresh water utilization in Jordan in the Water Management Working Group. But since the latter part of the 1990's, under the increasing difficulties of the peace process, this multilateral process has suffered a considerable slowdown.[56]

Japan maintains a stable relationship with Israel and a constant channel of dialogue. Japanese foreign ministers regularly visit Israel. Many members of the Israeli government have visited Japan, including Prime Minster Yitzhak Rabin in 1994 and Prime Minister Benjamin Netanyahu in 1997.

Since February 1996 Japan has taken part in the United Nations Peacekeeping Operation in the Middle East, and 45 Japanese are continuously participating in the UNDOF at the Golan Heights in Syria.

4. *New endeavours to enlarge the scope of foreign policy*

Afghanistan

As early as the mid-1980's there was recognition in Japan that Afghanistan's fate would have a deep impact on the Middle East situation and on the peace and stability in the southwestern part of the Eurasian continent. This recognition originated from a small number of regional specialists in MOFA and in general was supported by its leadership. It was not a coincidence that in 1988 the first Japanese political counsellor to the UN Peacekeeping operation was sent to Afghanistan (Chapter 12).

The Geneva Peace Agreement in April 1988 and the Soviet withdrawal in February 1989 did not bring peace and stability in Afghanistan. Civil war erupted and in 1996 the Taliban occupied Kabul. Since this period of turmoil, Japan had advocated convening an

---

[56] http://www.mofa.go.jp/mofaj/area/chuto/takoku.html 2002–11–13.

international conference for peace and for the reconstruction of Afghanistan.

Japan's major action in Afghanistan's assistance, however, began after 9/11. Japan's initial reaction was directed more towards its common fight against terrorism (Chapter 12). But Japan has, of course, not forgotten its traditional agenda of humanitarian and reconstruction assistance after the war. Japan and the United States organized a high-level conference on the reconstruction of Afghanistan in November 2001. It was immediately followed up by the first round of the Executive Assistance Group chaired by America, the EU, Japan and Saudi Arabia in December in Washington.

On 21 and 22 January 2002, the International Conference on Assistance and the Reconstruction of Afghanistan was held in Tokyo. 61 countries and 21 international organizations assembled and $4.5 billion was pledged. Japan's own pledge reached $500 million, covering such areas as reconstruction of the local community, the elimination of mines, education, medicine and welfare, media infrastructure, improvement of the position of women, etc. By early 2003, Japan had already implemented $375 million, including $282 million for reconstruction and $93 million for humanitarian assistance.[57]

Understanding Islam civilization

In January 2001 Foreign Minister Yohei Kono made a future-oriented speech at Doha, in the United Arab Emirates.[58] While acknowledging the importance of the oil connection with the Gulf countries, Minister Kono emphasized that future relations between Japan and these countries should develop on a multilayered basis. He underlined the need to deepen Japan's understanding of this world through direct and close contact and exchanges. The time of relying on the images Japan has accumulated over the years in such romantic novels as the 'Tales of the Arabian Nights' is over. He referred to serious works on Islamic civilization made by Japanese scholars in a study group conducted under the Minister's auspices and advanced

---

[57] MOFA, *Afuganisutan Gaikyou (Overall situation In Afghanistan)*, 20 February 2003 (www.mofa.go.jp/mofaj/area/afghanistan/kankei.html 2003–03–22).

[58] Y. Kono, *Wanganshokokutono Jyuusoutekina Kankeinimuketa Shinkousou (New initiatives for the Creation of Multilayered Relations with Gulf Countries)*, 9 January 2001, Doha (www.mofa.go.jp/mofaj/press/enzetsu/13/ekn_0109.html 2002–11–14).

several concrete proposals; inter alia, to enact a new dialogue with the Islamic world.

As an incarnation of his ideas a seminar-dialogue with the Islamic world began in Bahrain in March 2002. The seminar became especially timely after 9/11. A follow-up seminar in Japan in 2003 and in Iran in 2004 were agreed.[59] An embryonic effort has been made with the humble hope that a deeper understanding between the two civilizations will grow in the first decades of the 21st century.

---

[59] MOFA, *Isuramusekaitono Bunmeikantaiwa Seminaa (A Seminar Dialogue with the Civilization of the Islamic World)*, 28 March 2002 (www.mofa.go.jp/mofaj/area/islam/seminar_gh. html 2002–11–14).

CHAPTER TEN

OFFICIAL DEVELOPMENT ASSISTANCE: FROM RECIPIENT TO DONOR NUMBER ONE

1. *Japan's Official Development Assistance (ODA) in perspective*

There are several areas which have traditionally been identified as 'tools' or 'weapons' of foreign policy implementation. Military threat, economic power, scientific superiority, cultural richness, and economic assistance may be included in these tools. Economic assistance, known as Official Development Assistance (ODA), was probably the most consistent and effective tool of postwar Japanese foreign policy.

Japan's ODA can be analysed in four periods of its development since WWII:

(1) Postwar reconstruction and reparations (1945–1963) = Period I
(2) Expansion of economic assistance (1964–1976) = Period II
(3) Programmed expansion (1977–1988) = Period III
(4) A top donor (1989-to the present) = Period IV

Through fifty years of this historical development, Japan's ODA has several clear characteristics:

First, Japanese ODA continued to grow in volume. In 1989 Japan became the number one donor country in terms of the absolute amount of ODA, and since then, except for 1990 and 2001, for ten consecutive years from 1991 to 2000, Japan occupied the position of the world's number one donor.

Second, because Japan's ODA developed from its experience in implementing postwar reparations, it started with supplying Japanese products and Japanese services. In the course of ODA implementation this 'tied' aspect has fundamentally changed to become an 'untied' ODA.

Third, geographically Japan's ODA was exclusively earmarked for Asia, but that proportion declined to 75% by the middle of the 1970's, and to 50% by the end of the 1990's. Africa became the second largest recipient region followed by South America, the Middle East, Oceania, and Europe.[1]

Fourth, Japan's ODA consists of about 70% of bilateral aid and approximately 30% of assistance through multilateral international organizations. The bilateral aid is implemented through two channels: grant and loan. Loan aid had been the primary tool of assistance in the early years, but gradually the proportion of grant has increased. There are two types of grant aid. The first is hardware, which is supplying hospitals, equipment, food, and other items required by the recipient country. The second is software, which is technical cooperation, consisting of the transfer of technology required in the recipient country, through training and education. Training and education takes the form of dispatching Japanese experts or inviting relevant people for training in Japan.

Fifth, the greater the role of ODA in foreign policy, the more important it became to have a clear rationale for ODA, its priority areas, and its implementation. Efforts to conceptualize the function of ODA were necessary partly for effective ODA implementation and partly to convince taxpayers that their money was not wasted.

For the taxpayers, it was important to answer the question of 'why' Japan engages in ODA. Japan developed basically two answers to this question: one is the 'humanitarian consideration', that there are people who are suffering from social deprivation and economic difficulty, and as a wealthier country, that had received aid from other advanced countries during its difficult years, Japan should help these developing countries in their time of need. Another is the 'interest consideration', that helping those developing countries, as a final resort, would be in the interest of Japan. For example, some argued that the high esteem which a donor country would receive was in the ultimate interest of that donor country. Others argued that, in the world of interdependence, the economic development of the recipient country eventually would give greater economic benefits to the donor country. There was also the view that creating a stable and prosperous society in developing countries would increase Japan's security.

---

[1] European recipients were primarily former Yugoslavia and former East-European countries.

From the point of view of effective implementation of ODA, in addition to this question of 'why', the questions of 'how' and 'where' to implement ODA were important. Japan also developed answers to these questions.

Despite these efforts, Japan's ODA was not free from criticisms from other donor countries, in particular, in relation to the high percentage of loan assistance. Tense international debates were conducted. Furthermore, toward the latter part of the 1990's, Japan's inability to overcome non-performing loans and the ensuing deflationary economy increasingly put ODA under severe scrutiny from politicians and public opinion inside the country.

Japan's ODA is therefore at a turning point. Whether Japan continues to be a top leading donor and use ODA as an effective tool of foreign policy depends on efforts by the Japanese government and the support of the people of Japan.

2. *Postwar reconstruction and reparations*

America and the World Bank

Economic assistance for Japan in the immediate postwar period had an entirely different meaning: Japan was at the receiving end.

It was the United States that was the key donor country. From 1946 to 1951 an overall amount of $1.8 to $2 billion was granted to Japan through two funds: the Government and Relief in Occupied Areas (GARIOA), which handled primarily humanitarian emergency aid of food and medicine, and the Economic Rehabilitation in Occupied Areas (EROA), which basically assisted imports of raw materials for industrial production such as cotton or wool. After Japan gained independence in 1952, there were some debates in Japan whether this aid was a grant or a loan. Japan finally decided to reimburse this amount and from 1963 to 1973 completed the repayment.

After the entering into force of the San Francisco Peace Treaty in 1952, it was the World Bank which became the major donor to assist the economic reconstruction of Japan. For 14 years, from 1953 to 1966, the World Bank supplied loans to 31 projects, $863 million, including such worldfamous projects as the first *shinkansen*,[2] high-

---

[2] The literal translation is 'new major line', but it is generally understood to mean 'the bullet train'. It was first established between Tokyo and Osaka.

ways between Tokyo and Kansai, gigantic dams in Honshu, and other projects which created an indispensable infrastructure for Japan's industrial development. The last repayment of these loans terminated as late as July 1990, when Japan had just become the number one donor country (Chapter 11).[3]

This combination of humanitarian aid to cope with immediate necessities and loan assistance to contribute to the basic infrastructure for economic development became the basis of future Japanese assistance to developing countries in the form of Official Development Assistance (ODA).

War reparations

Reparations were another important basis from which Japanese economic assistance developed.

Japanese reparations were first prescribed in Article 14 of the San Francisco Peace Treaty. In this legally complex article, Japan was obligated to enter into negotiations "with Allied Powers so *desiring*, with a view to assisting to compensate those countries for the cost of repairing the damage done, by *making available the services of the Japanese people* in production, salvaging and other work for the Allied Powers in question."[4] Thus the first basic form of reparations, to pay an agreed amount of money *making available the services of the Japanese people*, took shape.

As we have already seen, the US and China did not *desire* to seek reparations and, in fact, the US became the first donor country to Japan. But most of the Asian countries sought reparations, based on the San Francisco Peace Treaty or otherwise,[5] and the majority of war reparations were settled during the latter half of the 1950's. In the negotiations with these countries the following three forms of reparations were formed: 1) reparations, actually so named, a transfer of money from Japan to the recipient country, 2) grants, in substance the same transfer of money from Japan to the recipient country, but conceptually different, and 3) loans, paid in the context of reparations.

---

[3] M. Shiratori, *Sekai Ginkou Gurupu (The World Bank Group)*, Kokusaikaihatu Journal, 1993, pp. 225–228.
[4] MOFA, *Principal Treaties, op. cit.*, p. 16, emphasis added.
[5] It was only the Philippines and Vietnam, which exercised the right of reparations based on Article 14 (a) of the San Francisco Peace Treaty. All other agreements were concluded on a bilateral basis (MOFA documents.

Thus, economic assistance in Japan began as an associated form of reparations. Japanese reparations were implemented in the form of purchases by the Japanese government of goods and services supplied by Japanese companies. As analysts observe, this reparations' structure supplied a basis for the aid structure in Japan (Chapter 6).[6]

The first Reparations and Economic Cooperation Agreement was concluded with Burma in 1954 and the last agreement in 1969 with Micronesia. This last agreement coincided with the end of the period of a fixed exchange rate of 360 yen per dollar. According to a MOFA calculation based on public figures, the total amount of Japanese reparations is the following (Chapter 6):[7]

– Reparations and grants (A): 604.75 billion yen (= 1. 679, 861 billion dollars)
– Loans (B): 340.78 billion yen (= 0.946, 611 billion dollars)
– Total amount (A) + (B): 945.53 billion yen (= 2. 626, 472 billion dollars)

Beginning of economic cooperation

In January 1950 an aid organization called the Colombo Plan was initiated by Great Britain and the Commonwealth countries with a view to enhancing social and economic development in the Asia-Pacific countries. In October 1954 Japan joined this organization and Japanese technical cooperation commenced under its auspices. Three years after the signing of the San Francisco Peace Treaty and two years before Japan joined the United Nations came the first signal that Japan had been received back into the community of nations.

During the 1950's Japan gained experience through its implementation of reparations agreements and the associated economic assistance agreements. This experience eventually became the basis of Japanese Official Development Assistance. The conclusion of a yen loan assistance agreement with India in 1958 marked the beginning of new Japanese initiatives in the area of bilateral economic cooperation.

---

[6] Sakamoto, *op. cit.*, p. 91; Tadokoro, *op. cit.*, p. 130.
[7] MOFA calculation based on public figures in yen, May 2000. The figures include South Korea but do not include North Vietnam. Calculated to dollars by the author with the exchange rate of 1$ = 360yen.

3. Development in volume

Growing figures (Period II)

In 1964 Japan's ODA reached $100 million. In the following decade that amount grew about 10 times and reached $1.1 billion in 1976. It was a period of quantitative and qualitative development. Powerful economic development through the 1960's was an important factor.

Introduction of numerical targets (Period III)

Symbolically enough, Japan's ODA entered a new phase after the last reparations had been paid to the Philippines in 1976. In 1977 Japan announced an ambitious objective of 'doubling ODA in five years'. In July 1978 at the Bonn Economic Summit, the Japanese government declared an even more audacious target of doubling ODA in three years[8] and introduced, for the first time, a numerical target entitled 'the Medium-Term Target'. This approach was met with success and in 1981, 1985, 1988 the second, third, and fourth Medium-Term Target was established.

As a result of these deliberate efforts the total amount of ODA calculated at $1.5 billion in 1977 reached $9 billion in 1988, a six fold expansion in 12 years.

As a top ODA donor (Period IV)

In 1989 Japan's ODA totalled $8.965 billion and Japan became volume wise, the largest donor in the world. This amount increased slightly in 1990 to $9.069 billion, but ranked second. In 1991 Japan became again the number one donor and since then for 10 consecutive years, until 2000, remained the world's largest donor:

---

[8] Ikei, *op. cit.*, p. 335.
[9] Yearly ODA Report 1999 (www.mofa.go.jp/mofaj/gaiko/oda/siryo/siryo_1/siryo_1f.html 2003-07-26).

Japanese ODA Total Amount 1989–2001[9]		
Year Amount($)	Rate of increase	GNP ratio
1989 8.965 billion	−1.9%	(0.31%)
1990 9.069 billion	1.2%	(0.31%)
1991 10.952 billion	20.8%	(0.32%)
1992 11.151 billion	1.8%	(0.30%)
1993 11.259 billion	1.0%	(0.27%)
1994 13.239 billion	17.6%	(0.29%)
1995 14.489 billion	9.4%	(0.28%)
1996 9.439 billion	−34.9%	(0.20%)
1997 9.358 billion	−0.9%	(0.22%)
1998 10.640 billion	13.7%	(0.28%)
1999 15.323 billion	44.0%	(0.35%)
2000 13.419 billion	−12.8%	(0.28%)[10]
2001 9.85 billion	−27.1%	(0.23%)[11]

Japan maintained its position as the number one donor, but the total amount of ODA began to decline. The fifth round of Medium-Term Target was established in 1993 for the period 1993–1997, but the Hashimoto cabinet decided to reduce—because of Japan's economic difficulties—the ODA budget by 10% for three years from 1996.[12] There was a conspicuous decline of ODA of −34.9% in 1996.

The Asian economic crisis in 1997, however, put a temporary halt to this policy of reducing ODA. Japan decided to extend substantial assistance to the Asian countries to overcome this crisis (Chapter 6). This decision resulted in a sharp rise in the loan sector and the Asian geographical distribution in 1998 and 1999. But in 2001, Japan's ODA saw a sharp decline, which put Japan in a position of donor number two, after the United States.

Here there emerges the first question in evaluating Japanese ODA. Volume-wise, is Japan making an adequate contribution to the developing world?

In this context, Japan declared its willingness to achieve 0.7% of ODA in proportion to that country's GNP in 1972 at the General

[10] ODA Hakusho, 2001, II–1 (www.mofa.go.jp/mofaj/gaiko/oda/siryo/siryo_2/siryo_2f.html 2003–03–28).
[11] ODA Hakusho, 2002, II–1 (www.mofa.go.jp/mofaj/gaiko/oda/siryo/siryo_2/siryo_2f.html 2003–07–26).
[12] Iokibe, *op. cit.*, p. 263.

Assembly of United Nations Conference on Trade and Development (UNCTAD).

Specifics of Japanese ODA 1997–2001 (1)[13]						
Year	1997	1998	1999	2000	2001	5 Y. Average
Total amount (b$)	9.43	10.78	15.32	13.42	9.85	11.76
GNP ratio	0.22%	0.28%	0.35%	0.28%	0.23%	0,27%
Per capita ODA	74.2$ (9th)	84.1$ (9th)		106.4$ (7th)		

From that perspective Japan's GNP ratio of 0.27% for 1997–2001 cannot be said to be very high. Even in 1999 when Japan reached its highest GNP ratio of 0.35%, it was far below North-European countries such as Denmark (1.01%), Norway (0.9%), the Netherlands (0.79%) and Sweden (0.70%).[14] Japan's yearly per capita ODA of around 80 dollars is not a high figure either in comparison to some of North-European countries which reach 300 dollars.[15]

However, there is a need for realism. The GNP ratio of those countries with a larger GNP is near that of Japan's ratio. In 1999, when Japan's GNP ratio was 0.35%, the US's ratio was 0.10%, the UK's 0.23%, Germany's 0.26% and France's 0.39%.[16] For those countries with a large GNP, achieving half of the UN target could result in a sizable ODA in absolute terms. Thus the UN target may be quite ambitious for those countries with a large GNP.

Japan is now facing a downward trend of the ODA volume, which we will be discussing at the concluding Section 8 below. Given the difficulty Japan already had to go through in maintaining the volume of ODA during the latter half of the 1990's, if Japan succeeds

---

[13] Tables of ODA 1997–2001 (1), (2), (3) are made from the MOFA homepage, annual report 1997–1999 and the White Paper 2001 and 2002. Some of the percentages are calculated by the author. Ranking figures in brackets are DAC ranking.

[14] ODA, Q&A series, Q4 (www.mofa.go.jp/mofaj/gaiko/oda/qa/q4.html 2002-11-24).

[15] K. Matsuura, *ODA Seisakuwo Ureu (Expressing concern on the ODA policy)*, Chuokoron, October 2002.

[16] ODA, Q&A series, Q4, *op. cit.*

in maintaining the current level of ODA, either in absolute terms or in GNP ratio, in my view Japan's efforts should be commended.

4. Qualitative improvement of yen loans

From reparations to assistance (Period II)

From the 1960's onwards, when Japan's assistance moved from the reparations period into a period of ODA implementation, the first area where qualitative improvement was sought was the yen loan. Yen loans were primarily directed to project loans. The recipient country needed railways, airports, ports, dams, and highways, etc., which would require a substantial amount of investment, but would be too expensive at normal commercial rates. Japan was prepared to provide loans with lower interest rates and longer reimbursement periods. The two governments had to conclude an international agreement, usually in the form of an Exchange of Notes, to establish respective rights and obligations. Then a loan agreement was concluded between the Overseas Economic Cooperation Fund, a semi-governmental implementing organization in Japan, and the recipient government.

In 1968 a new system of 'commodity loans' was introduced. This loan was not directed to big projects, and its main purpose was to initiate a system of lending for a relatively short period so as to help temporary economic and financial difficulties, such as trade imbalances, in the recipient country.

The most significant change, which began during this period, was the introduction of the 'untied yen loan'. As we have already seen, postwar Japanese economic assistance not only helped the recipient country, but also assisted Japanese business exports to the recipient country. The amount of money the Japanese government was prepared to spend was restricted to goods and services coming from Japan. This structure, known as 'tied yen loan' raised criticism from other donor countries as well as from the recipient country. It meant that the recipient country had to purchase Japanese goods and services, even when cheaper and qualitatively better goods and services were found from a third country. As a result the recipient country could become frustrated, seeing that an incremental yen could be used in a more effective way, while at the same time other donor countries claimed that 'tied yen loan' were a disguised form of Japanese export inducement.

The 'period of high growth' during the 1960's had released Japan from dependence on export-oriented assistance. The Japanese government began a new policy, that sought to untie the supply of goods and services to developing countries, called the 'LDC (least developed countries) untied'. Gradually a new system of 'untying across the board' followed.

Shift to untied assistance (Periods III and IV)

This policy bore clear results through the 1980's and 1990's and Japan made a significant shift from 'tied' to 'untied' economic assistance. In 1998, Japan's untied assistance within the whole of bilateral ODA reached 93.6%, the highest figure among the major donors, higher than the Netherlands (85.9%), the UK (79.6%) and France (65.1%). Untied assistance of the USA reached only 28.4% and Canada 34.5%.[17] Thus the first issue constantly debated in the initial years of Japanese ODA was overcome.

5. Regional diversification

Beginning of diversification (Period II)

Japanese ODA began exclusively in assistance to Asia. But substantial change occurred during the first half of the 1970's. In 1970 98% of Japanese assistance was still directed to Asia, but in 1975, that ratio declined to 75%. With some fluctuation, the ratio has continued to decline to this day.

Further geographical diversification (Period III)

Asia still remained the top recipient region. Japan took an important political decision to begin the first round of yen loans to China

---

[17] ODA, Q&A series, Q8 (www.mofa.go.jp/mofaj/gaiko/oda/qa/q8/html 2002–11–19).

in 1979, then the second round in 1984, and continued to the third round in 1988 (Chapter 4).

The proportion of ODA directed to Asia, however, continued to decline. From 75% of the total in 1975, it declined to 71% in 1980 and further to 68% in 1985. Just after the oil crisis particular attention was given to the Middle East and then the share of Africa rose rapidly. South America and Oceania followed.

A comment may be needed here to discuss Africa. In contrast to the relatively high growth in the Asian and Latin American economies, the economic difficulties of the African countries, which would later be named the 'Heavily Indebted Poor Countries (HIPs)', received greater attention. In particular, the issue of accumulated debt became a focal point of international debates from the end of the 1970's to the 1980's. In 1978 UNCTAD made an important resolution highlighting the necessity to tackle the issue.

Japan, which had always maintained the usefulness of loan assistance, could not remain aloof. In its postwar economic development Japan greatly benefited from the loans the World Bank had supplied. But if such a system creates problems in other countries these problems should be tackled squarely. Thus in 1987 Japan declared to the world financial and aid community its 'Financial Recycling Initiatives'. Japan emphasized the necessity of introducing structural changes on a global scale and resolving the accumulated debt issues within this broad context.

Regional diversification continued (Period IV)

ODA is now spread to all continents. But Asia is still by far the most important recipient region. Even on an individual country basis, the top three recipient countries of Japanese bilateral ODA from 1969 to 1999 were Indonesia ($16.393 billion), China ($14.479 billion) and the Philippines ($8.839 billion).[18]

---

[18] ODA White Paper 2000, 2–1–(note2) (www.mofa.go.jp/mofaj/gaiko/oda/00_hakusho/honpen/honpen_10.html 2002–11–20).

Specifics of Japanese ODA 1997–2001 (2)						
Year	1997	1998	1999	2000	2001	5 Y. Average
Total amount (b$)	9.43	10.78	15.32	13.42	9.85	
Percentage (%)						
Asia	46.5%	62.4%	63.2%	54.8%	56.6%	56.7%
Africa	12.1%	11.0%	9.5%	10.1%	11.4%	11%
South America	10.8%	6.4%	7.8%	8.3%	9.9%	8.64%
Middle East	7.8%	4.6%	5.2%	7.5%	3.9%	5.8%
Oceania	2.4%	1.7%	1.3%	1.2%	1.4%	1.6%
Europe	2.0%	1.7%	1.4%	1.2%		
Others	19.4%	12.2%	11.6%	16.5%		

Some might argue that Japan's assistance is too concentrated in Asia and that Japan lacks global perspectives. I do not think that this argument stands true. Every country has the right to develop its assistance in accordance with its historical, geographical and geopolitical interests. The recent five year average of just over 50% per year to Asia does seem to strike a right balance of Japan's regional diversification policy.

In addition, Japan's geographical distribution of ODA has to be considered with the growing importance Japan is attaching to Africa. Africa became a stable second recipient region. In the 1990's Japan increased its attention to the economic and social difficulty of this region. In 1993 Japan held a global conference on Africa entitled the Tokyo International Conference on African Development (TICAD). It was an initiative to attempt to direct the attention of the global community to Africa, when the world's attention was absorbed by the demise of the Soviet Union, the end of the Cold War and the War in the Gulf.

TICAD II was held in Tokyo in 1998 and adopted the Tokyo Action Plan which underlined two principles: that of 'ownership' on the part of the African countries, implying the principle of self-help, an underlying key concept of the Japanese aid policy, and that of 'partnership' on the part of the international community.

TICAD III took place in September-October 2003 and Japan committed another $1 billion of assistance in the coming five years, including medicines, foods and education.[19]

---

[19] http://www.mofa.go.jp/mofaj/area/ticad/tc_0.html 2002-11-20 (*Ashahi Shinbun,* 30 September 2003).

In January 2001 Prime Minister Mori visited Sub Saharan Africa
(South Africa, Kenya and Nigeria) the first postwar Japanese Prime
Minister to do so. In his African policy speech in South Africa he
declared, based on his recognition that "the stability and prosperity
of the 21st century cannot be achieved without resolving the problems which Africa faces now", that 'development assistance' and
'conflict prevention' were the two key factors of Japan's Africa foreign policy.[20]

One of the real difficulties in Africa was the issue of accumulated
debt. Many African countries were classified as Heavily Indebted
Poor Countries (HIPCs).[21] Japan took serious initiatives to contribute
to the resolution of this issue. MOFA published a position paper in
April 1999 just before the Cologne G8 Summit, announcing in particular that over the past twenty years Japan had provided grant
assistance to reduce the bilateral ODA debts of 27 countries, totalling
approximately 340 billion yen (approximately $3 billion) and that
any decision on future debt relief must take into consideration, among
other factors, ownership and economic reform in the HIPCs.[22]

6. *Forms of ODA and international polemics*

The beginning of grant aid (Periods II and III)

Japanese overseas assistance started with technical cooperation, by
joining the Colombo Plan in 1954, and yen loan, by initiating yen
loan assistance to India in 1958.

Grant assistance began at a later stage. In 1968 Japan joined the
scheme of grant aid for food within the framework of the GATT
Kennedy Round. In 1969 this experience in the Kennedy Round
opened a new gateway for grant assistance in general. Since then a
greater portion of grant assistance was given to projects of lower

---

[20] http://www.mofa.go.jp/mofaj/kaidan/kiroku/s_mori/arc_01/af_g01/gh.html
2002–11–23.

[21] IMF and the World Bank estimate that at the end of 2000, out of 41 countries as classified HIPCs 34 countries are from Africa and the Middle East. ODA,
Q&A series, Q11 (http://www.mofa.go.jp/gaiko/oda/qa/q11.html 2002–11–22).

[22] 28 April 1999, Japan's Comprehensive Plan for Development and Debt Relief
for HIPCs (www.mofa.go.jp/policy/oda/loanaid/plan9904.html 2002–11–22).

profitability (e.g. in medical or education areas), but some specific grant assistance was also given to fishery products (since 1972), cultural assistance (since 1975), natural disaster relief assistance (since 1976) and food production increase assistance (since 1977).

In 1987 non-project aid to promote economic reform started.

Grant, technical cooperation and loan (Period IV)

As for the proportion between grant, technical cooperation and yen loan, the average figures of the last five years (1997–2001) are 25%, 37% and 38%, respectively. In view of the high percentage of the loan assistance in early years of Japan's economic assistance, a stable 25% of grant assistance and technical cooperation almost equal to loan assistance seem to be a remarkable change. As we will see in Section 7 below, the high percentage of technical cooperation indicates the importance which Japan has attached to 'human resources development'.

Specifics of Japanese ODA 1997–2001 (3)						
Year	*1997*	*1998*	*1999*	*2000*	*2001*	*5 Y. Average*
Total amount						
(b$)	9.43	10.78	15.32	13.42	9.85	
Bilateral (b$)	6.61(70%)	8.65 (80%)	10.48 (68%)	9.64 (72%)	7.46 (76%)	73%
Grant (b$)	2.02 (31%)	2.18 (25%)	2.32 (22%)	2.11 (22%)	1.9 (26%)	25%
Techn. aid						
(b$)	3.02 (46%)	2.82 (33%)	3.16 (30%)	3.70 (38%)	2.84 (38%)	37%
Loan (b$)	1.57 (23%)	3.66 (42%)	5.00 (48%)	3.83 (40%)	2.72 (36%)	38%
Multilateral						
(b$)	2.82 (30%)	2.13 (20%)	4.85 (32%)	3.78 (28%)	2.39 (24%)	27%
Proportion of grant	43.5% (21st)	45.4% (last)		49.5% (last)		
Grant element		83.6% (last)		86.6% (last)		

An implementing organization called the Japan International Cooperation Agency (JICA), founded in 1974, played an important role in enhancing technical cooperation and grant assistance. JICA played a central role in developing human resources. JICA owned numerous training centres in Japan, and the training of thousands of experts there on a yearly basis was well appreciated by the recipient countries. A new type of assistance called 'project technical cooperation', composed of the dispatch of specialists, technical training in Japan, providing necessary equipment, sometimes combined with a substantial amount of grant aid in one specific project for several years, developed successfully in the 90's.

Despite these successes in the area of technical cooperation and grant, loan assistance continued to occupy an important part of the Japanese economic aid.

The issue of proportion between grant and loan has been a point of debate in the international donor community. As we saw in the figures in the table above, Japan's 'proportion of grant' and 'grant element'[23] are quite low among the DAC countries, so low that the average figure of 1998–1999 and 1999–2000 'proportion of grant' and 'grant element' were both the lowest among the DAC countries.

From the point of view of grant supporters, there was something incompatible in the concept of aid and lending. Japan was expected to improve her record on the 'proportion of grant' and 'grant element'.

Japan, however, has long maintained the validity of loan assistance. Japan greatly benefited in the postwar economic recovery from the loans she had received from the World Bank. The spirit of 'self-help', which Japan considers critically important for the development of a country, could be garnered by the working ethics related to loan transaction: borrowing money, creating things with that money, engendering profits and returning the borrowed amount to the lender. In addition, the conditions of Japanese loans were truly concessionary. In reality, loans provided for the mobilization of massive assistance. Recipient countries often showed appreciation.

It seems to me that there is certain compelling logic in Japan's argument for loan assistance. But nevertheless does Japan's 'grant element' and 'proportion of grant' have to be the lowest figure among major donors? Is there not further room for continuing the efforts so far done to lower the percentage of loan assistance? In the area of international polemics on ODA, if there is one area where Japan needs to give further thought, it may be this area.

---

[23] 'Proportion of grant' is calculated as the percentage of grant within the total amount of committed ODA. Grants include gifts without compensation, technical cooperation and multilateral cooperation.

'Grant element' is a format to calculate the degree of concession, taking into account the interest rate and reimbursement period for loan assistance. Grants will be calculated as 100% (ODA Hakusho, 2001, II–1, N.B.3; www.mofa.go.jp/mofaj/gaiko/oda/siryo/siryo_2/siryo_2f.html 2003–03–28).

At the same time, rather than continuing philosophical debates regarding the appropriateness of loan versus grant, it may be worthwhile to make efforts to harmonize these two types of assistance. Japan made such concrete efforts. At the initial stage of the construction of a society, there is a period when grant assistance is most useful. In a later stage, when the society has already been equipped with the necessary strength to handle loans, loan assistance could be incorporated gradually. The best combination of grant and loan assistance will engender the best results.[24]

Bilateral or multilateral channel

Japan's ODA has been implemented primarily through the bilateral channel. The five year average from 1997 to 2001 amounted to 73% through the bilateral channel and 27% through the multilateral channel.

Japanese multilateral assistance is channelled through such international financial institutions as the International Bank of Reconstruction and Development (IBRD), the International Development Association (IDA), the Asian Development Bank (ADB), and the United Nations Development Programme (UNDP; Chapter 11).

Japan's practice developed empirically. To start with, Japan had the economic strength sufficient to support the necessary organizations in implementing bilateral ODA. Bilateral assistance leaves a clear impression of the donor in the recipient country; this makes it easier to ensure public support in the donor country. It can also lead to the development of a sense of responsibility with the donor country. Competition among many donors can create a richer and finer output in the recipient countries as well.

However, some countries preferred multilateral assistance, maintaining that unified multilateral assistance would avoid duplication, lead to greater efficiency, and alleviate institutional burdens upon the recipient country.

Here again, rather than plunging into philosophical debates, Japan advocated closer consultation and coordination among the donor countries and international institutions. In May 1996 DAC/OECD

---

[24] ODA, Q&A Series, Q6 (www.mofa.go.jp/gaiko/oda/qa/q6.html 2002–11–19).

adopted the 'Development Partnership Strategy' (Chapter 11). Japan took a substantial initiative in formulating this initiative. While emphasizing the 'ownership' in the developing countries and the 'partnership' in the donor countries, the Strategy emphasized the need for enhanced cooperation among donor countries, NGOs and private companies to create a more comprehensive programme better attuned to respective situation in each recipient country.[25]

7. Conceptualization efforts of ODA

The question of conceptualization of Japanese ODA is not easy to grasp for an outsider. There are many documents produced by the government, mostly by the Ministry of Foreign Affairs, but reading them does not easily give a clear cut, unified view of Japan's concept of ODA. What one finds there are traces of the efforts made by many respectable diplomats, trying to explain several critical issues e.g. 'why' Japan has to implement ODA, 'how' it should be done, and 'where' the primary areas are to be focussed on. But these answers are often based on initiatives by individual diplomats and political forces surrounding them and the outcome was sometimes not well-coordinated and somewhat confused.

Nevertheless, it is important to follow the gist of Japan's vision and perspectives of ODA, because from these perceptions the future direction of ODA would be formed. Let me present my version of the conceptual development of Japan's ODA.

The first endeavour during the 1950's (Period I)

As we have already seen in Chapter 6, Prime Minister Kishi, in his foreign policy speech in February 1957, outlined the three principles of his Asian policy: 1) improvement of the status of Japan through the consolidation of neighbourly relations; 2) improvement of welfare in Asia through development cooperation; 3) and the development of the Japanese economy through reparations and economic cooperation.

---

[25] ODA, Q&A Series, Q7 and Q14 (www.mofa.go.jp/gaiko/oda/qa/q7.html (q14.html) 2002–11–19).

These principles were clear guidance not only to Japan's Asian policy but also to its economic assistance policy. Reading the three principles today, I feel that the two major principles 'why' Japan needs to implement ODA are well articulated here. The basic logic that ODA should serve the welfare of the recipient country, along the line of 'humanitarian consideration', is well formulated in the second principle. It is also made abundantly clear in the third principle that enhancing ODA is in Japan's own economic interest. The 'interest consideration' is clearly there.

Developing logics in the period of expansion of economic assistance (Period II)

I worked in the Bilateral Treaties Division of MOFA from 1976 and for about one year worked on all agreements related to economic cooperation. In principle all economic cooperation was conducted under government-to-government agreements. The primary purpose of concluding these agreements was to ensure correct implementation of assistance. Taxpayers' money was involved and the money could not be wasted. The best guarantee for that was to conclude a government-to-government international agreement and establish clear rights and obligations: the Japanese government bears an obligation to provide assistance, but the recipient government bears the responsibility of proper usage of this assistance.

This rigid system of requiring an assurance of proper usage in the form of a bilateral agreement sometimes hurt the pride of the people at the recipient end. All the more so, because the Japanese government, i.e. my division (!), insisted that the recipient government should accept a type of international agreement established in the Japanese ODA implementation. "The art of diplomacy is to convince the other side about the necessity of including these 'obligatory clauses' without offending their pride. If an objection is raised by the other side, you have to come up with the appropriate logic to convince the other side, but without offending their pride." This is what I was repeatedly told by my senior colleagues in the division.

Another point which was often discussed in the division was the importance of *yousei-shugi* or 'request first principle' from the recipient side. Japan should not enforce its will and the recipient

> side should always determine their request first. The ultimate responsibility to develop the country lies with the people of that country, and therefore, they should "request what they want". The principle of *jijyo-doryoku* or 'self-help' is crucially important in considering the question of 'how' to implement ODA. This is one of the basic philosophies of Japan's ODA, as I was taught. An interesting principle, I thought.

In answering the question of 'why' to implement ODA along the line of two principles, a new concept of 'basic human needs (BHN)' attracted attention among those engaged in economic assistance, particularly in Japan. The 'humanitarian consideration' and the importance of the welfare of the recipient state as stated in Prime Minister Kishi's 1957 speech took a clear formulation in BHN. On the other hand, after the first oil crisis a new notion of 'interdependence' surfaced in global economic relations. The 'interest' of the developed world and the developing world are interdependent; therefore Japan must assist the developing world ultimately to ensure its own 'interest'. So the logic developed.

Further conceptualization during the period of programmed expansion (Period III)

Toward the end of the 1970's the Ministry of Foreign Affairs seriously tried to redefine the concepts and objectives of ODA. There was a need to create a fresh vision to gain stronger domestic support for ODA, because it had already grown to a noticeable level, and because Japan's own economic difficulties, due to the oil shocks of 1973 and 1979 also compelled them to find convincing reasons to spend taxpayers' money outside the country.

Two documents produced by MOFA shed light in particular to the developing concept in defining Japan's own 'interest' in implementing ODA. In 1978 MOFA published 'The Current State of Economic Cooperation and its Outlook: The North-South Problem and Development Assistance', which clearly defined this notion:

> 1. Japan can ensure its security and prosperity only in a peaceful and stable world. One of the most appropriate means for Japan to contribute to the peace and stability of the world is assistance to developing countries.

2. Japan is closely interdependent with developing countries, since it is able to secure natural resources only through trade with those countries. Therefore, it is essential to maintain friendly relations with developing countries for Japan's economic growth.[26]

For the first time the notion of 'security, peace and stability' clearly appeared in Japan's thinking of ODA. The notion of 'interdependence' was further elaborated and received official recognition.

In 1980 another MOFA publication entitled 'The Philosophies of Economic Cooperation: Why Official Development Assistance?'. Japan's own experience and aid rationales commonly held by other donor countries were carefully studied. This document specifically concluded that Japan's economic cooperation is guided by two motives, among which 'the recognition of interdependence among nations' was one, and stated that providing ODA was the price to be paid for building an international environment to secure Japan's comprehensive security.[27]

In fact, an interesting analysis is given that during the first half of the 1980's Japan began deploying its ODA with 'strategic consideration' to Turkey in 1980 and 1981, to Somalia in 1982 and to Jamaica in 1983.[28]

As for the principle of 'humanitarian consideration', the 1980 document outlined as one of the two basic motives of ODA 'humanitarian and moral considerations'. The importance of meeting the 'basic human needs (BHN)' of developing countries was already recognized from the 1970's. Based on Japan's own experience during the postwar economic reconstruction, Japan became increasingly convinced that there was no-one else but the leaders and people of the recipient country who could ensure the BHN in that country.

Japan therefore very consciously began to emphasize the principle of *jijyo-doryoku* or 'self-help'. It was an important criterion in considering the question of 'how' to implement ODA.

From there Japan created a new concept of *hitozukuri* or 'human resources development'. This was an important new concept in answering the question of 'what' ODA should be directed towards.

---

[26] ODA Summary 1994, 1.(1) (www.mofa.go.jp/policy/oda/summary/1994/1.html 2002–11–22).
[27] Ibid.
[28] J. Inada, 'Japan's Aid Diplomacy: Economic, Political or Strategic?' in: K. Newland ed., *The International relations of Japan*, 1990, p. 105.

Human resources development assistance consisted mainly of technical cooperation in training experts in all areas relevant for the development of the recipient country. During the 1970's the proportion of technical cooperation increased rapidly from 5.6% (1974), 7.6% (1976), and 10.4% (1977) and continued to rise, as we have already seen in Section 6 above.

Conceptual efforts during the period as a top donor (Period IV)

(1) *ODA Charter*
In June 1992 the Japanese government adopted the ODA Charter in a cabinet decision so as to garner broader support at home and abroad and implement ODA more systematically. It reflected the past efforts of conceptualization and tried to answer new agendas which surfaced at the beginning of the 1990's, notably environmental concerns and some political values.

The ODA Charter is composed of four Basic Philosophies and four Principles and five Priority Issues:[29]

Basic Philosophy:

(1) Many people are still suffering from famine and poverty in the developing countries, which constitute a great majority among countries in the world. From a *humanitarian viewpoint*, the international community can ill afford to ignore this fact.

(2) The world is now striving to build a society where freedom, human rights, *democracy* and other values are ensured in peace and prosperity. We must recognize the fact of *interdependence* among nations of the international community and that stability and the further advancement of the developing world is indispensable to the peace and prosperity of the entire world.

(3) *Environmental conservation* is also a task for all mankind, which all countries, developed and developing alike, must work together to tackle.

---

[29] ODA, Japan's ODA Charter, June 30, 1992 (www.mofa.go.jp/policy/oda/summary/1999/refl.html 2003–04–04). The Basic Philosophy is slightly rearranged in accordance with the Q&A series, Q2 (www.mofa.go.jp/mofaj/gaiko/oda/qa/q2.html 2002–11–19).

(4) apan attaches central importance to the support of the *self-help efforts* of developing countries towards economic take-off. It will therefore implement its ODA—through *developing* a wide range of *human resources* and socio-economic infrastructure,—and through meeting *basic human needs (BHN)*—.

Principles:

(1) *Environmental conservation* and development should be pursued in tandem.

(2) Any use of ODA for *military* purposes or for aggravation of international conflicts should be *avoided*.

(3) Full *attention* should be paid to trends in recipient countries' *military* expenditures, their development and production of weapons of mass destruction and missiles, their export and import of arms, etc., so as to maintain and strengthen international peace and stability, and from the viewpoint that developing countries should place appropriate priorities in the allocation of their resources in their own economic and social development.

(4) Full attention should be paid to efforts for promoting *democratization* and the introduction of a *market-oriented economy*, and the situation regarding securing basic *human rights and freedoms* in the recipient country.

Priority Issues:

(1) Approach to global problems (such as the environment and population)

(2) Basic human needs

(3) Human resources development, research and other cooperation for improvement and dissemination of technologies

(4) Infrastructure improvement

(5) Structural adjustment

In answering the question of 'why' Japan is engaged in ODA, the Basic Philosophy point (1) referred to the well-established concept of 'humanitarian considerations' and point (2) quoted 'interdependence', which was a careful and quiet reference to national 'interest'.

Point (4) of the Basic Philosophy represented Japan's strong emphasis on the notion of 'self-help' in answering the question of 'how' ODA should be implemented.

The points in the Principles (2), (3) and (4) all referred to political values. They were innovative in this Charter in introducing a new factor of 'democratic and non-military values' in 'how' Japan should implement its ODA. During the Cold War, when the world was succinctly divided into three major blocs, namely, the western-democratic group, the socialist-communist group and the developing countries group (sometimes called the 'non-aligned movement' or 'the Third World'), political considerations were less relevant in the world of ODA. At least, that was the case in Japan. After the end of the Cold War when conflicts became more complex in their nature involving internal, regional, ethnic, religious, and cultural rivalries, a clearer political guideline for Japan's ODA became necessary. These democratic and non-military values were also an important and clear manifestation of the point Japanese democracy had reached nearly a half century after the end of the Pacific War.

Priority Issues gave an answer to the question of 'where' are the areas that Japan was directing its ODA.

– Basic human needs (2) was fairly obvious, given the importance this notion had in developing Japan's ODA.

– Infrastructure (4) and structural adjustment (5) may be necessary to supplement from a socio-economic point of view, the long-term objective to improve the welfare in developing countries.

– Human resources development (3) is the point to which Japan attached particular importance, closely linked with the notion of 'self-help'.

– It is interesting to note that global problems including environment (1) were placed in the top position among the Priority Issues. Both point (3) of the Basic Philosophy and point (1) of the Principles also referred to the environment. The importance of addressing key global issues affecting the fate of mankind became better perceived at the beginning of the 1990's and 'the environment' became the first and most representative issue towards this direction. As a matter of fact Japan's environment-related ODA occupied 33.5% of the total ODA in 1999.[30]

(2) Medium-term policy

The fifth round of the Medium-Term Target for 1993–1997 was established, but Japan's ODA saw an unprecedented reduction of

---

[30] ODA, Q&A Series Q9 (www.mofa.go.jp/mofaj/gaiko/oda/qa/q9.html 2002–11–22).

34.9% in 1996, as described above. Under such circumstances the traditional approach of establishing a Medium-Term Numerical Target received little sympathy among political leaders and budgetary authorities. Several visible efforts were made so as to overcome this difficult situation.

In January 1998 the Council on ODA Reforms for the 21st Century, a consultative body of 'wise men' for the Foreign Minister presented its final report. Other recommendations were made by the Prime Minister's consultative organ, parliamentary committees, and the Liberal Democratic Party's policy commission, etc.

As a basic direction of ODA policy at the beginning of the 21st century and with a view to replace the Medium-Term Numerical Objective, in August 1999 the Japanese government adopted a policy paper named 'Japan's Medium-Term Policy on ODA'.

The main characteristics of this complex and comprehensive document were the following:

(1) The Introduction[31] of this document outlines first the three following points as to 'why' should Japan engage in ODA. This is a continuation of the two pillars we have seen on many occasions:

> 1. Japan shoulders the important *responsibility* of contributing to *sustainable social and economic development* in developing countries;
> 2. This is a role through which Japan can *win the confidence* and appreciation of the international community; and
> 3. ODA plays a very significant role in ensuring Japan's own stability and prosperity. As such, economic assistance promotes *Japan's best interests*, including the maintenance of peace.

Subsequently this Introduction emphasizes the importance to "earn public understanding and support for the ODA programme in order to continue to respond to the high expectations of the international community" and outlines three points for attention:

> 1. Efforts must be continued to improve the effectiveness and efficiency of aid programmes;
> 2. Proper accountability must be established *vis-à-vis* the Diet and the general public; and
> 3. Japan's ODA programme must be coordinated with its foreign policies and with other important policies pertaining to the national interest.

---

[31] www.mofa.go.jp/policy/oda/summary/1999/ref2_01.html 2003–03–29, underlined by the author.

The underlying theme throughout these three points is the necessity of earning public understanding and support for ODA. This has become a new and serious outcry from all the ODA supporters in Japan.

(2) The Medium-Term Policy paper then elaborates on 'Basic Approaches (Chapter I)'.[32] This is partly to explain 'how' ODA should be implemented, and the notion of 'self-help' is naturally emphasized: "The key to realizing the goals of the Development Partnership Strategy (issued by DAC/OECD in 1996) lies in the self-help efforts and the initiatives of the developing countries as they work toward economic take-off. Japan will emphasize 'good governance' through the improvement of the policy management capabilities of developing countries and will work to support their initiatives in this area."

(3) The document also presents 'Priority Issues and Sectors (Chapter II)'.[33] The seven issues and sectors were probably the most representative list of areas to which Japan's ODA was then directed. In other words, this was the comprehensive list in response to the question of 'where' Japan's ODA was directed at. The two sectors outlined in the Basic Philosophy of the ODA Charter: 'human resources development' and 'environment' were included. The seven issues and sectors run as follows:

1. Support for *poverty alleviation and social development*: basic education, health and medical care, women in development
2. Support for economic and *social infrastructure*
3. *Human resources development* and intellectual support: human resources development, intellectual support, support for democratization
4. Responding to *global issues: environmental conservation*, population and aids, food, energy, drug abuse
5. Support for overcoming the *Asian* currency and economic *crisis* and the promotion of economic structural reform
6. *Conflict*, disaster, and development
7. Responding to issues of *debt relief*

(4) Finally, the Medium-Term Policy paper emphasized the necessity to understand further conditions of individual recipient developing countries and proposes the formulation of individual country-specific assistance programmes.[34]

---

[32] Ibid.

[33] www.mofa.go.jp/policy/oda/summary/1999/ref2_02.html 2003–03–29, underlined by the author.

[34] The Medium-Term Policy paper then comprises 'Priority issues and sectors by

It was then said that the Japanese ODA policy was governed in three layers: the ODA Charter at the top, Medium-Term Policy in the middle, and Country Assistance Programmes at the implementation level. By July 2002, 12 country programmes have been established and another nine programmes were under preparation.[35] The country programme for China adopted in October 2001 was one of the most important programmes thus far defined (Chapter 4).

8. *Current problems and future perspectives*

From the beginning of 2001 Japanese ODA faced dual difficulties.

One difficulty was the continuing economic stagnation and the resulting frustration by taxpayers that their money would be spent abroad and not in Japan. Politicians have reacted acutely to this popular antipathy toward ODA.

Another difficulty was related to the Ministry of Foreign Affairs, the central institution in charge of ODA in Japan. The Ministry entered into serious difficulty from the beginning of 2001 regarding a corruption and embezzlement scandal involving Ministry officials. The traditional sense of trust, by the people of Japan for the Ministry of Foreign Affairs and the Japanese diplomatic corps was shattered.

In March 2002 the Second Consultative Committee on ODA Reform finalized its report.[36] The report made it clear that "The very focus of the reform is how to reflect, in ODA, the mind, intellect and vitality of the Japanese people directed toward people in developing countries." Improved transparency and enhanced accountability toward the people were also emphasized.

Based on the recommendation of this report, a Board on Comprehensive ODA Strategy was established in June 2002 to discuss basic ODA policies. In August several board members made an

---

region (Chapter III)', 'Methods of AID (Chapter IV)' and 'Points to be followed in the implementation and management of ODA (Chapter V)'. A country specific programme is proposed in Chapter V (www.mofa.go.jp/policy/oda/summary/1999/ref2_03. (ref2_04. ref2_05.) html 2003–03–29).

[35] ODA, Country Assistance Programme, July 2002,
   www.mofa.go.jp/gaiko/oda/kuni/k_keikkaku.html 2002–11–24

[36] This committee, which basically succeeded the Council on ODA Reforms for the 21st Century, was established in May 2001 and had 15 meetings (http://www.mofa.go.jp/policy/oda/reform/report0203.html 2003–07–28).

emergency plea that for three consecutive years Japan's ODA budget had seen a sharp decline and that they feared that Japan's credibility in the international community could be seriously injured. They strongly warned not to cut ODA budget hastily.[37]

Against the background of these critical situations, in December 2002 MOFA decided to revise the ODA Charter adopted ten years previously in 1992. The initiative was taken primarily to regain credibility on Japan's ODA within the Japanese public. After the formal decision at ministerial level was taken for the revision in March 2003, the government draft was made public in July 2003.[38] A unique approach was taken to post the government draft for one month in order to gather views from the public through e-mail and letters.

The new ODA Charter, as formally adopted on 29 August,[39] expressed, with more emphasis than any previous documents, that ODA was a tool to enhance Japan's national interest. This effort toward the survival of ODA may result in greater understanding by Japanese people, and therefore greater dynamism, of Japan's ODA.

At any rate, the major characteristics of the new Charter are the following:

First, in describing the purposes of ODA there are ample statements that a positive approach to ODA "will in turn benefit Japan itself in a number of ways, including by promoting friendly relations and people-to-people exchanges with other countries, and by strengthening Japan's standing in the international arena," and "correlates closely with assuring Japan's security and prosperity and promoting the welfare of its people". It contrasts sharply to the cautious reference to 'interdependence' in the 1992 ODA Charter.

Second, the traditional hard core of Japan's ODA, 'request first principle, principle of self-help, and human resources development' are being modified. Already in March 2003 when the government decided to revise the 1992 Charter, it was made clear that 'request-based approach' would be under review. Instead, policy consultation where Japan's view may be better reflected is greatly emphasized in the new Charter. 'Principle of self-help' is more or less left intact as

---

[37] http://www.mofa.go.jp/mofaj/gaiko/oda/seisaku/seisaku_1/senryaku/kinkyu_1.html 2002-11-19.

[38] *Asahi Shinbun*, 7 July 2003.

[39] The new ODA text is found on the MOFA homepage (http://www.mofa.go.jp/policy/oda/reform/revision0308.html 2003-09-23).

the top item of the Basic Policies, but 'human resources development' ceased to be one of the Priority Issues.

Third, a new notion of 'human security' was included as an item of Basic Policy. It would probably become an interesting concept in further answering the question of 'how' to implement Japan's ODA (Chapter 12). 'Peace building' became one of the four Priority Issues. That is also quite a new approach in mobilizing ODA with greater dynamism.

Fourth, past efforts and the recent call to implement ODA with greater effectiveness and larger participation of the people are all there. Medium-term policy establishment and country assistance programme are confirmed. The role of the Japanese people is underlined in their participation, training and education, as well as in the emphasis given to accountability and public relations of ODA.[40]

Thus Japanese ODA is at a crossroads. Whether ODA will remain a powerful measure of Japanese foreign policy or, because of Japan's domestic situation, it will cease to play a leading role in its foreign policy is an important and as yet, an open question.

---

[40] Some of the major parts of the new Charter structures are as follows:

Basic Policies: (1) Supporting self-help efforts of the developing countries, (2) Perspective of 'human security', (3) Assurance of fairness, (4) Utilization of Japan's experience and expertise, (5) Partnership and collaboration with the international community

Priority Issues: (1) Poverty reduction, (2) Sustainable growth, (3) Addressing global issues, (4) Peace building

Principles of ODA Implementation The same four principles of the 1992 Charter are repeated.

CHAPTER ELEVEN

MULTILATERAL ECONOMIC DIPLOMACY: FROM PARTICIPANT TO POSITIVE CONTRIBUTOR

1. *Postwar international economic organizations and Japan's accession*

Establishment of major international economic organizations

From 1929 onwards the world economy plunged into a severe recession. Many countries resorted to trade barriers to protect their own industry and economy. Economic difficulties increased tension among the industrialized countries. Economic issues became an important underlying motive that led to World War II. When the war was still in full swing, the Allied Powers had already recognized the necessity of creating a new world economic order, which would ensure a stable economy, rising employment and enlarged production.

In July 1944 a conference of the Allied Powers was held in Bretton Woods in New Hampshire, USA, to discuss the postwar economic order. As a result of the agreement reached there two international organizations were established:

The International Monetary Fund (IMF) began its work in March 1947. The major purpose of IMF was to create an 'exchange fund', which would serve to stabilize the international financial situation. IMF also became the institutional basis for fixed exchange rates, based on the US gold convertible dollar, for more than 20 years in the postwar world economy.

The International Bank of Reconstruction and Development (IBRD), the so-called World Bank, began its work in June 1946. In the early years after the war IBRD concentrated its work in the area of postwar reconstruction. After this initial stage was over, its work was exclusively directed to the assistance of developing countries to help in resolving various problems related to development.

Parallel to these two organizations in charge of international financial issues, the General Agreement on Tariffs and Trade (GATT) was established to cover international trade issues. In 1948 a Charter to establish an International Trade Organization (ITO) was agreed upon in Havana. But in 1946–1947 the first round of negotiations had already been conducted among interested countries regarding the concession of tariffs in Geneva, and a schedule on tariff concessions was agreed upon. For fear that the ITO Havana Charter might not enter into force promptly, because of the ratification needed by each contracting party, the schedule agreed to in Geneva together with the relevant articles of the ITO Charter entered into force in the form of the General Agreement on Tariffs and Trade (GATT) from January 1948. The US Congress later rejected the ratification of the ITO Charter, and the previously agreed GATT formed the rules and organization to govern international trade.

The fundamental principles of GATT were the following:

1) Non-discriminatory and multilateral assurance of the Most-Favoured-Nation Treatment and National Treatment

2) General elimination of quantitative restrictions

3) Tariffs as agreed in the attached schedule to govern international trade.

4) Gradual reduction of trade barriers including tariff rates

5) Restriction of dumping and subsidies

But in reality, it was a complex organization which allowed many exceptions to meet the differing interests of the contracting parties. Idealism and realism had been dynamically interwoven.

Lastly, one more postwar international economic organization is worthwhile mentioning here: the Organization for Economic Cooperation and Development (OECD). This organization was first created as the Organization for European Economic Cooperation (OEEC) in Paris in 1948, primarily to implement the Marshall Plan in Europe. After that basic mission was accomplished, in 1960 it developed into a transatlantic cooperative organization where 18 European OEEC countries, America, Canada and three European Communities[1] joined. It was then renamed the Organization for Economic Cooperation and Development (OECD).

OECD became a gathering of major industrialized market economies, discussing important socio-economic issues for policy coordination, in particular, macroeconomic policy to ensure sustainable

---

[1] European Coal and Steel Community (ECSC), European Economic Community (EEC), and European Atomic Community (EURATOM).

growth; trade policy to strengthen free and multilateral trading systems; and Official Development Assistance (ODA) policy to establish effective coordination among donor countries. The Economic Policy Committee in charge of macroeconomic policy; the Trade Committee in charge of trade; and the Development Assistance Committee (DAC) in charge of assistance policy became the three pillars of OECD.

Japan's accession to major international economic organizations

After signing the San Francisco Peace Treaty in 1951, Japan immediately applied for membership to IMF. On 14 August 1952 Japan was accepted as a member and on 11 May 1953 the exchange rate of the yen was fixed at 1$ = 360yen.

Given the weakness of the Japanese economy, however, Japan was accepted only based on Article 14 of the IMF Agreement, i.e. as a country entitled to restrictive measures regarding international exchange dealings. It was on 1 April 1964 that Japan moved to the Article 8 status of the IMF Agreement, in which a country was not entitled to restrictive measures regarding international exchange dealings. It was a decisive turning point when Japan moved from the position of a postwar transition status to a developed country in the area of international finance.

On 14 August 1952 Japan also joined the IBRD. Japan was first a recipient country and from 1953 to 1966, the World Bank supplied loans to 31 projects of $863 million (Chapter 10).[2]

As with IMF, after the conclusion of the San Francisco Peace Treaty Japan immediately applied for membership to GATT in 1952. Japan's application was strongly backed by the United States, but was first opposed by major European countries, such as Great Britain and France (Chapter 8).

Japan was finally accepted into GATT in 1955, but 14 countries including major European countries invoked Article 35 of GATT which allows contracting parties to veto the Most-Favoured-Nation treatment to a new member state.[3] The Japanese government exerted

---

[2] It took another 20 years before, in 1984, Japan became the second contributor to the IBRD (Shiratori, *op. cit.*, p. 228).

[3] Article 35 of GATT prescribes that the Agreement shall not apply as between any contracting party and another contracting party, if either of the contracting parties, at the time either becomes a contracting party, does not consent to such application (MOFA, *Principal Treaties, op. cit.*, p. 1546).

considerable efforts to have this article removed from its application. Japan was assisted by America, which intended to create a world trade structure with reduced barriers, which eventually led to the Kennedy Round, as we will see below. Japan's rapid economic growth also gave compelling reasons for the European countries to treat Japan more as an economic equal partner. As the result of strenuous negotiations and Japan's concession in accepting the application of a 'safeguard clause' in case of emergency, the Treaty of Commerce and Navigation concluded with the United Kingdom was signed in 1962, and based on this Treaty the UK granted Most-Favoured-Nation treatment to Japan. France concluded the Treaty of Commerce in 1963 and MFN treatment was also granted to Japan (Chapter 8).

At the same time, when Japan joined GATT, it started with an Article 12 status, where a contracting party was allowed to introduce restrictions to safeguard its balance of payments. This status basically applied to developing countries, whose economy was still in a weaker position. But on 20 February 1963 Japan moved to the Article 11 status where a contracting party was in principle not allowed to apply quantitative restrictions. Article 11 was the GATT equivalent of Article 8 of the IMF Agreement. Japan was finally accepted as an integrated partner of the international trade community.

As we have seen in Chapter 3, the 1960's became a 'period of high growth' for Japan. Prime Minister Ikeda's policy of 'doubling the national income' in a decade was well met with an average annual rise in the GNP growth rate of more than 10% during the 1960's. In the process of this powerful economic growth, joining OECD became an important policy objective for Japan. On 28 April 1964, several months before the Tokyo Olympics, Japan finally joined OECD.

As if to commemorate Japan's full acceptance into GATT, IMF and OECD the Tokyo Olympic Games were held in the autumn of 1964. For many Japanese, it was a festival to mark Japan's economic recovery, the 'period of high growth' and its return to the international economic community.

Creation of other development-related organizations

In the development-related area, several important organizations were created during the 1960's. Japan became a founding member of all these organizations.

In 1960 a new institution called the International Development Association (IDA), sometimes called the Second World Bank, was created specifically to assist poorer countries. While IBRD supplied loans with conditions close to commercial lending, the IDA specialized in such concessionary loans as no-interest loans with a 35–40 year reimbursement period, including a 10 year period of grace.[4]

In 1964 the United Nations Conference on Trade and Development (UNCTAD) was established by a UN resolution and remained an active multilateral organization in charge of development. The developing countries formed a group within UNCTAD, the group of 77, which became the most representative group of developing countries during the 1960's and 70's.

In 1966 the United Nations Development Programme (UNDP) was founded by a UN General Assembly resolution. Since then it has specialized in all UN related technical cooperation.

2. Macroeconomic policy and international financial situation

Introduction of the float system and the establishment of the G7

In August 1971 President Nixon announced a new economic policy, including a temporary suspension of the exchange rate of dollars for gold (Chapter 3). New exchange rates were agreed upon in December 1971. The yen/dollar exchange rate was fixed at 1$ = 308yen. The agreement was called the Smithsonian Accord.

However, the demand for yen and other strong European currencies continued to increase. In February 1973 Japan moved to a floating exchange rate system. Europe followed in March. The postwar fixed exchange rate system virtually ended. IMF later introduced a formal revision of the Agreement in April 1978.[5]

IMF's role in maintaining an orderly international financial system waned after the introduction of floating exchange rates. Major global economies resorted to international financial markets to obtain financial resources rather than turning to the IMF facilities.

---

[4] From the beginning of the 1990's Japan assumed the position of second contributor to the IDA, bearing more than 20% of its budgetary share (Shiratori, *op. cit.*, p. 174, 228).

[5] MOFA, Foreign Policy Bureau, *Kokusaikikan Soran (Overview of International Organizations), IMF*, Japan Institute of International Affairs, June 1996, p. 509.

Meanwhile, as we saw in Chapter 9, Japan was fundamentally shaken by the oil crisis in 1973. The foundation of the world economy was shaken as well.

From the point of view of macroeconomic policy, OECD emphasized in particular the need for curbing inflation and enhancing coordination among the key leading economies of the world. In fact, under the new economic situation of high inflation, high unemployment and a balance of payments deficit, real policy coordination among the leading industrialized countries became more important than ever. French President Giscard D'Estaing took the initiative to convene a summit meeting of the leading industrialized countries in November 1975 at Rambouillet in France. Japan was invited to this forum right from the beginning, together with the US, the UK, West Germany and Italy. This was 20 years after Japan joined the United Nations and 12 years since Japan became an equal-footing member of the industrialized democratic countries in 1964. Canada joined in 1976 and the European Community in 1977.[6]

In the following years discussions at the G7 Economic Summit centred around the key issue of combating 'stagflation'—low growth and high inflation—in the world economy. At the London Economic Summit of May 1977 Prime Minister Fukuda took substantial leadership on the theory of 'locomotives', that "countries achieving high growth and a current account surplus should take a leadership role as 'locomotives' in leading the world economy, primarily by continuing high growth and by increasing imports." Japan successfully stabilized its economy after the oil crisis and achieved a 6.3% increase in GNP growth and $4.6 billion in its current account surplus in 1976 (Chapter 9). Thus Prime Minister Fukuda not only pledged a 6.7% increase in GNP growth, but also a $0.7 billion in current account deficits to absorb exports from other suffering nations. Japan was designated, together with the US, which had recorded a trade surplus in 1975[7] (Chapter 3), and West Germany as the three locomotives of the industrialized economy. At the Bonn Economic Summit in July 1978 Prime Minister Fukuda continued to pledge a 7% increase in economic growth and substantially increasing ODA (Chapter 10).[8]

---

[6] http://www.mofa.go.jp/mofaj/gaiko/summit/table/index.html 2003–07–31.
[7] Yabunaka, *op. cit.*, p. 10.
[8] Nakanishi, *op. cit.*, p. 177.

In October 1978 the yen hit a record high of 1$ = 176yen,[9] which was about twice as strong as the original fixed exchange rate of 1$ = 360yen.

Reaganomics, the Plaza Accord and Black Monday

But in 1979 the second oil crisis shook the world and the international economy plunged into three consecutive years of recession (Chapter 9). In particular the American economy suffered from 'stagflation'. President Reagan introduced a substantial tax reduction combined with a high interest rate and a strongly valued dollar to overcome this difficulty. As we saw in Chapter 3, the American economy grew and inflation was curbed, but the twin budgetary and trade deficits exploded and the sharp increase of foreign credit made America a debtor nation.

In order to overcome this situation, in September 1985 the Ministers of Finance of five leading industrialized countries (G5): the US, Japan, West Germany, Great Britain and France, gathered at the Plaza Hotel in New York and agreed on a common monetary policy of devaluing the dollar. This agreement bore concrete results and the dollar was devalued from 1$ = 240yen before the Plaza Accord to 1$ = 150yen in February 1987.[10]

These coordinated efforts, however, did not resolve the problems of the world economy. American twin deficits continued and policy surveillance to keep the level of exchange rates commensurate to the fundamentals of each economy continued. In February 1987 the five countries of the Plaza Accord, joined by Italy and Canada, agreed to the so-called Louvre Accord to "stabilize the exchange rate at the existing level".[11] The yen continued to appreciate and it reached almost 1$ = 120yen by the end of 1987.[12] Thus in a period just over two years the value of the yen almost doubled from 1$ = 240yen before Plaza to 1$ = 120yen after Louvre.

These efforts did not apparently inspire confidence in the world market and in October 1987 the world stock markets plunged into what came to be known as 'Black Monday'. As a part of a world-

---

[9] Ibid., p. 150.
[10] Murata, *op. cit.*, p. 204.
[11] Ibid., p. 216.
[12] Suzuta, *op. cit.*, p. 197.

wide operation to combat the collapse of the stock markets, Japan began to adopt a long-term policy of low interest rates.

Meanwhile in Japan, the rapid appreciation of the yen in turn devalued US bonds and securities and investors began selling them, seeking profitable investments in Japanese markets such as land and securities.

The Plaza Accord and the subsequent strengthening of the yen became one of the major reasons for the Japanese bubble economy in the latter half of the 1980's (Chapter 3). But in addition, the Japanese government policy to keep historically low interest rates further unleashed the yen, which resulted in soaring land and securities prices.

What happened in the 1990's in the Japanese financial situation, after the burst of the bubble economy, has already been described in Chapter 3. The full impact of the inability to overcome the outcome of the collapse of the bubble economy was only acutely felt in Japan in the latter part of the 1990's. During the first half of the 1990's the market continued to show strong confidence in the yen, and the yen crossed the line of 1\$ = 100yen in August 1993. The yen reached its most historic record to date of 1\$ = 79.75yen in April 1995.

3. International trade

The Kennedy Round and the Tokyo Round

GATT negotiations were usually conducted in the form of concentrated multilateral negotiations named 'round negotiations'. Starting from 1947 there had been altogether eight rounds of GATT negotiations. The first five rounds were primarily conducted to reduce tariffs and customs duties.

The sixth round convened from 1964 to 1967 and was named the Kennedy Round. In the field of the reduction of tariffs and customs duties, the creation of the European Community in 1967 became the focal point of negotiations. The US tried to ensure that EC internal tariffs would not become lower than its external tariffs. Negotiations were also conducted with the aim of achieving a 50% reduction in customs duties and it succeeded in achieving an average reduction of 35%. The Kennedy Round brought—for the first time—some attention to the problem of non-tariff barriers and an anti-dumping agreement was concluded.[13] During the 1960's Japan still had numerous items subjected to import restrictions. Although their numbers declined at the beginning of the 1970's they had not reached the level of other advanced industrialized countries.[14]

The seventh round of GATT negotiations conducted from 1973 to 1979 became an important round to roll back the temptation of protectionism when the world economy suffered from the first oil crisis. It also became an important round for Japan. Japan took the initiative to hold a ministerial meeting in September 1973 to inaugurate this round in Tokyo and it came to be called the Tokyo Round. Japan made efforts not only in this symbolic function, but also in reducing its tariff barriers during the difficult years after the first oil crisis. After the Tokyo Round, the average tariff rate attributed to foreign industrial products in Japan became one of the lowest among GATT member countries.

The Tokyo Round also became an important turning point in the history of GATT. It became the first round which devoted substantial energy and attention to the problem of non-tariff barriers. Altogether eleven treaties were concluded on the problems regarding non-tariff barriers,[15] such as anti-dumping, subsidies and countervailing duties, import permit procedures, government procurement, and civil aviation, etc.[16]

The Uruguay Round and the World Trade Organization

During the first half of the 1980's, when the world economy was suffering from the second oil crisis, conditions became ripe for the major economies to hold another major GATT round to tackle fundamental issues of the world economy.

For the United States, the resolution of the twin deficits and debtor nation status issues could not be left solely to the devaluation of the dollar and sectoral trade negotiations primarily with Japan. Further

---

[13] Kokusaihou Jiten (Dictionary of International Law), I. Mamiya, *Bouekishouheki (Trade Barriers)*, Sanseido, 1995, pp. 715–716.

[14] Tadokoro, *op. cit.*, p. 117.

[15] Kokusaihou Jiten (Dictionary of International Law), A. Shimizu, *GATT*, *op. cit.*, p. 146.

[16] Kokusaihou Jiten (Dictionary of International Law), I. Mamiya, *Tokyo Round of multilateral trade negotiations*, *op. cit.*, p. 577.

efforts were needed to strengthen the world trade and economic order through free and multilateral trade to ensure the expansion of the global economy, at the centre of which was the US economy. In particular, it became vitally important for the US administration to create new rules for such issues that had previously been neglected, such as agriculture, investment, services and intellectual property where America had developed a comparative advantage. That was also a worthwhile agenda for American political leaders and businessmen.

For Europe, which had been amidst a dynamic process of unification, it was critically important that the newly emerging unified Europe would be accepted by other major entities of the global economy and harmonized with existing world economic order. A new global round could serve Europe with such opportunities.

For Japan, the overall situation was not easy. Japan's trade surplus continued to accrue, the yen rose sharply, in particular, after the Plaza Accord and GDP grew by approximately 4%. Bilateral trade conflicts were heightened with America and Europe. Amidst this difficult period of trade disputes, it was particularly important for Japan to maintain the sound development of a free and multilateral trade system. It was indeed Japan that took the initiatives in convening the Uruguay Round, backed up strongly by America. Europe and other developing countries joined gradually.[17]

In September 1986 Foreign Minister Kuranari headed the Japanese delegation to participate in the inaugural meeting of the eighth round of GATT negotiations held in Uruguay. It was the first trip abroad for the Minister. The distance between Uruguay and Tokyo was vast; the travel time was almost 48 hours. Punta Del Este is a sea resort a few hours drive from the airport. Upon arrival, an exhausted Minister and his secretary (myself) were greeted with fresh breezes and ocean waves from the Atlantic. Given the positive role Japan had taken in inaugurating this round, it was no coincidence that the honour of naming this round the 'Uruguay Round' was given to my Minister in his opening speech on 15 September, the first day of the plenary session.

---

[17] M. Mizoguchi & M. Matsuo, *Uruguay Round*, NHK, 1994, pp. 32–40.

But the six days of negotiations in Punta Del Este were so tough for the Minister that he had hardly any time to enjoy the beauty of this resort. Agriculture was one of the highlights, but the major battle was conducted on the question of export subsidies between Europe and the Cairns group, as we will see below. Japan was not its focal point. New areas such as services were another key point of negotiations, but here Japan took positive initiatives in good harmony with the US delegation and made efforts to find a compromise acceptable to the developing countries. The most difficult issue was related to the nature of trade, proposed by the Europeans based on a new principle of 'Balance of Benefits (BOB)'. It clearly originated from European frustrations about the menacing character of Japanese trade. But this new concept just entailed endless discussions such as how to measure a 'Balance of Benefits' and it was totally unacceptable to Japan. Discussions reached such a tense point that the Japanese delegation counter-argued that Europe was trying to 'Bash Oriental Bums'. This counterargument was received favourably, particularly among Asian countries and BOB did not appear at all in the final communiqué.[18]

The Uruguay Round had been extended three times and finally was concluded on 15 April 1994 with a ceremonial signing of the Marrakesh Agreement establishing the World Trade Organization (WTO). The WTO formally began to function from 1 January 1995. Let us look at five salient points of this final round of GATT, which lasted for seven years and seven months, the longest round in the history of GATT:

(1) First, what really happened in the traditional agenda on trade? On the structural side, the so called 'Single Undertaking', which obligated all participant countries to undertake all WTO documents and obligations without exception was agreed. Another so-called 'grandfather's clause', which allowed the precedence of existing domestic law over such principles as National Treatment, was eliminated.

---

[18] My memory coincides exactly with that of a leading member of the Japanese delegation, Ambassador M. Mizoguchi (Ibid., pp. 22–23).

Thus the universality of the principles of free trade was strengthened.[19]

On the substantive side, the average tariff on non-agricultural products of the developed countries as calculated by the GATT Secretariat in accordance with the annexes to the Marrakesh Protocol would be reduced by 40%, from 6.3% before the Uruguay Round to 3.8% thereafter. Concessionary items would be enlarged to 99% from 78% in the case of the developed countries, and to 73% from 21% in the case of the developing countries.[20]

Japan made no small contributions in achieving these results. The reduction of the average tariffs on non-agricultural products in Japan was calculated at 56%, from 3.9% to 1.7% after the Uruguay Round.[21] Japan's initiative to convene the Tokyo Ministerial Meeting in July 1993 and, in particular, to agree among the US, the EC, Canada and Japan on eight areas of reciprocal tariffs' abolition, gave a substantial impetus to advance the negotiations toward the end of 1993.[22]

(2) Second, there was the issue of agriculture. Given the reality that for many countries agriculture constituted an important part of the internal economic, political and social structure, agricultural products had never fallen under such strict rulings as were applied to industrial products. For the first time in GATT history the Uruguay Round introduced a common ruling on all agricultural products, as an integral part of international trade. Agricultural exporting countries, the leader of which was America supported by the so-called 'Cairns Group'[23] were at the forefront of this direction. Japan and the EC, which were basically agricultural importing countries, opposed the introduction of too rigid a ruling. Thus, agriculture became one of the most difficult issues throughout the Uruguay Round and the primary reason for prolonging the negotiations.

---

[19] MOFA, First International Organizations Division, Economic Affairs Department, *Kaisetsu WTO Kyoutei, (Commentary on WTO Agreements)*, Japan Institute of International Affairs, May 1996, p. 14.

[20] Ibid., p. 92.

[21] Ibid.

[22] The 8 areas are: medicines, construction equipment, medical equipment, steel, furniture, agricultural machinery, beer, and whisky + brandy. Later in the process of the autumn negotiations, an agreement was also reached on paper and pulp and toys (Ibid., p. 91).

[23] For Japan, the political implication of the relationship with this group could not be underestimated. It was comprised of the most important countries of the Pacific region: Canada, Australia, New Zealand, Fiji, Thailand, the Philippines, Malaysia, Indonesia, Argentine, Brazil, Chile, Colombia, Uruguay, and Hungary (Mizoguchi & Matsuo, *op. cit.*, p. 156).

As mentioned above, one of the key issues discussed was the question of the abolition of export subsidies, implemented in European countries. Harsh debates took place in particular between Europe and the Cairns group.

But for Japan there was the issue of rice. Rice was traditionally the major nourishment for the Japanese people. It was the number one crop in Japan's farming industry and took a central position in the Japanese agrarian society throughout its history. Not only for the farmers who were directly involved in the production of rice, but also for many Japanese who were born in rural districts, the green and serene rice paddies which stretched narrowly at the foothills of the surrounding mountains held a special position in their childhood memories. In the period of rapid industrialization rice paddies began to bear a special significance in the preservation of nature as well.

Domestic political reasons also need to be mentioned. Since many deputies of the ruling Liberal Democratic Party were elected from rural districts, advocating a policy clearly against the interests of their own constituency was not an easy decision for any member of parliament.

At the same time, labour-intensive Japanese rice produced on a small scale for many centuries became expensive. Price-wise, it could not compete with the rice produced on a much larger scale in California or Thailand with the use of advanced technology. An understandable fear that an avalanche of rice imports from abroad could ruin the rice production and the basis of Japanese agriculture grasped the mind of Japanese farmers and politicians representing their interests. This inherent fear, however, developed into a rigid, fixed and emotional position that a single grain of imported rice would be the beginning of an avalanche which would eventually ruin Japanese agriculture. Not a single grain of rice was allowed to be imported. That was the situation the Japanese government found itself in at the time when the Uruguay Round started.

The general trend of negotiations at the Uruguay Round was far from supportive of the extreme Japanese position. Europe was sympathetic to measures which would protect the basis of agriculture, but the logic of 'a single grain of rice imports will result in an avalanche', resembling the image of 'a drop of water in a dike will destroy the whole *polder*', simply did not fly. The emerging consensus was that all agricultural products should be put under the GATT system of tariffs and that tariffs shall be reduced on average by 36%

within 6 years, with a minimum reduction of 15% for each product. Given the seriousness of the situation, Japan tried to keep rice under the quantitative restriction of 'minimum access', but it was already too late to command the sympathy of the negotiating partners. In December 1993, at the final stage of the negotiations, a proposal of ultimate compromise was launched by the chairman of the Market Access Group to make rice an item for exception, to allow a period of six years under quantitative restriction, to apply minimum access of 4% to 8% during this six year period, and to leave the regime open for the period starting from the seventh year.

On 14 December Japan accepted this proposal and also decided to accept a tariffs regime on all other agricultural products. Japan's decision became the last thing standing in the way of America and Europe in resolving their outstanding differences and on 15 December a de facto agreement was finally reached on all issues pertaining to the Uruguay Round.[24]

(3) Third, the Uruguay Round expanded its scope to such new areas as services, intellectual property and investment. All these important economic and business activities had not been covered under the traditional GATT ruling. The Uruguay Round broke the barrier.

Services cover a vital part of the economy, particularly for the developed countries. It is usually defined as an invisible transaction such as finance, transportation, communication, circulation, medicine, education and construction.[25] A list of the percentage of services in GDP prior to the Marrakesh agreement is shown below:

Percentage of Services in GDP 1980–1991[26]						
	Japan	Canada	France	Germany	Italy	England	America
1980	54.4	63.2	62.0	55.2	55.2	61.6	63.8
1991	56.1	68.5	68.2	59.8	64.6	68.7	68.8

Services are taking up an increasingly important position within global trade. Its share in international trade was 17% in 1980 and 21% in 1992.[27]

---

[24] Mizoguchi & Matsuo, *op. cit.*, p. 146, pp. 162–163, pp. 167–169.
[25] Ibid., pp. 94–96.
[26] Ibid., p. 98.
[27] Ibid., p. 99.

Against this background services had been discussed extensively during the Uruguay Round and the General Agreement on Trade in Services was concluded as an important part of the Marrakesh Agreement. Concrete agreements were reached in the areas of movement of natural persons, air transport, finance, maritime transport, basic telecommunications and professional services.[28] Throughout the negotiations Japan took a positive and leading position with a view to engendering a new multilateral framework to govern this important part of international trade. At the same time, Japan made its views clear not to be too demanding on concrete steps for liberalization, given the fact that the Uruguay Round was just the first occasion to introduce an international ruling in this new area. These Japanese initiatives were appreciated particularly by the developing countries.[29]

On the question of intellectual property the Agreement on the Trade-Related Aspects of Intellectual Property Rights (TRIP) was signed in Marrakesh. Japan, which relied heavily on technology for its economic development gave positive support to the conclusion of this agreement.[30] The Marrakesh Agreement also comprised of the Agreement on Trade-Related Investment Measures (TRIM) to govern international flows of investment, an entirely new development in the rule-making of the international economy.

(4) Fourth, the Uruguay Round marked a significant improvement by establishing a new Understanding of the Rules and Procedures Governing the Settlement of Disputes. Unlike the Tokyo Round, where different types of settlement were foreseen, subject to differing types of disputes, the new Understanding covered all disputes under a single criterion in the Marrakesh Agreement. The main features of this new Understanding are the introduction of a time limit; increased automatic nature of settlement such as the 'negative consensus approach',[31] and the contracting party's obligation to have

---

[28] MOFA, Services Trade Division, Economic Affairs Department, *WTO Sabisu Boueki Ippan Kyoutei (WTO GATS)*, Japan institute of International Affairs, 1997, p. vii.

[29] Mizoguchi & Matsuo, *op. cit.*, pp. 109, 209.

[30] Ibid., p. 210.

[31] It means that, unless it is decided positively by consensus that a conclusion of a committee or an approval of a countermeasure shall not be adopted, that

recourse only to the rules and procedures under this Understanding.[32]

During the latter part of the 1980's many instances occurred where America and the EC presented cases to the dispute settlement procedure of GATT. Cases were filed against Japan as well. For a while, Japan also saw the usefulness of this mechanism and at a time when the Uruguay Round negotiations were in full swing filed cases against the EC on the spare part dumping regulation in 1988 and the audio cassette case in 1992. The critical negotiations on auto and auto-parts with the US in 1995 were about to be brought to the WTO dispute settlement mechanism. It was a change in Japan's attitude to utilize the WTO dispute settlement mechanism for its own interest. But by 2001, although 225 cases were filed at the WTO trade disputes settlement mechanism, Japan filed only eight cases.[33]

(5) Fifth, the Uruguay Round coincided with the period of regional economic integration. Europe was undergoing a dynamic process of the Single European Act in 1987 and the Treaty of Maastricht agreed in 1991, signed in 1992 and entered into force in 1993 (Chapter 6). In America the US-Canada Free Trade Agreement was signed in January 1988 and entered into force in January 1989. The North American Free Trade Agreement (NAFTA) came to be negotiated between the US, Canada and Mexico from June 1990, was signed in December 1992, and entered into force in January 1994, just before the signature of the Marrakesh Agreement.

In this period of enhanced regionalism Japan had to think and act. The first question was: what position had Japan to take and what message did Japan have to give toward the newly established regional institutions in Europe and America? The key answer from Japan was that these new regional institutions should not create greater barriers to the flow of goods and services in the international economy. On the contrary, they should free the international economy and should be compatible with the principles and practices of GATT/WTO.

---

conclusion or approval prevails (MOFA First International Organization Division, *op. cit.*, p. 14).

[32] Ibid., p. 588.

[33] Gendaiyogono Kisochishiki (Encyclopedia of contemporary words) 2002, *WTOni Teisono Bouekifunsouanken (Trade Disputes filed to WTO)*, LogoVista.

The second question Japan had to answer was: how to think and to act in Japan's own region, the Asia-Pacific region? APEC was the answer, created with an underlying Japanese initiative in 1989, but with a typical Asian way of consensus and step by step approach (Chapter 6).

The Doha New Round

During the latter part of the 1990's the American economy was booming, Europe was preoccupied with the creation of the euro and the further deepening and expansion of the European Union, while Japan struggled through the legacy of the bubble economy and non-performing loans.

Meanwhile, the time frame agreed upon in Marrakesh for the six-year implementation period of Agreement on Agriculture was to expire by the end of 2000 and negotiations for continuing the process were to be initiated one year earlier, i.e. from the beginning of 2000.[34] In such a situation the US took the initiative that the new round should begin not only in agriculture, but also in all pertinent areas of WTO activities. The Seattle Ministerial Meeting in December 1999 should have inaugurated a comprehensive new round, as declared by President Clinton. The Seattle Meeting, however, collapsed, void of any agreement for a comprehensive round. Dissatisfaction among the developing countries; acute last minute conflicts regarding labour issues (the US wanted to prioritize it whereas the developing countries strongly objected its prioritization); division over anti-dumping legislation (many developed and developing countries agreed to include it in the agenda against a total rejection by the US); and huge NGO protests and demonstrations outside the conference finally led to this collapse.[35]

For Japan the collapse in Seattle was an unexpected blow. Japan in fact had many reasons to support America's comprehensive approach to the new round. Limiting the focus of the agenda to agriculture could have highlighted the 'protective' nature of Japanese agricultural policy. There were many areas where Japan wanted to further

---

[34] Agreement on Agriculture, Article 1 (f) and Article 20 (MOFA First International Organizations Division, *op. cit.*, pp. 126–127).
[35] Saga Shinbun, *Kyodo*, 5 December 1999.

strengthen the WTO ruling and the principle of free trade in the era of globalization, such as services, investment, trade ruling which harmonises with environment and consumer security and anti-dumping legislation.

Another crucial lesson to be learnt from Seattle was the issue of developing countries. Developing countries viewed the outcome of the Uruguay Round as having unfairly represented the interests of developed countries. Globalization engendered more serious divisions between the rich and the poor. The way things were handled in Seattle did not help in resolving their problems at all. The global economic community would enter into serious difficulty if the requests from the developing countries were not met adequately and quickly.

Against this background, the terrorist attack on September 11 triggered anxiety among WTO member countries on the danger of letting the WTO drift away. A deepening of the divisions between the developed and the developing countries in the age of globalization could have become one reason for fostering terrorists. Rules and principles which would satisfy the developing countries in principle have to be brought about and the developing countries should be firmly incorporated into the full process of WTO. This new process will, in the long run, help eliminate the seeds of fanaticism and extremism.[36] Such were Japan's views and so were the views of the ministers gathered in Doha, Qatar, in November 2001. An agreement was finally reached there to inaugurate a new round and the task of this new round was named the 'Doha Development Agenda'.

The Doha ministerial meeting formally invited China and Taiwan as WTO members and they became official members of the WTO in December 2001 and January 2002, respectively.

The home pages of MOFA, METI, and the Ministry of Agriculture, Forestry and Fisheries (MAFF) are full of encouraging messages to participate with vigour and sincerity in the Doha New Round. Some of the highlights of these messages at the end of 2002 are the following:

(1) MOFA emphasizes the importance of dealing squarely with the developing countries. Developing countries occupy three quarters

---

[36] MOFA, *WTOniokeru Kihonteki Senryaku, (Basic Strategy for WTO)*, "2. Why did the New Round begin?", 4 October 2002 (www.mofa.go.jp/mofaj/gaiko/wto/new_r_soron. html 2002–11–26).

of the WTO and they consider that the unfair agreement reached at the Uruguay Round cannot be repeated in the Doha Round. It is essential to ensure 'capacity building' of the developing countries, so that they would be equipped with the necessary power to observe the WTO rules. This 'capacity building' and active participation of developing countries in the WTO are in the precise interests of Japan, so declare the MOFA homepages.[37]

(2) After the agonizing decision on rice at the Uruguay Round to introduce a new system of quantitative restriction of 'minimum access', Japan moved into the long debated tariffs system in April 1999. The decision was taken nearly two years earlier than the expiry of the allowance period of six years. It was based on the assumption that the envisaged tariffs structure would import less rice than the continued system of 'minimum access' under quantitative restriction.

The most emotional stage might thus be over, but the level of optimal protection for expensive Japanese agriculture is far from being found. The fundamentals of Japanese rural life have to be protected, but reasonable competition with cheaper imported agricultural products has to be met as well.

Both MOFA and MAFF state that agriculture will become one of the crucially important subjects in the Doha Round.

In December 2000 Japan submitted its basic proposal on agriculture to the WTO. It announced five basic areas where due attention has to be paid: "1) consideration of the multifunctionality of agriculture, 2) ensuring food security, which is the basis of society in each country, 3) redressing the imbalance between rules and disciplines applied to agricultural exporting countries and those applied to importing countries, 4) consideration for developing countries, and 5) consideration for the consumers and the civil society."[38]

MAFF explains with colourful pictures the Japanese countryside, illustrating the essence of the multifunctionality of agriculture: maintenance of land, water resources, environment, scenery, culture, leisure and relaxation, regional community, and food security.[39] At the same time the MAFF homepage states that the Japanese proposal was met with sympathy by the EU, Korea and other likeminded countries,

---

[37] Ibid., "4. Concrete strategy".
[38] http://www.maff.go.jp/wto/wto_nihon_teian_e.html 2002–11–27.
[39] http://www.maff.go.jp/wto/iken/tamenteki.pdf 2002–11–27.

but was severely criticized by the US and the Cairns Group because of its protective nature that it went against the basic direction of reducing protection and subsidies in agriculture.[40]

(3) Both MOFA and METI devoted a fair amount of space in their homepages to Japan's approach to the Free Trade Agreement (FTA). After long and cautious deliberations, Japan concluded the first FTA with Singapore in January 2002 and moved to the next stage of negotiations with Mexico, ASEAN and Korea (Chapter 6). Japan considers that the FTA necessitates a strong WTO so as to avoid any trade distortion impact. MOFA states that WTO and FTA should be developed in parallel and supplement each other.[41] METI observes that WTO, FTA and other bilateral arrangements should compose a multilayered structure to allow a flexible implementation of external economic policy. The two Ministries seem to be very much in harmony on those basic principles.[42]

The WTO negotiations are moving with difficulty. As envisaged, agriculture and relations between the developed and developing countries became the two most contentious issues.

On agriculture, by March 2003, the Modality, that is the basic rule to be applied to all agricultural products and all countries, failed to be agreed upon. The Japanese media reported the danger that Japan's agricultural policy may hinder the achievement of an overall consensus and a too cautious policy, as a final resort, would not be to Japan's benefit.[43]

The US and EU began converging their position on agriculture before the Ministerial Meeting in Cancun, Mexico. But ultimately on 14 September 2003 the Cancun Meeting adjourned without an accord, due to the split between the developing and the developed countries.[44]

Observers began debating about the fate of Doha Round to be concluded by 1 January 2005.

<hr />

[40] http://www.maff.go.jp/wto/wto_agri_kousyou2.htm 2002-11-27.
[41] MOFA, *WTOniokeru Kihonteki Senryaku, (Basic Strategy for WTO), op. cit.*, "4. Concrete Strategy".
[42] METI, *Tsushou Hakusho (METI White Paper)* 2001, Chapter 4 > 3 > 3 > (1).
[43] *Yomiuri Shinbun*, 3 August 2003.
[44] *Asahi Shinbun*, 17 September 2003.

4. *Economic assistance through multilateral organizations*

Multilayered activities of numerous organizations

Since the postwar period, when the major developed countries discussed macroeconomic policy or trade issues so as to ensure the most dynamic development of the global economy, the question of the developing countries, or the question of development in general, was one of the key issues in their deliberations. What is happening in the Doha Round is exemplary, but it was so in IMF, OECD, G7, GATT, not to mention other development related organizations. Japan has tried to actively participate in the tasks conducted by these organizations, not only in its financial contribution, but also in influencing the direction of these organizations to follow Japan's philosophy regarding economic assistance.

UNCTAD was particularly active in the 1960's and 1970's. During the 1960's UNCTAD set forth three major objectives: to conclude commodity agreements on major commodities for which the developing countries seek stabilization of prices (nine such agreements have been concluded thus far); to establish a preferential tariff system for the developing countries called the Generalized System of Preferences (GSP; three rounds of GSP were committed since the 1970's for 30 years); to establish a country-wise objective of 0.7% ODA ratio in proportion to GNP (DAC average figure has reached only 0.22% in 2000).

IMF shifted its activities in helping the developing countries after the world financial system moved to floating exchange system. IMF had established new facilities, such as the stand-by arrangement (for ordinary situations), the extended fund facility (for long-term structural adjustments) and the supplemental reserve facility (for financial crises). The structural adjustment facility and the enhanced structural adjustment facility were established in 1986 and 1987, respectively, to cope with structural problems of middle-term nature. The systemic transformation facility was also established to assist the financial needs of countries in transition from a socialist to a market economy from 1993 to 1995. The 1994–95 Mexican and 1997–98 Asian financial crises were another challenge for IMF.[45]

---

[45] Gendaiyougono Kisochishiki (Encyclopedia of contemporary words) 2002, *IMF Yuushi (IMF financing)*, *op. cit.*

IMF assistance based on various facilities was made available to developing countries which faced with financial difficulties, provided that an economic stabilization plan established by IMF was observed. IMF played a central role in resolving accumulated debt issues in the developing countries in the 1980's through the establishment and monitoring of an economic stabilization plan.

By the 1980's Japan had become an active contributor to IMF facilities, fifth as a contributor, and second from 1992 together with Germany.[46] Strict conditionality required in IMF finance was a point of polemics among the donors and recipient countries. The IMF approach did not necessarily coincide with Japan's aid philosophy of 'self-help' and 'request first principle'. There was a debate within the Japanese administration during the first half of the 1990's whether a more flexible assistance principle could not be created regarding Russia and former Soviet countries, different from the IMF conditionality approach, and taking into account some inevitable local conditions. Stimulating though it was, Japan's position was not so well crystallized as to govern the aid philosophy toward these countries.

In 2000 the UNDP published a report entitled 'Human Rights and Human Development', in which it emphasized the critical role which 'human resources development' and 'respect of human rights' would play in the process of development. The work in UNDP was a publication in its series of reports on human development which UNDP has been publishing since 1990. It was resonant with the basic philosophy of Japan's ODA.[47]

Globalization and deeper division between the developed and developing countries

Since the 1990's, the global economy has faced a new dimension of 'globalization'. Activities of transnational corporations were the driving forces behind this globalization. Dynamic movements of capital and investments began to create a borderless economy.[48]

---

[46] MOFA Foreign Policy Bureau, *op. cit.*, pp. 508, 512.
[47] Gendaiyougono Kisochishiki (Encyclopedia of contemporary words) 2002, *UNDP*, *op. cit.*
[48] The origin of trans-national corporation dates back to the 60's when American megacompanies began their investments primarily in Europe, under the pressure of Japanese exports and European market-unification.

Technological innovation and development of information and communication technology enhanced the process of globalization. Politically, the end of the Cold War brought about a new perspective for a new global world order.

The impact of globalization first created an impression that discrepancies between the haves and the have-nots would diminish. But in reality discrepancies between the rich and poor became more acute than ever.

The positive and negative aspects of globalization began to attract serious attention from the world leaders, including the Japanese government and opinion leaders.

The adoption of 'Development Partnership Strategy' in 'Shaping the 21st Century: The Contribution of Development Cooperation' issued in May 1996 by DAC was a major effort in tackling the development assistance issue in this new situation. Japan took a substantial lead in adopting this report.

The first contribution made in this report was its urge to establish an assistance programme of a more comprehensive nature, as described in Chapter 10.

In 1999 the World Bank presented the concept of 'Comprehensive Development Framework (CDF)', which also underlined the importance of enhanced cooperation among donor countries and other organizations, based on the ownership of recipient countries and partnership of the donor countries and organizations. Japan naturally lead and supported this approach so resonant to DAC Development Partnership Strategy.[49]

The second contribution made was to squarely face the issue of poverty in the poorest countries, which among the many issues which developing countries face, came to be identified in this period as the most serious issue. The issue of accumulated debts, which had taken up world attention in the 80's now surfaced as a most serious issue in the least developed countries.

In this strategy, the target was set to reduce the poorest world population by half by 2015 including such targets in education, gender equality, child health and environment.

As a concrete implementation of this initiative, the accumulated debt issue of the HIPCs began to be addressed by the international

---

[49] ODA, Q&A Series, Q7, www.mofa.go.jp/gaiko/oda/qa/q7.html 2002-11-19.

community. At the Cologne Summit in 1999 a new initiative was proposed to relieve 41 HIPCs entirely from their ODA debts and 90% from their commercial debts. One calculation indicates that this proposal implies a reduction of $15 billion of ODA debts and $65 billion of commercial debts.[50]

In 2000, the millennium year, several initiatives were taken to more forcefully address these issues pertaining to poverty, particularly of HIPCs, and the negative aspects of globalization.

– From 2000 IMF opened a new facility named the poverty reduction growth facility, which replaced the enhanced structural adjustment facility, addressing the poverty issues of 80 countries. The Extended HIPCs Initiative was also introduced to address the issues of 41 HIPCs.[51]

– In February 2000 the 10th UNCTAD conference was held in Bangkok, urging the developed countries to ensure that globalization would also bring benefits to the developing countries.

– The Okinawa Summit in July 2000 focussed on the issue of globalization and took several initiatives on information and communication technology, infectious diseases, HIPCs, human science, the environment, etc.

– The Millennium Summit was held in September 2000 in New York. The concerns of world leaders centred on the issue of an increasing north-south divide through the rapid globalization. The Declaration adopted at the summit emphasized the need for concrete action so as to fill in this divide.

One aspect in UN Secretary-General K. Annan's report merits attention. He stressed in his report the need to establish 'global governance', so that the fruits of globalization could be shared by all.

The concept of global governance was first highlighted by a committee established by former German Chancellor Willy Brandt in 1992. In the age of globalization, it underlined the importance of creating new governance, based not only on traditional sovereign governments but also on such new entities as civil movements, non-government organizations (NGOs), transnational corporations, mass media, etc.

---

[50] Gendaiyougono Kisochishiki (Encyclopedia of contemporary words) 2002, *Köln Summit*.

[51] Ibid., *IBRD to IMF no Hinkon-taisaku (Measures against poverty in IBRD and IMF)*.

Japan was not the first country to have recognized the important role NGOs can play in the new era. But in 2000 a new organization called the Japan Platform was created as a consultative-cooperative body between the government, corporations and NGOs to enhance the implementation of emergency humanitarian aid. Fine attention was paid to the role of NGOs in holding the Okinawa Summit in 2000. The role of NGOs is becoming increasingly important in Japan in conducting foreign policy, particularly regarding such issues as development, the environment, globalization, etc.

5. New agenda: global environment, population and infectious diseases, and information technology

Global environment and sustainable development

The major direction of postwar economic development as we saw thus far was in the concept of 'growth'. In other words, economic values were in growth, development, and the creation of a greater amount of goods and services to be enjoyed by the people of the world.

At the same time there emerged such views which point out the limitations to growth and development. The first example we saw was energy. The two oil crises in the 1970's gave a clear message that energy resources are limited and that there is a need for many specific energy policies, such as conservation and the development of alternative energy to cope with this inherent limitation.

During the 1980's there emerged a new area where serious limitation to growth and development came to be recognized. The environment was the issue. Japan proposed to establish a committee on environment and development under the auspices of the United Nations and in 1987 this committee finalized its report entitled 'Our Common Future'. This was the first pronouncement of the concept of 'sustainable growth', i.e. people of the current generation should be able to enjoy the fruits of development, but only to the extent that the development is sustainable so as to allow future generations to also enjoy the fruits of development. Without the adequate preservation of the environment, future generations will not be able to enjoy the fruits of development.[52]

---

[52] Gendaiyougono Kisochishiki (Encyclopedia of contemporary words) 2002, *Jizokukanouna Kaihatsu (Sustainable Development)*, op. cit.

The United Nations Conference on Environment and Development, sometimes called the Earth Summit, was held in Rio de Janeiro in 1992. The Japanese delegation took an active part in realizing, in concrete terms, the concept of sustainable growth. In fact, there were several reasons why Japan was so active on environmental problems.

(1) During the decades of rapid economic growth Japan itself went through a horrible period of environmental contamination. Such unforgivable incidents of river pollution at the Minamata district by petrochemical waste came to be disclosed in the first half of the 1960's. Heavy Tokyo smog in the years of heightened economic development, which made it impossible for school children to play in courtyards in summer, left Japan with a clear memory that these environmental failures could not and should not be repeated.

(2) Series of measures and regulations were introduced and Japan became a country with successful anti-pollution legislation. The rivers and air in major Japanese cities were considerably cleaner over the 1990's in comparison to the situation in the 1960's and 1970's.

(3) Issues of global warming and acid rain began to catch the attention of the Japanese people. A feeling that something had to be done was felt much more acutely in the 1990's.

These experiences have developed the growing recognition among the Japanese people that Japan has to make further contributions to resolve such global issues, which mankind faces at the beginning of the new century. Japan must make the most of its own experience, financial strength and the willingness of the people to make concrete contributions. The environment became one of the most representative issues for Japan in overcoming the limitation of growth and development.

On the issue of global warming the Framework Convention on Climate Change, that was adopted in 1992 and entered into force in 1994, agreed to stabilize the greenhouse gases. Japan took a major initiative in December 1997 to host the third Conference of Parties (COP3) to the Framework Convention in Kyoto and succeeded in determining a quantitative target for the reduction of greenhouse gases. Since then Japan continued to make sincere efforts toward the early effectuation of the Kyoto Protocol and the determination of concrete rules for its implementation.[53]

---

[53] http://www.mofa.go.jp/mofaj/gaiko/kankyo/genjo.html 2003–08–02.

But the more concrete the agreement became the greater the difficulties have become. Environmentally meaningful reductions of greenhouse gases had to be harmonized with not-unduly-oppressed economic development.

Japan put particular efforts into trying to find a consensus point, which would allow the United States to join the Kyoto Protocol, but the US was not prepared to share the burden for fear of a negative impact on its own economic development. The Bush administration backed away.

The developing countries, on the other hand, considered that the burden of reduction of greenhouse gasses had to be born exclusively by the developed countries. While acknowledging an adequate share of responsibility, Japan also maintained that global warming had an additional detrimental impact on the economy of developing countries. Such issues as desertification or destruction of forests cannot be properly dealt with without serious participation by the developing countries themselves.

Japan put the Kyoto Protocol into force in June 2002.[54]

In June 2002 at the World Summit on Sustainable Development in Johannesburg, Prime Minister Koizumi launched a new initiative named the 'Environmental Conservation Initiative for Sustainable Development'. Human Security, Ownership and Partnership, and Pursuit of Environmental Conservation and Development are the three key concepts of this initiative. Concrete new initiatives such as educating 5,000 environmental experts in five years, starting from 2002, were also announced.[55]

Population and infectious diseases

The growing world population has long been a serious and long-term concern for world economic development. In 1998 the United Nations gave an estimate for a world population of 6.1 billion in 2000, 7.8 billion in 2025, and 8.9 billion in 2050.[56] The majority of this increase is expected to occur in the developing countries.

---

[54] http://www.mofa.go.jp/mofaj/press/danwa/14/dkw_0604.html 2002–11–26.

[55] http://www.mofa.go.jp/mofaj/gaiko/oda/seisaku/seisaku_2/wssd_gai.html 2003–08–02.

[56] Gendaiyougono Kisochishiki (Encyclopedia of contemporary words) 2002, *The UN Special General Assembly on Population and Development*.

How to curb this growth? What is the position of women in society, their education and their ability to practise birth control? Can the world economy achieve stable development without a stable perspective on population growth? These questions were debated in the International Conference on Population and Development, first held in Bucharest in 1974, in Mexico in 1984 and in Cairo in 1994. The Cairo Conference became a landmark conference in recognizing the population issue as an integral part of the problem of sustainable development. In 1999 the UN Special General Assembly on Population and Development was held to follow up the results of the Cairo Conference.

Japan has actively followed and participated in these efforts by the international community. At the same time, Japan found another critical issue related to world population, e.g. the issue of infectious diseases such as HIV/aids. Infectious disease had to be controlled from the humanitarian point of view, as well as from the point of view of ensuring the stable growth of the world population. Japan set up special ODA initiatives by contributing $3 billion to a 'Global Initiative on Population and HIV/aids' from 1994 to 2000. Japan actually made a contribution of $3.7 billion by the end of 1998.

At the Okinawa G7/G8 Summit in 2000 Japan took a careful look at the problems of infectious disease, where, on a yearly basis, three million are dying from HIV/aids, two million from tuberculosis, and one million from malaria. Japan pledged another $3 billion in contributions to combat these diseases in the five years ahead.[57]

Information technology

I need to mention a few words on information technology (IT) before concluding this chapter. At the beginning of the 21st century, it is not yet clear what impact IT could have upon the development of the global economy. But it has become evident that it has had a profound impact on the growth and nature of the global economy. In particular IT is affecting globalization in its ability to create an entirely new form of trans-border communication. But IT has already created a serious issue of the digital divide, where those who are unable to catch up with the new IT culture and way of life are

---

[57] www.mofa.go.jp/mofaj/gaiko/kansen/kansen.html 2002-11-26.

rapidly left behind. Some of the developing countries are presently in such situations, or strongly fear they will soon face it.

Thus in Okinawa in 2000, Japan made significant efforts in resolving the negative impacts of globalization and enhance its positive impact in the area of IT. So as to fill the gap in the digital divide between IT-developed countries and IT-underdeveloped countries, in July 2000 just prior to the Okinawa Summit, Japan announced an assistance programme of $15 billion in five years. The four pillars of this programme were intellectual assistance, strengthening the basis for information and communication, human resources development, and utilization of IT in the process of assistance.[58]

---

[58] www.mofa.go.jp/mofaj/gaiko/summit/ko_2000/genoa/it_1.html 2002-11-26.

CHAPTER TWELVE

MULTILATERAL POLITICAL DIPLOMACY:
THE UNITED NATIONS AND
PEACEKEEPING OPERATIONS

1. *Joining the United Nations*

During World War II discussions had already started among the Allied Powers to establish a new organization to replace the League of Nations in order to maintain international peace and security. From April to June 1945 the Charter of the United Nations was drafted in San Francisco, signed on 26 June and entered into force on 24 October 1945, with 51 countries as founding members.

After the San Francisco Peace Treaty came into force in April 1952, joining the United Nations became a priority for Japanese foreign policy. Politically, joining the United Nations meant recognition for Japan as a legitimate member of the international community. Japan no doubt strongly desired that. But from the point of view of Japan's security policy it entailed some complexity, which to this date is leaving traces in Japan's security-defence policy.

Under the United Nations Charter all members of the UN are obligated to "refrain from the threat or use of force (Article 2–4)", with two exceptions: the first is "such action by air, sea, or land forces as may be necessary to maintain or restore international peace and security (Article 42, Chapter VII)" taken by the Security Council and the second is "the inherent right of individual or collective self-defence (Article 51)". Not only were these two exceptions acknowledged, UN member countries were obligated to "undertake to make available to the Security Council, on its call and in accordance with a special agreement or agreements, armed forces, assistance, and facilities—(Article 43, Chapter VII)".

But Article 9 of the Constitution of Japan "renounces war as a sovereign right of the nation" and does not recognize "the right of belligerency". The accepted interpretation of Article 9 was that the right of individual self-defence can only be exerted. In terms of Article 51, it meant that the exertion of the right to collective self-

defence was not allowed. That aspect did not create problems for
Japan in joining the United Nations. But in terms of the other aspect,
the right and obligation under Chapter VII, the issue was not that
simple.

Analysts say[1] that at the time Japan applied to the UN, there were
views by the government that Japan would not be able to fulfil its
obligation under Article 43 because of Article 9 of the Constitution
and that adequate reservations had to be made at the time of the
application. But after careful deliberation the Japanese government
formulated the following position in the letter written by Katsuo
Okazaki, Minister of Foreign Affairs as of 16 June 1952:

> The government of Japan hereby accepts the obligations contained in
> the Charter of the United Nations, and undertakes to honour them,
> by all means at its disposal from the day when Japan becomes a mem-
> ber of the United Nations.[2]

Since then the government has taken the position that this part
does not imply reservations because the obligation under Chapter
VII, Article 43 is discharged in accordance with a special agreement
and that Japan's constitutional problem could be dealt with in that
agreement.[3]

However, the issue of constitutional limitation and Japan's obligation based on the UN Charter have not ceased to be widely debated
in Japan. In that context, one cannot deny that the critical part of
Foreign Minister Okazaki's letter—"by all means at its disposal"—
has left a certain ambiguity. The Japanese government has also continuously argued that since Chapter VII UN forces were never
established, Japan's final disposition to these forces is "under study".[4]
Whatever the intentions of those who formulated these positions
many decades ago, the remaining ambiguity bears an interesting seed
for discussion of future Japanese security policy.

While the Japanese government spent a lot of energy in settling
the constitutional issue in relation to the Japanese application, Japan's

---

[1] Fukushima, *op. cit.*, pp. 56–58.

[2] Ibid., p. 57.

[3] S. Yanai, Director General of the Treaties Bureau, at the House of Councillors,
Settlement Committee, 21 November 1990; Foreign Minister Ikeda, at the House
of Representatives, Foreign Relations Committee, 30 May 1996, No. 10, p. 24.

[4] A. Kudo, Director General of the National Legislation Bureau of the Prime
Minister's Cabinet, at the House of Representatives, Budget Committee, 19 October
1990.

accession to the United Nations was first hampered by the Cold War reality. The Soviet Union exercised its veto. But against the background of the politics of 'thaw', in 1955, Japan's membership received serious consideration. A group accession proposal of 18 countries including Japan was presented to the General Assembly. But the Republic of China (Taiwan) vetoed Mongolia's accession, and the Soviet Union proposed to exclude both Mongolia and Japan from the group of 18 countries.[5]

It was precisely during this period that negotiations on the Peace Treaty between Japan and the Soviet Union began in London. As we have seen in Chapter 7, the Soviet Union withdrew its veto after the conclusion of the Joint Declaration of 1956 and on 18 December 1956 Japan became the 80th country to join the UN.

The United Nations became the driving force behind the Japanese foreign policy immediately after Japan joined the UN. As mentioned in Chapter 6, in February 1957 Foreign Minister Kishi announced in his parliamentary policy speech the three pillars of postwar Japanese foreign policy: 'United Nations-centred diplomacy', 'Cooperation with the free world', and 'Maintaining the position as a member of Asia'. In September 1957 when the first 'Diplomatic Bluebook' was published by the Foreign Ministry, 'United Nations-centred diplomacy' again became one of the three pillars together with the other two.[6]

2. The United Nations during the Cold War

The initial euphoric period of 'United Nations-centred diplomacy' proved to be short-lived.

Partly the waning enthusiasm was due to the inability on the part of the United Nations to function as the guardian of global peace and security.

The Korean War of 1950–53 was probably the only example during the Cold War of UN forces acting effectively, in spite of various criticisms from the socialist countries.

---

[5] Ikei, *op. cit.*, p. 262.
[6] Fukushima, *op. cit.*, p. 80; Sakamoto, *op. cit.*, p. 88. Both Kishi's speech and the Diplomatic Bluebook showed the order of the three principles as UN-Free world-Asia. Although nothing clearly defined that this order meant policy priorities, it might have been a reflection of the political mood then prevailing.

North Korea attacked South Korea on 25 June 1950. The Security Council reacted with the successive Resolutions 82 (25 June), 83 (27 June) and 84 (7 July). These resolutions created the United Nations armed forces and authorized the use of the UN flag. Significantly, unified command of these forces was granted to the United States.

Thus the United Nations armed forces in Korea were not the armed forces created on the basis of Article 42 and 43 of Chapter VII *per se* but they had a substantial 'UN basis'. Under the Cold War climate it could be done only in the absence of the Soviet Union in the successive Security Council meetings that prevented it from exercising its veto power. Whatever the reason for its absence, the Soviet Union must have thought that it could not see further United States led armed forces acting on behalf of the United Nations.

Therefore all subsequent missions or troops organized by the United Nations could not take the form even close to the United Nations Korean forces. Thus UN forces with far more limited functions, intended to maintain or preserve peace after the ceasefire, were created based on specific Security Council resolutions. The activities of these missions or troops became known as 'peacekeeping operations'[7] and they took the form of military observer missions consisting of unarmed officers or peacekeeping forces consisting of troops under UN command.

The first peacekeeping operation mission was sent to the Middle East in 1948, and by the time Japan joined the United Nations in December 1956, there were only three missions of this kind sent to the areas of conflict in the world.[8]

In addition to the limitations on the UN side, Japan's involvement in UN peacekeeping operation missions was limited due to self-imposed restrictions. In July 1958 the US and the UK dispatched troops to Lebanon and Jordan, respectively, in response to the rising tension in the Middle East caused by a revolution in Iraq. Japan,

---

[7] Peacekeeping operations were sometimes called 'Chapter 6 and a half' activities. Chapter 6 of the UN Charter deals with 'Pacific Settlement of Disputes'. Solutions through negotiations or mediation are envisaged. Chapter 7 deals with 'Action with respect to Threats to the Peace, Breaches of the Peace, and Acts of Aggression'. It envisages military and non-military (such as economic sanctions) measures to resolve disputes which went beyond the level of possible peaceful solutions. UN measures taken based on Security Council resolutions discussed in this Section could be construed as being somewhere in between these two Chapters.

[8] From 1948 until 1987 there were only 13 missions of this kind.

which was elected for the first time as a non-permanent member of the Security Council in October 1957, presented a resolution calling for the strengthening of the UN Mission already dispatched there in June 1958 and the withdrawal of American troops. The resolution was vetoed by the Soviet Union, but was appreciated by the international community as a serious attempt by Japan to play an active role in matters of peace and security.

However, when UN Secretary-General Dag Hammarskjöld asked Japan to send ten officers to join the UN military observer mission Japan refused, on the basis that the domestic law which governed the Self-Defence Forces lacked the legal basis for such a dispatch.[9] Sending Self-Defence Forces was not unconstitutional, but politically unacceptable in Japan in 1958. Japan's reaction was inescapably met with disappointment by the UN community.

Thus because of UN limitations and Japan's self-imposed restrictions, the initial enthusiasm toward UN-centred diplomacy in Japan rapidly waned. In fact, the Diplomatic Bluebook refrained from describing UN-centred diplomacy as one of the three pillars of the Japanese foreign policy as early as 1959.[10] Instead of UN-centred diplomacy a new expression 'UN-cooperative diplomacy'[11] began to be used in the foreign ministry's documents.

There were two issues, however, which still caught political attention regarding the United Nations during the Cold War days.

The first issue was the question of China's representation. The anomaly of leaving continental Communist China outside the scope of the UN was increasingly felt and from the 1960's to the beginning of the 1970's this had become a serious issue for deliberation at each UN session in autumn. We have already seen how it was resolved in 1971 in Chapter 4.

The second issue was the question of the composition of the Security Council. During the 1970's, particularly at the time of Detente, Japan began to make explicit statements calling for its inclusion in the Security Council as a permanent member. In spite of self-imposed restrictions in assuming responsibilities for international

---

[9] Sakamoto, *op. cit.*, pp. 89–90.
[10] Fukushima, *op. cit.*, p. 80.
[11] UN-centred diplomacy is *Kokuren Chuushin Gaikou* and UN-cooperative diplomacy is *Kokuren Kyouchou Gaikou*.

peace and security, Japan sought a political role which was commensurate with its growing economic power and its increasing contributions to the UN budget. The political climate under Detente
helped to develop Japan's aspirations. Japan's desire was often expressed
in its call for the need to reform the Security Council.

Foreign Minister Kiichi Aichi and Zentaro Kosaka, respectively,
made statements calling for a reform of the Security Council at the
UN General Assembly in 1971 and in 1976. America expressed open
support of these aspirations. In the Nixon-Tanaka Joint Communiqué
in 1973 and the Carter-Fukuda Joint Communiqué in 1977, explicit
support by the US for Japan's permanent Security Council membership was included.

Japan's interest in the Security Council waned after the Soviet
invasion of Afghanistan in 1979 and following the UN's inability to
resolve this situation.[12]

3. *After the Cold War: UN reforms and Japan*

Gorbachev's assumption of power in the Soviet Union in 1985, the
introduction of his policy of *perestroika* (reconstruction) in internal policy and *novoe myshlenie* (new thinking) in foreign policy, the end of
the Cold War and the demise of the Soviet Union, all of these
unprecedented events opened entirely new perspectives in the work
of the UN. UN peacekeeping activities underwent an impressive
change and the scope of their activities was greatly enlarged from
this period. Japan's participation in UN peacekeeping operations was
substantially enlarged as well. We will analyse these phenomena in
the next Section.

In this new situation where the Security Council began to play a
more substantial role in the international community, Japan's participation in UN peacekeeping activities also became more active.
Greater participation in UN activities, notably in the field of peacekeeping, evoked greater interest in Japan toward UN reforms. These
reforms were perceived in two areas: Security Council reforms and
budget reforms.

---

[12] Fukushima, *op. cit.*, p. 87.

Security Council reforms

The United Nations began in 1945 as an organization with 51 member states, 11 of which were Security Council members (5 permanent members). The member countries increased dramatically throughout the 1960's, particularly as a result of the independence of former colonies and reached 118 in 1965, at which time the Security Council was expanded to 15 countries (5 permanent members). In 2000 the total number of member countries rose to 189.[13] The structure of the Security Council did not change during this period. The Security Council members / UN member countries ratio declined from 22% in 1945, to 13% in 1965, and to 8% in 2000.

There were two major issues in discussing Security Council reform. The first issue was the number of the countries represented therein. Given the importance the Council bears regarding the issues pertaining to international peace and security, a natural desire was expressed to expand the Security Council so that more countries could join and contribute therein.

The second issue was the increase in permanent member countries in the Council. This issue became a matter of primary concern for larger countries like Japan, Germany, and Brazil. The status these new permanent member countries would acquire, for instance on the veto question, was another issue debated in this context.

At the beginning of the 1990's, the issue of Security Council reform became actively debated in New York at the United Nations and in the capitals. In 1993 the General Assembly decided to create an open-ended working group on the questions of equitable representation and increase in membership of the Security Council.

The time had come for Japan to speak out. But to the disappointment of those who expected Japan to express intelligibly what it wanted and what it was prepared to do, Japan's statements were subdued.

Prime Minister Hosokawa came to the United Nations General Assembly in September 1993 and stated that "Japan is prepared to do all it can to discharge its responsibility in the reformed United Nations."[14] This subdued expression was said to have been influenced by Shusei Tanaka, special assistant to the Prime Minister, who did

---

[13] http://www.mofa.go.jp/mofaj/gaiko/jp_un/rekishi.html 2002-12-04.

[14] Fukushima, *op. cit.*, p. 88.

not agree to express directly Japan's wish to become a permanent member of the Security Council. Tanaka argued that because of the limitations derived from Article 9 Japan should not explicitly claim a permanent seat.[15]

When Foreign Minister Yohei Kono came to New York in the autumn of 1994, his statement was clearer than Hosokawa's statement made in the previous year: "Japan, with the endorsement of many countries, is prepared to discharge its responsibilities as a permanent member of the Security Council in accordance with its basic philosophy of not resorting to the use of force prohibited by its Constitution."[16] Thus, Japan's wish to become a permanent member had been expressed, while Japan's limitation had been articulated.

From then on, Kono's position became the basis of a series of statements made by Japanese representatives to the United Nations on the question of Security Council reforms and Japan. Tense discussions continued for four years.

In March 1997 the Malaysian Ambassador to the UN, Razali Ismail, who had been elected as the President of the General Assembly, made a proposal. The Razali Proposal consisted of enlarging the number of Council members from 15 to 24, adding 5 permanent members (one country each from the developing countries in Asia, Africa and Latin America, and two from developed countries, generally recognized as Japan and Germany), and 4 non-permanent members (one country each from the developing countries in Asia, Africa, Latin America and the East European countries). The proposal was made as a result of Razali's efforts in identifying where UN consensus could be found. The gist of the proposal seemed to be acceptable to Japan.

Foreign Minister Obuchi came to the UN General Assembly in September 1997 and after reiterating Kono's statement of 1994, firmly stated that "If Japan's assessment [contributions] were to increase further out of proportion, with reform of the Security Council not yet realized, I must say there would be a problem with respect to the fairness of such a situation."[17]

Japan's expectation proved to be premature if not naive. Italy, Korea and other countries, which thought that Razali's proposal did

---

[15] Ibid., pp. 88, 99.
[16] Ibid., p. 88.
[17] http://www.mofa.go.jp/policy/un/pamph96/o_un.html 2003-04-12.

not ensure their interest in proportion to the degree of their representation in the Council, worked actively against this proposal and in November 1997 it was decided that Razali's proposal would not be put to vote by the General Assembly. The decision for postponement virtually crushed Japan's aspiration for a permanent seat, at least for the time being.[18]

It was a great disappointment for Japan. Five years have passed since then, efforts are going on to regain momentum, but so far without success.

The MOFA homepage announces that Japan is willing to fulfil further obligations as a permanent member in a reformed Security Council based on the following considerations[19]:

(1) The reform of the Security Council must improve the effectiveness of its work in implementing decisions and enhance its legitimacy in representing the international community.

(2) The effectiveness of the Council's work should be improved by adding a limited number of countries which have the ability and willingness to bear global responsibility for the maintenance of international peace and security.

(3) Japan has already fulfilled the role of non-permanent member of the Security Council eight times in the past. Japan has made various contributions and cooperated in such areas as development, disarmament, non-proliferation, and human security inside and outside the UN framework. Such contributions can be made on a more continuous and effective basis if Japan was a permanent member.

(4) Developing countries must also become permanent members of the Council. Non-permanent members of the Council have to be increased as well. The total number of countries in the reformed Council should be 24.

This homepage underlines the merit of having Japan as a permanent member of the Council, rather than emphasizing the unfairness of not letting Japan, the second largest financial contributor (20%) to the organization, participate, on a permanent basis in the key decision-making process in the United Nations.

---

[18] Fukushima, *op. cit.*, pp. 96–97.
[19] http://www.mofa.go.jp/mofaj/comment/q_a/topic_4.html 2002–12–04.

The homepage does not address the question concerning the limitations Article 9 of the Japanese Constitution might impose on participating in the collective security of the United Nations. The role which Japan may or may not play in the current hypothetical UN forces based on Articles 42 and 43 of Chapter VII is naturally not touched upon. But the role which Japan may or may not play in the UN peacekeeping operation forces, and in the Multinational forces sent to the Gulf in 1991, to Afghanistan in 2001 and to Iraq in 2003, are all real issues. It is true that in the past UN history, all permanent member countries of the Security Council were not necessarily active in participating in the UN-based PKO or multi-national forces. But in a situation where Japan might become a permanent member of the Security Council, Japan cannot avoid greater scrutiny from its own public opinion, debates in the Diet and international Japan watchers asking what role Japan wants to play in contributing to global peace and security within the framework of the United Nations.

Against this sensitive background the same MOFA homepage touches on an interesting legal issue related to the obligation incurred in becoming a permanent member of the Security Council.

Article 47 of the UN Charter prescribes that a Military Staff Committee shall be established to advise the Council and that the Committee shall consist of the Chiefs of Staff or their representatives of the permanent members of the Council. The primary purpose of the Committee seems to be advising the Council in Article 42 and 43 situations. Such a committee has never been established thus far, nor is it likely that it will be established in the foreseeable future.

The homepage does not refer to Article 9 of the Constitution, but states that "there are no differences in terms of legal obligations for a permanent member and a non-permanent member country", with an explicit reference to the obligations of allowing its Chief of Staff to become a member of the UN Military Staff Committee.

Reforms in the financial area

The revitalization of the UN from the end of the 1980's resulted in growing budgetary expenditure. The UN budget is divided into two categories: the regular budget and the PKO budget.

The PKO budget, reflecting the increased activities in the post-Cold War era, grew rapidly during the first half of the 1990's, up to the level of $3 billion. Then it declined to $1 billion but because of the creation of large-scale PKOs in the latter half of the 1990's it reached \$2.154 billion in 2000. The regular budget has been kept under a virtual zero growth after Kofi Annan became Secretary-General and the bi-annual budget was \$2.533 billion for 2000/2001.[20]

Japan took active initiatives on financial reform.

First, Japan had continuously advocated improving efficiency, implementing further reforms, and keeping the UN budget under constant review.

Second, Japan put a lot of effort in resolving the huge amount of arrears in the UN budget. By the end of 2000 arrears in the UN budget totalled \$2.26 billion. A greater part of this was owed by the United States to the term of \$1.32 billion.[21] Foreign Minister Obuchi stated in September 1997 at the UN General Assembly that "I would emphasize again that it is the obligation of member states to pay their assessed contributions in full, and that member states in arrears should make every effort to eliminate them."[22]

Third, Japan maintained an equitable share of assessment contributions. The table below shows the share of assessment contributions in the regular budget of top 15 countries from 2001 to 2003 as agreed by the member countries in December 2000.[23]

Share of assessment contributions of the UN regular budget % As of December, 2000							
Share % 2000		2001		2002		2003	
USA	25.000	USA	22.000	USA	22.000	USA	22.00000
Japan	20.573	Japan	19.629	Japan	19.669	Japan	19.51575
Germany	9.857	Germany	9.825	Germany	9.845	Germany	9.76900
France	6.545	France	6.503	France	6.516	France	6.46600
Italy	5.437	UK	5.568	UK	5.579	UK	5.53600
UK	5.092	Italy	5.094	Italy	5.104	Italy	5.06475
Canada	2.732	Canada	2.573	Canada	2.579	Canada	2.55800
Spain	2.591	Spain	2.534	Spain	2.539	Spain	2.51875
Netherl.	1.632	Brazil	2.231	Brazil	2.093	Brazil	2.39000
Australia	1.483	Netherl.	1.748	Korea	1.866	Korea	1.85100
Brazil	1.471	Korea	1.728	Netherl.	1.751	Netherl.	1.73800
Belgium	1.104	Australia	1.636	Australia	1.640	Australia	1.62700
Argentine	1.103	China	1.541	China	1.545	China	1.53200
Sweden	1.079	Russia	1.200	Russia	1.200	Russia	1.20000
Russia	1.077	Argentine	1.156	Argentine	1.159	Argentine	1.14900

---

[20] http://www.mofa.go.jp/mofaj/gaiko/jp_un/kaikaku.html 2002–12–14.

[21] Ibid.

[22] www.mofa.go.jp/policy/un/pamph96/o_un.html 2003–04–12.

[23] www.mofa.go.jp/mofaj/gaiko/jp_un/yosan.html 2002–12–04.

The slight decline in Japan's share is the result of the efforts made
on the part of Japanese government and its UN delegation. Japan
maintained the following points strenuously and gained sympathy
from other member countries that resulted in the decline of its assessment contributions:[24]

– Genuine efforts have to be made to substantially decrease the
areas of assessment contributions;
– The UN budget must undergo severe scrutiny to cut back non-
indispensable expenditure;
– Fair burden-sharing has to be introduced, taking into account
the existing economic situation in each individual country;
– Japan will pay its assessment contribution, responsibly and without any delay, once that amount has been decided upon after sincere debates among member countries.

4. *After the Cold War: multinational forces and peacekeeping operations*

Initial stage of Japan's participation in peacekeeping operations

As I have already mentioned, UN peacekeeping operations were substantially activated from the end of the 1980's. The end of the Cold
War opened a real possibility for consensus-building within the Security
Council, without always being hampered by vetoes from a permanent member. At the same time, regional and intrastate conflicts
suppressed under the heavy weight of US-Soviet rivalry during the
Cold War became unleashed, such as in the case of the former
Yugoslavia. The increased regional and intrastate conflicts necessitated closer involvement by the United Nations for the maintenance
of peace and stability.

Thus from 1988 till the summer of 2003 altogether 42 UN peace-
keeping missions were sent to various areas of conflict in the world.
Volume-wise, it was nine times more in comparison with the Cold
War days.[25]

---

[24] http://www.mofa.go.jp/mofaj/comment/q_a/topic_5.html 2002–12–04.
[25] http://www.mofa.go.jp/mofaj/gaiko/pko/pdfs/ichiran.pdf 2003–08–04. During
the Cold War 13 missions were sent in 40 years (1948–1987); after the Cold War
42 missions in 15 years (1988–2002); this makes a 9-fold increase calculating with
the same base years.

Japan began its first deliberation on enhanced contribution to the cause of international peace and security primarily in the Ministry of Foreign Affairs under the general guidance of Prime Minister Takeshita, who succeeded Prime Minister Nakasone in November 1987. Japan's new initiatives were announced by Prime Minister Takeshita in May 1988 as his 'International Contribution Initiatives'. These initiatives consisted of three pillars: economic cooperation (ODA), cultural cooperation, and cooperation for peace.

As a footnote, during the period when the Foreign Ministry was fully involved in the preparatory works for the Takeshita Initiatives, I was working in the Economic Affairs Department. My department also wanted to contribute to this initiative and proposed several ideas, including a liberalization policy of immigration of foreign workers. Given the growing interest over this issue in the 2000's and against the background of Japan's demographic change to an ageing society, my department's proposal was a far-sighted one, but unfortunately, it was not accepted as a major pillar of Takeshita's Initiative.

The third pillar, cooperation for peace, was the first pronouncement of Japan's policy towards the contribution to international peace and security. Three issues were discussed as threats to the peace in the Asia-Pacific region: Cambodia, Korea and the Northern Territorial Issue between Japan and the Soviet Union.[26] But it was in Afghanistan that the first Japanese 'Cooperation for Peace' was realized. In May 1988, after ten years of silence, the United Nations dispatched a PKO mission to the border area of Afghanistan (UNGOMAP), where peace was being realized under Gorbachev's 'New Thinking' foreign policy. In June 1988 a Foreign Ministry official was sent to UNGOMAP as a political counsellor. In August 1988 another political counsellor was sent to the Inspection Mission on Iran and Iraq (UNIIMOG), and from 1989 to January 1991 four election monitoring missions were sent to various part of the world.[27]

---

[26] T. Ikeda, *Cambodia Waheiheno Michi (Road to Cambodian Peace)*, Toshishuppan, 1996, pp. 19–20.

[27] http://www.mofa.go.jp/mofaj/gaiko/pko/kyoryoku.html 2002-12-04.

These Japanese officials were sent to their missions under the Ministry of Foreign Affairs Law; therefore the civilians sent were limited to the numbers prescribed by MOFA Law, making it impossible to send more than 20 to 30 people. It also made the dispatch of Self-Defence Forces virtually impossible.[28] Nevertheless hopes for enhanced Japanese participation to PKO were clearly growing.

The Gulf War: Japan failed in multinational forces cooperation, but later succeeded in peacekeeping operations

The Gulf Crisis erupted in August 1990. Sadly Japan's preparation for participation in the cause of international peace and security under Prime Minister Takeshita could not create a basis sufficient to cope with this situation. Japan was engulfed in the huge torrent of its own history.

The Kaifu cabinet was well aware that financial cooperation alone was not sufficient and that some physical participation was essential. In October 1990 the government presented to the Diet the 'Bill on Peace Cooperation with the United Nations'. The essence of this bill was to create a United Nations Peace Cooperation Force, separate from the Self-Defence Forces, in order to conduct ceasefire monitoring, logistic support and medical care. In reality, it was envisaged that the Self-Defence Forces would constitute a major portion of the UN Peace Cooperation Forces. It was also clearly stipulated that the Cooperation Forces must not take actions which might constitute a threat by force or a use of force.

A fundamental difficulty emerged, however, in relation to Article 9 of the Constitution. In 1980 the Japanese government submitted a written statement to the Diet that "Participation of Self-Defence Forces to a UN operation is unconstitutional and inadmissible, if the purpose and duty of that UN force involves the use of force."[29] It was quite obvious that the purpose and duty of the multinational forces gathering near Kuwait involved a possible use of force to redress the situation created by the Iraqi invasion of Kuwait. Following this logic, the Japanese UN Peace Cooperation Forces could not

---

[28] Fukushima, *op. cit.*, p. 65.

[29] H. Nakajima, *Kokusaiheiwakyouryoku Nyuumon (Introduction of International Peace Cooperation)*, *Chapter 5*, T. Shinyo ed., Yuuhikaku, 1995, p. 179.

'participate' in multinational forces because it was unconstitutional. The Japanese government argued that the activities envisaged under the new bill constituted 'collaboration' and not 'participation'. Fierce parliamentary debates continued around such issues, for example, whether "the transportation of water to units on the front line would be considered contributing to the use of force".[30] Finally the parliamentary debates came to a halt, because the government could not clearly explain where to draw the line between 'participation' and 'collaboration'. The bill was withdrawn in November 1990.[31]

Meanwhile, the United Nations Security Council adopted a decisive Resolution 678 on 29 November, granting member countries to take all the necessary measures to restore peace and security in the area. It was not exactly in the same manner as the UN armed forces in Korea, but the multinational forces gathering around Iraq had clearly acquired a status to act under the auspices of the United Nations. But in Japan, the withdrawal of the Bill on Peace Cooperation with the United Nations from the Diet was fatal in terms of its 'human' contribution to the Gulf Crisis. The limited amount of medical doctors and civilian transportation were far from satisfactory to indicate Japan's contribution in international peace and security. In the summer of 1991, six months after the war had ended, the Self-Defence Forces sent mine sweepers to the Persian Gulf. They made substantial contributions in clearing mines in the Gulf area, but their contributions could not alter the image that Japan had stayed away from the crisis when its presence had been so greatly expected.

There was awareness though in Japan that something had to be done to remedy the situation. When the UN Peace Cooperation Bill was withdrawn in November 1990, the three ruling parties, the Liberal Democratic Party, the Komeito Party, and the Japan Democratic Socialist Party had already agreed to enact a new law, which would enable Japan to participate in UN peacekeeping operations and humanitarian relief operations.[32]

In September 1991 a new bill concerning cooperation with United Nations peacekeeping operations (International Peace Cooperation Bill) was presented to the Diet. This time, the objective of Japan's

---

[30] Fukushima, *op. cit.*, p. 69.
[31] Nakajima, *op. cit.*, pp. 178–180.
[32] Fukushima, *op. cit.*, p. 69.

cooperation was limited primarily to UN peacekeeping operations. Other humanitarian relief activities based on resolutions by the UN or other international organizations were also included in the objective, but the most controversial point under the previous bill, cooperation in multinational forces, was excluded. The scope of activities governed by this bill could be divided into core activities (observance of ceasefire, collection of weapons, and exchange of prisoners, etc.), rear area support and humanitarian relief activities.

In order to keep Japan's participation strictly within Article 9 of the Constitution, the bill prescribed that "international peacekeeping activities shall not be construed as the use of force" and following five conditions to be observed by Japanese participants were also stipulated:

1) The existence of a ceasefire agreement;
2) The existence of consent for Japan's participation by the conflicting parties;
3) That peacekeeping forces maintain an impartial position;
4) In the event that the above three conditions are not met, Japanese peacekeeping forces will be withdrawn; and
5) Use of weapons shall be limited to the minimum for protection of personnel.

The first three conditions were shared by the international community when peacekeeping operations were considered during the Cold War. The last two were uniquely Japanese. The fourth condition created an impression of extreme cautiousness. The fifth condition, excluding the use of weapons even when the 'mission was obstructed' was a singularly limited interpretation pertaining to the use of weapons, directly deriving from Article 9 of the Constitution.

In addition to these limitations, two more substantial conditions were attached to this bill during the parliamentary debate: first, abovementioned core activities would be 'frozen', i.e. the core activities would not be allowed to be implemented until such time as conditions become matured, and second, even after they become 'unfrozen' in the future, each dispatch on core activities has to be approved by the parliament.

When the bill was debated, the opposition from the socialist party, the communist party and pacifist public opinion was very strong. Thus the bill had to be subjected to the limitations mentioned above.

And yet the bill was approved and became law on 15 June 1992.[33] Despite these limitations, the enactment of the new law was a significant step forward for Japan to become actively engaged in international peacekeeping operations.

Cambodian peacekeeping operations and after

Just before the International Peace Cooperation Law was enacted in June 1992, the international community, particularly Asia-Pacific nations, had seen a dramatic achievement in establishing peace in Cambodia. For Japan, the new law was enacted in time to enable Japanese participation in Cambodian peacekeeping operations from the initial period of their activities. Let us turn our eyes for a while to Cambodia, to see how the situation had been evolving.

The Peace Accord on Vietnam was signed in January 1973 and Saigon fell in April 1975. The American objective to protect a democratic South Vietnam failed, but the situation in Vietnam was stabilized. However, for nearly two decades since then Cambodia underwent a painful era of massacre, invasion, and indescribable civil strife.

Terror under the Khmer Rouge led by Pol Pot first started in April 1975. It ended in December 1978, when Vietnam invaded Cambodia. China intervened, opposing Vietnam in February 1979, which resulted in 29 days of warfare. A new regime in Phnom Pen, backed by Vietnam and joined by Hun Sen, then began to represent Cambodia. Opposition to this regime, a triple alliance consisting of Prince Norodom Sihanouk (supported by China), the Son Sann group (a group of pre-Pol Pot political forces) and the Khieu Samphan group (Khmer Rouge) was formed. Together they waged a prolonged civil war against Phnom Penh which lasted for about a decade. More than 300,000 refugees fled to the border area between Cambodia and Thailand.[34]

In the latter half of the 1980's Vietnam changed its policy, envisaging its withdrawal from Cambodia. From December 1987 to January 1988 meetings between Prince Sihanouk and Hun Sen took place

---

[33] Ibid., pp. 69–73; Nakajima, *op. cit.*, p. 180, pp. 191–193, pp. 195–196.
[34] Ikeda, *op. cit.*, pp. 45–48.

in Paris and new hopes for Cambodian peace emerged. After the withdrawal of Vietnam from Cambodia in September 1989, these hopes were interrupted for a while by the resumption of hostilities between Phnom Pen and the triple alliance. Nevertheless the scales were tipped toward Cambodian peace through 1990 and 1991.

Japan realized that an opportunity for participating in an issue critically important for peace and security in the Asia-Pacific region had been opened. Japan became actively involved in this process, through numerous contacts and dialogue with all four groups in Cambodia; convened the Tokyo Conference on Cambodian Peace in June 1990; and participated fully in the International Peace Process on Cambodia in Paris.

The Comprehensive Peace Accord on Cambodia was signed in Paris on 23 October 1991. The UN peacekeeping forces in Cambodia (UNTAC) began their work in March 1992. For Japan the enactment of the International Peace Cooperation Law in June 1992 created an indispensable basis for its participation in the UN peacekeeping operations in Cambodia.

Thus from September 1992 Japan began an unprecedented participation in the UNTAC. Japan dispatched eight ceasefire observers, 600 construction troops, 75 civilian police officers, and 41 election observers.[35]

Everything started well. But Japan's participation to the Cambodian peacekeeping operation had to face another challenge in April and May of 1993. The Khmer Rouge broke away from the Paris Accord and resorted to violence to regain their power. The overall situation became tense and on 28 April 1993 a UN volunteer Mr. Nakata was killed, followed by the death of a civilian policeman, Mr. Takada, on 4 May. Strong public opinion mounted in Japan calling for the withdrawal of Japanese participants. They argued that since the ceasefire arrangement had not been maintained, the very first condition for dispatching Japanese peacekeepers no longer applied.

But the government, led by Prime Minister Miyazawa, remained firm. The Cambodian situation was in a precarious situation. The Paris Accord had to be maintained. That was the only way to save peace and security in Cambodia. Japan's withdrawal from Cambodia could have critically damaged UNTAC and ruined the fragile peace

---

[35] http://www.mofa.go.jp/mofaj/gaiko/pko/kyoryoku.html 2002–12–04.

based on the Paris Accord. Japan stayed and Cambodia slowly but firmly began to stride toward peace and stability.[36] It was a real success in the history of Japan's contributions to the cause of peace and security in the Asia-Pacific region.

Thus, based on the new International Peace Cooperation Law of 1992, Japan began participating in UN peacekeeping operations and humanitarian relief mission. But Japan faced limitations through its own experience. The humanitarian relief mission sent to Rwanda in autumn 1994 was allowed to operate only outside Rwanda, in Zaire and Kenya, because of the limitations under the International Peace Cooperation Law.[37] Another limitation was that Japan could not even participate in election monitoring conducted outside the auspices of the United Nations.

Faced with these limitations, in 1998 the law was revised in two aspects: first, material contributions to humanitarian relief activities when a ceasefire agreement was not in place were included; second, Japanese participation to election monitoring conducted by regional organizations, such as the OSCE was allowed. Based on this revision 30 election monitors were sent to Bosnia in summer 1998 under the auspices of the OSCE.

Thus Japan, though slowly and gradually, succeeded in somehow overcoming its 'defeat in the Gulf War', and with its centripetal energy toward positive participation in UN peacekeeping operations, began to make real contributions to the cause of international peace and security.

5. September Eleven and Eastern Timor

Japan's reaction to September 11

And then, on 11 September 2001, terrorists attacked the United States. America immediately announced that the attack had been made by a group of Islamic fundamentalists called Al Qaeda, led by Osama bin Laden, and they also declared that Afghanistan was

---

[36] Ikeda, *op. cit.*, pp. 180–188.
[37] Caroline Rose, 'Japanese role in PKO and Humanitarian Assistance', in T. Inoguchi and J. Purnendra (ed.), *Japanese Foreign Policy Today*, Palgrave, 2000, p. 123.

responsible for harbouring these terrorists. It became clear that a decisive attack against the terrorists was imminent. The key question was how Japan would respond to this situation.

I arrived in the Netherlands as ambassador just two months before the terrorist attack. On 11 September, as I watched television images of the collapsing twin tower buildings in New York, many questions came to my mind: How would Tokyo react? Would Japan clearly support international efforts against terrorism? Are we going to contribute, not by financial means, but through human actions, to the international efforts against terrorism? Japan's 'defeat in 1991' was strongly embedded in our memory. But at the same time, political decision-making in Tokyo might be subjected to many uncertainties. Until a clear decision was made, no-one could really be sure.

As it turned out, a series of decisions taken in Tokyo in the fall of 2001 were truly beyond my expectations. As the newly arrived ambassador, no greater back-up could be expected from Tokyo than these swift and forthcoming decisions. Each time Tokyo took a substantive decision, my staff in the embassy immediately added it to the embassy homepage. Whenever I made calls to my Dutch interlocutors, I often quoted passages from the homepage to explain the essence of Japan's decisions.

In fact, when the Dutch government took concrete decisions on their participation in the coalition of forces against terrorism, both Prime Minister Kok and the Defence Minister de Grave specifically referred to and commended Japan's participation in the coalition of forces against international terrorism.

On 19 September, Prime Minister Koizumi announced Japan's basic policy. It was a clear and unmistakable message of support for the common action of the international community against terrorism.

(1) Japan will actively engage in the combat against terrorism, which it regards as Japan's own security issue.

(2) Japan strongly supports the United States, its ally, and will act in concert with the United States and other countries around the world.

(3) Japan will take concrete and effective measures which will

clearly demonstrate its firm determination. These measures will be implemented in a swift and comprehensive manner.[38]

On 5 October, only three weeks after the initial reaction on 19 September, the government presented the Anti-Terrorism Special Measures Bill to the parliament. The essence of this bill was to send Self-Defence Forces to provide rear area support in the war against international terrorism:

> "The purpose of the Law is to specify the measures in order to enable Japan to makeactive and positive contributions to the efforts of the international community towards the prevention and eradication of international terrorism.
> 1. The measures include:
> (1) Cooperation and Support Activities, to be provided by the Self-Defense Forces, such as supply, transportation, repair and maintenance, medical services, communications, airport and seaport operations, and base operations;
> (2) Search and Rescue Activities;
> (3) Assistance to Affected People.
> 2. These measures shall be implemented in (a) Japanese territory and (b) the High seas and airspace above as well as foreign territories, where combat operations are not conducted or not expected.
> 3. Use of weapons is allowed to protect the lives of members of the Self-Defense Force, as well as the lives of those conducting relevant activities with them or those who come under their command while implementing the measures mentioned above."[39]

On 29 October, the bill was approved by the Diet.[40] It was indeed a miraculously fast operation to enact a bill of that complexity and have it approved altogether in 40 days after the basic policy was announced. Clearly Japan was different from that country that battered down the hatches during the Gulf War in 1990 and 1991. What the Kaifu government wanted to achieve in assisting the UN multinational forces during the Gulf War was basically accepted in relation to the common fight against international terrorism. The key question which pulled down government logic, whether Japan was 'participating' or 'collaborating' with the multinational forces, did not appear in the forefront of the parliamentary debate. The

---

[38] http://www.emb-japan.nl/information2/statement/news4.htm 2001–11–09.
[39] http://www.emb-japan.nl/information2/statement/news7.htm 2001–11–09.
[40] http://www.kantei.go.jp/jp/koizumispeech/2001/1029danwa.html 2003–04–14.

question of constitutionality was overcome by the government affirmation that Japan's action "must not be the threat or use of force"
(Article 2–2) and that measures based on this law will be implemented in areas where "combat operations are not conducted or
expected" (Article 2–3).

The accumulated records of the JSDF sent abroad under the 1992
International Peace Cooperation Law were an important psychological factor which prepared Japanese people for this sea change.
At the same time, the 1999 Surrounding Situations Law also provided a solid basis, both legal and substantial, for the enactment of
this new law against terrorism. The similarity in the scope of cooperative activities envisaged by the two laws, as described above and
in Chapter 2, is striking. The major difference between the two laws
was the purpose of cooperation: the Surrounding Situation Law envisaged cooperation to achieve the goals of the Security Treaty, whereas
the new law envisaged cooperation for a common fight against international terrorism. On the issue of the use of weapons, taking into
account the various criticisms against the two laws enacted in the
1990's, the scope of the usage of weapons under the new Anti-
Terrorism Law was enlarged to include "those who come under the
command of" Japanese forces.

On 16 November the Basic Plan of the Self-Defence Forces, based
on the Anti-Terrorism Special Measures Law was adopted.[41] The
Basic Plan prescribed rear area support for those troops engaged in
a common fight against international terrorism. It envisaged the
involvement of five ships, eight aircraft and 1,380 troops.[42]

On 30 November the Basic Plan was approved by the parliament.[43] Since then, these ships and aircraft have been continuously
in action. Ships were primarily engaged in supplying fuel at the
Indian Ocean and the Arabian Sea to American and British vessels
engaged in combat activities against international terrorism in
Afghanistan. Aircraft were primarily engaged in transport between
American bases inside Japan and the Guam Islands.[44]

On 7 December a long awaited law to 'defreeze' the core activities of the International Peace Cooperation Law was approved by

---

[41] http://www.kantei.go.jp/jp/tyokan/koizumi/2001/1116danwa.html 2003–04–14.
[42] Saga Shinbun, *Kyodo*, 17 November 2001.
[43] Saga Shinbun, *Kyodo*, 1 December 2001.
[44] Nihon Keizai Shinbun, 7 November 2002.

the Diet. The scope of the usage of weapons was enlarged to protect the lives of "those who come under the command" of respective Self-Defence Forces, in line with the Anti-Terrorism Special Measures Law.[45]

Peacekeeping operations in East Timor

Probably the most important Japanese peacekeeping operations after the autumn of 2001 were its participation in UN PKO in East Timor.

East Timor's independence from Indonesia became a serious concern to the international community toward the end of the 1990's. In August 1999 under UN supervision (UNAMET) an epoch-making election was held and a substantial majority voted for independence. But immediately thereafter, an uprising of pro-Indonesian factions erupted. The UN and the international community reacted sharply and in September UN multinational forces, with Australia as a major player, were dispatched (UNTTERFET). In October a UN-based administrative organ was also created (UNTAET) and as the situation came under control, it took over the military responsibility of UNTERFET in February 2000. In 2000 and 2001 the overall situation continued to improve. In August 2001 an election to establish a Constitutional Assembly was held, and in 2002 the constitution was enacted, the presidential election was held in April, and finally East Timor became independent on 20 May 2002. Upon its independence UNTAET terminated its function and a smaller scale UN PKO replaced the activities (UNMISET).[46]

Japan was involved in the East Timor situation from the beginning. But the limitation of Japanese peacekeeping operations became clear through these East Timor operations. From November 1999 to February 2000, during the crucial period of peacekeeping operations under UNTAET, Japan sent only airborne relief missions to East Timor. Japanese monitors went to the election of the Constitutional Assembly in summer 2001. But it could not participate in UNTAET itself, because no ceasefire agreement had yet been reached. Finally, from March 2002, at the concluding period of UNTAET, 680 Self-Defence Forces personnel were sent to facilities construction,

---

[45] www.mofa.go.jp/mofaj/gaiko/pko/ho_kaisei.html 2002–12–04.
[46] www.mofa.go.jp/mofaj/gaiko/pko/unmiset.html 2002–12–07.

10 commanding officers were dispatched and they were carried over to UNMISET.

As a UN report of August 2000 indicated,[47] the common practice of the international community had already moved toward dispatching peacekeeping forces without requiring a ceasefire agreement. Commonly accepted international practices allowed the use of weapons when their "mission was obstructed", whereas the Japanese law did not.

But all in all, from the enactment of International Peace Cooperation Law in 1992 to the summer of 2003 Japan has sent 17 missions based on this law, 8 in UN peacekeeping operations, 4 in humanitarian relief activities and 5 in election monitoring.

From 1988 to the summer of 2003, altogether 25 missions continued to be sent based on the Ministry of Foreign Affairs Law, including 10 in UN peacekeeping operations and 15 others, primarily in election monitoring.[48]

6. *Japan's participation in Iraq reconstruction and further challenges*

When we look back at the history from the beginning of the 1990's to this day, in the area of Japan's contribution to international peace and security the changes which have actually taken place are quite amazing.

In the field of UN peacekeeping operations a new 1992 law has now been well established and has produced results such as those in Cambodia, East Timor, the Golan Heights and other areas of conflict. There are certainly gaps between international and Japanese practices as mentioned above, but things have been moving forward.

In the direction of cooperation to the UN multinational forces, after the 'defeat' in 1990 in relation to the United Nations Peace Cooperation Bill, a spectacular step was taken in relation to the 2001 Anti-Terrorism Special Measures Law.

And yet, the momentum gained from the end of 2002 to 2003 seems to exceed the speed which the 1990's have seen.

---

[47] On August 23, 2000, a panel created by UN Secretary-General Kofi Annan announced a report on UN peacekeeping operations. The report is called the Brahimi Report after the chairman of the panel (http://www.mofa.go.jp./mofaj/gaiko/pko/kento_p/html 2003-08-04).

[48] http://www.mofa.go.jp./mofaj/gaiko/pko/pdfs/jinteki.pdf 2003-08-05.

In December 2002 a private advisory committee under the chairmanship of Mr. Yasushi Akashi, former Deputy Secretary-General of the UN, formulated a report and presented it to the Prime Minister. The report indicated that the "ten years of Japanese peacekeeping operations after the Cambodian involvement lagged far behind compared to other advanced countries". The report advised a new law to enable the SDF to engage in all multinational forces based on UN resolutions, and substantially soften the five principles prescribed in the International Peace Cooperation Law. The general reception by the media was not negative.[49]

And then what actually happened in the summer of 2003 in relation to the War in Iraq added further momentum.

Right from the beginning Prime Minister Koizumi's basic position was to ultimately support President Bush. In my view, that option was the best option for Japan's security and defence policy, as I have described in Chapter 9. But in doing so, from summer 2002 till mid-February Japan conducted a quiet diplomacy, advising America that it was in the best interest of America to go through the UN procedures, with credible evidence, in particular on weapons of mass destruction. Consensus among the international community was important for America, the Japan-US alliance and the United Nations. For Japan, the role of the UN was particularly important, because Japan's contribution to the peace and security of the world could best be implemented through the UN, be it through peacekeeping operations or multinational coalition of forces.

Japan began openly supporting American policy just before the Security Council on 16 February 2002, where French Foreign Minister Dominique de Villepin made an impressive intervention and the Security Council preferred the continuation of the inspector's work with a majority of 12 to 3. Why did Japan not endeavour a little more, seeking a resolution which might have gathered all members of the Council?[50] Even Prime Minister Blair continued his efforts until the last moment toward that direction. If Japan's basic position

---

[49] *Asahi Shinbun*, 19 December 2002.
[50] The Japanese ambassador in the United Nations announced on 18 February that Japan supported a second UN Resolution, but in the then existing political condition this meant that Japan did not support the continuation of inspectors work and did support the decision to go to war.

was 'Blair without armed forces' and if the United Nations had importance as a basis on which Japan's international contribution could further be developed, then why could not Japan have followed the same path?

Be it as it may, the war began and Koizumi unambiguously supported President Bush, but did not participate in the war. As the result of two months of deliberation after the war ended, the government presented a new bill concerning Japan's assistance in Iraq on 13 June. The bill was approved by the House of Representatives on 3 July and by the House of Councillors on 26 July.

The new Law concerning the Special Measures in Iraq prescribed humanitarian and reconstruction activities and rear area support activities of coalition forces by the JSDF.

The structure of the new law was similar to the Anti-Terrorism Special Measures Law of 2001 in many respects. Constitutionality was overcome in principle in the same manner by government affirmation that Japan's action "must not be the threat or use of force" (Article 2–2) and that measures based on this law will be implemented in areas where "combat operations are not conducted or expected" (Article 2–3). The emphasis of the 2001 law was on the high seas, whereas the new law was on foreign territories.

The new law also has clear traces to harmonize Japan's action with the past UN resolutions. As for the 1991 Gulf War and the 2001 Anti-Terrorism War, the multinational forces were created on the basis of a clear Security Council endorsement. The 'legal' position of the Japanese government was to defend the War in Iraq with likewise legitimacy. Thus the Security Council Resolution 1483 of 22 May 2003 was referred to as the triggering element for Japan's action.[51] In addition, Security Council Resolutions 678, 687 and 1441 were quoted to show that the war *per se* was conducted on their basis. But in reality, the failure of the second Resolution just before the outbreak of the war is in everyone's memory. The real issue of re-establishing a politically effective role for the United Nations goes beyond this legal victory.

---

[51] It was reported that already as early as 10 February Japan requested the US that a UN resolution was necessary for postwar Iraqi reconstruction. The urge addressed to member countries to contribute to the stability and security in Iraq incorporated in the Resolution 1483 was based upon Japan's proposal (*Asahi Shinbun*, 7 August 2003).

At any rate, Koizumi continued his efforts. The experience of the 2001 Anti-Terrorism Law and the 2003 Iraqi Assistance Law engendered precisely the same view as expressed in the Akashi Report of December 2002, that a 'permanent legal basis' which would enable Japan to participate in a multinational coalition of forces would be necessary. On 1 August 2003, a special task force was established at the Cabinet Secretariat.[52] Numerous issues are waiting for political and legal deliberation, including the role of the United Nations, the use of weapons, and the nature of the multinational forces.

Based on the new Law concerning the Special Measures on Humanitarian and Reconstruction Assistance in Iraq, Koizumi started sending SDF units to Iraq in December 2003.

Thus, from the end of 2003 onwards Koizumi's cabinet has a lot to do within the realm of Article 9 of the Constitution to take a more responsible role in the international community: the revision of the 1992 International Peace Cooperation Law to harmonize Japan's practice and the commonly accepted international practice of peacekeeping operations is one task; The bill studied by the special task force at the Cabinet Secretariat to create a 'permanent legal basis' for Japan's participation in rear area support to the coalition of forces is another (Chapter 2).

7. New agenda: disarmament and non-proliferation, conflict prevention, and human security

Disarmament and non-proliferation

Disarmament and non-proliferation have been areas to which Japan has paid continued attention and tried to take initiatives in its postwar foreign policy. It could be explained by its determination to become a peace-loving nation and its experience of being subjected to nuclear bombs in 1945.

In May 2002 MOFA published, through the Japan Institute of International Affairs and the Disarmament and Non-Proliferation Enhancement Centre, a white paper entitled 'Japan's Foreign Policy on Disarmament'.[53]

---

[52] *Asahi Shinbun*, 3 August 2003.
[53] http://www.mofa.go.jp/mofaj/gaiko/gun_hakusho/2002/index.html 2003–08–06.

The paper underlines three major areas on which Japan has recently focussed its attention:

(1) *Disarmament and non-proliferation of weapons of mass destruction, including nuclear weapons.* There has been some progress made in this area during the latter part of the 1990's, e.g. the indefinite extension of the Non-Proliferation Treaty in 1995 and the adoption of the Comprehensive Test Ban Treaty (CTBT) by the UN General Assembly in 1996. Japan actively supported them. Japan has put a lot of effort in improving the safeguard function of the International Atomic Energy Agency (IAEA), persuading the US, China, India, Pakistan and North Korea to join the CTBT, and adopting a UN resolution which declares the ultimate abolition of nuclear weapons.

(2) *Disarmament and non-proliferation of conventional weapons.* Japan has taken initiatives in two areas:

In the area of small arms and light weapons, based on a UN resolution which was proposed by Japan, expert meetings and UN conferences were held to prevent illicit trade and to further increase attention of the international community on this issue.

In the area of anti-personnel landmines, Japan joined the Anti-Personnel Mines Convention on 30 September 1998 and the Convention entered into force in March 1999. Japan has lobbied diligently to increase member countries of this treaty. Japan has made concrete efforts in de-mining and in victim assistance. As of August 2000, Japan had extended $56 million in mine removal and victim assistance.[54]

(3) *Consolidation of the general system of non proliferation.* Japan has been particularly concerned with the area of the proliferation of missiles capable of delivering weapons of mass destruction. Japan has actively supported the work of the Missile Technology Control Regime (MTCR), the sole multilateral framework aimed at missile non-proliferation. Japan also made efforts in strengthening the non-proliferation system in Asia and has held seminars on export control and missile non-proliferation.

Conflict prevention

For Japan, 2000 was a particularly important year, because Japan had taken concrete initiatives in this area. Having chaired the G8

---

[54] *Diplomatic Bluebook,* 2001 (www.mofa.go.jp/policy/other/bluebook/2001/chap2–1–b.html 2003–04–15).

Summit, Japan prepared the G8 Miyazaki Initiatives endorsed by the G8 Foreign Ministers in July. The following five areas were highlighted to promote conflict prevention:

1) Small arms and light weapons;
2) Conflict and development;
3) Illicit trade in diamonds;
4) Children in armed conflict;
5) International civil police.

Among the five aforementioned points Japan has put particular emphasis on the first two; small arms and light weapons and conflict and development. The Diplomatic Bluebook 2001 states that "Overall, conflict prevention has become one area where Japan should move forward with more concrete measures".[55]

Human security

On 2 December 1998 an international conference called 'Intellectual dialogue to create the future of Asia' was held in Japan in which Prime Minister Obuchi spoke and highlighted the notion of 'human security' as an important objective of Japanese foreign policy. In March 1999 a Trust Fund for Human Security was created in the UN with Japanese funds. The introductory passage of the brochure on the Trust Fund reads as follows, and shows the reasoning behind Japanese foreign policy in this new and creative area:

> Each human being is equal in having his own potential. A person should be respected as an individual, regardless of nationality, race, sex, etc. Human development has been promoted by the accumulation of creative activities by free individuals. However, it is extremely difficult for individuals to realize their potential and capabilities if their lives and livelihoods are threatened, and their dignity impaired. Under such conditions, the future of the whole society could be at stake, as well as that of individual citizens.
>
> In order to meet such diversified challenges in the post-Cold War international community, it is important that governments work with various international organizations and civil society including non-governmental organizations (NGOs), to create and sustain societies that enable individual human beings to realize their potential. This is the

---

[55] Ibid.

goal of the concept of human security, which is one of the key perspectives of Japan's foreign policy.[56]

The Japanese government continued to contribute to this fund and
by the end of 2001 the overall contribution amounted to 18.8 billion yen. Wherever the dignity of human beings suffers and requires
protection against poverty, medical failure, civil and international
conflicts, this Trust Fund is made available.

---

[56] http://www.mofa.go.jp/policy/human_secu/t_fund21/what.html 2003–04–15.

CONCLUSION

PAST PERSPECTIVES AND FUTURE AGENDAS

1. *Past perspectives*

In August 1945 World War II ended and Japan was defeated. Never before in its entire history had Japan experienced defeat. The country was in ruins, values were lost. The hearts and souls of the people of Japan were deeply scarred and an indescribable hollow engulfed the nation.

From this vacuum, however, Japan gradually re-emerged with new values: peace and democracy. These new values were brought to Japan by the occupying forces, but at the same time, the majority of the Japanese people intuitively desired and accepted them. The Imperial tradition, which dates back to Japan's ancient history and which played an important role since the Meiji Restoration, was also preserved in postwar Japan. The Constitution adopted in November 1946 embodied these three political values of the postwar Japan: peace, democracy and the Emperor.

But the way some of these political values were formulated in early postwar years left deep divisions in society. One issue was the emergence of a passive pacifism, that because war was wrong Japan should never again engage in any war, and should entrust its security to the goodwill of the community of nations. Article 9 of the Constitution became a substantial and symbolic stronghold for these views.

But the rising Cold War tension and the outbreak of the Korean War in 1950 shook this passive pacifism. The US occupation policy changed substantially from encouraging pacifism in Japan, to building Japan into a stronghold of democracy. Prime Minister Shigeru Yoshida (1946.5–1947.5, 1948.10–1954.12) chose the path towards democracy. Conflicts between the passive pacifists in the opposition parties and public opinion and the realists in the government heightened.

The realists made three policy choices: concluding the San Francisco Peace Treaty in September 1951 with only those countries prepared to do so—excluding China, Korea and the Soviet Union—called the 'partial peace'; accepting security ties with the United States; and agreeing to maintain minimum forces for self-defence. Strong public opinion favoured passive pacifism advocating 'comprehensive peace', neutrality and no armament, but the government realists and their leadership remained firm. The issue of passive pacifism, however, crystallized around Article 9 of the Constitution, remained as an unresolved issue.

Another unresolved issue was the question of war responsibility. The abovementioned passive pacifism was often linked with the view that everything that Japan had done before the war was wrong. But there were Japanese who did not agree with this. Was everything Japan had done really wrong? Had all the soldiers died in vain? Was the International Military Tribunal for the Far East not a 'victor's justice'? Thus, although the Japanese began to develop a general sense of remorse and regret for the deeds committed before and during the war, in particular in Asia, some aspects of the question of war responsibility were left unanswered and later caused difficulties in Japan's external relations.

Parallel to the political and security issues, economic development and economic values had already become dominant themes in the immediate postwar era in Japan. After the enactment of the constitution and a series of political and economic reforms, Japan's energy was directed towards economic reconstruction. The Korean War resulted in the first economic boom in Japan's postwar economic development.

In this book Chapter 1 described this postwar situation up to the San Francisco Peace Treaty in a horizontal manner. The subsequent eleven Chapters dealt with eleven subjects vertically. In order to give a general perspective of Japan's postwar foreign policy, I would like to give a brief summary of the horizontal development since the San Francisco Peace Treaty in the five decades leading to the present.

(1) The 1950's (September 1951–June 1960)[1]

After the signing of the San Francisco Peace Treaty, Japan entered a period of postwar recovery. Japan directed all its energy, both eco-

---

[1] The San Francisco Peace Treaty was signed on 8 September 1951. The revised Japan-US Security Treaty entered into force on 23 June 1960.

nomic and political, to rising from destruction and becoming an accepted member of the international community.

Prime Minister Yoshida made efforts to restrict the scope of the Self-Defence Forces, which were established in 1954, to a minimum level in order to concentrate the limited resources of the country on the reconstruction of the economy. These efforts to rebuild the economy were successful. The economy continued to develop, and after the Korean War boom, the *Jinmu* boom and the *Iwato* boom followed. Japan joined IMF in 1952 and GATT in 1955.

Politically Japan's major efforts in the 1950's were directed towards resolving those issues yet unsettled by the San Francisco Peace Treaty.

In 1952, during the Cold War tensions, Japan resumed its diplomatic relations with the Republic of China (Taiwan). The normalization of relations with Communist China, however, took another two decades. With other Asian countries, primarily in Southeast Asia, Japan began relations by regulating reparations. Reparations were agreed upon to compensate the damages caused by war, but also served the purpose of stimulating Japanese exports to the region. Prime Minister Nobusuke Kishi (1957.2–1960.7) added further impetus in developing the relations with his vision and a series of visits to the region. With South Korea, negotiations to establish diplomatic relations began, but up to the mid-60's no results were seen.

With the Soviet Union, Prime Minister Ichiro Hatoyama (1954.12–1956.12) concentrated his efforts on normalizing the relationship, and in October 1956 diplomatic relations were established, but a territorial issue over four islands northeast of Hokkaido was left unresolved. In December 1956, the Soviet Union withdrew its veto and Japan joined the United Nations.

Another dramatic event in foreign policy during this decade was the revision of the Security Treaty with the United States. Prime Minister Kishi took the lead in revising this treaty, originally concluded in September 1951 together with the San Francisco Peace Treaty, to bring Japan to an equal status with the US. The new Security Treaty was successfully concluded in 1960 and became the cornerstone of Japan's security policy and Japan-US relations. But protests by passive pacifists became so strong that Kishi had to resign upon the conclusion of the new treaty.

(2) *The 1960's (June 1960–June 1971)*[2]

Japan continued its efforts towards postwar recovery and by the end of the 1960's had in principle achieved this objective.

In the economic area, these efforts became so successful that the 1960's came to be known as 'the period of high growth' and brought about a remarkable growth rate of 10.9%. Prime Minister Hayato Ikeda (1960.7–1964.11) led this policy of rapid growth.

In 1963 Japan became a member, with full responsibility as an advanced economy, to GATT, to IMF in 1964 and in the same year joined OECD. The Tokyo Olympic Games held in the autumn of 1964 are remembered by many Japanese as a symbol of Japan's economic success and the return to the international economic community. In 1966 Japan received its last loan assistance from the International Bank of Reconstruction and Development (IBRD). Japan became an active donor of Official Development Assistance (ODA) in the 1960's.

In the political arena, Prime Minister Eisaku Sato (1964.11–1972.7) resolved two major outstanding agendas and closed the 'postwar period'. First, in 1965 Japan and South Korea finally concluded 14 years of negotiations and established diplomatic relations. Political relations with South Korea remained fragile, but at least economic relations began to develop quickly.

Second, the Agreement on the reversion of Okinawa in June 1971 marked an end of the 'postwar period'. Okinawa had been under American administration and played a vital role for the security of the Far East. Prime Minister Sato declared in August 1965 during his visit to Okinawa that: "unless Okinawa is returned to her homeland, the postwar period for Japan shall never end." The negotiations were difficult, Okinawa's pivotal role in the maintenance of security in the Far East could not be jeopardized, but Japan's request to keep nuclear arms out from Okinawa had to be met. After strenuous negotiations, in November 1969 the Sato-Nixon Joint Communiqué announced that the reversion of Okinawa would take place in 1972 and that the most difficult issue of nuclear weapons in Okinawa would be handled in accordance with the prior consultation mechanism of the Security Treaty. Upon the reversion of Okinawa,

---

[2] The Agreement concerning the reversion of Okinawa was signed on 17 June 1971.

Japan moved into a new decade with a greater responsibility and a different vision.

(3) *The 1970's (June 1971–June 1980)*[3]

Thus by the end of the 1960's Japan appeared to be an economic giant in international relations, had overcome the basic political agendas of postwar recovery, and should have been able to fulfil a new role in the international community. The 1970's became a decade in which Japan tried to play a responsible role commensurate with its massive economic power.

Up until the middle of the 1960's the US retained its position as the dominant political and economic power in the democratic camp. But as Japan and Europe, particularly Germany, recovered from the devastation of World War II and the US became increasingly involved in the war in Vietnam, a new approach was required in the global strategy of the United States.

In the political arena of international relations, 'Detente' became the key word. President Nixon sought to open new relations with major communist countries, based on negotiations and restraint, and aimed at bringing about greater leverage for US foreign policy. Relations between the East and the West began to thaw and several significant changes occurred. In 1971 President Nixon announced his plan to visit the People's Republic of China and US-PRC Shanghai Communiqué was issued in 1972; the US-Soviet SALT I and ABM Treaty were signed in 1972; the Peace Accord on Vietnam was concluded in 1973 (though Saigon fell in 1975); and the Helsinki Final Act was adopted in 1975.

Japan, an economic giant but a minor political figure in international relations, nevertheless had already become too important not to be affected by these fundamental changes. The change in US-China relations had direct repercussions on Japan's China policy to move forward its relationship with the PRC. Prime Minister Kakuei Tanaka (1972.7–1974.12) visited Beijing and opened diplomatic relations with the People's Republic of China in September 1972. Diplomatic relations with Taiwan ended.

---

[3] Incumbent Prime Minister Masayoshi Ohira died on 12 June 1980. A caretaker cabinet lasted until 17 July 1980.

The improvement in the US-China-Japan triangle raised Soviet concerns regarding encirclement. Prime Minister Tanaka visited the Soviet Union in October 1973 with a view to making a breakthrough in the unresolved territorial dispute. It brought limited progress: Soviet General Secretary Brezhnev verbally acknowledged that the object of territorial negotiations was four islands.

The international climate under the 'Detente' in the first half of the 1970's waned, when the Soviet Union's influence clearly began to grow in Indochina and Africa. 1976 came to be known as the 'end of Detente'.

In the latter half of the 1970's Japan's Asia-Pacific policy was conducted in the midst of this changing international climate. Prime Minister Takeo Fukuda (1976.12–1978.12) advocated an 'omnidirectional diplomacy for peace', but in reality Japan-China relations moved fast, whereas Japan-Soviet relations stagnated. The Treaty of Peace and Friendship between Japan and China, which was concluded in 1978, strengthened the relationship. In 1978 China also adopted a new economic policy toward 'reform and opening' under Deng Xiaoping, and economic ties between Japan and China began to develop rapidly. But in relation to the Soviet Union, after its invasion of Afghanistan in 1979, Japan immediately sided with other 'Western' countries in introducing economic sanctions and boycotting the Moscow Olympic Games in 1980.

During this period of fallout of the 'Detente' Japan gradually and quietly succeeded in creating more solid relations with the countries in Southeast Asia. In 1977 Prime Minister Fukuda made also an important visit to ASEAN and emphasized the importance of 'heart-to-heart' relations between Japan and ASEAN. In 1980 Prime Minister Masayoshi Ohira (1978.12–1980.7) took an initiative in establishing the first Asia-Pacific multilateral institution called the Pacific Economic Cooperation Conference (PECC), recruiting people from government, business and academia, to deepen mutual understanding and cooperation.

Turning our eyes to the world economic situation, the 1970's began with a relative decline in American global economic power. In 1971 a new economic policy, including a temporal suspension of the dollar's convertibility with gold was announced by President Nixon, which was followed by a new exchange rate with a weakened dollar, and moved to a floating exchange rate system in 1973.

The 1973 oil crisis resulted in unemployment, inflation and trade deficits in most of the advanced industrialized countries. Japan was also subjected to considerable economic fall-out, but managed to overcome this and became one of the most successful economies in the advanced industrialized countries.

With this success story in overcoming the oil crisis, Japan began taking initiatives so as to strengthen the fundamentals of the world economy. When the Economic Summit was convened in Rambouillet in 1975 to discuss global economic issues, Japan was invited as a founding member. Two years later Prime Minister Fukuda took an important initiative at the London Economic Summit in furthering Japan's role as a 'locomotive' of the world economy. His efforts continued at the Bonn Economic Summit in 1978.

Japan also took a positive initiative in convening the GATT/Tokyo Round from 1974 to 1979. After this round Japan's tariff rate for industrial products became one of the lowest among the developed countries.

Japan's economic power developed, as exemplified in its strengthened yen which reached 1 dollar = 176 yen in 1978. ODA increased from 1977 with a new tactic involving numerical targets.

As Japan's economic power grew the era of trade conflicts began. Japan's powerful exports inflicted damage on counterpart industries in the USA and calls to restrict Japanese exports mounted there. The first trade conflicts focussed on textiles from the end of the 1960's and in the early 1970's and the second on steel, colour television sets and automobiles in the latter half of the 1970's. Trade conflicts with Europe followed then as well. Japan agreed to introduce Voluntary Export Restraints (VERs), but the trade conflicts continued into the 1980's.

(4) *The 1980's (June 1980–December 1989)*[4]

During the 1980's Japan's economy remained strong. The yen became stronger and stronger, and combined with many other factors, this brought about an unprecedented economic bubble in Japan, led by soaring land prices and securities. Backed up by this ever evolving economic strength, Japan began asserting itself to play a greater and more responsible political role in the area of international diplomacy.

---

[4] On 3 December 1989, The US-Soviet Summit in Malta declared the end of the Cold War.

It was particularly under Prime Minister Yasuhiro Nakasone (1982.11–1987.11) that Japan displayed the most vigour in its foreign policy. Nakasone's success was partly due to his relations with the United States, or rather with President Reagan, who was in the White House from 1981 to 1988.

At the Williamsburg Summit in 1983 Nakasone appeared as a strong leader from a country with overwhelming economic power, and one which was prepared to exert political leadership. Nakasone, in close collaboration with President Reagan, spoke with a clear message that the security of the West was indivisible, and in this context, that Soviet Intermediate-Range Nuclear Forces (INF) such as SS20s had to be dismantled not only in European Russia, but also in Siberia and the Russian Far East. Japan-US cooperation was exemplified in the handling of the shooting down of a Korean airliner by a Soviet fighter plane in September 1983.

Japan's overall relations with China and South Korea developed as well. But they became conditioned by the wounded feelings from the war. The 'textbook' issue appeared in the spring-summer of 1982, which was resolved, although painfully. After Nakasone became Prime Minister a similar issue was reopened in 1986 but he succeeded in overcoming it. But Nakasone's own visit to the Yasukuni Shrine in 1985 resulted in fierce protests from China and South Korea. Nakasone had to refrain from visiting Yasukuni from then on.

In the field of economics, during the 1980's, the world economy was strongly affected by the US economic policy, often called 'Reaganomics'. President Reagan advocated a drastic tax cut to overcome stagflation which had resulted from the second oil crisis. He succeeded in boosting the American economy, but invited the twin budget and trade deficits.

As Japan's economy continued to grow and the US economy faced serious twin deficits, trade friction between the two countries heightened during the 1980's. The US administration initiated several measures to overcome the situation and on the Japanese side Nakasone tried to respond positively, sometimes taking his own initiatives.

First, the major industrialized countries coordinated their international financial policies to devalue the dollar: the Plaza Accord in 1985 and the Louvre Accord in 1987 brought about concrete results. The yen's value doubled in two years to 1 dollar = 120 yen in 1987. Second, sector-led negotiations between Japan and the US such as MOSS (Market-Oriented, Sector-Selective), semi-conductors, construction market, beef and citrus followed one after another. These negotiations were different from those in the 1970's, because they concentrated on opening up Japanese markets. Third, Nakasone took his own initiatives in making Japan's society better attuned to the outside world, such as the Maekawa Report formulated in April 1986. Fourth, under President George Bush, unprecedented talks on a wide range of structural reforms in both countries named SII (Structural Impediment Initiatives) were successfully conducted from September 1989 until June 1990. In the latter part of the 1980's Japan's investment in the US also reached unprecedented heights, ranging from $10 to $30 billion annually.

With Europe, the same type of trade conflicts occurred, but Europe specifically emphasized the increase of its exports to Japan and Japan's enhanced investment in Europe. Japan tried to respond positively as well.

In the multilateral economic fora, serious efforts were made by leading industrialized countries to consolidate the GATT system through the Uruguay Round (1986–1994). Japan made efforts in opening up imports of agricultural products, including rice. At the same time, the 80's were a period when enhanced regionalism flourished; in Europe with the strengthening of the European Community and in the American continent in the form of the North American Free Trade Agreement (NAFTA). In response to these moves, Japan took cautious leadership in establishing the Asia Pacific Economic Cooperation (APEC) in 1989. Japan's ODA continued to grow, guided by its numerical targets, and by the end of the 1980's reached the position of the world's number one donor.

Toward the end of the 1980's, both American and European trade deficits with Japan declined. So, all in all, the 80's seemed to have produced positive results in the area of Japanese economic diplomacy.

(5) *The 1990's and beginning of the 2000's (December 1989–2003)*

That image of continued Japanese success waned in the 1990's. This decade is sometimes referred to in Japan as the 'lost decade'. This was primarily due to the bursting of the bubble economy at the beginning of 1991 and Japan's inability to overcome its aftermath and resolve the ensuing deflationary economy.

For Japanese foreign policy, the international situation was more complex. The major event of the last decade of the 20th century was the end of the Cold War. The end of the Cold War meant that the heavy weight of US-Soviet rivalry was lifted from the world. The demise of the Soviet Union brought about fundamental changes in Europe. Changes were not that drastic in Asia, but Japan was also seriously affected, because she was exposed to the reality of world politics much more directly than during those Cold War years.

Starting with security issues, the first trial Japan had to go through was the Gulf War in 1990–1991. Despite government efforts, Japan's inability to provide a 'human' contribution and its financial assistance, which was viewed as 'too little and too late', left an impression of 'defeat for Japan in 1991'. But this 'defeat' became the springboard of substantial changes in security policy in Japan: a new law to ensure the participation of the Self-Defence Forces in UN peacekeeping operations was enacted in June 1992. Based on the new law an unprecedented number of Japanese peacekeepers went to Cambodia in September 1992.

In the Korean peninsula, South Korea opened its relations with the Soviet Union in 1990 and with China in 1992. The second trial which Japan had to go through was the nuclear weapons crisis, which erupted over North Korea in 1993–94. Tensions also rose over the Taiwan Strait in 1995–96. Against this background, the Japan and US administrations addressed the key question of how to consider security relations in the post-Cold War period. In 1996 President Clinton and Prime Minister Ryutaro Hashimoto (1996.1–1998.7) reaffirmed their security relations and the new Defence Guidelines were adopted in 1997. The law to ensure the implementation of these Guidelines was enacted in May 1999.

And then, the third trial came when international terrorists attacked America on 11 September 2001. This time, Prime Minister Junichiro Koizumi's (2001.4–) reaction was totally different from Japan's reaction in 1990 and 1991. Koizumi reacted swiftly and almost immediately enacted a new law, and already from November Japanese aircraft, ships and troops provided rear area support to US and British forces in the Indian Ocean.

In the War in Iraq in 2003, Koizumi unambiguously supported President George W. Bush in his decision to 'dismantle' Saddam Hussein. After the war ended Koizumi enacted a new law to send the SDF for humanitarian and reconstruction assistance and rear area support in Iraq and started to send SDF units in December 2003. The government established a special task force to study a 'permanent legal basis', which would enable Japan to participate in multi-national coalitions of forces.

In the new era of American unilateralism, there are growing voices in Japan arguing that Japan should express more clearly her own views regarding key issues pertaining to international peace and security. Whether or not Koizumi could be criticized for overly eager acceptance of the US position, these actions *per se* are clear steps towards sharing greater responsibility and as such, in my view, cannot but be welcomed.

The Parliamentary Research Commission on the Constitution is expected to terminate its five years work by 2005. This may become an important timing to consider the question of the revision of the Constitution, including that of Article 9.

Turning to other political aspects in the Asia-Pacific region, there are some significant moves as well. In September 2002 Prime Minister Koizumi visited Pyongyang, but the negotiations for establishing diplomatic relations encountered difficulties because of the abduction issue.[5] The disclosure of the North Korean nuclear weapons issue in October and the North Korean declared intention to start the process of possessing nuclear weapons in December made the situation in the Korean peninsula extremely tense and uncertain. It has become a paramount security/foreign policy objective for Japan to stop the North Korean nuclear weapons programme. The Six-party Talks which began in the summer of 2003 may become a new challenge to test Japan's foreign policy capability at the beginning of the century.

With China and South Korea, the issue of wounded feelings from the past war lingered over the 1990's. Prime Minister Tomiichi Murayama (1994.6–1996.1) made a historic statement of "deep remorse and heartfelt apology" in August 1995. In 1998 both President Kim Dae-Jung and President Jiang Zemin made an important visit to Japan. But a new textbook controversy and Prime Minister Koizumi's visit to the Yasukuni Shrine in 2001 reopened the old wounds. And yet under the new situation of a North Korean nuclear threat and the new era of American unilateralism, greater opportunity for a strategic dialogue between the three countries seems to be emerging.

---

[5] At the end of the 1970's, North Korea abducted at least thirteen Japanese citizens. In September 2002 Kim Jong-Il acknowledged this fact, apologized and later returned five of them who were still alive.

In this connection, it is noted that the Asia-Pacific region has seen the proliferation of multilateral institutions at various levels after the end of the Cold War, where Japan, in general, took a positive approach. APEC was elevated to a leadership level meeting from 1993. In the security area the ASEAN Regional Forum (ARF) was established in 1994. ASEAN plus Three (China, Japan and South Korea) began in 1997. In the early 2000's enhanced regional cooperation around ASEAN, including Free Trade Agreements (FTA) caught the attention of countries in the region.

As for Japan's relations with Russia, where another unresolved issue from WWII was still lingering, the post-Cold War climate activated the process of negotiations. Under Presidents Gorbachev, Yeltsin and Putin a decade of negotiations continued with a gradual warming of the overall relationship, including economic relations, regional cooperation and security exchanges. All these endeavours peaked at the Irkutsk Meeting in March 2001 but the negotiations basically came to a halt after this meeting. Prime Minister Koizumi's visit to Moscow in 2003 and the establishment of an Action Plan keeps the relationship at a moderate temperature.

In relation to Europe, in the dramatic post-Cold War decade, efforts were being made to strengthen a more meaningful political dialogue, including the 1991 Joint Japan-EC Declaration and the 2001 Action Plan for EU-Japan Cooperation, 'Shaping our Common Future'.

On the economic front Japan began the 1990's with the image of unstoppable success, and therefore, with continued trade conflicts particularly with America. Under President Clinton, with his emphasis on 'measurable criteria', tensions rose between the two administrations, but an agreement on automobiles in June 1995 brought an end to the heated negotiations.

By the mid-90's it became apparent that it was not easy for Japan to overcome the aftermath of the bursting of the bubble economy. For the first time in the postwar era, Japan suffered a long period of economic recession. GDP growth stagnated, the unemployment rate rose, the economy went into a deflation and yet, the issue of non-performing loans remained unresolved.

Thus a paradoxical phenomenon occurred in the latter part of the 1990's: Japan's trade surplus grew to a historical high *vis-à-vis* both America and Europe, but because of economic stagnation in Japan and the economic boom in the US and the vigour toward a single currency market in Europe, political turmoil did not occur either in the US or in Europe.

Despite the hardship of a 'lost decade' Japan continued its efforts in assuming a responsible role in multilateral economic institutions. Japan made efforts for the successful conclusion of the Uruguay Round and the establishment of the WTO and decided to begin rice imports in 1994. Japan took a positive step in initiating the WTO/Doha Round from 2001. During the 1990's Japan continued to hold the position of number one donor among DAC countries. Japan's $80 billion assistance at the Asian financial crisis in 1997–98 was also an expression of acting responsibly to a crisis of common concern. Japan also took initiatives on such global issues as sustainable development, the environment, population, infectious diseases and the information technology.

2. *Seven agendas for the future*

General views

The purpose of this book has been to explain the major issues of Japanese foreign policy from 1945 to 2003. It is not written to give an overall analysis on the future tasks in the early decades of the 21st century. Nevertheless, in concluding this book, brief perspectives on future agendas, where the major focus of Japanese foreign policy can be found, may be useful.

During my last few years in the Foreign Ministry, I had always thought that there were only two major agendas for Japanese foreign policy on the 'voyage without a chart' at the beginning of the 21st century: first, the fundamental issue of security based on the geopolitical conditions in which Japan is placed; second, global issues such as the development of the world economy, the problems of the developing countries, the environment, human security, taking into account the extraordinary developments in information and technology.[6]

Why are geopolitical security issues crucially important to Japan? During the Cold War, when the security of the world was clearly

---

[6] Kazuhiko Togo, in Taiheiyou wo kangaeru (Thinking of the Pacific), *Gaiko Forum*, No. 141, May 2000, p. 20.

divided between East (socialist countries) and West (democratic countries), there was probably no real need to consider geopolitical security interests for many countries, including Japan. But as the Cold War ended, this issue became a reality.

One approach to answer this question is to go back to the period when the world was not yet governed by the Cold War divide, e.g. the geopolitical conditions which surrounded Japan from the Meiji Restoration to World War II. As we have seen briefly in the Prologue, there were clearly two areas where prewar Japan found its geopolitical strategic interest: the first was Northeast Asia, including Korea, Manchuria, and China, eventually spreading to include Indochina and Southeast Asia; the second was the Pacific Ocean and the United States, looming on the other horizon. These were Japan's priorities as it developed from the Meiji era through to the 1930's, and the Pacific War. Europe,—in particular Great Britain and Germany—it must be understood, was not an area of vital interest to Japan, but it was essential in maintaining Japan's geopolitical interest.

Considering the many events that have taken place in the world since the 1990's, one may observe that critical events occurred precisely in the same areas as in pre-war history. The context and implications differ entirely, but their similarity in geopolitical location is striking. Two major areas of geopolitical security interest coincide completely. The role of Europe, though from a different perspective, is also resonant, and the list would be complete if we were to add the Middle East to this consideration. The first focus will be, taking into account that prewar history ended with the war with America: the United States across the Pacific, the second: Northeast Asia, including Korea, China, Southeast Asia and Russia, the third: Europe, and the fourth: the Middle East.

What global agendas are of critical importance to Japan?

A great part of the postwar Japanese strength was concentrated on economic development. If one thinks economics, then one has to think global. This is the axiom of economics in the world we live. At the same time there is no reason to consider that global thinking should be monopolized by the socio-economic agenda. Thus, in line with how it is explained in this book, I would like to mention three areas: first, the key question of development and developing countries, and the way Japan can contribute, at the heart of which lies the matter of ODA; second, the general framework of global trade and investment, and a wide range of issues pertaining to 'globalization' and sustainable development; third, agendas for peace and security from a global perspective.

Let me summarize very briefly the key characteristics of these seven agendas.

Geopolitical issues of vital importance for Japan

(1) *Across the Pacific Ocean: the United States*

The importance of the United States for Japan's security interests need not be underlined here. Nevertheless, it should be noted that particularly during the period after the demise of the Soviet Union, security relations between Japan and the United States were redefined and reconfirmed.

In the summer of 2003, the bilateral security relations stand on a firm basis. Japan's post-Cold War policy to bear greater responsibility in her own defence and in making a real contribution in matters of peace and security put alliance relations with the US on such a firm basis. It was no coincidence that the Bush-Koizumi friendship developed in that sound soil of strategic relationship. Koizumi's support of President Bush in March as well as his decision in July to send the JSDF to Iraqi humanitarian-reconstruction activities symbolizes this sound relationship.

At the same time, Japan has reached an important point in its alliance relations. The war in Iraq created an overwhelming impression of US unilateralism, a serious transatlantic split, resentments from the Islamic world, many difficult postwar issues in governing Iraq, and a new search for the role which the United Nations could play in the coming decades. As a true alliance partner, it is critically important that Japan expresses her views even if they differ from those of the US and will become engaged in a serious discourse with the United States on these difficult issues.

The North Korean nuclear weapons crisis is another reason for the necessity of maintaining and deepening a real discourse as alliance partners.

Japan needs to create an independent, pro-active foreign policy, which fully takes into account the interest of the alliance partner, but which at the same time, unambiguously asserts her own judgement and national interest consideration. The future of the relationship will then be in good shape.

(2) *Toward the adjacent areas: East Asia*

In summer 2003 Northeast Asia stands at the crossroads of new strategic relations. The North Korean nuclear crisis has become a real security threat for the region. Particularly for Japan, it poses the most acute security danger in the whole post-WWII period. The historical perception of the early Meiji period that security threats come from the Korean peninsula proved to be right, but certainly in a very different nature compared to the Meiji period.

The emergence of the Six-party Talks concerning the North Korean nuclear issue may be opening interesting strategic perspectives. At the end of 2003, each member of the Six-party Talks is finding its own interest in participating in this framework. If this framework plays a useful role in squeezing out an ultimate agreement between North Korea and the US, multilateral dialogues regarding peace and security could bear a more dynamic character in the region thence onwards.

For Japan, a new challenging task may be opened: through consultation and coordination in this framework Japan might be able to strengthen her relations with each of the member countries. Relations with South Korea count heavily, China is undoubtedly a key player, dialogue with Russia helps, policy coordination with the US naturally has a crucial importance. Strengthening the ties with each may open for Japan a new strategic position in the region for many years to come.

In the mid to long-term perspectives the most important strategic task facing Japan in Northeast Asia is the People's Republic of China. What type of relationship will Japan maintain with China, with its massive economic potential, its growing military strength, and increasingly assertive political role? As a potential threat to the security of the region, the question of Taiwan cannot be underestimated.

Supporting the development of a strategic dialogue in Northeast Asia, the Asia-Pacific region generally has seen a gradual consolidation of mechanisms for multilateral dialogue. From Japan's perspective these structures fan out from nearest neighbours with: the Three (Japan, China and South Korea); ASEAN plus Three; and ARF and APEC which cover the entire Asia-Pacific region.

In these newly emerging geopolitical relationships, issues lingering from the past might have a more productive context for their ultimate resolution.

(3) *Toward a relevant dialogue partner: Europe*

Japan and Europe did not share vital security interests from a geopolitical perspective before World War II, and I cannot say that today much has changed in this respect. However, I do believe, that during the four decades of the Cold War Japan and Europe came to share common values, common problems and common responsibilities. If I say 'common values', I do not mean that, for example, Japan and Europe have now created an identical democratic society. The difference in history, culture and political structure is, of course, evident in their respective approaches regarding this issue. But generally speaking, after World War II Japan and Europe moved together in the same direction and toward the same goal.

Decades of trade disputes are, at least for now, over. During the 1990's, after the end of the Cold War, Japan and Europe began to move in their common efforts toward the consolidation of these 'common values' as defined above. The Japan-EC Joint Declaration of 1991 and the Japan-EU Action Plan in 2001 symbolize these efforts.

In 2003, the War in Iraq and the American unilateralism in the background presented a real test to the nature of the political dialogue between Japan and Europe. There was no issue more important than this one for Japan and Europe to seriously engage in an exchange of views.

The Japan-Europe link was long said to be the weakest in the chain of trilateral relations between Europe, America and Japan. Against the background of a transatlantic split Japan has gained an unprecedented opportunity to redress this weaker part of the relationships. Will Japan and Europe be able to strengthen the dialogue and their ties? An important strategic challenge for the future is opened here.

(4) *From the perspectives of oil and security: the Middle East*

Traditionally Japan's interests in the Middle East were closely linked with Japan's dependence on oil.

But events in the 1990's, after the end of the Cold War, lead us to conclude that problems originating from this region could affect fundamental geopolitical interests of so many countries on a global scale. If this is the case, Japan's foreign policy will face new challenges and tasks that will call for a rapid response.

The root of all tension, the Middle East peace process, is still so far from being resolved. The first phase of the war against terrorism after 9/11 was successfully completed after the collapse of the Taliban regime in Afghanistan, but the origins of international terrorism were far from being eradicated. The War in Iraq in 2003 brought an end to Saddam Hussein's regime, but the repercussions of this war are yet unknown. Reactions from the Arab world, the future reconstruction of Iraq, the transatlantic rift, and the legitimacy of the United Nations, all these issues are left unanswered in light of the overwhelming power and unilateralism demonstrated by the United States.

For Japan, to answer these questions and participate usefully in global security issues related to this region, are formidable challenges in the coming years.

Global issues of critical significance for Japan

In the half century of postwar development, Japan became an economic giant. Since the 1990's Japan has encountered difficulties never before experienced during the previous decades of rapid development. Still Japan's economic power cannot be dismissed lightly. Japan has to fulfill global responsibilities commensurate with its economic power, not only in global economic diplomacy, but in global political diplomacy as well.

(5) Filling the gap between the developed and the developing countries: Official Development Assistance (ODA)

One of the major issues facing the world economy at the threshold of the 21st century is the question of development and the increasing discrepancies between the developed and the developing nations. Japan's postwar diplomacy endeavoured to fill in the gap and contribute toward the advancement of the developing countries. ODA was its vehicle and it was perhaps the most consistent and effective tool of Japan's postwar foreign policy.

In the latter half of the 1990's, ODA reached a turning point. The economic recession put a pressure on ODA to downsize and in 2001 Japan ceased to be the number one donor. Accountability to taxpayers became a determining factor for its future. In the summer of 2003 the Japanese government made a serious attempt to create a stronger consensus on ODA implementation in the form of a new ODA Charter.

Whether ODA can continue to play its role as a major foreign policy tool is one of the crucial tasks which Japan's foreign policy is now facing. It is sincerely hoped that Japan will not weaken the best tool in its foreign policy implementation.

(6) *Toward the creation of values and rules to be shared by all countries: Multilateral Economic Diplomacy*

Despite the 'lost decade' of the 1990's Japan is still an economic giant. As an economic giant, Japan naturally has a responsibility to create values and rules which will enable all countries to enjoy greater wealth and prosperity. Bilateral ODA is one of the important tools in achieving this objective, but making an active contribution to multilateral economic diplomacy is another.

When one focuses on Japan's leadership role in the global efforts for the enhancement of the free and multilateral flow of trade and investment, the political necessity of protecting a part of domestic production often appears as a stumbling block. Agriculture is one of the most quoted examples.

Japan has taken active leadership in promoting the WTO/Doha Round. But by the summer of 2003 it is reported that Japan's position in agriculture might create difficulty for the achievement of a general consensus. It goes without saying that agriculture is a difficult issue. It is hoped that Japan would have the political strength to satisfy the dual agenda to take a leadership role in advancing the causes of the Doha Round and to meet the domestic necessity over agriculture inside Japan.

In all areas pertaining to the global economy, Japan is expected to play a leadership role, based on a political determination to find an answer to satisfy the diverging interests of the international community, while meeting legitimate internal demand. The answer is not easy, but it is the only basis upon which Japan can make a 'sustainable' contribution for the strengthening of global, free and multilateral economy.

(7) *Sharing responsibly in enhancing global peace and security: Multilateral Political Diplomacy*

During the 1990's Japan began to make positive contributions in UN peacekeeping activities. Despite the continuing constitutional limitation, Japan's participation in the UN peacekeeping forces in

Cambodia, the Golan Heights, and East Timor, as well as in the rear area support of the coalition forces against international terrorism in Afghanistan from December 2001, in Iraq, as prospected, and its preparations in considering a 'permanent law' for Japan's participation to multinational coalition forces were substantial steps forward.

At the same time, after the War in Iraq in March/April 2003, the United Nations were put under new tension in search of its role under American unilateralism. Japan has quietly underpinned the role of the United Nations: before the war started, by persuading the American administration to go through the Security Council resolution, and after the war ended, again by letting the Security Council adopt a resolution which urges member countries to contribute to Iraqi humanitarian and reconstruction assiatance.

Still, the overwhelming memory of the failure in getting the second resolution before the attack is alive in the minds of participants and observers. Repeated attacks against UN peacekeepers in Iraq make UN missions' activities there very difficult.

Despite all the changes, which had taken place in the 1990's and the beginning of the 2000's, the influence of public opinion inclined towards pacifism cannot be negated in Japan. In such a situation, the consensus of international society, which can be formulated only through the United Nations, is a critically important basis for enlarging Japan's contribution and participation to the cause of international peace and security.

What is Japan's view and what role will Japan play in the process of redefining UN activities? An important and challenging agenda for the future is opened for Japan's foreign policy.

3. *Five unresolved issues from the past*

Past conditions present-day foreign policy

The seven agendas described in the previous Section are agendas for the future. They are tasks, objectives, and challenges for Japan's foreign policy in the early decades of the 21st century. The more Japan is able to develop a creative and dynamic policy in these areas, the greater Japan's national interest should become. Ultimately, this should bring about greater peace and prosperity in the world.

But the more you analyse these agendas for the future, the more you realize that the past is closely interwoven with the present. Sometimes it seemed as though heavy anchors of the past weighed down the ship of "Japanese foreign policy".

During my 34 years in the Foreign Ministry, the past has also cast shadows on my work in many ways. Having written the twelve Chapters of this book, I reconfirm the impression of just how much the past has affected the present Japanese foreign policy in many important fields.

Dealing with the issues from the past might require additional energy and imagination, because you not only need to address the present consequences, but you also need to have an understanding of what the past meant for the people who lived through it in its historical context. Lack of understanding for the values which were so important a few decades ago in their proper historical context makes the content of the foreign policy shallow.

Eight years ago, when I lectured on Japan's foreign policy in Moscow, it also occurred to me that certain agendas from the past weighed heavily in the conduct of the present-day Japanese foreign policy. I included these specific issues in the conclusion of my book published in Russia in 1996 '50 Years of Japanese Foreign Policy (1945–1995)'.

During the eight years since then, many people have worked hard to alleviate this weight from the past. It was my fervent desire that Japan's foreign policy be liberated from these burdens from the past and I viewed it as my primary task to devote my energy to this end in the areas where I was assigned.

It now saddens me somewhat to see that the five issues I am going to describe as the 'burdens from the past' are identical to those I included in the conclusion of my book published eight years ago. This does not mean, however, that no progress has been made in the past eight years. Certainly in some areas progress was made, but there were also missed opportunities.

Five unresolved issues

(1) Resumption of diplomatic relations with North Korea
Present-day foreign policy toward North Korea is dominated by the issue of nuclear weapons as the most urgent security matter in the

Far East. The Koizumi government is exerting great efforts in playing a useful role in the international coalition to prevent North Korea from possessing nuclear weapons. This is an inevitable course for Japan to take in the field of foreign policy.

Domestically, public opinion is determined that before relations with North Korea can be normalized, the issue of the abduction of Japanese nationals must be completely resolved. Given the traumatic experiences of the families of the abductees the views of the public are, to say the least, understandable.

But at the same time, Japan-North Korea relations are conditioned by the past and can be traced back to the Japanese involvement in the Korean peninsula and the Japanese annexation of Korea during 1910–1945. The establishment of a diplomatic relationship is an objective which must be achieved if we are to overcome this past, which has lasted for 58 years.

On two occasions in the past, when a window of opportunity might have been opened: Shin Kanemaru's visit to North Korea in September 1990 and Koizumi's visit in September 2002, both opportunities were missed. From the point of view of national interest, I am saddened by these missed opportunities.

In principle the establishment of diplomatic relations not only resolves the burden from the past, but also consolidates Japan's geopolitical position in Northeast Asia, because dialogue *per se* should, in principle, engender greater room for exerting influence.

One may also add that in the long term, the improvement of North-South relations and the eventual unification of North and South Korea are bound to happen. In order for Japan to create harmonious ties with a united Korea, an early normalization of relations with North Korea and the establishment of stable relations are in the interest of Japan.

(2) *Conclusion of the Peace Treaty with Russia*

After the heightened exchanges during the 1990's the Peace Treaty negotiations on the territorial issue over the four islands failed to produce a breakthrough. For Japan, the territorial problem with Russia is not an economic or security problem. Rather, it is an acute reflection of wounded national pride from the tragic events between Japan and the Soviet Union during the spring and summer of 1945. It is an issue of victim consciousness in the context of wounded national pride.

Thus at the beginning of the 21st century, Japan and Russia entered into a low profile and moderate state of relations. Economic relations, regional cooperation and security exchanges are conducted with moderate enthusiasm.

The Japanese have reached the point of measuring the weight of territorial issue in the context of overall relations. This can certainly be considered as a positive development. But how important is it that it be resolved in the context of the postwar wounded national consciousness? Leaving the situation as it stands now means that an issue so important in the past is left neglected. It also means a lost opportunity for Japan. A drastically improved bilateral relationship leading to much increased diplomatic leverage for Japan is not achieved.

The reconstruction of a dynamic Russian policy is a difficult, but unavoidable task for Japan's foreign policy.

(3) *How to overcome the question of war responsibility*
This is a complicated and complex issue. It is even more difficult to define its essence, but I will try:

1) When the Pacific War ended, the Japanese were faced with total devastation and an abrupt rupture from past values;

2) They re-emerged with a general sense of remorse and apology for the suffering Japan had caused, particularly in Asia;

3) But the situation was also confusing. On the one hand, there were strong 'leftist' beliefs that everything Japan had done in the prewar period had been wrong. On the other hand, there were people who were convinced that many soldiers had died with good faith and love for the country and that their honour had to be protected. This split became so deep that solid and unified views did not emerge;

4) In the 1980's open criticism from China and Korea began, particularly on the textbook issues and visits to the Yasukuni Shrine. Some analysts argue that their positions were determined by the domestic situations in their respective countries. Subsequently statements were made by Japanese politicians defending prewar activities, which soon resulted in their resignation, when criticisms from neighbouring countries were raised. These events also added to the confusion;

5) Thus for many decades, Japan was not able to create a national consensus on its actions prior to and during the war or what should be negated and what should be defended;

6) The Murayama Statement of 1995 set the tone of remorse and apology. Real signs of reconciliation began, particularly with South Korea and the Netherlands. Improvement was seen with China and Great Britain;

7) And yet this issue is far from resolved. A more articulate 'nationalist view' has emerged from within Japan. The way this view is transmitted is not helping in bringing about reconciliation with the Asian countries. Prime Minister Koizumi's visit to the Yasukuni Shrine and the approval of controversial textbooks recently re-emerged with no sign of a clear answer.

It is my view that Japan needs to have two types of courage: the courage to acknowledge and apologize for the deeds which were wrong, which Japan committed as perpetrator; but at the same time to have the courage to stand firm against wrong accusations and to defend her honour and her soldiers who were acting in good faith.

But then, what was right and what was wrong? It is not easy. But now, nearly 60 years after the war ended, has not the time come to face history with greater wisdom? There should be a way that governments reach certain basic understandings, without delving into the past, but by agreeing on certain protocols which will prevent further politicization of this issue. The Japanese government should base its position on the Murayama Statement. And then, it is primarily academics and scholars who should bear the task of facing the history and the discourse to find a common approach toward the past.

Admittedly, this will take time. It took Japan 50 years to get to the Murayama Statement. Without losing the momentum, efforts should be continued to find the means to reach a real reconciliation.

The ultimate objective of Japan's foreign policy toward adjacent countries is to create relations based on mutual trust and friendship. This alone can ensure maximum benefits to Japan and optimize Japan's diplomatic leverage. But in order to achieve this objective, with China and Korea in particular, there is a need for genuine reconciliation over the past.

Japan, together with China and Korea are in great need of 'future-oriented' relations, but in my view, it cannot be accomplished by ignoring the past. On the contrary, the time has come to face history from both sides more seriously than ever, in an objective and scholarly manner.

(4) *Article 9 of the Constitution*

I cannot overemphasize the weight of pacifism in postwar Japanese foreign policy. Serious continuing opposition between the passive pacifists and realists conditioned Japan's security policy. But as the years went by, such emotional and controversial issues as 'partial or comprehensive peace', 'security ties with the US or neutrality' and 'minimum forces for self-defence or no armament' were resolved one by one.

From the 1990's, after the end of the Cold War, the JSDF began actively participating in UN peacekeeping operations and in the rear area support of the coalition of forces which were acting with the endorsement of the Security Council of the United Nations. All these activities were within the realm of Article 9 of the Constitution in the sense that 'use of force' was excluded from the purpose of their activities. But in comparison to the pre-1991 Gulf War situation it was clearly a sea change.

Japan still has several agendas to fulfil before she completes everything she could have done within the realm of Article 9. Outstanding laws in relation to the Laws concerning the Response to an Armed Attack have to be put in place. The bill studied by the special task force in the Cabinet Secretariat to create a 'permanent legal basis' for Japan's participation in rear area support to the coalition of forces is one task. The revision of the 1992 International Peace Cooperation Law to harmonize Japan's practice and commonly accepted international practice of peacekeeping operations is another task.

What is going to happen when all these agenda are completed? What will happen after the report by the Parliamentary Research Commission on the Constitution is finalized in 2005? Will the critical moment come that Japan ultimately revises Article 9 of the Constitution?

It is not easy to draw a clear conclusion. However, one thing is clear. Any significant revision of Article 9 would require not only the strong support of the Japanese people, but also the understanding of the international community, particularly from the neighbouring Asian countries. Sensitivity toward adjacent countries, a theme strongly underlined by pacifists, would be critical in this scenario.

It must therefore be noted that the interpretation of Article 9 and the issue of war responsibility are closely tied in the deep current of postwar Japanese foreign policy. For many years it was the surrounding Asian countries that had criticized Japan for not assuming the responsibilities of its prewar conduct and had voiced the sharpest concern regarding the possible revival of Japanese militarism. Enhanced trust with these countries would no doubt give a stronger basis for greater participation for Japan in matters related to international peace and security.

(5) *Reforms in the domestic economy*
Domestic economy is usually not a vital foreign policy issue. But in the case of Japan, postwar economic development has been so powerful that the very structure of the Japanese domestic economy has become the subject of international dispute. During the period of trade disputes, particularly from the 1980's to the early 1990's, the key theme of "making Japanese society more attuned to the outside world" permeated reformist thinking.

But by the middle of the 1990's the period of trade conflicts had gradually waned. Japan's primary policy objective became revitalizing its economy: overcoming non-performing loans, pulling the Japanese economy out of the deflationary spiral, and implementing structural reforms to stimulate the Japanese economy.

The task of the revitalization of the Japanese economy is still difficult. Some maintain that vigorous measures are necessary to squeeze the non-performing loans out from the markets, but others argue that hasty measures might result in widespread bankruptcy and massive unemployment. Some argue that reforms have to be implemented as quickly as possible, but others stress that getting out from under the deflationary spiral is the government's primary task. Some argue that budgetary expenditure has to be curbed to resolve the accumulated debt, but others maintain that enhanced public investment is necessary to boost the economy, because economic growth will eventually bring about greater tax revenues.

Regardless of the immediate priorities, deregulation, increased foreign investments, enhanced competition in the markets are some of the major policy guidelines toward recovery. It is interesting to note that these measures coincide exactly with the measures discussed in the 1980's to "make Japanese society more attuned to the outside world".

Japan has an enormous task ahead: to revitalize its economy and gain the confidence of the market and, above all, the confidence of the people on the future of their own society. A new aspiration is slowly developing toward a life in harmony with nature and modern technology. The real task is to achieve these internal visions in a manner 'harmonious with the outside world'.

The task of creating a strong and harmonized economy in Japan might exceed the narrow realm of foreign policy, but this is a task which absolutely needs to be resolved successfully, because the foreign policy implications of this agenda are indeed immeasurable.

4. *Epilogue: the flow of history and human efforts*

During the 58 years of postwar Japanese foreign policy, there have always been two crucial factors in achieving important policy objectives: the flow of history and human efforts.

The effective implementation of foreign policy requires a correct sense of history. One must know and feel the conditions which surround particular policy objectives. If one senses a surge in these conditions one must go forward, it could be the moment of truth.

At the same time, if one does not act at this moment of truth, or does not even realize that a moment of truth has arrived, nothing will ever be accomplished. A once opened window of opportunity will close quietly, and it will take years, sometimes decades, to open it again. The responsibility each individual is given at certain moments in history must not be taken lightly.

A common difficulty one faces at these important decision-making times is the question of how to define the national interest in that particular circumstance. This is a difficult question which one does not answer easily. On the one hand, there are usually some clear domestic values. They may take the form of specific material interests or some abstract values, be it nationalistic or otherwise. They may be strongly supported by public opinion, and the media may often be on their side. Would it serve the interest of the country to simply follow their views? No. A country's national interest has to be considered in a wider context. All surrounding conditions, historical legacies and future perspectives must be taken into account. If the subject of dispute is important—as a final resort—it is the Prime Minister alone who must make the decision. The responsibility of a diplomat is to advise the leadership of the best possible policy option to meet the national interest taking into account all necessary factors.

My mother, Ise Togo, died in July 1998. She was born as the only child of Shigenori Togo and his wife Edi De Lalande, a German woman from Hamburg. My mother accompanied Shigenori Togo to Berlin and Moscow, where he was sent as ambassador before the Pacific War and from that period onwards, including the period when he was appointed as foreign minister, stayed with him very closely until he died in the Sugamo prison hospital in 1950.

In the summer of 1998 my mother was already suffering severely from cancer. Just shortly before she passed away, when I was at her bed side, she suddenly began to ask me:

"Kazu, do you know what your grandfather used to say what the most important factor in diplomacy is?"

Since I could think of no immediate answer, I replied "No."

Then she said, "Well, he used to say that the most important thing in diplomacy is, when you come to a critical point in negotiations, be prepared to give 51(%) to your counterpart and be satisfied with 49(%) on your side."

My mother's answer surprised me. Shigenori Togo was known to be a person of strong will. He was remembered for his toughness in negotiations, e.g. with his Soviet counterpart V. M. Molotov in concluding the armistice in the Nomonhan Incident and in his unfaltering will in bringing the Pacific War to an end. This image of a principled and rigorous approach to the foreign policy did not fit in well with this compromise of giving 51 to the other side. Seeing that I did not grasp the essence of the answer, my mother continued:

"Usually we say in the foreign service that winning too much is not good for one's own country."

"Yes, that I have heard many times."

"If you win too much, then the other side will become frustrated and this will leave seeds for future contention. So the best outcome of a negotiation is a result of 50 to 50. It is a no winner and no loser situation."

"Well, that I have heard often too."

"But what your grandfather said was a little more. He said that a mutually satisfactory result would emerge if a negotiator ultimately thinks deeply about the position of the other side, even to the extent of contemplating giving 51 to the other side, i.e. a little more than the position of one's own country. This is the most difficult part. There are so many forces pressuring you to think about the immediate interest of your own country. Someone has to think about the position of the other side. And that is the way to secure ultimately the best interest of your country. That is the challenge and art of diplomacy."

Since then, whenever I found myself at a crucial point of a negotiation, I always asked myself what this 51 would have meant in order to find a solution in that particular circumstance.

BIBLIOGRAPHY

General

Gendaiyougono Kisochishiki (Basic Knowledge of Contemporary Vocabulary) 2002, Jiyuu-Kokuminsha, 2002.
Kokusaihou Jiten (Dictionary of International Law), Sanseido, 1995.
Microsoft Encarta Reference Library, 2003.
MOFA, *Gaikou Seisho (Diplomatic Bluebook)*, various years.
MOFA, *Shuyo Jyouyaku-shuu (Principal Treaties)*, 1991.

Peter Duus, *Modern Japan*, Houghton Mifflin, 1998.
Bert Edstrom, *Japan's Evolving Foreign Policy Doctrine-From Yoshida to Miyazawa*, Palgrave, 1999.
Craig C. Garby and Mary Brown Bullock ed., *Japan—A New Kind of Superpower?*, The Woodrow Wilson Center Press, 1994.
Michael Green, *Japan's Reluctant Realism*, Palgrave, 2001.
Glenn D. Hook, Julie Gilson, Christopher W. Hughes, Hugo Dobson, *Japan's International Relations-Politics, Economics and Security*, Routledge, 2001.
C. Hosoya, *Nihongaikouno Kiseki (Traces of Japanese Foreign Policy)*, NHK, 1993.
M. Ikei, *Nihongaikoushi Gaisetu (Overview of Japanese Foreign Policy)* 3rd Edition, Keio University, 1997.
Takashi Inoguchi and Jain Purnendra ed., *Japanese Foreign Policy today*, Palgrave, 2000.
M. Iokibe (also ed.), K. Sakamoto, M. Tadokoro, H. Nakanishi, and K. Murata, *Sengo Nihongaikoushi (Post-War Japanese Foreign Policy)*, Yuuhikaku, 1999.
A. Iriye, *Nihonno Gaikou (Japanese Foreign Policy)*, Cuukou Shinsho, 1966.
A. Iriye, *Shin-Nihonno Gaikou (New Japanese Foreign Policy)*, Cuukou Shinsho, 1991.
Y. Kawashima, *Japanese Foreign Policy at the Crossroads, Challenges and Options for the Twenty-First Century*, Brookings Institution Press, 2003.
Jeffery Kingston, *Japan in Transformation 1952–2000*, Pearson Education Limited, 2001.
Richard D. Leitch, Jr., Akira Kato, and Martin E. Weinstein, *Japan's Role in the Post-Cold War World*, Greenwood, 1995.
J.A.A. Stockwin, *Governing Japan*, Blackwell, 1999.

Prologue

S. Izumi, *Dodotaru Nihonjin (The Dignified Japanese)*, Shodensha, 1997.
H.Takeuchi, *Ano sensouha ittai nandeattaka (What was that War?)*, Harashobou, 1997.
Shigehiko Togo, *Sofu Togo Shigenorino Shougai (Life of my grandfather Shigenori Togo)*, Bungeishunjyu, 1993.
Shigenori Togo, *Jidaino Ichimen*, Chuukoubunko, 1989, translated by Ben Bruce Blakney and Fumihiko Togo, *The Cause of Japan*, Simon and Schuster, 1956.

Chapter 1

Bruce Cumings, 'Japan's position in the world system', in: Andrew Gordon (ed.) *Postwar Japan as History*, Oxford 1933.
John W. Dower, *Embracing Defeat: Japan in the Wake of World War II*, New York: W.W. Norton, 1999.
Norma Field, *In the Realm of a Dying Emperor*, New York: Pantheon, 1991.

C. Hosoya, *Sanfuranshisuko kouwaheno michi (Road to the San Francisco Peace)*, Chuoukouron, 1984.

I. Sato, *Nihonkokukenpo Gaisetsu (The Constitution of Japan)*, Gakuyou Shobou, 1993.

Chapter 2

JDA, *Bouei Hakusho (Defence White Paper)*, various years.

Y. Funabashi, *Doumei Hyoryuu (Alliance Adrift)*, Iwanami, 1997.

Michael J. Green, 'Defense or Security? The US-Japan Defense Guidelines and China', in: David M. Lampton (ed.) *Major Power Relations in Northeast Asia: Win-Win or Zero-Sum Game*, Tokyo, 2001.

F. Togo, *Nichibeigaiko 30 Nen (Thirty years of Japan-US foreign relations)*, Sekaino Ugokisha, 1982.

K. Wakaizumi, *Tasakunakarishiwo Shinzentohossu (I wanted to believe that there was no other option)*, Bungeishinjyu, 1995.

Chapter 3

METI, *Tsushou Hakusho (METI White Paper)*, various years

K. Akiyama, *Nichibei Tsushoumasatsuno Kenkyuu (Research on Japan-US Trade Conflict)*, Dobunkan, 1994.

M. Fukuoka, *Keizaigaku Nyuumon (Introduction to Economics Third Edition)*, Nihonkeizai Shuppansha, 2000.

T. Nishino, *Keizaiyougoni Tsuyokunaruhon (Mastering the Language of Economics)*, PHP Bunko, 2000.

M. Satake, 'Trade conflicts between Japan and the United States over Market Access: The case of Automobiles and Automotive parts', *Pacific Economic Paper*, no. 310, Australia-Japan Research Centre, Dec. 2000.

A. Suzuta, *Konoissatsude Keizaiga Wakaru (Understanding Economics in One Book)*, Mikasa Shobou, 2000.

M. Yabunaka, Taibei Keizaikoushou (In Search of New Japan-US Economic Relations), Simul Press, 1991.

Chapter 4

Shen Caibin, *The China Shock (Japanese)*, Nihon Nouritsukyoukai Manejimento Centre, 2002.

H.G. Hilbert, 'China and Japan: Conflict or Cooperation? What does Trade Data say?', in: H.G. Hilbert and Haak (ed.), *Japan and China*, New York, 2002A.

A. Ishii, K. Shu, Y. Soeya, Lin Xiao Guang, *Nichuu Kokkouseijyouka, Nicchuu Heiwa Yuukoujyouyaku Teiketsu Koushou (Normalization of Japan-China diplomatic relations, Negotiation of the Japan-China Peace and Friendship Treaty)*, Iwanami, 2003.

I. Kayahara (also ed.), Y. Onishi, and others, *Chuugokuha Dokoni Mukau (Where does China go?)*, Sousousha, 2001.

Ma Licheng, 'Nichuu Kankei no Shin Shikou (New thinking in China-Japan Relations)', in: *Strategy and Control*, translated and published in *Chuuoukouron*, March 2003.

M. Nakajima and Y. Komori, *2008 nen Chuugokuno Shinjitsu (Supremacy or Collapse Reality of China until 2008)*, Business-Sha, 2002.

A. Tanaka, *Nichuu Kankei 1945–1990 (Japan-China Relations 1945–1990)*, Tokyo University, 1991.

Chapter 5

K. Kobayashi, K. Odagawa, K. Yokobori, and others, *Kitachou sen—Sono Jitsuzouto Kiseki (North Korea, its Reality and Locus)*, Kobunken, 1998.
T. Shigemura, *Kankokuhodo Taisetuna Kunihanai (There is no country more important than Korea)*, Touyoukeizai Shinpousha, 1998.

Chapter 6

James Hsiung ed., *Asia Pacific in the New World Politics*, Lynne Rienner Publishers, 1993.
A. Fukushima (also translator), David Capie, Paul Evans, *Lexicon Asia-Taiheiyou Anzenhoshoutaiwa (The Asia-Pacific Security Lexicon)*, Nihonkeizai Hyouronsha, 2002.
A. Fukushima, *Japanese Foreign Policy, The Emerging Logic of Multilateralism*, Macmillan, 1999.
Y. Funabashi, *Asia Pacific Fusion (Japanese)*, Chuuou Kouronsha, 1995.
T. Kikuchi, *APEC Asia Taiheiyou Shinchitujyono Mosaku (APEC, Search for a New Order in the Asia-Pacific)*, Japan Institute of International Affairs, 1995.
Wolf Mendl, *Japan's Asia policy*, Routledge, 1995.
John Ravenhill, *APEC and the Construction of Pacific Rim Regionalism*, Cambridge University press, 2001.
A. Rix, 'Japan and the Region: leading from behind', in: R. Riggot, R. Leaver and J. Ravenhill, *Pacific Economic Relations in the 1990's: Cooperation or Conflict*, St. Leonards, Australia, 1993.

Chapter 7

MOFA, *Warerano Hoppou Ryoudo (Our Northern Territory)*, 2000.
MOFA, Japan and Russia, *Nichiroryoudomondaino Rekishinikansuru Kyoudousakuseishir-youshuu (Joint Compendium of Documents on the history of Japan Russian Territorial Problem)*, 1992.

S. Edamura, *Teikoku Kaitai Zengo (Before and After the Demise of an Empire)*, Toshi Shuppan, 1997.
T. Hasegawa, *Hoppouryoudomondaito Nichirokankei (Northern Territorial Issue and Japan-Russia Relations)* Chikuma, 2000.
T. Hasegawa, *The Northern Territories Dispute and Russo-Japanese Relations*, volume 1 *Between War and Peace 1697–1985* and volume 2 *Neither War nor Peace 1985–1998*, University of California at Berkeley, 1998.
H. Kimura, *Nichirokokkyoukoushoushi (History of Border Negotiations between Japan and Russia)*, Chuukou Shinsho, 1993.
H. Kimura, *Distant Neighbors*, volume One *Japanese-Russian Relations under Brezhnev and Andropov*, and volume Two *Japanese-Russian Relations under Gorbachev and Yeltsin*, M.E. Sharpe, New York, 2000.
H. Kimura, G.T. Alison, K. Sarkisov, *Nichibeiro Shinjidaiheno Shinario (A Scenario of New Era between Japan, US, and Russia)*, Dayamondosha, 1993.
K. Ogawa, *Saigono Nyuufurontia (The Last New Frontier)*, Daiichi-Insatsu, 1993.
A. Panov, *Fushinkara Shinraihe (Beyond Distrust to Trust)*, Simul Press, 1992.
K. Sato and A. Komaki, *Nichiro-Shunou Koushou (Japan-Russia Leaders Negotiations)*, Iwanami Shoten, 2003.
Gilbert Rozman, *Japan's Response to the Gorbachev Era, 1985–1991*, Princeton University Press, 1992.
Gilbert Rozman (ed.), *Japan and Russia—The Tortuous Path to Normalization, 1949–1999*, St. Martin's Press, 2000.
N. Shimotomai, *Hoppouryoudo Q&A 80 (80 Q&A on Northern Territory)*, Shougakkan, 2000.

K. Togo, *Nichiroshinnjidaiheno Jyosou (Japan and Russia, in Search of Breakthrough)*, Simul Press, 1993.
H. Wada, *Hoppouryoudomondai (Northern Territorial Problem)*, Asahi Sensho, 1999.

Chapter 8

Henri-Claude de Bettingnies, 'Japan and the E.C.' 92', in: Craig C. Garby and Mary Brown Bullock (ed.) *Japan: A new kind of superpower?* Baltimore, 1994.
Marie Conte-Helm, *Igirisuto Nihon (Japan and the North East of England)*, Simul Press, 1989.
Julie Gilson, *Japan and the European Union, A Partnership for the Twenty-First Century?* Palgrave, 2000.
K. Kusaka, *EU Tougou Kusanoneno Genjitu (EU Unification, Grass Roots Reality)*, Nihon Keizai Shinbunsha, 1995.
T. Onishi & S. Nakasone, *EU Seido to Kinou (EU, System and Function)*, Waseda University Press, 1995.
T. Togo, *20 Seikino Yoroppa (Europe in the 20th Century)*, Sekainougokisha, 1991.
M. Watanabe, Grand Chamberlain of the Emperor, *Koushitsuto Orandaoukeno 50nen (Fifty years between the Imperial family and the Dutch Royal family)*, Chuoukoron, 2003.1
H. Yamane, *EU/EC Ho-Oushuurengouno Kiso (European Community Law and Legal Foundations of the European Union)*, Yuushindo, 1995.

Chapter 9

J. Eto, 'The Japanese Constitution and the Post-Gulf War World', in: *Japan Echo*, vol. XVIII, No. 3, Autumn 1991.
K. Ijiri, 'Japan's Defeat in the Gulf War', in: *Japan Echo*, vol. XVIII, No. 3, Autumn 1991.
T. Kagami, *Chuutoufunsou Sonohyakunennno Soukoku (100 Years of Middle East Conflict)*, Yuuhikaku Sensho, 2001.
S. Koyama, *Saudiarabia (Saudi Arabia)*, Chuukousensho, 1994.
T. Sudo, *Darenidemowakaru Chuutoufunsou (Middle East Conflict for everyones' understanding)*, Chuutou Chousakai, 1995.
N. Tanaka, *Enerugiimondai Nyuumon (Introduction to Energy Issues)*, Nihon Keizaisha, 2000.
R. Teshima, *1991 Nihonno Haiboku (Japan's Defeat in 1991)*, Shinchousha, 1993.

Chapter 10

MOFA, *ODA Nenji Houkoku, Yearly Report of ODA*; *ODA Hakusho, ODA White Paper*, various years.

J. Inada, 'Japan's Aid Diplomacy: Economic, Political or Strategic?' in: K. Newland ed., *The International relations of Japan*, 1990.

Chapter 11

MOFA, First International Organizations Division, Economic Affairs Department, *Kaisetsu WTO Kyoutei (Commentary on WTO Agreements)*, Japan Institute of International Affairs, May 1996.
MOFA, Foreign Policy Bureau, *Kokusaikikan Soran (Overview of International Organizations)*, Japan Institute of International Affairs, June 1996.

Y. Funabashi, *Tsuuka Retsuretsu*, Asahi Shinbun-sha, 1988.
K. Hamada, 'Japan's Prospective Role in the International Monetary Regime', in: C.C. Garby and M.B. Bullock ed., *Japan—A New Kind of Superpower?*, The Woodrow Wilson Center Press, 1994.

M. Mizoguchi & M. Matsuo, *Uruguay Round*, NHK, 1994.

M. Shiratori, *Sekai Ginkou Gurupu (The World Bank Group)*, Kokusaikaihatu Journal, 1993.

Chapter 12

Maurice Bertrand, *Kokurenno Kanouseito Genkai (L'ONU)*, Kokusai Shoin, 1995.

T. Ikeda, *Cambodia Waheiheno Michi (Road to Cambodian Peace)*, Toshishuppan, 1996.

Caroline Rose, 'Japanese role in PKO and Humanitarian Assistance', in: T. Inoguchi and J. Purnendra (ed.), *Japanese Foreign Policy Today*, Palgrave, 2000.

T. Shinyo (also ed.), H. Nakajima and others, *Kokusaiheiwakyouryoku Nyuumon (Introduction to International Peace Cooperation)*, Yuuhikaku, 1995.

Website Addresses
(as of November 2003)

Prime Minister's Residence	http://www.kantei.go.jp
Prime Minister's Office	http://www.sorifu.go.jp
Ministry of Foreign Affairs	http://www.mofa.go.jp
Japan Defence Agency	http://www.jda.go.jp
Ministry of Finance	http://www.mof.go.jp
Ministry of Economy, Trade and Industry	http://www.meti.go.jp
Ministry of Agriculture, Forestry and Fisheries	http://www.maff.go.jp
JETRO	http://www.jetro.go.jp
Asahi Shinbun	http://www.asahi.com
Mainichi Shinbun	http://www.mainichi.co.jp
Yomiuri Shinbun	http://www.yomiuri.co.jp
Nihon Keizai Shinbun	http://www.nikkei.co.jp
Sankei Shinbun	http://www.sankei.co.jp
Tokyo Shinbun	http://www.tokyo-np.co.jp
Hokkaido Shinbun	http://www.hokkaido-np.co.jp
Saga Shinbun	http://www.saga-s.co.jp
Kyodo News	http://www.kyodo.co.jp
Jiji News	http://www.jiji.com

APPENDICES

- Treaty of Peace with Japan (excerpts) (1951)
- Treaty of Mutual Cooperation and Security between Japan and the United States of America (1960)
- Treaty on Basic Relations between Japan and the Republic of Korea (1965)
- Joint Communiqué of the Government of Japan and the Government of the People's Republic of China (1972)
- Joint Declaration on Relations between the European Community and its Member States and Japan (1991)
- Japan-U.S. Joint Declaration on Security: Alliance for the 21st Century (1996)
- Japan-Republic of Korea Joint Declaration: A new Japan-Republic of Korea Partnership towards the Twenty-First Century (1998)
- Irkutsk Statement by the Prime Minister of Japan and the President of the Russian Federation on the Continuation of the Future Negotiations on the Issue of a Peace Treaty (2001)
- Japan-DPRK Pyongyang Declaration (2002)

TREATY OF PEACE WITH JAPAN (EXCERPTS)

8 September 1951

CHAPTER I

PEACE

Article 1

(a) The state of war between Japan and each of the Allied Powers is terminated as from the date on which the present Treaty comes into force between Japan and the Allied Power concerned as provided for in Article 23.

(b) The Allied Powers recognize the full sovereignty of the Japanese people over Japan and its territorial waters.

CHAPTER II

TERRITORY

Article 2

(a) Japan recognizing the independence of Korea, renounces all right, title and claim to Korea, including the islands of Quelpart, Port Hamilton and Dagelet.

(b) Japan renounces all right, title and claim to Formosa and the Pescadores.

(c) Japan renounces all right, title and claim to the Kurile Islands, and to that portion of Sakhalin and the islands adjacent to it over which Japan acquired sovereignty as a consequence of the Treaty of Portsmouth of 5 September 1905.

(d) Japan renounces all right, title and claim in connection with the League of Nations Mandate System, and accepts the action of the United Nations Security Council of 2 April 1947, extending the trusteeship system to the Pacific Islands formerly under mandate to Japan.

(e) Japan renounces all claim to any right or title to or interest in connection with any part of the Antarctic area, whether deriving from the activities of Japanese nationals or otherwise.

(f) Japan renounces all right, title and claim to the Spratly Islands and to the Paracel Islands.

Article 3
Japan will concur in any proposal of the United States to the United Nations to place under its trusteeship system, with the United States as the sole administering authority, Nansei Shoto south of 29deg. north latitude (including the Ryukyu Islands and the Daito Islands), Nanpo Shoto south of Sofu Gan (including the Bonin Islands, Rosario Island and the Volcano Islands) and Parece Vela and Marcus Island. Pending the making of such a proposal and affirmative action thereon, the United States will have the right to exercise all and any powers of administration, legislation and jurisdiction over the territory and inhabitants of these islands, including their territorial waters.

Article 4
(a) Subject to the provisions of paragraph (b) of this Article, the disposition of property of Japan and of its nationals in the areas referred to in Article 2, and their claims, including debts, against the authorities presently administering such areas and the residents (including juridical persons) thereof, and the disposition in Japan of property of such authorities and residents, and of claims, including debts, of such authorities and residents against Japan and its nationals, shall be the subject of special arrangements between Japan and such authorities. The property of any of the Allied Powers or its nationals in the areas referred to in Article 2 shall, insofar as this has not already been done, be returned by the administering authority in the condition in which it now exists. (The term nationals whenever used in the present Treaty includes juridical persons.)

(b) Japan recognizes the validity of dispositions of property of Japan and Japanese nationals made by or pursuant to directives of the United States Military Government in any of the areas referred to in Articles 2 and 3.

(c) Japanese owned submarine cables connection Japan with territory removed from Japanese control pursuant to the present Treaty shall be equally divided, Japan retaining the Japanese terminal and adjoining half of the cable, and the detached territory the remainder of the cable and connecting terminal facilities.

CHAPTER III

SECURITY

Article 5
(a) Japan accepts the obligations set forth in Article 2 of the Charter of the United Nations, and in particular the obligations

(i) to settle its international disputes by peaceful means in such a manner that international peace and security, and justice, are not endangered;

(ii) to refrain in its international relations from the threat or use of force against the territorial integrity or political independence of any State or in any other manner inconsistent with the Purposes of the United Nations;

(iii) to give the United Nations every assistance in any action it takes in accordance with the Charter and to refrain from giving assistance to any State against which the United Nations may take preventive or enforcement action.

(b) The Allied Powers confirm that they will be guided by the principles of Article 2 of the Charter of the United Nations in their relations with Japan.

(c) The Allied Powers for their part recognize that Japan as a sovereign nation possesses the inherent right of individual or collective self-defense referred to in Article 51 of the Charter of the United Nations and that Japan may voluntarily enter into collective security arrangements.

Article 6
(a) All occupation forces of the Allied Powers shall be withdrawn from Japan as soon as possible after the coming into force of the present Treaty, and in any case not later than 90 days thereafter. Nothing in this provision shall, however, prevent the stationing or retention of foreign armed forces in Japanese territory under or in consequence of any bilateral or multilateral agreements which have been or may be made between one or more of the Allied Powers, on the one hand, and Japan on the other.

(b) The provisions of Article 9 of the Potsdam Proclamation of 26 July 1945, dealing with the return of Japanese military forces to their homes, to the extent not already completed, will be carried out.

(c) All Japanese property for which compensation has not already been paid, which was supplied for the use of the occupation forces and which remains in the possession of those forces at the time of the coming into force of the present Treaty, shall be returned to the Japanese Government within the same 90 days unless other arrangements are made by mutual agreement.

CHAPTER V

CLAIMS AND PROPERTY

Article 14
(a) It is recognized that Japan should pay reparations to the Allied Powers for the damage and suffering caused by it during the war. Nevertheless it is also recognized that the resources of Japan are not presently sufficient, if it is to maintain a viable economy, to make complete reparation for all such damage and suffering and at the same time meet its other obligations.

Therefore,

1. Japan will promptly enter into negotiations with Allied Powers so desiring, whose present territories were occupied by Japanese forces and damaged by Japan, with a view to assisting to compensate those countries for the cost of repairing the damage done, by making available the services of the Japanese people in production, salvaging and other work for the Allied Powers in question. Such arrangements shall avoid the imposition of additional liabilities on other Allied Powers, and, where the manufacturing of raw materials is called for, they shall be supplied by the Allied Powers in question, so as not to throw any foreign exchange burden upon Japan.

2. (I) Subject to the provisions of subparagraph (II) below, each of the Allied Powers shall have the right to seize, retain, liquidate or otherwise dispose of all property, rights and interests of

(a) Japan and Japanese nationals,

(b) persons acting for or on behalf of Japan or Japanese nationals, and

(c) entities owned or controlled by Japan or Japanese nationals,

which on the first coming into force of the present Treaty were subject to its jurisdiction. The property, rights and interests specified in this subparagraph shall include those now blocked, vested or in the possession or under the control of enemy property authorities of Allied Powers, which belong to, or were held or managed on behalf of, any of the persons or entities mentioned in (a), (b) or (c) above at the time such assets came under the controls of such authorities.

(II) The following shall be excepted from the right specified in subparagraph (I) above:

(i) property of Japanese natural persons who during the war resided with the permission of the Government concerned in the territory of one of the Allied Powers, other than territory occupied by Japan, except property subjected to restrictions during the war and not released from such restrictions as of the date of the first coming into force of the present Treaty;

(ii) all real property, furniture and fixtures owned by the Government of Japan and used for diplomatic or consular purposes, and all personal furniture and furnishings and other private property not of an investment nature which was normally necessary for the carrying out of diplomatic and consular functions, owned by Japanese diplomatic and consular personnel;

(iii) property belonging to religious bodies or private charitable institutions and used exclusively for religious or charitable purposes;

(iv) property, rights and interests which have come within its jurisdiction in consequence of the resumption of trade and financial relations subsequent to 2 September 1945, between the country concerned and Japan, except such as have resulted from transactions contrary to the laws of the Allied Power concerned;

(v) obligations of Japan or Japanese nationals, any right, title or interest in tangible property located in Japan, interests in enterprises organized under the laws of Japan, or any paper evidence thereof; provided that this exception shall only apply to obligations of Japan and its nationals expressed in Japanese currency.

(III) Property referred to in exceptions (i) through (v) above shall be returned subject to reasonable expenses for its preservation and administration. If any such property has been liquidated the proceeds shall be returned instead.

(IV) The right to seize, retain, liquidate or otherwise dispose of property as provided in subparagraph (I) above shall be exercised in accordance with the laws of the Allied Power concerned, and the owner shall have only such rights as may be given him by those laws.

(V) The Allied Powers agree to deal with Japanese trademarks and literary and artistic property rights on a basis as favorable to Japan as circumstances ruling in each country will permit.

(b) Except as otherwise provided in the present Treaty, the Allied Powers waive all reparations claims of the Allied Powers, other claims of the Allied Powers and their nationals arising out of any actions taken by Japan and its nationals in the course of the prosecution of the war, and claims of the Allied Powers for direct military costs of occupation.

Article 16
As an expression of its desire to indemnify those members of the armed forces of the Allied Powers who suffered undue hardships while prisoners of war of Japan, Japan will transfer its assets and those of its nationals in countries which were neutral during the war, or which were at war with any of the Allied Powers, or, at its option, the equivalent of such assets, to the International Committee of the Red Cross which shall liquidate such assets and distribute the resultant fund to appropriate national agencies, for the benefit of former prisoners of war and their families on such basis as it may determine to be equitable. The categories of assets described in Article 14(a)2(II)(ii) through (v) of the present Treaty shall be excepted from transfer, as well as assets of Japanese natural persons not residents of Japan on the first coming into force of the Treaty. It is equally understood that the transfer provision of this Article has no application to the 19,770 shares in the Bank for International Settlements presently owned by Japanese financial institutions.

TREATY OF MUTUAL COOPERATION AND SECURITY BETWEEN JAPAN AND THE UNITED STATES OF AMERICA

19 January 1960

Article I

The Parties undertake, as set forth in the Charter of the United Nations, to settle any international disputes in which they may be involved by peaceful means in such a manner that international peace and security and justice are not endangered and to refrain in their international relations from the threat or use of force against the territorial integrity or political independence of any state, or in any other manner inconsistent with the purposes of the United Nations. The Parties will endeavor in concert with other peace-loving countries to strengthen the United Nations so that its mission of maintaining international peace and security may be discharged more effectively.

Article II

The Parties will contribute toward the further development of peaceful and friendly international relations by strengthening their free institutions, by bringing about a better understanding of the principles upon which these institutions are founded, and by promoting conditions of stability and well-being. They will seek to eliminate conflict in their international economic policies and will encourage economic collaboration between them.

Article III

The Parties, individually and in cooperation with each other, by means of continuous and effective self-help and mutual aid will maintain and develop, subject to their constitutional provisions, their capacities to resist armed attack.

Article IV

The Parties will consult together from time to time regarding the implementation of this Treaty, and, at the request of either Party, whenever the security of Japan or international peace and security in the Far East is threatened.

Article V

Each Party recognizes that an armed attack against either Party in the territories under the administration of Japan would be dangerous to its own peace and safety and declares that it would act to meet the common danger in accordance with its constitutional provisions and processes. Any such armed attack and all measures taken as a result thereof shall be immediately reported to the Security Council of the United Nations in accordance with the provisions of Article 51 of the Charter. Such measures shall be terminated when the Security Council has taken the measures necessary to restore and maintain international peace and security.

Article VI

For the purpose of contributing to the security of Japan and the maintenance of international peace and security in the Far East, the United States of America is granted the use by its land, air and naval forces of facilities and areas in Japan. The use of these facilities and areas as well as the status of United States armed forces in Japan shall be governed by a separate agreement, replacing the Administrative Agreement under Article III of the Security Treaty between Japan and the United States of America, signed at Tokyo on February 28, 1952, as amended, and by such other arrangements as may be agreed upon.

Article VII

This Treaty does not affect and shall not be interpreted as affecting in any way the rights and obligations of the Parties under the Charter of the United Nations or the responsibility of the United Nations for the maintenance of international peace and security.

Article VIII

This Treaty shall be ratified by Japan and the United States of America in accordance with their respective constitutional processes and will enter into force on the date on which the instruments of ratification thereof have been exchanged by them in Tokyo.

Article IX

The Security Treaty between Japan and the United States of America signed at the city of San Francisco on September 8, 1951 shall expire upon the entering into force of this Treaty.

Article X

This Treaty shall remain in force until in the opinion of the Governments of Japan and the United States of America there shall have come into force such United Nations arrangements as will satisfactorily provide for the maintenance of international peace and security in the Japan area. However, after the Treaty has been in force for ten years, either Party may give notice to the other Party of its intention to terminate the Treaty, in which case the Treaty shall terminate one year after such notice has been given.

IN WITNESS WHEREOF the undersigned Plenipotentiaries have signed this Treaty.

DONE in duplicate at Washington in the Japanese and English languages, both equally authentic, this 19th day of January, 1960.

TREATY ON BASIC RELATIONS BETWEEN JAPAN AND THE REPUBLIC OF KOREA

22 June 1965

Japan and the Republic of Korea,

Considering the historical background of relationship between their peoples and their mutual desire for good neighborliness and for the normalization of their relations on the basis of the principle of mutual respect for sovereignty;

Recognizing the importance of their close cooperation in conformity with the principles of the Charter of the United Nations to the promotion of their mutual welfare and common interests and to the maintenance of international peace and security; and

Recalling the relevant provisions of the Treaty of Peace with Japan signed at the city of San Francisco on September 8, 1951 and the Resolution 195 (III) adopted by the United Nations General Assembly on December 12, 1948;

Have resolved to conclude the present Treaty on Basic Relations and have accordingly appointed as their Plenipotentiaries,

Japan:
Etsusaburo Shiina,
Minister for Foreign Affairs of Japan
Shinichi Takasugi

The Republic of Korea:
Tong Won Lee,
Minister of Foreign Affairs of the Republic of Korea
Dong Jo Kim,
Ambassador Extraordinary and Plenipotentiary of the Republic of Korea
Who, having communicated to each other their full powers found to be in good and due form, have agreed upon the following articles:

Article I

Diplomatic and consular relations shall be established between the High Contracting Parties. The High Contracting Parties shall exchange diplomatic envoys with the Ambassadorial rank without delay. The High Contracting Parties will also establish consulates at locations to be agreed upon by the two Governments.

Article II

It is confirmed that all treaties or agreements concluded between the Empire of Japan and the Empire of Korea on or before August 22, 1910 are already null and void.

Article III
It is confirmed that the Government of the Republic of Korea is the only lawful Government in Korea as specified in the Resolution 195 (III) of the United Nations General Assembly.

Article IV
(a) The High Contracting Parties will be guided by the principles of the Charter of the United Nations in their mutual relations.
(b) The High Contracting Parties will cooperate in conformity with the principles of the Charter of the United Nations in promoting their mutual welfare and common interests.

Article V
The High Contracting Parties will enter into negotiations at the earliest practicable date for the conclusion of treaties or agreements to place their trading, maritime and other commercial relations on a stable and friendly basis.

Article VI
The High Contracting Parties will enter into negotiations at the earliest practicable date for the conclusion of an agreement relating to civil air transport.

Article VII
The present Treaty shall be ratified. The instruments of ratification shall be exchanged at Seoul as soon as possible. The present Treaty shall enter into force as from the date on which the instruments of ratification are exchanged.

IN WITNESS WHEREOF, the respective Plenipotentiaries have signed the present Treaty and have affixed thereto their seals.

DONE in duplicate at Tokyo, this twenty-second day of June of the year one thousand nine hundred and sixty-five in the Japanese, Korean, and English languages, each text being equally authentic. In case of any divergence of interpretation, the English text shall prevail.

JOINT COMMUNIQUÉ OF THE GOVERNMENT OF JAPAN AND THE GOVERNMENT OF THE PEOPLE'S REPUBLIC OF CHINA

29 September 1972

Prime Minister Kakuei Tanaka of Japan visited the People's Republic of China at the invitation of Premier of the State Council Chou En-lai of the People's Republic of China from September 25 to September 30, 1972. Accompanying Prime Minister Tanaka were Minister for Foreign Affairs Masayoshi Ohira, Chief Cabinet Secretary Susumu Nikaido and other government officials.

Chairman Mao Tse-tung met Prime Minister Kakuei Tanaka on September 27. They had an earnest and friendly conversation.

Prime Minister Tanaka and Minister for Foreign Affairs Ohira had an earnest and frank exchange of views with Premier Chou En-lai and Minister for Foreign Affairs Chi Peng-fei in a friendly atmosphere throughout on the question of the normalization of relations between Japan and China and other problems between the two countries as well as on other matters of interest to both sides, and agreed to issue the following Joint Communique of the two Governments:

Japan and China are neighbouring countries, separated only by a strip of water with a long history of traditional friendship. The peoples of the two countries earnestly desire to put an end to the abnormal state of affairs that has hitherto existed between the two countries. The realization of the aspiration of the two peoples for the termination of the state of war and the normalization of relations between Japan and China will add a new page to the annals of relations between the two countries.

The Japanese side is keenly conscious of the responsibility for the serious damage that Japan caused in the past to the Chinese people through war, and deeply reproaches itself. Further, the Japanese side reaffirms its position that it intends to realize the normalization of relations between the two countries from the stand of fully understanding "the three principles for the restoration of relations" put forward by the Government of the People's Republic of China. The Chinese side expresses its welcome for this.

In spite of the differences in their social systems existing between the two countries, the two countries should, and can, establish relations of peace and friendship. The normalization of relations and development of good-neighborly and friendly relations between the two countries are in the interests of the two peoples and will contribute to the relaxation of tension in Asia and peace in the world.

1. The abnormal state of affairs that has hitherto existed between Japan

and the People's Republic of China is terminated on the date on which this Joint Communique is issued.

2. The Government of Japan recognizes that Government of the People's Republic of China as the sole legal Government of China.

3. The Government of the People's Republic of China reiterates that Taiwan is an inalienable part of the territory of the People's Republic of China. The Government of Japan fully understands and respects this stand of the Government of the People's Republic of China, and it firmly maintains its stand under Article 8 of the Postsdam Proclamation.

4. The Government of Japan and the Government of People's Republic of China have decided to establish diplomatic relations as from September 29, 1972. The two Governments have decided to take all necessary measures for the establishment and the performance of the functions of each other's embassy in their respective capitals in accordance with international law and practice, and to exchange ambassadors as speedily as possible.

5. The Government of the People's Republic of China declares that in the interest of the friendship between the Chinese and the Japanese peoples, it renounces its demand for war reparation from Japan.

6. The Government of Japan and the Government of the People's Republic of China agree to establish relations of perpetual peace and friendship between the two countries on the basis of the principles of mutual respect for sovereignty and territorial integrity, mutual non-aggression, non-interference in each other's internal affairs, equality and mutual benefit and peaceful co-existence.

The two Governments confirm that, in conformity with the foregoing principles and the principles of the Charter of the United Nations, Japan and China shall in their mutual relations settle all disputes by peaceful means and shall refrain from the use or threat of force.

7. The normalization of relations between Japan and China is not directed against any third country. Neither of the two countries should seek hegemony in the Asia-Pacific region and each is opposed to efforts by any other country or group of countries to establish such hegemony.

8. The Government of Japan and the Government of the People's Republic of China have agreed that, with a view to solidifying and developing the relations of peace and friendship between the two countries, the two Governments will enter into negotiations for the purpose of concluding a treaty of peace and friendship.

9. The Government of Japan and the Government of the People's Republic of China have agreed that, with a view to further promoting relations between the two countries and to expanding interchanges of people, the two Governments will, as necessary and taking account of the existing non-governmental arrangements, enter into negotiations for the purpose of concluding agreements concerning such matters as trade, shipping, aviation, and fisheries.

JOINT DECLARATION ON RELATIONS BETWEEN THE EUROPEAN COMMUNITY AND ITS MEMBER STATES AND JAPAN

July 18, 1991

(1) PREAMBLE

The European Community and its member States on the one part and Japan on the other part,

- conscious of their common attachment to freedom, democracy, the rule of law and human rights
- affirming their common attachment to market principles, the promotion of free trade and the development of a prosperous and sound world economy;
- recalling their increasingly close ties and acknowledging growing worldwide interdependence and, acknowledging growing worldwide interdependence and, consequently, the need for heightened international cooperation;
- affirming their common interest in security, peace and stability of the world;
- aware of the importance of deepening their dialogue in order to make a joint contribution towards safeguarding peace in the world, setting up a just an stable international order in accordance with the principles and purposes of the United Nations Charter and taking up the global challenges that the international community has to face;
- mindful of the accelerated process whereby the European Community is acquiring its own identity in the economic and monetary sphere, in foreign policy and in the field of security;
- have decided to intensify their dialogue and to strengthen their cooperation and partnership in order that the challenges of the future may be met.

(2) GENERAL PRINCIPLES OF DIALOGUE AND OF COOPERATION

The European Community and its member States and Japan will firmly endeavour to inform and consult each other on major international issues, which are of common interest to both Parties, be they political, economic, scientific, cultural or other. They will strive, whenever appropriate, to coordinate their positions. They will strengthen their cooperation and exchange of information both between the two Parties and within international organizations.

(3) OBJECTIVES OF DIALOGUE AND COOPERATION

The two Parties will set out to explore together areas of possible cooperation, including where appropriate common diplomatic action. They will endeavour to strengthen their cooperation in a fair and harmonious way in all areas of their relations taken as a whole in particular with respect to the following:

- promoting negotiated solutions to international or regional tensions and the strengthening of the United Nations and other international organizations;
- supporting social system based on freedom, democracy, the rule of law, human rights and market economy;
- enhancing policy consultation and, wherever possible, policy coordination on the international issues which might affect world peace and stability, including international security matters such as the non-proliferation of nuclear, chemical and biological weapons, the non-proliferation of missile technology and the international transfer of conventional weapons;
- pursuing cooperation aimed at achieving a sound development of the world economy and trade, particularly in further strengthening the open multilateral trading system, by rejecting protectionism and recourse to unilateral measures and by implementing GATT and OECD principles concerning trade and investment;
- pursuing their resolve for equitable access to their respective markets and removing obstacles whether structural or other, impeding the expansion of trade and investment, on the basis of comparable opportunities;
- strengthening their dialogue and cooperation on various aspects of multi-faceted relations between both Parties in such areas as trade, investment, industrial cooperation, advanced technology, energy, employment, social affairs and competition rules;
- supporting the efforts of developing countries, in particular the poorest among them, to achieve sustained development and political and economic progress, along with fostering respect for human rights as a major factor in genuine development, with due regard for the objectives set by international organizations;
- joining their efforts in meeting transnational challenges, such as the issue of environment, the conservation of resources and energy, terrorism, international crime and drugs and related criminal activity, in particular the laundering of the proceeds of crime;
- strengthening cooperation and, where appropriate, promoting joint projects in the field of science and technology with a view to contributing to the promotion of scientific knowledge which is essential for the future prosperity of all mankind;
- developing academic, cultural and youth exchange programmes aiming to increase knowledge and improve understanding between their respective peoples;
- supporting, in cooperation with other States or organizations, Central and Eastern European countries engaged in political and economic reforms aimed at stabilizing their economies and promoting their full integration into world economy;
- cooperating, in relation with the countries of the Asia-Pacific region, for the promotion of peace, stability and prosperity of the region.

(4) FRAMEWORK FOR DIALOGUE AND CONSULTATIONS

Both Parties are committed to engage in continuous dialogue to give substance to this Declaration. To this end, in addition to the full use of all existing regular consultation mechanisms, both Parties have decided to strengthen their mechanisms for consultation and substantial cooperation on global and bilateral issues;

- especially they have decided to hold annual consultations in Europe or in Japan between, on the one hand, the President of the European Council and the President of the Commission and, on the other, the Japanese Prime Minister;
- an annual meeting continues to be held between the Commission and the Japanese Government at ministerial level;
- six-monthly consultations continue to be held between the Foreign Ministers of the Community and the Member of the Commission responsible for external relations (Troika) and the Japanese Foreign Minister;
- the representatives of Japan are briefed by the Presidency of European Political Cooperation following ministerial political cooperation meetings, and Japan informs the representatives of the Community of Japanese Government's foreign policy.

In order to give substance to this declaration, both Parties will make use of the existing and above-mentioned fora with a view to regularly review its implementation and to provide a permanent stimulus to the development of EC-Japan relations.

JAPAN-U.S. JOINT DECLARATION ON SECURITY: ALLIANCE FOR THE 21ST CENTURY

17 April 1996

1. Today, the Prime Minister and the President celebrated one of the most successful bilateral relationships in history. The leaders took pride in the profound and positive contribution this relationship has made to world peace and regional stability and prosperity. The strong Alliance between Japan and the United States helped ensure peace and security in the Asia-Pacific region during the Cold War. Our Alliance continues to underlie the dynamic economic growth in this region. The two leaders agreed that the future security and prosperity of both Japan and the United States are tied inextricably to the future of the Asia-Pacific region.

The benefits of peace and prosperity that spring from the Alliance are due not only to the commitments of the two governments, but also to the contributions of the Japanese and American people who have shared the burden of securing freedom and democracy. The Prime Minister and the President expressed their profound gratitude to those who sustain the Alliance, especially those Japanese communities that host U.S. forces, and those Americans who, far from home, devote themselves to the defense of peace and freedom.

2. For more than a year, the two governments conducted an intensive review of the evolving political and security environment of the Asia-Pacific region and of various aspects of the Japan-U.S. security relationship. On the basis of this review, the Prime Minister and the President reaffirmed their commitment to the profound common values that guide our national policies: the maintenance of freedom, the pursuit of democracy, and respect for human rights. They agreed that the foundations for our cooperation remain firm, and that this partnership will remain vital in the twenty-first century.

THE REGIONAL OUTLOOK

3. Since the end of the Cold War, the possibility of global armed conflict has receded. The last few years have seen expanded political and security dialogue among countries of the region. Respect for democratic principles is growing. Prosperity is more widespread than at any other time in history, and we are witnessing the emergence of an Asia-Pacific community. The Asia-Pacific region has become the most dynamic area of the globe.

At the same time, instability and uncertainty persist in the region. Tensions continue on the Korean Peninsula. There are still heavy concentrations of military force, including nuclear arsenals. Unresolved territorial disputes, potential regional conflicts, and the proliferation of weapons of mass destruction and their means of delivery all constitute sources of instability.

THE JAPAN-U.S. ALLIANCE AND THE TREATY OF MUTUAL COOPERATION AND SECURITY

4. The Prime Minister and the President underscored the importance of promoting stability in this region and dealing with the security challenges facing both countries.

In this regard, the Prime Minister and the President reiterated the significant value of the Alliance between Japan and the United States. They reaffirmed that the Japan-U.S. security relationship, based on the Treaty of Mutual Cooperation and Security between Japan and the United States of America, remains the cornerstone for achieving common security objectives, and for maintaining a stable and prosperous environment for the Asia-Pacific region as we enter the twenty-first century.

(a) The Prime Minister confirmed Japan's fundamental defense policy as articulated in its new "National Defense Program Outline" adopted in November, 1995, which underscored that the Japanese defense capabilities should play appropriate roles in the security environment after the Cold War. The Prime Minister and the President agreed that the most effective framework for the defense of Japan is close defense cooperation between the two countries. This cooperation is based on a combination of appropriate defense capabilities for the Self-Defense Forces of Japan and the Japan-U.S. security arrangements. The leaders again confirmed that U.S. deterrence under the Treaty of Mutual Cooperation and Security remains the guarantee for Japan's security.

(b) The Prime Minister and the President agreed that continued U.S. military presence is also essential for preserving peace and stability in the Asia-Pacific region. The leaders shared the common recognition that the Japan-U.S. security relationship forms an essential pillar which supports the positive regional engagement of the U.S.

The President emphasized the U.S. commitment to the defense of Japan as well as to peace and stability in the Asia-Pacific region. He noted that there has been some adjustment of U.S. forces in the Asia-Pacific region since the end of the Cold War. On the basis of a thorough assessment, the United States reaffirmed that meeting its commitments in the prevailing security environment requires the maintenance of its current force structure of about 100,000 forward deployed military personnel in the region, including about the current level in Japan.

(c) The Prime Minister welcomed the U.S. determination to remain a stable and steadfast presence in the region. He reconfirmed that Japan would continue appropriate contributions for the maintenance of U.S. forces in Japan, such as through the provision of facilities and areas in accordance with the Treaty of Mutual Cooperation and Security and Host Nation Support. The President expressed U.S. appreciation for Japan's contributions, and welcomed the conclusion of the new Special Measures Agreement which provides financial support for U.S. forces stationed in Japan.

BILATERAL COOPERATION UNDER THE JAPAN-U.S. SECURITY RELATIONSHIP

5. The Prime Minister and the President, with the objective of enhancing the credibility of this vital security relationship, agreed to undertake efforts to advance cooperation in the following areas.

(a) Recognizing that close bilateral defense cooperation is a central element of the Japan-U.S. Alliance, both governments agreed that continued close consultation is essential. Both governments will further enhance the exchange of information and views on the international situation, in particular the Asia-Pacific region. At the same time, in response to the changes which may arise in the international security environment, both governments will continue to consult closely on defense policies and military postures, including the U.S. force structure in Japan, which will best meet their requirements.

(b) The Prime Minister and the President agreed to initiate a review of the 1978 Guidelines for Japan-U.S. Defense Cooperation to build upon the close working relationship already established between Japan and the United States.

The two leaders agreed on the necessity to promote bilateral policy coordination, including studies on bilateral cooperation in dealing with situations that may emerge in the areas surrounding Japan and which will have an important influence on the peace and security of Japan.

(c) The Prime Minister and the President welcomed the April 15, 1996 signature of the Agreement Between the Government of Japan and the Government of the United States of America Concerning Reciprocal Provision of Logistic Support, Supplies and Services Between the Self-Defense Forces of Japan and the Armed Forces of the United States of America, and expressed their hope that this Agreement will further promote the bilateral cooperative relationship.

(d) Noting the importance of interoperability in all facets of cooperation between the Self-Defense Forces of Japan and the U.S. forces, the two governments will enhance mutual exchange in the areas of technology and equipment, including bilateral cooperative research and development of equipment such as the support fighter (F-2).

(e) The two governments recognized that the proliferation of weapons of mass destruction and their means of delivery has important implications for their common security. They will work together to prevent proliferation and will continue to cooperate in the ongoing study on ballistic missile defense.

6. The Prime Minister and the President recognized that the broad support and understanding of the Japanese people are indispensable for the smooth stationing of U.S. forces in Japan, which is the core element of the Japan-U.S. security arrangements. The two leaders agreed that both governments will make every effort to deal with various issues related to the presence and status of U.S. forces. They also agreed to make further efforts to enhance mutual understanding between U.S. forces and local Japanese communities.

In particular, with respect to Okinawa, where U.S. facilities and areas are highly concentrated, the Prime Minister and the President reconfirmed their determination to carry out steps to consolidate, realign, and reduce U.S. facilities and areas consistent with the objectives of the Treaty of Mutual Cooperation and Security. In this respect, the two leaders took satisfaction in the significant progress which has been made so far through the "Special Action Committee on Okinawa" (SACO), and welcomed the far reaching measures outlined in the SACO Interim Report of April 15, 1996. They expressed their firm commitment to achieve a successful conclusion of the SACO process by November 1996.

REGIONAL COOPERATION

7. The Prime Minister and the President agreed that the two governments will jointly and individually strive to achieve a more peaceful and stable security environment in the Asia-Pacific region. In this regard, the two leaders recognized that the engagement of the United States in the region, supported by the Japan-U.S. security relationship, constitutes the foundation for such efforts.

The two leaders stressed the importance of peaceful resolution of problems in the region. They emphasized that it is extremely important for the stability and prosperity of the region that China play a positive and constructive role, and, in this context, stressed the interest of both countries in furthering cooperation with China. Russia's ongoing process of reform contributes to regional and global stability, and merits continued encouragement and cooperation. The leaders also stated that full normalization of Japan-Russia relations based on the Tokyo Declaration is important to peace and stability in the Asia-Pacific region. They noted also that stability on the Korean Peninsula is vitally important to Japan and the United States and reaffirmed that both countries will continue to make every effort in this regard, in close cooperation with the Republic of Korea.

The Prime Minister and the President reaffirmed that the two governments will continue working jointly and with other countries in the region to further develop multilateral regional security dialogues and cooperation mechanisms such as the ASEAN Regional Forum, and eventually, security dialogues regarding Northeast Asia.

GLOBAL COOPERATION

8. The Prime Minister and the President recognized that the Treaty of Mutual Cooperation and Security is the core of the Japan-U.S. Alliance, and underlies the mutual confidence that constitutes the foundation for bilateral cooperation on global issues.

The Prime Minister and the President agreed that the two governments will strengthen their cooperation in support of the United Nations and other international organizations through activities such as peacekeeping and humanitarian relief operations.

Both governments will coordinate their policies and cooperate on issues such as arms control and disarmament, including acceleration of the Comprehensive Test Ban Treaty (CTBT) negotiations and the prevention of the proliferation of weapons of mass destruction and their means of delivery. The two leaders agreed that cooperation in the United Nations and APEC, and on issues such as the North Korean nuclear problem, the Middle East peace process, and the peace implementation process in the former Yugoslavia, helps to build the kind of world that promotes our shared interests and values.

CONCLUSION

9. In concluding, the Prime Minister and the President agreed that the three legs of the Japan-U.S. relationship—security, political, and economic—are based on shared values and interests and rest on the mutual confidence embodied in the Treaty of Mutual Cooperation and Security. The Prime Minister and the President reaffirmed their strong determination, on the eve of the twenty-first century, to build on the successful history of security cooperation and to work hand-in-hand to secure peace and prosperity for future generations.

JAPAN-REPUBLIC OF KOREA JOINT DECLARATION: A NEW JAPAN-REPUBLIC OF KOREA PARTNERSHIP TOWARDS THE TWENTY-FIRST CENTURY

8 October 1998

1. President Kim Dae Jung of the Republic of Korea and Mrs. Kim paid an official visit to Japan as State Guests from 7 October 1998 to 10 October 1998. During his stay in Japan, President Kim Dae Jung held a meeting with Prime Minister Keizo Obuchi of Japan. The two leaders conducted an overall review of past relations between Japan and the Republic of Korea, reaffirmed the current friendly and cooperative relations, and exchanged views on how the relations between the two countries should be in the future.

As a result of the meeting, the two leaders declared their common determination to raise to a higher dimension the close, friendly and cooperative relations between Japan and the Republic of Korea which have been built since the normalization of their relations in 1965 so as to build a new Japan-Republic of Korea partnership towards the twenty-first century.

2. The two leaders shared the view that in order for Japan and the Republic of Korea to build solid, good-neighborly and friendly relations in the twenty-first century, it was important that both countries squarely face the past and develop relations based on mutual understanding and trust.

Looking back on the relations between Japan and the Republic of Korea during this century, Prime Minister Obuchi regarded in a spirit of humility the fact of history that Japan caused, during a certain period in the past, tremendous damage and suffering to the people of the Republic of Korea through its colonial rule, and expressed his deep remorse and heartfelt apology for this fact. President Kim accepted with sincerity this statement of Prime Minister Obuchi's recognition of history and expressed his appreciation for it. He also expressed his view that the present calls upon both countries to overcome their unfortunate history and to build a future-oriented relationship based on reconciliation as well as good-neighborly and friendly cooperation.

Further, both leaders shared the view that it was important that the peoples of both countries, the young generation in particular, deepen their understanding of history, and stressed the need to devote much attention and effort to that end.

3. The two leaders shared the recognition that Japan and the Republic of Korea, which have maintained exchanges and cooperation throughout a long history, have developed close, friendly and cooperative relations in various areas since the normalization of their relations in 1965, and that such

cooperative relations have contributed to the development of both countries. Prime Minister Obuchi expressed his admiration for the Republic of Korea which, through the untiring efforts of its people, has achieved dramatic development and democratization and has grown into a prosperous and mature democratic state. President Kim highly appreciated the role that Japan has played for the peace and prosperity of the international community through it security policies, foremost its exclusively defense-oriented policy and three non-nuclear principles under the postwar Japanese Peace Constitution, its contributions to the global economy and its economic assistance to developing countries, and other means. Both leaders expressed their determination that Japan and the Republic of Korea further develop their cooperative relationship founded on such universal principles as freedom, democracy and the market economy, based on broad exchanges and mutual understanding between their peoples.

4. The two leaders shared the view that there was a need to enhance the relations between Japan and the Republic of Korea in a wide range of areas to a balanced cooperative relationship of a higher dimension, including in the political, security and economic areas as well as in personnel and cultural exchanges. They also shared the view that it was extremely important to advance the partnership between the two countries, not only in the bilateral dimension but also for the peace and prosperity of the Asia-Pacific region and the international community as a whole, and in exploring in various ways to achieve a society in which individual human rights are better respected, and a more comfortable global environment.

In order to bring the relationship between Japan and the Republic of Korea in the twentieth century to a fitting conclusion as well as to build and develop the partnership between the two countries as a common goal based on true mutual understanding and cooperation, the two leaders therefore concurred on the following. They formulated the action plan annexed to this Joint Declaration in order to give concrete form to this partnership.

The two leaders decided that the Ministers for Foreign of Affairs of their countries would serve as the overall supervisors of this Japan-Republic of Korea partnership and that their Governments would review regularly the state of progress in the cooperation based on it and strengthen the cooperation as necessary.

5. Both leaders shared the view that consultations and dialogue between the two countries should be further promoted in order to develop the present Japan-Republic of Korea relationship to a higher dimension.

Based on this view, the two leaders decided to maintain and strengthen the mutual visits and the close consultations between them, to conduct these visits and consultations regularly and to further enhance Minister-level consultations in various areas, in particular those between their Foreign Ministers. They also decided that a gathering of Ministers of the two countries would be held as soon as possible to provide an occasion for a free exchange of views among the concerned Ministers responsible for policy implementation.

In addition, the two leaders expressed appreciation for the positive results of exchanges among parliamentarians of Japan and the Republic of Korea, and welcomed the positions of the Japan-Republic of Korea and the Republic of Korea-Japan parliamentarian friendship leagues to expand their activities, and decided that they would encourage increased exchanges among young parliamentarians who will play a prominent role in the twenty-first century.

6. The two leaders shared the view that it was important for Japan and the Republic of Korea to cooperate on and to participate actively in international efforts to build a more peaceful and safer international order in the post-Cold War world. They shared the view that the role of the United Nations should be strengthened in order to respond more effectively to the challenges and tasks in the twenty-first century and that this could be achieved through strengthening the functions of the Security Council, increasing the efficiency of the United Nations Secretariat, ensuring a stable financial base, strengthening United Nations peace-keeping operations, cooperation for economic and social development in developing countries and other means.

Bearing these views in mind, President Kim Dae Jung expressed appreciation for Japan's contributions to and the Japanese role in the international community, including the United Nations, and expressed the expectation that these kinds of contributions and role will be increased in the future.

The two leaders also stressed the importance of disarmament and non-proliferation. In particular, they emphasized that all kinds of weapons of mass destruction and their proliferation posed a threat to the peace and security of the international community, and decided to further strengthen cooperation between Japan and the Republic of Korea in this field.

The two leaders welcomed the security dialogue as well as the defense exchanges at various levels between the two countries and decided to further strengthen them. The leaders also shared the view on the importance of both countries to steadfastly maintain their security arrangements with the United States while at the same time further strengthen efforts on multilateral dialogue for the peace and stability of the Asia-Pacific region.

7. The two leaders shared the view that in order to achieve peace and stability on the Korean Peninsula, it was extremely important that North Korea pursue reform and openness and take through dialogue a more constructive attitude. Prime Minister Obuchi expressed support for the policies of President Kim Dae Jung regarding North Korea under which the Republic of Korea is actively promoting reconciliation and cooperation while maintaining a solid security system. In this regard, both leaders shared the view that the implementation of the Agreement on Reconciliation, Nonaggression, Exchanges and Cooperation between the South and North, which entered into force in February 1992, and the smooth progress of the Four-Party Talks are desirable. Furthermore, both leaders confirmed the importance of maintaining the Agreed Framework signed in October 1994 between the

United States of America and North Korea and the Korean Peninsula Energy Development Organization (KEDO) as the most realistic and effective mechanisms for preventing North Korea from advancing its nuclear program. In this connection, the two leaders shared the concern and regret expressed by the President of the United Nations Security Council on behalf of the Security Council over the recent missile launch by North Korea, as well as the view that, North Korea's missile development, if unchecked, would adversely affect the peace and security of Japan, the Republic of Korea and the entire Northeast Asian region.

The two leaders reaffirmed the importance of close coordination between the two countries in conducting their policies on North Korea, and shared the view that policy consultations at various levels should be strengthened.

8. The two leaders agreed that in order to maintain and develop the free and open international economic system and revive the Asian economy which is facing structural problems, it is important that Japan and the Republic of Korea further strengthen their mutual cooperative relations in the economic field in a balanced manner while each overcomes its respective economic difficulties. For this end, the two leaders shared the view that they would further strengthen bilateral economic policy consultations as well as to further promote policy coordination between the two countries at such multilateral fora as the World Trade Organization (WTO), the Organisation for Economic Co-operation and Development (OECD) and the Asia-Pacific Economic Cooperation (APEC).

President Kim appreciated the economic assistance to the Republic of Korea from Japan in the past in a wide range of areas including finance, investment and technological transfer, and explained the efforts of the Republic of Korea to resolve its economic problems. Prime Minister Obuchi explained the various measures for reviving the Japanese economy and the economic assistance which Japan is providing to assist in overcoming the difficulties faced by Asian economies, and expressed Japan's intention to continue support for the efforts being made by the Republic of Korea to overcome its economic difficulties. Both leaders welcomed that a basic agreement was reached on loans from the Export-Import Bank of Japan to the Republic of Korea which properly utilizes the fiscal investment and loan program.

The two leaders sincerely welcomed that the negotiations on the new Japan-Republic of Korea fisheries agreement, which had been a major outstanding issue between the two countries, had reached basic agreement, and expressed the hope that under the new fishing order based on the United Nations Convention on the Law of the Sea, relations between Japan and the Republic of Korea in the area of fisheries would develop smoothly.

The two leaders also welcomed the signing of the new Japan-Republic of Korea Tax Convention.

They shared the common view that they would enhance cooperation and exchanges in various areas including trade and investment, industrial technology, science and technology, telecommunications and exchanges between governments, employers and workers, and to exchange information and views on their respective social welfare systems at an appropriate time in the future, bearing in mind the probable conclusion of a Japan-Republic of Korea Agreement on Social Security.

9. The two leaders shared the view that both Governments would cooperate closely on resolving various global issues which transcend national borders and which are becoming new threats to the security and welfare of the international community. They also shared the view that both countries would promote Japan-Republic of Korea environmental policy dialogue in order to strengthen their cooperation on various issues concerning the global environment, such as reducing greenhouse gas emissions and countermeasures against acid rain. They further shared the determination to promote bilateral coordination further on overseas assistance so as to strengthen their support for developing countries. In addition, the two leaders shared the view that both Governments would commence talks on concluding a Japan-Republic of Korea Extradition Treaty and further strengthen cooperation on countermeasures against international organized crime such as on illicit narcotics and stimulants.

10. Recognizing that the foundation for effectively advancing cooperation between Japan and the Republic of Korea in the areas mentioned above lies not only in intergovernmental exchanges but also in profound mutual understanding and diverse exchanges among the peoples of the two countries, the two leaders shared the view that they would expand cultural and personnel exchanges between the two countries.

The two leaders shared their determination to support cooperation between the peoples of Japan and the Republic of Korea for the success of the 2002 Soccer World Cup and to use the occasion of this event to further promote cultural and sports exchanges.

The two leaders decided to promote exchanges among various groups and region at various levels in the two societies, inter alia, researchers, teachers, journalists, civic circles and other diverse groups.

The two leaders decided to continue the ongoing measures to simplify visa requirements as a means to create a foundation on which to promote such exchanges and mutual understanding. The two leaders agreed that, in order to contribute to the expansion of exchanges and to the furthering of mutual understanding between Japan and the Republic of Korea, efforts would be made to enhance governmental programs for the exchange of students and youths including the introduction of such programs for junior and senior high school students, and that both Governments would introduce a working holiday program for youths of both countries from April 1999. Recognizing that Korean nationals residing in Japan could serve as a bridge for mutual exchanges and understanding between the peoples of Japan and the Republic of Korea, the two leaders also shared the determination to continue ongoing consultations between the two countries for the enhancement of their social status.

The two leaders highly appreciated the significance of intellectual exchanges between Japan and the Republic of Korea being conducted by the concerned individuals and groups such as the Japan-Republic of Korea Forum and the Japan-Republic of Korea Joint Committee to Promote Historical Research, and decided to continue support for such efforts.

President Kim Dae Jung conveyed his policy of opening the Republic of Korea to Japanese culture. Prime Minister Obuchi welcomed this policy as contributing to true, mutual understanding between the peoples of Japan and the Republic of Korea.

11. Prime Minister Obuchi and President Kim Dae Jung expressed their shared faith that the new Japan-Republic of Korea partnership towards the twenty-first century can be enhanced to an even higher dimension through the broad-based participation and untiring efforts of the peoples of the two countries. The two leaders called on the peoples of both countries to share the spirit of this Joint Declaration and to participate in joint efforts to build and develop a new Japan-Republic of Korea partnership.

IRKUTSK STATEMENT BY THE PRIME MINISTER OF JAPAN AND THE PRESIDENT OF THE RUSSIAN FEDERATION ON THE CONTINUATION OF FUTURE NEGOTIATIONS ON THE ISSUE OF A PEACE TREATY

25 March 2001

On 25 March 2001, Prime Minister Yoshiro Mori of Japan and President Vladimir Vladimirovich Putin of the Russian Federation held talks in Irkutsk. Both parties expressed their satisfaction that bilateral relations are demonstrating further progress in all areas following the visit to St. Petersburg of the Prime Minister of Japan in April 2000 and the visit to Tokyo of the President of the Russian Federation in September 2000.

The two leaders had an in-depth exchange of views regarding peace treaty issues based on the points agreed in the Statement by the Prime Minister of Japan and the President of the Russian Federation on the Issue of a Peace Treaty signed on 5 September 2000.

Both parties state that, in the 1990s, qualitative activation of the negotiation process led to a more profound understanding of each other's position. The Krasnoyarsk Agreement, in which both sides agreed to make their utmost efforts to conclude a peace treaty by the year 2000 on the basis of the 1993 Tokyo Declaration on Japan-Russia Relations, provided a crucial, positive impetus to negotiations. Both parties pointed out that work toward the realization of the Krasnoyarsk Agreement had achieved important results, and that such creative drive must be sustained into the future.

In this connection, based on the conviction that the conclusion of a peace treaty will encourage further activation of progressive development in Japan-Russia relations and herald a qualitatively new stage in those relations,
Both parties,

- Agreed to further negotiations regarding the conclusion of a peace treaty on the basis of documents adopted thus far, including the 1956 Japan-Soviet Joint Declaration, the 1973 Japan-Soviet Joint Communique, the 1991 Japan-Soviet Joint Communique, the 1993 Tokyo Declaration on Japan-Russia Relations, the Moscow Declaration on Building a Creative Partnership between Japan and the Russian Federation, the 2000 Statement by the Prime Minister of Japan and the President of the Russian Federation on the Issue of a Peace Treaty, and this Statement;
- Confirmed that the 1956 Japan-Soviet Joint Declaration is a basic legal document that established the starting point in the negotiation process for the conclusion of a peace treaty subsequent to the restoration of diplomatic relations between both countries;

- Based on this confirmation, agreed to promote future negotiations to accomplish complete normalization of Japan-Russia relations by means of concluding a peace treaty through the solution of issues concerning the attribution of the islands of Etorofu, Kunashiri, Shikotan and Habomai, on the basis of the 1993 Tokyo Declaration on Japan-Russia Relations;
- Agreed to activate negotiations and to decide at the earliest possible date a concrete direction for progress toward the conclusion of a peace treaty, aiming to reach a solution acceptable to both sides;
- Confirmed to continue cooperation surrounding the islands of Etorofu, Kunashiri, Shikotan and Habomai aimed at improving the environment for the early conclusion of a peace treaty;
- Confirmed the importance of the implementation of the Memorandum on the Preparation of a New Version of the Joint Compendium of Documents on the History of Territorial Issues and Enlightenment of the Public as to the Importance of the Conclusion of a Peace Treaty signed by Minister for Foreign Affairs Yohei Kono of Japan and Minister of Foreign Affairs Igor Sergeyevich Ivanov of the Russian Federation on 16 January 2001.
- Both parties consider it fundamental that the maintenance of an atmosphere based on mutual understanding, trust and wide-ranging mutually beneficial cooperation in various aspects in Japan-Russia relations is extremely important in conducting negotiations.

In Irkutsk, the twenty-fifth day of March two thousand and one.

JAPAN-DPRK PYONGYANG DECLARATION

17 September 2002

Japanese Prime Minister Junichiro Koizumi and Chairman Kim Jong-Il of the DPRK National Defense Commission met and had talks in Pyongyang on September 17, 2002.

Both leaders confirmed the shared recognition that establishing a fruitful political, economic and cultural relationship between Japan and the DPRK through the settlement of unfortunate past between them and the outstanding issues of concern would be consistent with the fundamental interests of both sides, and would greatly contribute to the peace and stability of the region.

1. Both sides determined that, pursuant to the spirit and basic principles laid out in this Declaration, they would make every possible effort for an early normalization of the relations, and decided that they would resume the Japan DPRK normalization talks in October 2002.

Both sides expressed their strong determination that they would sincerely tackle outstanding problems between Japan and the DPRK based upon their mutual trust in the course of achieving the normalization.

2. The Japanese side regards, in a spirit of humility, the facts of history that Japan caused tremendous damage and suffering to the people of Korea through its colonial rule in the past, and expressed deep remorse and heartfelt apology.

Both sides shared the recognition that, providing economic co-operation after the normalization by the Japanese side to the DPRK side, including grant aids, long-term loans with low interest rates and such assistances as humanitarian assistance through international organizations, over a period of time deemed appropriate by both sides, and providing other loans and credits by such financial institutions as the Japan Bank for International Co-operation with a view to supporting private economic activities, would be consistent with the spirit of this Declaration, and decided that they would sincerely discuss the specific scales and contents of the economic co-operation in the normalization talks.

Both sides, pursuant to the basic principle that when the bilateral relationship is normalized both Japan and the DPRK would mutually waive all their property and claims and those of their nationals that had arisen from causes which occurred before August 15, 1945, decided that they would discuss this issue of property and claims concretely in the normalization talks.

Both sides decided that they would sincerely discuss the issue of the status of Korean residents in Japan and the issue of cultural property.

3. Both sides confirmed that they would comply with international law and would not commit conducts threatening the security of the other side. With respect to the outstanding issues of concern related to the lives and security of Japanese nationals, the DPRK side confirmed that it would take appropriate measures so that these regrettable incidents, that took place under the abnormal bilateral relationship, would never happen in the future.

4. Both sides confirmed that they would co-operate with each other in order to maintain and strengthen the peace and stability of North East Asia.

Both sides confirmed the importance of establishing co-operative relationships based upon mutual trust among countries concerned in this region, and shared the recognition that it is important to have a framework in place in order for these regional countries to promote confidence-building, as the relationships among these countries are normalized.

Both sides confirmed that, for an overall resolution of the nuclear issues on the Korean Peninsula, they would comply with all related international agreements. Both sides also confirmed the necessity of resolving security problems including nuclear and missile issues by promoting dialogues among countries concerned.

The DPRK side expressed its intention that, pursuant to the spirit of this Declaration, it would further maintain the moratorium on missile launching in and after 2003.

Both sides decided that they would discuss issues relating to security.

INDEX